THE MILLENNIAL CITY

A New Urban Paradigm
for 21st-Century America

EDITED WITH AN INTRODUCTION BY

Myron Magnet

Ivan R. Dee

CHICAGO 2000

147864

Library of Congress Cataloging-in-Publication Data:
The millennial city : a new urban paradigm for 21st-century America / edited with an introduction by Myron Magnet.
     p. cm.
    Selection of articles from City journal magazine.
    Includes index.
    ISBN 1-56663-285-4
    1. Cities and towns—United States.   2. Sociology, Urban—United States.
I. Magnet, Myron.
HT123.M535 2000
307.76'0973—dc21   99-088326

Contents

The Millennial City

MYRON MAGNET

Introduction

ANY YOUNG PERSON must find it incredible that for a quarter of a century—until very recently—newspapers and newsweeklies all over the world regularly published stories about the imminent death of America's cities. From the urban riots of the sixties to the municipal bankruptcies and near-bankruptcies of the seventies to the crime wave of the eighties, the news from the cities looked bleak and bleaker. But in the nineties urban America almost miraculously came back to life, with breathtaking speed. From New York to Los Angeles, from San Diego to Milwaukee, cities vigorously rebounded.

Each successful city accomplished its renaissance in its own particular way, with its own special twist. But looking across the spectrum of flourishing cities, one can perceive a clear set of principles that lead to urban health. Over the years *City Journal* has tried to flesh out this new blueprint for urban success, and the nation's most innovative mayors have kindly acknowledged that the magazine's intellectual framework undergirds many of their reforms. Collected here are those *City Journal* articles that best articulate this new urban vision. Taken together they serve as a handbook of how to make a city prosper.

To start with, the new urban vision totally rejects the old municipal welfare-state ideology, whose decades of failed policies led the nation's cities to the brink. Urban government, that idea went, was above all supposed to achieve social justice and the uplift of the poor. It seemed to make sense: cities always had large concentrations both of poor people to help and of wealth to tax. So cities piled on welfare benefits and social services, created huge bureaucracies to administer them, and taxed heavily to fund them.

But things didn't work out as expected. With the information revolution, all those companies whose great skyscrapers made them appear eternally rooted in the cities no longer *had* to be there in order to be near their suppliers, customers, or bankers. And global competition *required* them to become efficient and cut costs. No more could they justify paying high corporate income taxes, commercial rent taxes, or inflated utility taxes. So the number of Fortune 500 companies headquartered in New York, for example, fell from 140 in 1947 to 31 now. And most of the new, smaller businesses that have generated *all* the new jobs of the last decade or more never started up in many of the old cities. Result: a city like New York, even though it seems to be booming now, lags far behind the rest of the nation in job creation. Indeed, it has hardly created a single net new job since World War II.

Worse, the costly municipal welfare state turned out not to work. Most social indicators are *worse*, not better, than when the whole rescue effort began. The inner-city illegitimacy rate is way up, the urban high school graduation rate way down, and—until the recent new-paradigm reforms—the welfare dependency rate had soared into the stratosphere. All these trillions of dollars made things worse, because, we learned, if communities don't make their citizens personally responsible for themselves and their families, but instead tell them that they're victims, they will become dependent and demoralized. If the welfare state tells people that it's fine to have illegitimate children, that poverty excuses crime, that welfare payments are appropriate reparations for historical victimization, and that working in "dead-end" jobs for "chump change" is undignified, what can possibly result but illegitimacy, crime, welfare dependency, and nonwork? So even if we could afford our municipal welfare states, they wouldn't produce the uplift we desire. Like the bleeding of patients in the eighteenth century, the treatment only worsens the illness.

The new urban paradigm has four chief elements. First is a new approach to crime. Government has only a very few core functions, the new paradigm holds, and the first of them is making sure that citizens are safe. How to do it? The old view was that crime was the result of poverty, racism, and job scarcity, so we couldn't reduce it until we cured these so-called "root causes." All we could do was to trot along behind crime with a magnifying glass and deerstalker cap after it happened—remembering that criminals were probably victims too, so we shouldn't come down too hard on them.

The new view is that the government can *prevent* crime by a new style of policing that New York pioneered and that cut crime by more than half in only four years—the most impressive urban governance success I know. The theory is this: just as, if you don't fix a broken window in an empty factory you'll soon end up with every window broken because vandals believe nobody cares, so too if you allow low-level disorder to flourish—vagrancy, aggressive panhandling, graffiti, fare-beating—you'll soon get the prostitutes and drug pushers, then the muggers and rapists. The message sent by permitting so-called victimless crimes to flourish is that nobody is in charge: you can get away with anything. But if you come down hard on the little crimes of disorder, if you police with zero tolerance and make sure that public spaces are orderly, people will be less emboldened to commit the big crimes. If, in addition, you work to get guns off the street and to dismantle the infrastructure that criminals need, from fences to chop shops; if you gather intelligence forcefully and track crime carefully so you can put your resources where the problems are—you can make a gigantic difference.

The results have been spectacular. In New York, when people stopped being afraid to go out at night, moribund Broadway theaters boomed, tourists flocked in, hotels were full. New Yorkers felt their city had a future; it wasn't destined to wither away. Big beneficiaries included minority neighborhoods, where the decline in crime was greatest. For example, murder—down 68 percent in the city overall—fell 81 percent in Hunts Point and 89 percent in Central Harlem. At the start of the 1990s we used to read in the tabloids every week of housing projects crackling with gunfire every night, with residents so fearful of stray bullets that they sat on the floor instead of chairs in order to keep their heads below window level. They were afraid to take night classes or to send their kids out to buy milk because of crime. We don't read of such things any more. Minority neighborhoods have stopped being anarchies now that the cops police them—something that didn't happen for decades before the new-paradigm reforms. The result is that minority communities now have the most fundamental civil right of them all: the right to be safe in the streets and in one's home.

The second new-paradigm element is the reform of welfare—on which the United States has spent well over $5 *trillion* since the mid-1960s. In New York or Washington, total spending on low-income assistance eats up a third of the budget—twice the proportion spent on such basic services as police and fire protection, transportation, and parks *combined*. These are the city services that the vast majority of the population really needs and wants, and some of them get short shrift.

Even before the 1996 national welfare-reform law, cities were beginning to change their welfare policies. The idea at the heart of the new policies is that no one is "entitled" to the unconditional support of his or her neighbors; a welfare recipient has an obligation—a personal responsibility—to do something in return.

Welfare reform begins by trying to keep people off the rolls. That means careful checks of eligibility. It means that welfare authorities must encourage applicants to find a private sector job or help them find any conceivable way to avoid dependency. If just Medicaid will keep someone off the rolls, or even an interest-free loan from the state, authorities arrange it. But if the applicant signs up, he or she gets a government-funded workfare job—not job training, which studies have shown to be useless. This requirement prods people to get serious about finding better-paying private-sector work, since they will have to work anyway. Such initiatives cut the nation's welfare rolls in half in a mere four years. Nor did the homeless shelter population rise substantially, and children did not starve in the streets, as welfare-reform opponents had predicted. As one workfare participant told *City Journal* contributing editor Heather Mac Donald: "They shoulda done this a long time ago." After all, work is something that gives people self-respect: it is not punishment.

Troublingly, though, even as the welfare rolls have come down, illegitimacy—which has made the welfare problem perennial—has remained high. If the children of single welfare mothers generally succeeded, maybe we could live with illegitimacy. But overwhelmingly they don't, because they typically come from such weak families, unable to give them the cognitive and moral nurture they need. New urban thinkers are just beginning to consider how to reduce illegitimacy and promote strong families, the best child-welfare program of them all. Practical politicians on the local and national levels are backing them up.

The third element in the new urban vision is what's been called "reinventing government"—making government smaller but more effective, so that it stops gobbling tax money and sucking the vitality out of the private economy. Bloated and inefficient, city governments have long been jobs programs for political supporters, and they are sclerotic with union work rules and bureaucratic procedures. One key solution is privatization. Former Indianapolis mayor Stephen Goldsmith paved the way in this effort: he invited private companies to bid against public agencies for the pothole-filling contract, the bus repair contract, the contract to run the airport or the jails. There's nothing inherently more efficient about a private worker than a public one, he explained. What counts is competition, which in the 80-odd services he privatized produced savings from 25 to 40 percent.

Of course, some services need not to be delivered more efficiently but not delivered at all—everything from alternatives to detention programs for teen thugs to services to teen mothers that make illegitimate childbearing seem acceptable. No big city has yet started really to dismantle the municipal welfare state, taking on the politically powerful unions and social-service bureaucrats who are its beneficiaries. What's needed is a mayor who won't say, What programs do we need and how much in taxes must we raise to pay for them? but rather, How much do our taxes need to be cut in order to make our city economically viable, and what are the least essential programs we can junk to get there? Companies and individuals are willing to pay a reasonable premium to locate in a great city, but a tax burden that in New York is 2.75 times higher than in the average Eastern and Midwestern city—and more than 4 times higher than in the rising cities of the South and Southwest—is more than most people find tolerable. The result, according to a *City Journal* study by economists Steven Craig and Andrew Austin, is that New York has 1 million fewer jobs than it probably would have if its taxes were equal to those of the average Eastern and Midwestern city. In Washington, D.C., or Philadelphia the numbers are comparable. And it goes without saying that a vibrant economy that churns out new jobs creates opportunity for the poor as well as for the prosperous.

Finally, education reform. For generations of immigrants, urban schools were the great institution of acculturation into American life and values, and for decades they amply provided city kids with the skills they needed to move as far up the economic ladder as they had the talent and enterprise (and luck) to go. No more. Today urban schools are dreadful, especially those in inner-city neighborhoods whose pupils most desperately need what schools can offer. City systems are Soviet-style bureaucratic monopolies made all the more dysfunctional by politically invincible teachers' unions concerned about teachers rather than children. Seniority, not performance, determines raises and promotions. The incompetent never get fired. No one is accountable. If you don't like it and can't afford private school, tough.

More and more, new-paradigm thinkers have concluded that vouchers are the answer. Instead of forcing kids to go to government-run schools, why not give parents a voucher worth, say, $3,000 or $3,500, so their kids can attend any accredited private school that will take them? That would most often turn out to be a Catholic school, which typically educates inner-city kids *successfully* at one-third the cost of government schools, which in New York now spend some $10,000 per pupil annually. The goal wouldn't be to replace the government schools but to force them to change. They'd know that if they didn't improve quickly, they'd lose their formerly captive clientele and go out of business. So they'd have to reward excellence and fire incompetence. That is beginning to happen in Milwaukee and Cleveland, cities where publicly funded voucher programs are already established. No wonder minority parents are so enthusiastic about vouchers: in philanthropist Theodore Forstman's recent lottery for privately funded vouchers, an incredible 40 percent of the eligible pupils in Baltimore and one-third of those in New York and Philadelphia applied. You could hardly find a more sweeping indictment of government schools—or more convincing evidence that radical school reform, as *City Journal* contributing editor Sol Stern puts it, is the last civil rights battle.

Behind all these new principles lies a well-established vision of what cities are for. Cities are humanity's hothouses, where human potential develops to its fullest pitch of excellence and variety. With their complex, sophisticated economies and the opportunities for collaboration and competition that such differentiation and specialization present, cities are arenas of ambition and achievement, fostering the best neurosurgery or opera singing or deal-making of which mankind is capable. Pulsating with opportunity, cities constantly renew themselves by attracting the talented and enterprising from everywhere else, however distant or foreign. Above all, cities are realms of freedom: freedom to invent yourself, to choose your friends, to better yourself, to enjoy privacy and anonymity, to think new and dangerous thoughts—which makes cities engines of invention and progress. Cities offer freedom from the merely utilitarian facts of life too: the wealth that their ingenuity and industriousness generate allows them to create a man-made world that embodies the highest aspirations of what life can be, in art and sculpture, in splendid buildings, in public works, in the work of art that is the city itself.

So the new urban thinkers also ponder ways to preserve and extend the riches we inherit just by being residents of a city—the magnificent buildings; the transportation and communications infrastructure; the museums, hospitals, concert halls, theaters, universities, and parks that together make the city someplace special. They think about how to enhance the quality of urban life, making public spaces orderly and public behavior civil, keeping streets and parks clean and well maintained, fostering housing and office development that allows the city to flourish and grow. And, based on the urban renaissance of the last decade of the twentieth century, they are certain that cities are not destined to crumble under the weight of their own social problems or wither away as the information age allows people and companies ever greater mobility. On the contrary: as knowledge and invention increasingly become the principal sources of wealth creation, the spur that urban life gives to intellect and enterprise will keep cities indispensable.

I
CITIES

*At the turn of the millennium, cities are the nation's great
laboratory of domestic policy, and they have repeatedly
shown how intelligent new measures can radically
transform the urban landscape. This section begins with
a description of urban America's near-death experience at
the end of the 1980s, when the political will to resuscitate
the nation's cities seemed nowhere in sight, even though
theorists were beginning to lay out a program for renewal.
The section provides a spectrum of case studies, showing
how cities that clung to the old urban orthodoxy
languished while those that put the new urban thinking
into practice flourished.*

NATHAN GLAZER
Fate of a World City

WHAT DO WE MEAN by a "world city"? A current book on New York City, edited by Martin Shefter, is titled *Capital of the American Century: The National and International Influence of New York City*. The American Century ran from 1945 to . . . well, there is some indeterminacy as to its completion. But the United States is still the most powerful country—economically, militarily, diplomatically—in the world, and its culture is as significant as that of any other country in the world. The Capital of the American Century would surely qualify as a "world city." But is New York City eligible for the title "Capital of the American Century"? New York's role as a capital of anything is somewhat clouded. It is not the capital of the United States, not even the capital of New York State, yet the book's title does claim that New York is a city of world significance—and not because the United Nations is located here.

The title evokes Walter Benjamin's reference to Paris as the "Capital of the Nineteenth Century." Paris made its claim because of the significant world events that began there and influenced all of Europe, and because of the worldwide significance of its culture, even as France's military, economic, and diplomatic power declined. Each world city makes a claim on a different basis; I believe New York's was based on two factors: the preeminence of the United States in the world economy; and the significance of New York City as the place where key decisions affecting that economy—not the political decisions, but the decisions implied by its role as the center of financial markets—were taken. But of course other elements contributed: its population, twice the size of the next American city; its role as the great immigrant city in a great immigrant nation; its increasing attractiveness in the course of the nineteenth and twentieth centuries to those who made American art, music, and literature a significant force in world culture and to those who carried on the business of culture.

And one can add other elements, such as its monuments and icons. New York would be less of a world city without the Statue of Liberty. Indeed, *Capital of the American Century* bears on its cover a photograph of the Statue of Liberty, with the World Trade Center in the background.

When I ask what is the fate of New York as a world city, what I have in mind is its capacity to play in the league of world cities. I think of a world city primarily as a hub of transactions in an internationally enmeshed economy. And the question asks: Whatever happens throughout the world economy, will New York remain a city in which much of consequence will take place?

We know that the headquarters of most large companies have already moved from New York. But that has been going on for decades. We also know that the banks, law firms, and accounting firms they deal with, as well as many of the people who design their new out-of-town headquarters and logos—in short, the entire multifarious system of support for business—remain centered in New York. The city also contains the major centers of mass media and the major cultural institutions that the rich and powerful will want to group around them—or group themselves around. All these are part of what makes a world city.

Some decline from New York's eminent position has a certain inevitability. There is such a thing as the sweep of world history, in which Japan closes the distance between itself and what is still the world's largest economy, in which we surprisingly find huge China joining the little Asian dragons on the heels of Japan, in which a European Community, with an economy much larger than that of the United States, comes into being. Along with these global trends, there are others, in our own country, that must affect New York and its fate. New York has the same population, more or less, that it had in 1930 or 1940—rather remarkable, since most old northeastern industrial cities have lost a great part of their populations. But in the meantime, the rest of the population of the United States has doubled, and New York's weight in the United States—in particular its political weight, which is reckoned in large part by numbers—has been much reduced. In 1970, New York was still the largest state, and half its population lived in New York City. Today New York is far out-distanced by California, and New York City is a smaller share of the state's population. The city's role in the state government, which exercises so much power over its political and financial affairs, is reduced, as is its role in the federal government.

But it remains a center of world significance in the roles that have come to define a great world city. It is where one goes to consummate the largest deals, to gain access to the largest pools of capital; it is home to the largest news-gathering institutions, a place of access to the most immediate commercial intelligence in a host of fields. It is a headquarters, if not of many industrial corporations, then of the service and financial industries and of the new consumption industries that produce and market images, music, and information. These are industries whose sales and significance rival those of the old ones—steel, railroads, mineral extraction, and mass manufacture—that made the United States the largest economy in the world at the turn of the century. The giants of the Industrial Age, regardless of where their facilities were located, came to New York to transact their most important business. So do the new industries that are replacing them.

New York became a remarkably distinctive and powerful icon of such transactions. With its awe-inspiring collection of skyscrapers, its great bridges, its huge railroad terminals, and its vast underground transit system, New York emerged as the very symbol of modernity and mega-urbanism. If one sees an art or photography exhibition on "the city," almost anywhere, one can be sure images of New York will predominate.

A city can live, of course, without emblems or icons. But a world city gains identity and pride by the immediate recognizability of such symbols. For New York, they are the product of a distinctive site transformed by great works of man. In recent years, unfortunately, emblems such as skyscrapers, bridges, the Statue of Liberty, and the grand entrance to New York Harbor— all the things we saw in the movies of the 1930s and 1940s—have been joined by new emblems: garbage-strewn streets, graffiti-marred subways and buildings, half-abandoned housing, an ever more visible disturbed and derelict population.

It is true that superficially similar images of the underside of urban life were once prominent in movies of New York, and as recognizable as its skyscrapers: the crowded tenements, the slums from which came gangsters and prizefighters. But there was a certain romance and glamour in the city of slums and poverty then; there is none, alas, in the pictures we now see projected against the background of a world city—the images of housing projects and drug use and meaningless crime. Undoubtedly, to speak of movies and their characterization of New York seems frivolous when we consider the economic and political problems of New York. Yet one should not underestimate the power of these images in affecting where people and businesses locate themselves. After all, as we have been told so often by the analysts of the information revolution, they can do it anywhere.

Where people and businesses will locate themselves is the key question when we consider the fate of New York as a world city. Where will immigrants, with great skills or hardly any, settle? Where will entrepreneurs start up? Where will people of talent in a host of fields go to realize it? Where will major financial and service and media institutions locate themselves? (We can kiss manufacturing good-bye: it employed 30 percent of the city workforce in 1960, but only 11 percent in 1990.) Images of the quality of life, as well as real levels of crime and taxes and services, will play a role. It is in connection with these decisions of hundreds of thousands of individuals to come, to stay, to invest, that one is concerned about the future of New York as a world city.

New York City is now going through hard times, as is southern California, as are London and Paris, as is even, by its standards, Tokyo. But unless we are on the verge of a shift in the cyclical pattern of economic development that no one of consequence expects, there will be recovery of a sort. The *Wall Street Journal* tells us that knowing investors with deep pockets are now looking at urban real estate again. Those of us who sometimes wonder what can possibly happen to those enormous office buildings when the back-office operations shift to New Jersey, or when electronic trading makes the markets unnecessary, will probably soon be revealed as pessimists, as these huge buildings, their values driven way down and rents reduced, fill up again.

New York has recovered in the past from disastrous downturns. In the 1980s it recovered from the crisis of the mid-1970s, which brought it to the edge of bankruptcy. The loss of 600,000 jobs in the 1970s was two-thirds made up with a gain of 400,000 jobs in the 1980s; the loss of 700,000 people in the 1970s was somewhat made up with an increase in population of 200,000 in the 1980s. (With immigration and social disorder hiding a good number of people from the census taker, the recovery in population might have been greater than the census records show.) Undoubtedly there will be some kind of recovery in the 1990s.

But at the same time, we are becoming more aware of conditions that have taken on a kind of permanence and that hobble New York by placing enormous and largely unnecessary obstacles in the way of its performing as a world city—or even as a reasonably efficient city. The distinctive political culture of New York City, seconded by that of New York State, has produced a structure of business disincentives unique in the United States and unique, too, when contrasted with the league of world cities in which New York has to play. New York City's taxes, city and state, are overwhelming; its public services perform poorly; it seems to have lost the ability to maintain and extend the facilities the city needs to perform effectively.

I am saying nothing new, but the evidence for these things becomes stronger and stronger. Whatever else is not working in New York, research on the city is flourishing. In such sources as the admirable series of studies by Charles Brecher and Raymond Horton on New York City's budget and services, *Setting Municipal Priorities*; in their recent capstone to the project, *Power Failure* (from which the statistics I have just cited come); in the *City Journal*; and in a variety of other studies, we have a sharper light on New York than we have had in some decades.

I conclude from these studies that New York's government, as defined by how it spends its money and what it tries to do, underwent a massive change in the 1960s, as a result of which it still suffers. I would define that change in one sentence: New York stopped trying to do well the kinds of things a city can do, and started trying to do the kinds of things a city cannot do. The things a city can do include keeping its streets and bridges in repair, building new facilities to accommodate new needs and a shifting population, picking up the garbage, and policing the public environment. Among the things it can't do are redistributing income on a large scale and solving the social and personal problems of people who, for whatever reason, are engaged in self-destructive behavior—resisting school, taking to drugs and crime, indulging in self-gratification at the expense of their children, their families, their neighbors. I realize this distinction is much too crude, too broad, but on the whole, I believe, it will hold.

Consider the evidence on how New York shifted from the things it can do to the things it can't do. In *Power Failure*, Brecher and Horton take 1960 as a comparison date. That was the year when Wallace Sayre and Herbert Kaufman's massive study, *Governing New York City*, was published. Sayre and Kaufman's book ended on a note of self-satisfaction; its last paragraph is worth quoting in full:

> The most lasting impressions created by a systematic analysis of New York City's political and governmental system as a whole are its democratic virtues: its qualities of openness, its commitments to bargaining and accommodation among participants, its receptivity to new participants, its opportunities for the exercise of leadership by an unmatched variety and number of the city's residents, new and old. Defects accompany these virtues, and in some situations overshadow them, but the City of New York can confidently ask: What other large American city is as democratically and as well governed?

Brecher and Horton quote this summing up, but they then go on to tell us they would be hard put to say the same thing today.

Consider first the pattern of public spending by the city over these 30 years. For the first half of this period, we learn, spending rose at an astonishing rate—in constant dollars, it tripled over 15 years. During this same period the population of the city declined substantially. What could have occasioned this remarkable increase in public spending? The increase could not, of course, be maintained; it was checked by the economic crisis of 1975. Spending declined somewhat, in constant dollars, until it began rising in 1983, to reach the 1975 level in 1990. It is as if the tripling of expenditure in those 15 years, 1960 to 1975, had established a new norm, and even if the city was driven away from it for a while by threat of bankruptcy, it strove mightily to return.

But in addition to the simple volume of public spending, we must look at its relation to the local economy. Was New York becoming so much richer that it could indulge itself in a much higher level of public spending? Brecher and Horton estimate the amount of city spending as a percentage of "local value added" (one measure of the size of the local economy). In 1961 this proportion was under 10 percent. It rose steadily, reaching 22 percent in 1975. The crisis then forced government spending down to a low of 17 percent of local value added in 1983, when it began rising again. It reached 19 percent in 1989. Again, a new norm had been established: city spending amounts to one-fifth of local value added.

It is astonishing that after 1960, city spending rose from one-tenth of local value added to more than one-fifth and that, despite great economic difficulties since, this has remained the norm. The *Wall Street Journal* often points out that the federal government, after all the permutations and changes in its tax policies, takes one-fifth of the gross national product, year in and year out, whether under Republican or Democratic administrations. It seems that whatever the tax structure and rates, people manage to avoid contributing more than one-fifth of the national income to the federal government. The citizens of New York are less successful. In 15 years the city's political system managed to double its exactions from the people of New York. On top of that, the city is located in New York State, which has one of the heaviest tax burdens in the nation.

It would be superfluous to add that there was no observable improvement in the functioning of the city as a result of all this. Where, then, did the money go? It went to what Brecher and Horton call, quite directly, "primarily redistributive functions." This included public assistance, health, social services, and housing. From 26 percent of New York City's expenditures in 1961, "redistribution" rose to 36 percent in 1969—from a quarter to more than a third—and it has stayed at close to one-third of the city's expenditures, just as total expenditures as a proportion of local value added have stayed at close to one-fifth: another norm established.

Where did this increase in spending on redistribution come from? Largely from two sources: a reduction in what Brecher and Horton call "development," from 11 percent in 1961 down to 6 percent in 1969 (it did struggle back to regain the loss); and from what the authors call "other allocative functions"—that is, the regular work of city government, such as sanitation and fire fighting (but not including criminal justice or education), which dropped from 22 percent of all city expenditures in 1961 to 18 percent in 1969, and to 15 percent in 1975. (There has been some recovery in the percentage of money that goes to these basic functions since.) It is hard to avoid the conclusion that something drastic happened in the 1960s.

What could explain these seismic shifts in the city's spending? One thing that we know happened was that money from the federal government began to flow more freely to cities (and states) for various social policies we can call redistributive. The cities were encouraged to go into such activities, tempted into a level of expenditure they could not maintain except by raising taxes. In Brecher and Horton's book we learn that intergovernmental aid (state as well as federal), 18 percent of city expenditures in 1961, rose to almost 40 percent in 1979, before going down to 31 percent in 1990. That is 31 percent of a level of expenditure that was triple that of 1961. Federal subsidies may explain why the city went into this business with such enthusiasm, but why did it not reduce its commitment when federal aid was cut back?

Was New York inescapably driven to this expenditure because it had become a poorer city? By various measures, one notes no marked increase in the percentage of the population in poverty while expenditures were shooting up: it was 16 percent in 1960, 15 percent in 1970. It did rise to 20 percent in 1980 and a peak of 24 percent in 1986, but came down to 19 percent in 1990. New York did become a somewhat poorer city, but the great increase in expenditure came while poverty was falling. Of course, many other things were happening: a great outflow of the older white population in the 1960s and 1970s, an inflow of Caribbean, Hispanic, and Asian immigrants. This might well have required a higher level of redistributive expenditure; it could also have been taken as a signal that belt-tightening was necessary. In any case, the argument that New York's expenditures rose to accommodate an increase in poverty will not hold for the mostly prosperous 1960s, when New York's welfare population tripled, to about a million—again, a new norm of city life.

How was this expenditure maintained? By the development of the most complex, irritating, and, indeed, destructive tax system of any city. Most city budgets are maintained principally by property taxes. In 1961, New York was more like other cities—64 percent of its tax revenue came from property taxes. But then began an inexorable growth of those special New York City taxes that seem almost designed to drive business out: the city personal income tax, the commercial rent tax, the business income tax, the sales tax. By 1990, the property tax accounted for only 44 percent of city tax revenues.

One must now speak of another new norm, established in the 1960s, that maintains this perverse system: the norm of city employment. There are 325,000 or so city jobs at any given time. In 1960, government jobs (almost all city jobs) accounted for 11.5 percent of all jobs in the city; this figure rose to 14.4 percent by 1969, during a decade in which the total number of jobs citywide increased 16 percent. Government employment rose yet further to 17 percent of all jobs in 1977, while the total number of jobs dropped almost 20 percent. In 1990, before the recession had bitten hard, the public sector again accounted for 17 percent of all jobs. The number dropped during the crisis beginning in 1975, but snapped back in the 1980s. It was never evident that the growth in employment did the city all that much good.

If one asks what maintains the new norms, it is not hard to find the answer: 85,000 teachers are a more powerful force in the city today than 45,000 were when Sayre and Kaufman wrote. The city population and public school enrollment have remained pretty much the same, while the number of school-system employees has doubled. And so with other unionized city employees.

"Redistribution" suggests handouts to the poor, and indeed some redistributive expenditures consist of cash payments to the poor. But far more go for salaries to those who serve the poor. Redistribution meant a huge increase in the number of city employees and in their influence over city decisions. As *The Economist* sardonically notes, only $3 billion of the $14.5 billion the city spends on social and medical services goes to the poor in direct payments. "That leaves $11.5 billion to be handled by umpteen intermediaries."

This analysis could be repeated for New York State. One might think that if New York City spends so much, it must be because New York State spends so little, forcing the city to spend more for what should be state functions. There is something to this: Medicaid, for example, is entirely covered by the state in most places, but not in New York. Still, the state is as much enchanted as the city with the idea of an activist government dealing energetically with poverty and other social problems. New York State is notorious for its high taxes. The 1960s were not an era of restrained expenditure in the New York State of Nelson Rockefeller—college campuses sprouted like weeds across the state, and a good part of central Albany was leveled for the awful Albany Mall. And in the 1980s, while New York City gradually recovered to the levels of expenditure it had attained in the 1960s, New York State increased spending much more.

The 1980s saw an amazing explosion of state spending, even though New York was already well ahead of most other states. In 1983, economist Edwin Rubenstein tells us, New York State already spent 29 percent more per capita, and 13.8 percent more relative to personal income, than the average of the other states. During the next eight years, state spending rose 91 percent. By 1988, the state was spending 47.3 percent more per capita than the average of the other 49 states, and 24.4 percent more relative to personal income.

The money, Rubenstein notes, goes primarily to three areas: education, on which New York regularly spends more than virtually any other state; welfare, on which New York's spending is first in the nation as a percentage of personal income; and Medicaid, where New York also leads the nation. Perhaps New York's people are poorer and sicker—but New York's welfare and Medicaid spending for 1986–87, state and local, was almost twice as high on a per-capita basis as the national average, even taking into account such factors as population characteristics, crime rates, and high local salary levels, according to an analysis by Robert W. Rafuse Jr. of the Advisory Committee of Intergovernmental Relations.

Naturally, this means that New York has far more state and local workers than the nation as a whole—634 per 10,000 residents versus 494 in the other states. This does not mean that in those areas where one can judge quality, New York is ahead. The Empire State, for example, leads the nation in the percentage of its bridges in the federal-aid highway system that are structurally deficient and in need of repair—56 percent, against a national figure of 13 percent. In New York State, as in New York City, there is an irredeemable attachment to doing the things that can't be done very well, while those that can be done—like repairing the bridges—are considered old hat, hardly relevant to New York's deep social problems.

New York City's massive social problems, which scarcely need be rehearsed here, are themselves a constant menace to its capacity to act as a home base for economic activity. From the humblest taxi driver or storekeeper to the grandest international corporation, all are threatened by the city's public disorder. But the problem has been compounded by the city's pouring resources into problems on which it can make little or no headway, adding to the injury of social disorder the insult of heavy and unmatched taxation.

The argument for the primacy of greater expenditure on social problems is easily made: there are so many of them, they are so urgent. If a probation officer has a caseload of 160, for example, wouldn't things be better if it were 80—or why not 40? It is not easy to know what conclusions to draw from the fact that, after doubling or tripling expenditure on a problem, one has detected no particular improvement. Would another doubling help? Possibly.

On the other hand, a sharp reduction in expenditures does not seem to hurt. The recent experience of Massachusetts, which has had to tighten its belt severely and has had a governor willing to do it, is some evidence for that. And when the city workforce underwent a sudden and precipitate decline beginning in 1975, no one noticed that the problems became any worse. (One must agree, however, that they were no better, either.)

For some problems, one doesn't know what to do, even with great resources. I am skeptical, for example, that we know much about solving drug addiction, which contributes mightily to crime, homelessness, and dependency. I wonder even how much worse off the poor were when we were spending a few billion less on Medicaid.

This is not an easy argument to make, but I am willing to make it because there are things that the city, in principle, knows how to do, once did better, and doesn't do well anymore: fix up and maintain the streets, bridges, and tunnels; collect the garbage; maintain the water system—all the essentials of city living.

Beyond that, there are things the city did until about 30 or 40 years ago and now can't do at all: extend the subways; build new bridges, tunnels, and other facilities. All this was once done with a celerity that is, in these latter days, unbelievable. The city suffers from a garbage crisis. In 1979, the mayor proposed to build eight giant incinerators; 14 years later, the first has yet to be started, while the only remaining landfill will not be able to take any more refuse in only a few years. When I say these are the things the city can do, I contrast the doable against the uncertain efforts to solve social problems—drug treatment, rehabilitating criminals, changing the capacities and motives of people on welfare. We do know how to build. We can estimate the costs and time to completion; there is no way to do that with social problems.

It is true that in New York City today, as in so many other cities, knowing how is not enough: there is an enormous distrust of government, and community groups have developed skills in agitation and obstruction they did not have when Sayre and Kaufman wrote about New York City. But it would be a counsel of despair to say that even the things that can be done technically cannot be done politically. There must be a way in which Westway or its equivalent can be built, in which public transit connections to the airports can be built, in which the crowded tunnel connections to New Jersey can be supplemented, in which better garbage collection and disposal systems can be created, in which great monuments of the sort we once built can again be erected. Ominously, we see all these things being done in the other world cities that are New York's competitors. If it is to remain a world city, New York must find the political leaders who can do them here.

—Autumn 1993

FRED SIEGEL AND KAY S. HYMOWITZ
Why Did Ed Rendell Fizzle Out?

RALPH, who works in a restaurant near South Philadelphia's Italian market, and Virgil, an African-American bus driver, both agree that Ed Rendell is a great mayor. "He brought pride back to the city," says Ralph. "He's out there every day in the streets getting the job done," says Virgil, with an approving smile. Polls echo their enthusiasm, giving Rendell, who's term-limited out of office come January 2000, an extraordinary 77 percent approval rating. When asked how, if Rendell has been so successful, Philadelphia has lost almost 150,000 people since 1990—more than any other city—Ralph is incredulous. "It can't be!" he exclaims. That's the same answer Mayor Rendell gave to the Census Bureau when he heard the bad news.

At the end of the Rendell era, Philadelphia is a city that has solved its age-old image problem but has hardly begun to address its reality problem. Its national reputation stands high. Center City looks great, with its futuristic office towers and classy new hotels and restaurants. The upgraded airport sparkles, and new jobs are starting to sprout after a slow start following the last recession. The city finally seems free of the self-denigrating spirit that produced one adman's tourist slogan in the late 1970s: "Philadelphia isn't as bad as Philadelphians say it is." But while Center City and citizen self-esteem are flourishing, Philadelphia remains a crime- and tax-ridden city of collapsing schools and continued middle-class flight, still suffering from economic decline. Much of the last decade's new urban thinking that has put the bloom back on cities from coast to coast has yet to reach the City of Brotherly Love. One lesson of the Rendell era is that to revive a city a mayor must draw on the full array of urban policy reforms; and if he's unwilling to force change on almost every front, he will at best preside over managed decline.

Rendell at first seemed a Hercules of a mayor, able to tame mighty unions and bring a dying city back to life. He was, proclaimed Vice President Gore shortly after Rendell's legendary success in municipal contract negotiations, "America's Mayor." But Rendell turned out not to be the vision-ary and heroic reformer he first appeared to be. Aside from his genuine com-mitment to budget balancing and his energetic boosterism, he has proved an old-style big-city mayor, who has fought welfare reform, despite its successes in so many other cities, and he has looked to Washington subsidies to solve local problems instead of fixing his own faltering economy. The few real re-forms he has accomplished since his battle with the unions have come late, in response to outside pressures.

So why, on the eve of an election to pick his successor, does he con-tinue to rate so high with Philadelphians like Virgil and Ralph? Part of the answer lies in the trauma of 30 years of miserable mayors and long-standing municipal corruption. After leaders like Frank Rizzo and Wilson Goode, people are relieved to embrace Rendell's implied message: be happy, I'm a big improvement. Beyond that, Philadelphians have a peculiarly local and provincial sense of resignation. "People here don't think you can do any-thing about cities," says one political insider. "It's like the seasons changing or the stars moving." So, though Philadelphians have found Rendell's showy optimism infectious, deep down they have few expectations for substantive change—even though other American cities have shown how it can be done.

When Ed Rendell took office in 1992, Philadelphia was on the verge of total collapse. It had lost 400,000 people and 200,000 jobs in the previous 30 years. Crime had jumped 16 percent the year before; the Center City side-walks reeked of human waste. The City Council, distinguished for fistfights and fierce yearlong debates over such questions as whether to designate June as Gay and Lesbian Pride Month, was such a joke that *Fodor's Travel Guide* included it under "Entertainment." The low point came in 1985, on Wilson Goode's watch, when city agencies failed to act as garbage piled up in the street outside of the headquarters of the armed African-American cult MOVE, and a howitzer appeared on the building's roof. Dithering police of-ficials finally overreacted by dropping a bomb on the headquarters. It seemed symbolic of this dysfunctional government that it managed acciden-tally to burn down two entire city blocks and kill 11 people in the process.

Once the home of hundreds of small factories—as well as the head-quarters of the Pennsylvania Railroad, the nation's then-largest corporation, and Stetson, the country's largest hatmaker in an era when everyone wore hats—the city had ceased growing in the 1920s. Before World War II, Philadelphia's neighborhoods, urban villages organized around their local factories, had been what one historian has ambivalently called "ghettos of opportunity." But as factories moved out during the postwar era, these varied ethnic neighborhoods lost their economic centers and their identity. Fanned by decline, ethnic and racial resentments grew, and the row-house populace became fodder for the populist politics of mayors like James Tate and his successor Frank Rizzo, who ran the city from the mid-1960s to the late 1970s.

Though reforming Democratic mayors Joseph Clark and Richard Dilworth had briefly attempted to move Philadelphia into a post-industrial economy in the 1950s, their successors, especially Rizzo, tried to ease the pain of industrial decline by expanding government to fill the vacuum. It was this public sector approach, backed by the political clout of public sector unionists, that sent the city into an economic death spiral. Mayors governed with the permission of city workers—all of them voters, by way of residency requirements. As Rendell quipped after he came into office, "There hasn't been a bad day for these guys in thirty years"—despite the state of the local economy.

Unsurprisingly, the bloated workforce was inefficient and unaccountable. Work rules required—no joke—three workers to change lightbulbs at the city-owned airport. City custodians had to clean only shoulder high—when they showed up. When you added up holidays, vacation, and sick leave, the average first-year worker could take 47 days off, or one working day in five.

The city's takeover of the Philadelphia Gas Works perfectly exemplifies its recipe for governing: ever-swelling public employment and patronage, coupled with poor service. In 1972, Rizzo arranged to take over the privately managed PGW, despite the fact that for the previous 75 years the American Gas Association had held it up as a model, with some of the lowest rates in the country and almost no debt or delinquent accounts. Justified on the grounds that the city would save money by eliminating management fees, the takeover in reality offered irresistible patronage opportunities. Rizzo turned the outfit into an arm of his political operation, putting 32 ex-cops on the payroll among many other political hires. Since then, according to the *Inquirer*, PGW has continued to "provide . . . jobs for the well-connected, pinstripe patronage for campaign contributors, special handling for influential customers, across-the-board discounts for the elderly—regardless of need—and costly bill-paying assistance for the poor." Debt and delinquent accounts have ballooned. Prices—and complaints—have risen to the highest in the region. When economic journalist Andy Cassell recently confronted a top PGW official with the accusation of running a patronage pit, he "bristled indignantly; only a third of the gas-works employees," he protested, "were straight patronage hires."

To pay the fat and happy municipal workforce, mayors kept rejiggering the fiscal calendar and rattling the tin cup in Washington, making Philadelphia increasingly dependent on federal money. But the principal method of financing expenditures was to increase taxes. In perhaps the most egregious example, Mayor Rizzo, while campaigning for a second term in 1975, gave the city's 20,000 blue-collar workers a 12.8 percent raise, 100 percent reimbursement of health-insurance costs, and union control of the health and welfare fund, only to declare a fiscal emergency two weeks after his reelection and to pass the largest tax increases in Philadelphia history.

Above all, Philadelphia expanded taxes on wages. Initiated as a temporary measure in 1940, the wage tax became increasingly popular with elected officials, because it shifted the tax burden away from property owners and onto business and commuters, no small matter in a city that had the highest percentage of homeowners in the country, a significant number of whom were current or onetime public employees. Over time the wage tax evolved into the highest in the U.S., at nearly 5 percent for residents and 4.3 percent for commuters. Combined with the nation's largest transfer tax on real estate (also almost 5 percent) and a "business privilege tax" (a tax on gross revenues, whether a company is profitable or not), it served as an open invitation for business to leave Philly—which it did. The city's remaining business elite offered little resistance; its members, mostly commuters from the Main Line suburbs, withdrew even further from civic affairs as they came under increasing ethnic and racial resentment in the sixties and seventies.

Philadelphia might have continued to stumble along if it hadn't been for comptroller Jonathan Saidel, a levelheaded CPA. In 1991, toward the end of the Goode administration and shortly before Rendell took office, Saidel refused to back the annual sale of tax anticipation notes that rolled the city's debt over from one year to the next. He was deliberately provoking a crisis. "It was," he said, time "to get back to the basics of what municipal government is all about." Staggering under the weight of a $206 million deficit and a junk-bond credit rating that made it almost impossible to borrow, the city simply stopped paying its bills and couldn't fund its basic pension contributions. *City and State* magazine ranked its fiscal condition the lowest of the nation's 50 largest cities. To meet the crisis, the state appointed an oversight board, PICA (the Pennsylvania Intergovernmental Cooperation Authority), to borrow for the city and supervise its fiscal practices, placing Philadelphia in what amounted to limited receivership.

When Rendell assumed the mayoralty in 1992, it didn't take him long to realize the magnitude of the problem he had inherited. Philadelphia was facing a cumulative deficit of nearly $1.25 billion over the next five years— larger than the entire budget of the city of Houston—and an immediate deficit that had grown to $230 million. Rendell understood that, in a city that had raised taxes 19 times in 11 years, this approach was no longer an option. If the city did any more to drive out its middle class, he said, it would become "Detroit without automobiles." And while Frank Rizzo, his opponent in the election in a comeback campaign, had insisted that there was a "federal responsibility to come to the aid of Philadelphia," Rendell saw that the national political climate of the 1990s had blocked that route. Stop looking to Washington and Harrisburg, he announced in a speech on the looming budget disaster: "The only resources that we can rely on to solve our problem is ourselves." And he meant it—at least for the time being.

Rendell's finest hour—his pivotal struggle over the city's fiscal future—came in the summer of 1992, during contract negotiations with the four primary municipal unions. His goal was almost unfathomable in past Philadelphia terms: he had to trim $110 million from their departmental budgets. In the last ten years alone, employee compensation had doubled from about $25,000 per employee to more than $50,000. The city was paying an astounding $475 per employee per month for health and welfare benefits, one of Rizzo's many onerous legacies. And to make matters worse, some of this money, which was administered by union officials, appeared to be paying for mortgages on union buildings and union patronage jobs. Equally important were noneconomic issues, such as work rules that made it almost impossible for the city to fire or transfer incompetent or extraneous employees. In sum, what the mayor needed to do was to roll back decades' worth of perks and redefine totally the way the city managed its workforce.

In the negotiations, Rendell faced not only the usual threat of strikes and a loss of significant support in the next election but racial violence as well. According to journalist Buzz Bissinger in his much-praised book, *A Prayer for the City: They Said It Was a Place That Couldn't Be Saved—One Man Decided to Save It*, the mayor's most stubborn and powerful adversary was the largely African-American District Council 33 of the American Federation of State, County, and Municipal Employees. AFSCME leader Jim Sutton threatened: "If you think L.A. had a bad time, mess with District Council 33." Nor was it seen as an idle threat. With a lingering memory of the race riots of 1964, and highly conscious of their 59 percent black and 39 percent white population (as of 1996), Philadelphians had lived for over 30 years in a racially charged political atmosphere. Official appointments were carefully vetted for racial propriety; elections tended to fall along strict racial dividing lines. In the 1987 mayoral election, for instance, Wilson Goode received 98 percent of the black vote, while Rizzo (in yet another comeback effort) won 97 percent of the white vote. Rendell himself, though now popular with blacks like Virgil the bus driver, knew at the time that he owed his Democratic primary victory in 1991 to the efforts of two African-American opponents to "out-black each other," in the words of one local observer, and that one of the greatest challenges ahead of him was to earn the support of his city's black population.

Despite these pressures, Rendell, his back to the wall, did not blink at

Sutton's threats. He waged a brilliant battle. His counter-threat was to privatize Sutton's political base, the sanitation department. On another front,
Rendell leaked to the press doomsday scenarios of massive layoffs and lists of
some of those work rules most likely to enrage the public, such as 14 paid
holidays, including Flag Day. And in a bargain that would eventually come
to mar his legacy, he elicited the support of the mercurial African-American
City Council president John Street, boss of North Philadelphia, who like
Rendell opposed further tax increases. Famous for never forgetting a slight,
Street was feared as much as admired, but his cooperation was essential for
Rendell's agenda.

For months, the unions thought Rendell, facing the threat of chaotic
strikes and race riots, was bluffing. They tried delay; they brought in national
labor leaders to hurl their standard slogans and intimidate the mayor. But
with public opinion firmly behind Rendell and with the City Council quies-
cent under Street's command, none of it worked. The mayor triumphed in
October with a four-year contract stipulating no raises in the first two years,
only minimal ones in the following two, and a lowering of health benefits to
$360 a month per employee. The contract reduced paid holidays from 14 to
ten and gave the city greater control over worker productivity. Though no
one knew it at the time, Rendell had secured union boss Sutton's quiescence
by signing a secret agreement not to contract out sanitation, regardless of the
$30-million-a-year savings and improved efficiency it would have brought.

Before his election, Rendell, having lost the Democratic primaries for
governor in 1986 and mayor in 1987, and dogged by a reputation for frat-boy
antics and a failure to pay parking tickets, had seemed a less than stellar pol.
But in the battle with the unions, he showed he was much more than that,
capable of outstanding skill and courage. He not only reversed out-of-control
spending and entitlements but also introduced what seemed to be a new
model of urban management. After contracting out 15 different city functions, including the guarding of the art museum and the cleaning of City
Hall, he had saved the city $35 million a year. By the fall of 1993, without
raising taxes and through a host of cost-cutting measures, including renegoti-
ating city vendor contracts, his administration had eliminated the structural
deficit it had inherited when Rendell first took office.

On top of that, Rendell as mayor radiated ethnic warmth and helluva-
guy ebullience—just the qualities that won him the chairmanship of the
Democratic National Committee in September 1999. Attending as many as
a dozen events in a single day, making tearful visits to the relatives of
wounded police officers, jumping into city swimming pools, on his hands
and knees scraping off years of accumulated dirt from the walls of City Hall's
men's room, downing hoagies, he raised Philadelphia's spirits and hopes. It
began to seem as if the city might become as lively, lovable, and entertaining

as Ed Rendell himself. And to raise their spirits even more, Philadelphians woke up to the morning papers to discover that they had been clever enough to elect a mayor worthy of glowing articles in the *New York Times*, the *Wall Street Journal*, and the *Washington Post*.

Yet there were ominous signs. The mayor himself, the city's Booster-in-Chief, was privately gloomy about his city's future. "We're dying," Bissinger recounts the mayor saying mournfully to the White House aide in charge of intergovernmental affairs. "Forget all the good things I've done; Philadelphia is dying." He had cause to worry. Black and white middle-class families with children were continuing—as they do today—to pour out of the city. They always cited the same reasons: schools, crime, and taxes. Schools, crime, and taxes: it was a recurrent chant—but not one to which Rendell was able to respond. Caught up in conventional assumptions, the mayor, after his budgetary triumph, was ultimately unwilling to grapple with the deeper structural problems that virtually guarantee Philly's continuing decline—showing that even a brush with disaster isn't always enough to galvanize an administration into pursuing wholesale reform.

High taxes head those problems. A study by Penn professor Robert Inman found that the wage tax had cost the city 100,000 jobs between 1966 and 1992. The taxes needed to pay for an aging population of pensioners and current public employees, according to a study by Vertex, a publisher of business tax software, gave Philly the highest business costs of the nation's 27 largest cities, squelching employment. Despite adding 10,000 jobs in 1997 and 1998, during a red-hot national boom, Philadelphia is still down 57,000 jobs from the start of the decade. The city doesn't attract the kinds of start-up businesses flourishing elsewhere. In 1997, Philadelphia had one new business started for every 275 residents, compared with one in 97 in San Francisco and one in 66 in Houston. Meanwhile, the surrounding counties experienced such a boom that a city resident is now more likely to commute to the suburbs than a suburbanite is likely to commute into the city. Though why city residents would want to stay remains a puzzle: a family of four paid 15 percent more in local tax than it would in high-tax New York or Chicago, and twice what it would pay in L.A.

Rendell has made job creation a top goal, yet in response to what he himself calls Philadelphia's "oppressive tax structure," he has managed only a fractional reduction of both the wage and gross-receipts tax. Once he had successfully balanced the budget, he failed to seek other ways of saving the city money—such as further privatization or shrinking the city's workforce—that might have allowed greater reductions. The result: during his entire tenure, city expenditures have risen faster than inflation, and taxes are nowhere near the level that would make Philly attractive to business.

Still, Rendell did understand that Philadelphia's economic future lies not in neighborhoods centered on local factories but in a vibrant Center City, home to what East-Coast developer Bill Rouse calls a "new, hospitality-driven economy" that takes advantage of Philadelphia's rich colonial history. The new convention center, begun before Rendell's election but opened early in his mayoralty, has helped him make the city a tourist and convention stop. In addition to an explosion of new hotels—15 of them in the last five years—Rendell's hands-on promotional efforts produced the groundbreaking for a new performing-arts center, a Disney Quest entertainment center, the 2000 Republican Convention, and probably, courtesy of money from Harrisburg rather than the city treasury, two new sports stadiums. Today, Center City contains 40 percent of the city's jobs, a fact that sometimes provokes grumbling from the neighborhoods that Rendell is really only the mayor "from Pine to Vine," the two streets that mark the boundaries of downtown.

Rendell's personalized deal-making, though, has an old-fashioned, big-city-mayor quality that has blinded him to the opportunities that the new biotech and finance firms blossoming in nearby Chester and Montgomery Counties present, even though many of these firms along booming suburban Route 202 had their start at the city's universities and medical schools. Instead, the mayor has sought to revive—expensively—the antiquated but historic Philadelphia Naval Yard. He and Governor Tom Ridge have given the Anglo-Norwegian firm Kvaerner over $400 million in subsidies, for which Kvaerner was obligated to create between 700 and 1,000 jobs—a $400,000 subsidy per job, at best. Worse still, Kvaerner, faced with low-cost competition from other countries, has now withdrawn from the shipbuilding business, as if to mock the city's superannuated approach to job creation. So that $400 million—which, notes David Thornburgh of the Pennsylvania Economy League, could have begun buying down the wage tax that is chasing off more innovative businesses—bought virtually nothing.

Nowhere are the limitations of Ed Rendell's public-subsidy, deal-making approach to job creation clearer than in his agenda for impoverished North Philadelphia. Rendell had once described the area as a "tumble-down, emptied-out, garbage-strewn sprawl . . . , where seven of ten adults are unemployed and where children by age 12 develop a total lack of hope." In truth, North Philadelphia's "badlands" are probably the worst American slums of the last half century, more like the shantytowns of Santo Domingo than anything we associate with the United States. With their collapsed houses, abandoned lots, and daytime drug zombies, areas like Kensington, ten minutes north of Center City, compare unfavorably to the South Bronx of the 1970s. This is the district of City Council president John Street, a man who often casts himself in the familiar Philadelphia role of defender of the neighborhood against Center City interests. "We pay and pay," he once cried (with some hyperbole), "and all we see is fancy buildings going up in the center of town."

This sort of charge must have made Rendell wince, for he had often worn his compassion for the inner-city poor on his sleeve. More than any other big-city mayor, he continuously opposed welfare reform because of the "fiscal and human catastrophe" that he warned would ensue once thousands of former recipients looked for work in his job-hungry city—despite the mounting evidence that seemed to contradict him in his own streets. He displayed some of the same moral urgency when he set out to get federal money for an empowerment zone in North Philadelphia, aimed at bringing jobs to those same welfare recipients. Author Bissinger, who makes Rendell's testimony before the Senate Finance Committee hearing on empowerment zones the emotional high point of his book, describes him as speaking of the city's plight and its economic decline "with passion that reached just a notch below outrage, . . . urgently as if his words couldn't keep up with the fervor of his belief in them." His plea for federal funds, Bissinger assures us, wasn't just another request for a handout from Washington. Instead, says Bissinger, he was "seeking a way, at minimal public expense, of bringing an obliterated portion of the American landscape back to life."

It was quite a performance, but its outcome casts doubt on its sincerity. In a series of searing articles in the *Daily News*, investigative reporter Paul Davies described how both Street and Rendell looked the other way as the empowerment zone degenerated into a useless patronage operation. It appears that Rendell's administration rested on an alliance that was at once a stroke of political genius and a devil's bargain. Street delivered the City Council for Rendell's agenda of relative fiscal restraint and downtown development, while Rendell gave Street a free hand in North Philly and the promise of support when the councilman ran for mayor, as he is now doing. Their cooperation has cooled racial passions, but at the cost of the continuing collapse of North Philadelphia.

Now, five years and many millions of dollars after the mayor's dramatic performance before the Senate, the empowerment zone has produced numerous jobs and contracts for John Street's allies, several large holes in the ground where the Billie Holiday Entertainment Complex was supposed to be, and hundreds of thousands of dollars in unpaid bills. And the response from Philadelphians? Davies's stories have produced a collective "What did you expect?" True, as the zone has come under federal and state investigation, Rendell has felt compelled to take action: the sign touting Rendell and Street at one of the sites has been removed.

Rendell's crime policies have been feckless and outdated, too, though this time some Philadelphians refused to be satisfied. The Philadelphia police needed reforming, for sure. The department, notes Temple professor and former New York cop James Fyfe, "has never been accused of professionalism." It had the dubious distinction of being the first police force sued for systematic brutality and the only big-city force, Fyfe says, "where even white ethnics feared the police." Still, the citizens' fear paled next to city officials' fear of the police as a political force. Thanks to a residency requirement, the Fraternal Order of Police (FOP), which includes commanding officers, patrolmen, and retirees, is a powerful voting block in Philly as well as a big campaign contributor. Judges, D.A.s, mayors, and other elected officials criticize the cops at their political peril.

Rendell played by the old political rules. Trumpeting "statistics" proving that Philadelphia was the safest big city in America—even though as a former D.A. he probably knew that the numbers had been cooked, as has since come to light—Rendell not only pooh-poohed ex–New York City police chief William Bratton's innovative and successful zero-tolerance policing strategy; he also refused requests for a New York–style Mollen Commission to look into systematic, widespread police misconduct. Meanwhile, bowing to pressure from both the FOP and black ministers, who, now that they had a white mayor, were determined to have an African-American police chief, he gave the job to the ineffectual Richard Neal, a department lifer. The mayor's "crime policy," explains *Inquirer* columnist David Boldt, "reflects a tacit deal with black leaders," which made Neal the figurehead, while Rendell and his indispensable aide, David Cohen, ran the force on a business-as-usual basis.

Rendell, the FOP, and John Street might passively have let crime ravage North Philadelphia through the mayor's second and final term, had it not been for a North Philadelphia state legislator named Dwight Evans. Evans, who understood the lessons of successful police reform elsewhere, couldn't stomach the toll that crime was taking on North Philadelphia—or Rendell's stubborn provincialism. He asked Bill Bratton to give a Convention Center speech on how he had dramatically cut crime in New York. But in a bravura performance, Rendell continued to insist it was all a perception problem and stole the show back with a handout "proving" that crime had dropped 17 percent in Philly. A few days later, the *Inquirer* showed that, even using Philadelphia's phony statistics, which systematically downgraded those crimes that were allowed to be reported, the numbers had gone up 9 percent. It was only under continued pressure from the African-American Evans and the so-called Gang of Five—a biracial, bipartisan group of state legislators from Philly—that Rendell finally took action. Despite the protest of the NAACP and the black ministers, he pushed Neal aside and brought in Bratton's former top aide, John Timoney, in March 1998.

The FOP has fought Timoney—only the third top cop ever brought in from outside the ranks—tooth and nail. Since the Philadelphia police commissioner can appoint and dismiss only his two top deputies—the rest have both union and civil service protection—it's been a lonely battle. When Timoney tried to bring in Penn cartographers to help reproduce New York's successful Compstat crime-mapping system in Philly, the FOP filed a grievance that those had to be union jobs.

Even so, the formidable Timoney, who holds two masters degrees and likes to quote Yeats and Joyce, has mobilized popular support for his reforms through virtually nonstop meetings with community and church groups. He has brought hope to neighborhoods that city government had long abandoned. When he launched Operation Sunrise, a full-throttle assault on gun and drug dealing in the "badlands," residents stood on their porches and applauded as police cars and sanitation trucks paraded into Kensington to start the operation, the *Inquirer* reports. Police morale (especially for those cops who had been chafing under the old regime) and public confidence in the force have been rising as crime and complaints against the police have dropped. Murders fell from 418 in 1997 to 338 in 1998, and 1999 looks to be even better, with 166 homicides as of August 16, compared with 200 in same period last year.

Rendell seems of two minds about the policing success forced on him. Though he's been publicly supportive of Timoney, he clings to his old illusions that crime can't fall as a result of better policing but only as a result of an improvement in its supposed "root causes": poverty and racism. Even after Timoney had begun to reduce Philly's crime, Rendell told the *Washington Post* that a growing economy and the decline of crack use were "as responsible as anything for the decline in homicides." It's a slow learning curve.

On education, Rendell has shown more interest in reform than earlier Philadelphia mayors, but even here, because he is ultimately wedded to an obsolete orthodoxy—and because he has been unwavering in supporting a prickly superintendent who has offended everyone—his efforts haven't borne fruit. When he took office, the Philadelphia District—over 75 percent black and Hispanic—looked like any other failed big-city system, with only a quarter of the elementary school children reading at grade level and high school seniors scoring more than 200 points under the national average on their SATs. For every 100 high school kids, there were six incidents of crime during the school year, and 25 students suspended. A cumbrously bureaucratic Board of Education oversaw everything from hiring the superintendent to the toilet-paper contracts, often enough granted to board members' relatives. The mighty Philadelphia Federation of Teachers had, among other perks, one of the shortest school days in the nation, so short it didn't meet the state requirement for minimum hours of schooling. So bad was the situation that Philadelphia's ordinarily passive business community began to get involved.

When Rendell named David W. Hornbeck superintendent in 1994, he must have thought he was truly living up to his reputation as America's Mayor. Unlike past in-house appointees, Hornbeck had won a national reputation as a visionary reformer as Secretary of Education in Maryland and the architect of statewide reform in Kentucky. The business community, the City Council, even usually wary state officials, greeted his arrival enthusiastically. Board Chairman of the Children's Defense Fund and both a lawyer and doctor of divinity, Hornbeck is an old-fashioned civil-rights liberal, zealously dedicated to the plight of poor minority children.

In a ten-point agenda, with which even his now-numerous enemies have few quarrels, Hornbeck imposed tough standards, testing, and full-day kindergarten, and he sought increased accountability and longer workdays from teachers. But in one key respect, Hornbeck took Philadelphia back to the tired approaches that America's Mayor was supposed to have transcended: he blamed poor school performance chiefly on inadequate funding from Harrisburg—and he did so in the most pious and provocative terms. Philadelphia spends a little over $7,000 per student—a bit more than the state average—and about half of that money comes from the state. But as Hornbeck has pointed out, suburban Lower Merion spends about $12,000 per student. Never mind that most of that money comes from local taxes or that the state provides considerably less money per pupil to wealthy districts than to poor. For Hornbeck, the conclusion was obvious: the gap between Philadelphia and Lower Merion was a consequence of racism.

He has lectured relentlessly—hectoringly—about the need for more state money. In one indignant speech, he likened Harrisburg's distribution of education funds to apartheid in South Africa. "Our children," he self-righteously intoned in another, "have been held in bondage, . . . condemned to a modern form of slavery." The climactic moment came in the spring of 1998, when Hornbeck, with Rendell at his side, announced that he was submitting a $1.5 billion budget that would require another $85 million or so from Harrisburg, though the state had not agreed to it. Should the district run out of money, he implied, he would merely close the schools.

By then, Hornbeck had managed to enrage everyone from whom he needed help—not just Republicans like Governor Ridge but several black Democratic legislators, his most likely allies. Appropriations Committee head Dwight Evans, for instance, took offense at Hornbeck's charges of racism. Other legislators blasted his strategy as "blackmail." Fed up, Harrisburg passed an emergency measure that would allow the state to take over the district and, for good measure, would significantly weaken the teachers' union by forbidding strikes and bringing entitlements like the assignment and transferring of teachers under state control if the schools did indeed shut down. Radicalized by Hornbeck's hectoring, some legislators got further fired up by the idea of taking over the troubled district. They began to look at school reform in innovative Cleveland, Houston, and Milwaukee. With the governor, they formulated the Academic Recovery Act, a radical attempt at reform that offers distressed districts cutting-edge possibilities, from vouchers to the power to convert existing schools to charter schools or to contract out the running of schools to for-profit companies.

And what was Ed Rendell's view of all this? Just when the state legislature seemed on the verge of passing the Academic Recovery Act, it's widely reported in Harrisburg that the ever-dealing mayor called several Philly legislators to help block it temporarily—which they successfully did—arguing that they could trade their support for the measure later in exchange for more money for city schools. The truth is, though Rendell doesn't strongly disbelieve in charter schools or vouchers, he is no real education reformer; he is stuck in the increasingly outworn belief that more money, rather than systemic restructuring, is the true key to fixing the public schools. A memo from pollster Neil Oxman warned Rendell that schools were going to become the number-one issue in the next election if he didn't do something as dramatic as he had finally done with crime. Oxman went on to say that few citizens believed the argument that insufficient funds were the problem, and fewer than a third of Philadelphians thought Hornbeck should be rehired. According to the *Inquirer*, Rendell pronounced the memo "bizarre" and extended Hornbeck's contract into the next mayoralty. And in 1996 he accepted a teacher's contract that was a sorry decline from his heroic 1992 struggle with the unions. It managed to win another 19 minutes of teaching time from the teachers—just barely enough to satisfy state minimums—but that was about it.

Rendell claims that the Philadelphia schools are improving under Hornbeck. True, test scores have risen in the lower grades, but too little, too late. Almost half of fourth-graders and two-thirds of eleventh-graders still can't read at grade level, and Hornbeck has failed to inspire confidence in the very minority families he was dedicated to helping. They want out of his system. When Ted Forstmann and John Walton's Children's Scholarship Fund offered private vouchers to poor families, Philadelphia received 41,000 applications for 5,000 positions, 33 percent of those eligible—a proportion second only to Baltimore. Philadelphia blacks and Hispanics support vouchers by over 72 percent and 78 percent, respectively, according to a recent poll from the Annenberg Public Policy Center. And now African-American leaders like Evans and Tony Williams are calling for what Williams calls a "family-driven process, not a system-driven process."

Morale is low for everyone in the system. Only 38 percent of newly appointed teachers are still on the job after two years, while 15 percent of the principals and assistant principals have left in the last 13 months alone, in what Michael Axelrod, president of the Commonwealth Association of School Administrators, calls a "massive brain drain." As for the students, up to a third of them do not show up regularly in some high schools, prompting Pennsylvania Secretary of Education Eugene Hickok to scoff, "Class size is not a problem in Philadelphia. No one is going to school."

Shipping executive Steve Van Dyck, until recently Governor Ridge's top appointee to PICA, the city's financial oversight board, summarizes the Rendell years accurately: "Ed did a nice job of picking the low-lying fruit. But he did not fight the big battles that need to be fought." The danger is that the big battles will continue to be put off, because, after eight years of Rendell's irrepressible boosterism, Philadelphians believe their city is in better shape than it is. Councilman John Street, the mayor's "partner" and designated heir, is running for mayor on the premise that there is no need to disturb the current era of good feeling, no need to tackle school and tax reform. In fact, Street, who seems unenthusiastic about Timoney's attempt to curb patronage in the police department, may not even want to hold on to the low-hanging fruit that Ed Rendell picked.

Street's opponent, Sam Katz, though a Republican, is the true successor to the Rendell who warned that "what's dangerous is the belief out there that we've got it licked." One of the financial advisors behind Rendell's first-term success, Katz argues that "Philadelphia must end denial and face up to reality" with "sharply lower taxes" and substantial school reform, including charter schools and vouchers. He promises to leverage the Rendell-era self-esteem into wider reforms. He can't be the favorite in a city that is three-to-one Democratic. But Street's "I'll get even" personality and Katz's ties to black, homosexual, and Jewish voters provide the possibility of a competitive race.

Ed Rendell has kept his bargain and thrown his support behind John Street. But in a moment of stunning candor, he told *Philadelphia* magazine, "If I woke up the day after the election and Sam Katz was the mayor, there'd be no reason to be concerned." It's as if he senses that his own legacy may well be judged on the success of his successor. Rendell saved the city from immediate disaster, but he didn't stop Philly's long, slow, downward slide. The question for this election is whether Katz can, without undermining the city's newfound optimism, convey enough urgency to the voters to get the chance to try. If he can't, expect the city's decline to continue.

—Autumn 1999

BRIAN C. ANDERSON AND MATT ROBINSON

Willie Brown Shows How Not to Run a City

TWO YEARS AGO, *Newsweek* ran a story on America's new urbanism, featuring Mayors Rudy Giuliani of New York and Willie Brown of San Francisco on its cover as exemplars of the innovative policies that are reviving the nation's cities. But *Newsweek* got it only half right: while Mayor Giuliani's bold, mold-breaking approach has slashed Gotham's crime rate, shrunk its welfare rolls, and civilized its public spaces, Mayor Brown has turned San Francisco into a museum of the discredited urban policies of the past. And with predictable results. San Francisco is overrun with homeless people, crimes go unpunished, the public schools fail, and the city's municipal budget rockets higher and higher. As an aide to California governor Pete Wilson put it, "San Francisco is the anti-New York." It is today's Exhibit A of how not to run a city.

In San Francisco, the countercultural ideas that ravaged America's cities—that one has a right to the state-subsidized "lifestyle" of one's choice, that the homeless are victims of a cruel economy, that crime is society's fault, that the purpose of education is to attack discrimination—still prevail, as if nothing has been learned about their destructive real-world effects. For a moment a few years ago, under then-mayor Frank Jordan, San Francisco seemed ready to liberate public space from the panhandlers and junkies who had made the city a crime-ridden dystopia by the end of the eighties. No more: under the flamboyant Brown, San Francisco's first black mayor, the city now stands with its back to the future, clinging to its old-paradigm past.

Brown himself, in his resplendent fedoras, $3,000 suits, and $500 Italian shoes, seems like a throwback to the past, a figure more like former Detroit mayor Coleman Young than like Rudy Giuliani. Born 64 years ago in segregated, depression-ridden East Texas, Brown grew up poor, shining shoes as a teenager. After earning a college diploma from San Francisco State University and a law degree from the University of California's Hastings College of the Law in San Francisco, Brown got swept up in the vortex of sixties' radicalism, angrily fighting for the rights of victims of America's racism, as he saw it—who often enough were merely "hustlers and pimps," as *San Francisco Examiner* columnist Rob Morse observes.

But Brown's career as a lawyer was short-lived: he proved a born politician. Elected to the California Assembly in 1964 as a left-wing Democrat with the backing of the Marxist W. E. B. Du Bois Club, a hothouse of sixties' radicalism, Brown spent the next 31 years in Sacramento, the last 15 as assembly speaker. Until term limits finally drove him out of the Legislature, Brown favored friends and crushed enemies like a modern-day Florentine, becoming one of California's most powerful politicians—ever—and one of the leading black political figures in the country. Though he had allies in the corporate world—including the tobacco companies, from which he's taken more money than Jesse Helms—Brown relentlessly defended liberal causes, from affirmative action to the expansion of the welfare state, throughout his legislative career.

When Brown ran for mayor of San Francisco three years ago, his formidable political skills were on ample display. He forged a sizable leftist voting base out of quarrelsome feminists, homosexual activists, homeless advocates, minorities, municipal unions, and social workers. Yet Brown probably wouldn't have won the election if not for the self-sabotage of his opponent, incumbent Frank Jordan, a former police chief who drew support from middle-class home owners on the city's western edge. The mayoral campaign ran tightly until Jordan, seeking to loosen up his straitlaced image, posed naked in his shower with two popular male talk-show hosts—also naked. Nobody took him seriously thereafter, and his campaign died from embarrassment.

Three years later, Brown holds on to his patched-together support, though his imperial manner continues to get him into trouble. Until voters rejected the idea, Brown wanted to evict 350 workers from City Hall to make room for an opulent ballroom and a kingly new protocol office, part of an ongoing renovation of the old building—"Taj Ma Willie," critics dub it—which will cost taxpayers upward of $140 million. He'd like, too, to establish an official mayoral residence at Nimitz House, a beautiful navy-owned mansion on Yerba Buena Island in San Francisco Bay.

Then there's the chunk of landfill and mud next to Yerba Buena Island: the mile-wide Treasure Island. Still owned by the Department of Defense, "Willigan's Island," as critics call it, features a striking vista of the city from San Francisco Bay, though it's off-limits to most San Franciscans. Last year, the city's Board of Supervisors gave Brown control of the nonprofit corporation that will buy Treasure Island from the navy and supervise its development. Since then, Brown has used it as a private preserve, hosting lavish parties and offering development contracts to cronies. Last June, though, voters grew suspicious of the mayor's plans for the island and passed a nonbinding measure that calls on the Board of Supervisors to dissolve the Brown-stacked nonprofit corporation and hand the island over to existing city agencies. The board has refused to do so. "Da Mayor," as he calls himself, rules with such grandiosity that, Rob Morse complains, "the only job left is swinging the pot of incense."

Royal pretensions aside, it's in propping up the crumbling edifice that old-style urbanism built that Brown has done the most harm to San Francisco. The most striking result is the city's homelessness problem—and nothing threatens San Francisco's future more. Under the pressure of homelessness, the collapse of public order has grown intolerable. A stroll down Haight Street—the counterculture's ground zero—shows how bad the problem really is. Sallow-faced teenage runaways, sullenly propped against storefronts, beg for money, while wild-eyed street people harass pedestrians on every corner. Drug dealers brazenly ply their trade on the filthy, urine-drenched sidewalks. Once home to flower children and free love, Haight Street now mocks the emancipatory ideals of the sixties, its atmosphere of menace the Summer of Love's legacy. As even neighborhood civil libertarians admit these days, Haight Street's 70 social service organizations—many aimed at the homeless—inexorably draw in disorder. "In the 20 years I've been here, Haight Street has never looked worse—it has gone from cutting edge to ominous and dangerous," a grim resident told a local journalist a few months back. The owner of Haight Street's Ben & Jerry's—the self-advertised liberal ice cream chain—agrees. He has to paint over graffiti on his storefront three times a week, and, like other merchants, he frequently replaces store windows, cracked or shattered in the night. He's had enough, as have many in the neighborhood.

Dorothy Williams is a former nurse who now panhandles for a living near City Hall. She's still pretty, though it's clear that living on the street has started to take its toll. Bundled against the chilly wind in a blue down jacket, she is one of San Francisco's estimated 16,000 homeless; and looking past her, toward City Hall itself, one sees at least 50 homeless men and women hitting up tourists for spare change, slowly pushing shopping carts as if in a waking dream, or huddling in corners and on steps, half asleep.

"It can't stay like this," Williams admits, surveying the scene below her. She thinks homelessness has grown worse in the past few years—because of the city's lax policies. "Oakland, Fremont, Berkeley—they all make it harder," she says. "San Francisco makes everybody lazy." She's right: San Francisco's homeless population has more than doubled under Willie Brown's lax regime.

Things were already pretty bad during the eighties. As the Reagan years brought economic prosperity to America, San Francisco's then-mayor Art

Agnos held the wrongheaded notion that homelessness results from lack of affordable housing, not from self-destructive behavior. San Francisco subsequently extended the most generous benefits to the homeless the country has yet seen, all of which remain in place: a $345-a-month general assistance grant for single adults, thousands of beds in dozens of shelters, free health and dental care, no time limits on receiving help, and an array of special services, from rental assistance to "permanent supportive housing."

As benefits ballooned, Agnos also told cops not to arrest homeless squatters in public parks—they weren't hurting anybody, he pronounced, and shouldn't be punished for being victims. Predictably, hordes of homeless people, many addicted or addled, descended on the city, transforming Civic Center Plaza—the open space in front of City Hall—into what the *San Francisco Chronicle* aptly dubbed the "Mecca of America's unwashed." Others sarcastically called it "Camp Agnos." As the homeless settled in, San Francisco's quality of life plummeted, and the city's public spaces became haunts for drug pushers and prostitutes soliciting the homeless. The financial cost to the city's business community was considerable: more than $170 million a year lost in retail and restaurant sales, according to an April 1992 study, as frightened customers stayed away. San Francisco was a city under siege.

In 1991, beleaguered San Franciscans had had enough; though they're normally bleeding hearts, they're also prosperous yuppies. They elected Frank Jordan to clean up Camp Agnos. Though at first he dithered with talk of tackling the "root causes" of homelessness—exactly the mind-set that created the mess in the first place—Jordan, feeling public heat, launched Operation Matrix. The program rested upon criminologist George Kelling's "broken windows" theory: that an unrepaired broken window or a stripped car left abandoned and untowed sends the message that no one cares, encouraging would-be thugs to act on their darker impulses. Conversely, a window quickly repaired sends the opposite message: that an energetic lawful order exists, and that a potential hood should think twice before he commits a crime. No longer, then, would San Francisco tolerate "victimless" crimes such as public urination: using the crime-fighting strategy that has since worked wonders in New York, police enforced long-unused ordinances that forbade public drunkenness, sleeping in public, obstructing sidewalks, and a host of other quality-of-life offenses. Operation Matrix worked: the homeless moved to friendlier locales or entered the city's abundant shelters, serious crime dropped 25 percent, public feelings of safety grew, and tourists, who bring $4 billion into the Bay area, flooded in.

Willie Brown changed all that. During the 1995 mayoral race, Brown made undoing Operation Matrix key to his campaign, describing the program, in language that recalled the fever years of the sixties, as "persons in uniforms operating as if they are occupational officers in a conquered land." In one of his first mayoral acts, he junked Matrix. Result: the homeless are back, in force. Though police claim to write citations for quality-of-life offenses as furiously as in the days of Operation Matrix (14,000 in 1997), no one tracks how many citations get paid or result in prosecution, and it's clear that, since Brown became mayor, few do. As one cop grumbled to the *San Francisco Chronicle*'s Ken Garcia, the homeless advocates' sway with Mayor Brown ensures that police citations for quality-of-life offenses disappear by the time they reach the municipal court system.

By 1998, the homelessness problem had sprawled out of control — worse than in the days of Camp Agnos. The city's Department of Human Services, wielding a gigantic annual budget of $320 million, will spend $66 million this year on the homeless through its Division of Homeless Programs and $50 million more through general assistance grants, given out to 13,000 adults every month — half of whom are employable, the department itself admits. All this in a city with a total population of 780,000 or so. "We're humanistic," Brown explains, defending the city's approach. But what's humanistic about allowing 16,000 folks, 70 percent of whom are substance abusers, 40 percent of whom are mentally disturbed, to continue their self-destructive and community-damaging behavior isn't clear.

These days, panhandling Dorothy Williams has a clearer grasp on the homeless problem than do city officials. City Supervisor Amos Brown (no relation to the mayor) is a case in point: he proposed that San Francisco supply the homeless with shopping carts in which they could store their worldly possessions — an encouragement to stay homeless. Supervisor Brown's foolish plan went even further: he wanted the city to create special parking areas for the homeless to lock up their city-provided carts — officially institutionalizing homelessness. While Mayor Brown hasn't yet endorsed the shopping-cart idea, a few months back he floated a notion just as absurd: setting up a mobile car park, replete with showers, toilets, and garbage service, for the 2,000 or so people in the city who live out of their cars — still technically a crime in San Francisco.

The mayor has also supported one of the pet projects of the city's homeless advocates: making the Presidio, formerly a military base and now a national park, into a fortress of homelessness. The activists want the complex's 466 vacant residential units, breathtakingly located at the mouth of San Francisco Bay, for the homeless, and San Francisco's Board of Supervisors agrees: last year, it unanimously approved a resolution asking the Presidio's board to lease the space to the city. But because many San Franciscans remain unenthusiastic about the idea, rightly fearing it would attract more vagabonds to the city, it has stalled.

For all his efforts to placate advocates, though, the homeless may yet prove Brown's undoing. San Franciscans are losing their patience—even those from San Francisco's Castro district, perhaps the most permissive community in the U.S. Castro residents and business owners, tired of frayed nerves and the drain on property values and profits that the legions of homeless sleeping in doorways and harassing customers have caused, recently formed an activist group, Community Pride and Revitalization. Their motto: Create change, don't hand it out.

In response, the mayor has grown defensive and testy on the subject. Last fall, Brown bragged that once-resplendent Golden Gate Park was vagrant-free, only to have a local television station show him, as he sat and seethed, live footage of the homeless shuffling through the park. Shortly afterward, a frustrated Brown suggested using city helicopters with heat-sensing cameras to locate and scatter homeless encampments, a sadly familiar story of unlimited tolerance suddenly giving way to authoritarian crackdown—and a plan the city thankfully hasn't yet used.

San Francisco, like most of the country, has benefited from a steep drop in crime over the past five years. Much of the credit should go to Operation Matrix and to California governor Pete Wilson's 1994 "Three Strikes" law, which metes out automatic jail sentences for third-time offenders and which by 1998 had brought about a 40 percent drop in California's homicide rate. Even after Mayor Brown took office, San Francisco continued to participate in the wider trend: in 1997 the city's reported crime fell 6.8 percent, and there were only 45 murders all year—a 27.4 percent decrease from 1996. But the city's lax law enforcement under Brown and his longtime ally, D.A. Terence Hallinan—rooted in sixties-style ideas that so-called victimless crimes shouldn't be punished and that crime in general is society's fault— threatens to make San Francisco dangerous again.

Terence Tyrone Hallinan is the hardest-left D.A. in the country and easily as colorful a figure as the mayor. As cultural historian Stephen Schwartz recounts, Hallinan was a student radical at Berkeley in the sixties, teaching seminars on Marxism-Leninism in his father's law offices, rechristened the "San Francisco School for Social Science." Back in those heady days he went by the *nom de guerre* "Kayo." He also helped run the communist W. E. B. Du Bois Club at Berkeley, where he first met—and cultivated—a young lawyer, Willie Brown. Police arrested Kayo frequently in his youth for theft and several violent assaults, one of which landed a stranger in the hospital with a broken jaw in an unprovoked attack. A light-heavyweight boxer at Berkeley, Kayo was not averse to pounding political opponents—Trotskyists particularly irked him—into submission with his well-practiced fists.

While Hallinan might have toned down his Marxism in recent years, his ideas on crime remain vintage radicalism. The D.A.'s spokesman, John Shanley, for example, attributes San Francisco's plunging crime rates to prosperity. "With a better economy, there is less need to go out and commit crimes," he says, in a classic restatement of the "root causes" theory of criminal behavior that got America's cities into so much trouble over the past 30 years. "We target violent crimes rather than low-end drug crimes," Shanley adds—an inversion of New York's quality-of-life policing approach that has made Gotham's streets safer by orders of magnitude.

Without fail, Hallinan refuses to prosecute "victimless" crimes. He wants to legalize prostitution and has appointed a hooker to a task force formed to overhaul prostitution laws. Earlier this year, Hallinan openly flouted a Justice Department crackdown on the city's "medical" cannabis club, until San Francisco superior judge William Cahill, ruling it a "public nuisance," ordered him to comply. The poorly regulated club, which preexisted the 1996 California state referendum that legalized the medical use of marijuana for gravely or terminally ill patients, was a haven for illegal drug-selling and drug use. Prior to the judge's ruling, the D.A., perhaps wistful for his student radical days, eagerly joined a street demonstration in support of the dope club, haranguing the small crowd of activists.

Unsurprisingly, Hallinan resists implementing Governor Wilson's popular Three Strikes law. As David La Bahn, deputy director of the California District Attorneys Association, complains, "It is well known within the association that San Francisco doesn't support Three Strikes." Shanley admits as much: "No one is going to go to prison for 25 years to life for stealing a pizza." With Brown and Hallinan running the show, it won't be long before even the official crime rates start to creep up again.

In fact, there are already signs that crime is on the rise. For the first six months of 1998, murder is up a frightening 43 percent, and rape has increased too, up 21 percent. Burglaries have bumped up as well, though less dramatically. And many San Francisco residents report a heightened fear of crime. Typical is historian Stephen Schwartz: "I go outside for a walk and I think: this place has so much to love about it," Schwartz says, "but that lasts about five seconds. Then I think: God, am I going to get killed in my house?"

A San Francisco Board of Supervisors meeting in May offers further evidence that crime is worsening. Frustrated merchants, prosecutors, and police argued that the city's low bail for drug-related crime has made San Francisco the place to go to sell drugs. For selling powdered cocaine, San Francisco sets bail at a paltry $2,500–$13,500 lower than any nearby county. Even for selling drugs to a child, San Francisco sets bail at only $10,000, while nearby Alameda County requires a more forbidding $25,000. Lieutenant Kitt Crenshaw, a narcotics cop, told the board that drug dealers flock to San Francisco from as far away as Pittsburg and Richmond to sell their wares. Along San Francisco's border with Daly City, dealers won't close a sale until they're safely on the San Francisco side, according to Assistant D.A. Vernon Grigg III.

Nor is it just on Haight Street or in the Castro district that drug dealers reign. They've also taken over Dolores Park, a wooded, 13-acre, former Jewish cemetery in the city's Mission district. Garry Trudeau's graying counterculture comic strip *Doonesbury* recently poked fun at the ease with which you can buy drugs at Dolores Park. Police say they're doing what they can, but unless the city frees up more money for overtime, the cops can't increase their park presence, and the lax bail requirements mean that dealers are back in the park soon after they're arrested.

Criminality has made its way even into city agencies. San Francisco's Housing Authority, bringing back memories of such harebrained Great Society schemes as New York's Mobilization for Youth, has squandered taxpayer dollars employing neighborhood reprobates supposedly to organize their inner-city communities, according to a federal audit released last July. The audit excoriated the agency's Office of Community Relations and Involvement, headed by Brown's crony Thomas Mayfield, for pouring $1.7 million in grant funds targeted to fight drug abuse in the projects into either no-show jobs or into a pet program of Mayor Brown's that hires "at-risk" youth to patrol the projects. The patrols, critics charge, are often no more than government-subsidized drug runs by young hoodlums.

The fed-up feds have cut the authority's funding, and the city has reassigned Mayfield and given his duties to a man who turns out not to have the clinical social worker's license claimed on his résumé, because he lost it for embezzling funds from a nonprofit organization. The farce goes on.

Old-paradigm urban policies haunt San Francisco's public schools, too. Submerged in race and identity politics, they have among the worst math and reading scores of all California school districts. With Willie Brown as mayor, things won't change anytime soon.

To grasp what's wrong with San Francisco's public schools, start with a deal made 15 years ago between the NAACP and the San Francisco Unified School District. The NAACP had sued, claiming that black and Hispanic students weren't getting an education equal to that of whites. Rather than fighting the suit—despite no real evidence of discrimination—the district agreed to enter into a federally supervised consent decree.

The consent decree sets up a social engineer's paradise. It divides San Francisco's 63,000 public school students into nine ethnic groups: American Indian, Black, Chinese, Filipino, Japanese, Korean, Other Non-White, Other White, and Hispanic. Though California has allowed parents to enroll kids near work or day care since 1987, effectively making public school choice widespread, the decree limits the share of any one racial group to no more than 45 percent at any school. Thus Asian students, who score high on entrance exams, get shunted from the top schools, where they'd soon exceed the 45 percent quota, to less prestigious ones.

At distinguished Lowell High School, for instance, a Chinese-American must score 64 out of a maximum 69 on city admissions evaluations to get in, while a black student has to score only 56. "It's just absurd," says Amy Chang of the Asian American Legal Foundation. "The school district moves children around like racial objects." A group of Asian-American parents has sued to end the consent decree, but the NAACP arrogantly dismisses them, claiming to represent all minorities, including Asian-Americans. The suit has yet to be adjudicated.

Racial vigilance permeates the entire school system. The San Francisco Unified School District, for example, has sought to limit the number of blacks and Latinos suspended or kicked out of its schools. The district's false assumption, that only racism can explain the greater number of black and Hispanic students expelled, sends exactly the wrong message to unruly minority kids—that if they're black or Hispanic, they don't have to behave. In the same vein, several members of the board of education tried unsuccessfully to block a state-sponsored test that requires teachers to display tenth-grade-level reading and math skills, claiming it is racially discriminatory. And in March the board debated—and may yet adopt—a proposal to require that 40 percent of the books used in high school classes be by minority authors, as if a black or Asian kid can't learn anything from reading Dickens, because he's white.

The educational result of all this race consciousness? Though the district boasts of rising scores over the past five years, the numbers are highly deceptive. For while scores have gone up, the number of students taking the test has fallen each year, as the district prevents kids who would drag test scores down—"limited English proficient" students, special-education students, and non-English speakers—from taking the test. Moreover, the black and Hispanic students who are the supposed beneficiaries of these policies have woefully low grade-point averages: 1.86 out of 4 for blacks, 2.04 for Hispanics—which, in the context of grade inflation, means that most of these kids are failing. As journalist Debra Saunders laments, the board of education "thinks more about race than they think about excellence."

Columnist Rob Morse has called on Willie Brown to help free the public schools from the quagmire of identity politics: "By the power of his personality," Morse wrote in the *San Francisco Examiner*, "Willie could influence what goes on in the schools. . . . I'd like to see him use his moral capital to bring change." Fat chance: after all, Brown has played the race card throughout his political career. Though pressing for an end to the consent decree would win him kudos even from blacks, increasingly frustrated with the public school system, Brown isn't likely to take on the NAACP, which has supported him for decades.

Brown's supporters argue that San Francisco's economy is healthy, and with unemployment at a remarkably low 3.5 percent—the statewide rate is 6 percent—and the city enjoying a $100 million budget surplus, what's to complain about? Vacancy rates in the city's central business district are a tiny 2 percent, while tourists, who flock to the city at the rate of 130,000 a day, spent over $4 billion last year in San Francisco. The city cannily used its surplus to refinance debt and improve its bond rating. Tax revenues are up 12 percent. The mayor has won grudging respect from the business community by not increasing taxes—a good thing, since San Francisco already has the highest city taxes in California, making it one of the most expensive cities in the nation. Property values have soared. The picture certainly seems rosy.

Look closely, however, and you'll see it's a bit of an illusion: San Francisco is fast becoming a strange, theme-park suburb of high-tech Silicon Valley, south of the city. San Francisco's manufacturing industry left town in the fifties, and the military, long a major employer in the area, closed up shop earlier this decade. Though 10 percent of the city's workforce still toils in finance, insurance, and real estate, San Francisco's economy increasingly depends on the spending of single, childless, twenty-something city dwellers who love the city's hip cafés, chic restaurants, and libertine culture but who work in Silicon Valley, where the average salary is a healthy $75,000. Traffic up and down Interstate 280 and Highway 101, the roads to Silicon Valley, has increased 20 percent in the past few years as a result. These cyber-yuppie reverse commuters, reflexive life-style liberals, have put up with the mayor's Great Society rerun so far, but whether they will continue to support Brown as the city's quality of life nose-dives remains to be seen.

As for San Francisco's internal economy, storm clouds are forming on the horizon. BankAmerica, which merged with NationsBank earlier this year to form a $64 billion banking colossus, plans to move its executive suite from San Francisco's financial district to lower-cost Charlotte, North Carolina, though its international operations will remain in the city. Since the firm employs more than 9,000 people in San Francisco, the move is sure to mean thousands of lost jobs. A spate of other recent mergers, swallowing up such San Francisco–based firms as Pacific Telesis, Montgomery Securities, and Robertson Stephens, threatens further corporate flight from this expensive city.

Equally worrisome, disgruntled noises are emanating from Multimedia Gulch, a ten-square-block area of converted warehouses that burst with software companies specializing in CD-ROMs, Internet services, and the like.

Revenues of interactive media firms in San Francisco increased 150 percent last year, and Multimedia Gulch now employs 35,000 workers, up 70 percent from 1995. The highly mobile industry is worth approximately $2 billion to the city's economy. Multimedia executives could probably live with the city's inflated rents, but they grumble ominously about the long wait for required permits that makes expanding a successful business time-consuming and costly. A study by the Coopers & Lybrand accounting firm reports that close to a third of these innovative companies are considering leaving San Francisco. Should the industry trickle out of town, San Francisco's economic horizon will darken further.

San Francisco depends on its rich cyber-yuppies, its growing local high-tech sector, and its booming tourism industry to fund a grossly bloated municipal welfare state. Mayor Brown has fattened the city budget by over $1 billion in three years—a whopping 30 percent increase. Taxpayers must support both a vast empire of social services, eating up 33 percent of San Francisco's $3.9 billion 1998–99 budget, and an expensive municipal workforce represented by powerful unions. Brown refuses to consider privatization seriously, and he has hiked city worker salaries 12.9 percent since taking office and has added 2,000 city jobs. San Francisco's municipal workers now earn up to 50 percent more than government workers elsewhere in California, making them among the best-off public employees in the nation.

Brown has also showered the city's private sector unions with favors. In February, he pushed through a new city ordinance that makes it much easier for labor activists to unionize hotels and restaurants that operate on city property or that have received financial help from the city. Unions can now duck the formal secret-ballot elections, overseen by the National Labor Relations Board, that were once obligatory before a union could gain representation of a particular shop. Now a union rep just hands out authorization cards and asks workers to sign them. If the union gets a majority of workers to sign, it's in. San Francisco is the first jurisdiction in the country to agree to this procedure, which makes unionizing a workplace quick and easy; if it spreads beyond hotels and restaurants, San Francisco businesses will crowd toward the exits.

In March, Brown gave the unions another gift: the Displaced Worker Protection Act, which protects the jobs of San Francisco's 10,000 janitors and security guards. The act requires, with few exceptions, that any contractor taking over another contractor's work must keep its janitors and security guards on its payroll for at least three months, regardless of whether it works for a city agency or a private firm. When the act passed, Ken Cleveland of San Francisco's Building Owners and Managers Association grimly concluded: "The business community got a blow to the solar plexus today." In addition, the city's Board of Supervisors will soon pass, with the mayor's blessing, a New York–style "living wage" law that guarantees anyone working on a city contract a minimum $11 per hour.

In exchange for Brown's piled-on gifts, the unions offer unflagging support. The city's powerful Labor Council just gave the mayor an unprecedented early endorsement for the November 1999 mayoral race. After hearing the council's decision, Brown told them, "I don't think democracy is well served with me having an opponent"—a sentiment more befitting a Third World dictator than the mayor of a major American city.

San Francisco has always courted the counterculture, embracing everything from Beat poetry (Lawrence Ferlinghetti was named the city's first poet laureate in August) to the frazzled music, easy sex, and psychedelic drugs of the sixties, to the decadent gay bathhouses of more recent times. In what other American city, after all, could the city's entire political elite, including the mayor, attend a much-publicized birthday party—for Brown's campaign manager Jack Davis—that featured a leather-masked sadomasochist first carving a bloody pentagram into the back of a naked man and then urinating on him? As birthday-boy Davis later gushed to the local media, "It wasn't anything compared to the after-party at my house." The mayor's only response? "This is a messed-up city." In fact, San Francisco's tradition of indiscriminate tolerance goes back even further than the sixties. When poet Kenneth Rexroth came to the city in the 1920s, he noted that "it was the only city in the United States not settled overland by the spreading Puritan tradition. . . . Nobody cared what you did as long as you didn't commit any gross public crimes."

What Rexroth didn't anticipate, though, is how fiercely intolerant San Francisco would turn in pursuit of a politically correct agenda. In November 1996, Willie Brown signed local legislation that requires any agency or firm contracting with the city to offer the same benefits it offers to employee spouses to the domestic partners—homosexual or heterosexual—of unmarried employees, on pain of having its operations in the city shut down. One of the law's first targets: Catholic Charities. Like other organizations tapping city money, the city's Board of Supervisors ruled, Catholic Charities must offer domestic partnership benefits to employees—in effect, sanctioning homosexual "marriage"—or give up its $6 million in city funding. Catholic Charities buckled. By contrast, the Salvation Army commendably refused to comply and continued to offer services without city reimbursement. When it became clear the city wouldn't offer it a waiver on the domestic partnership requirement—as it has for hundreds of other charitable and non-charitable groups—the Salvation Army left town.

San Francisco's intolerance has taken on international scope. In early 1997, it demanded that United Airlines extend domestic partnership benefits to all its 86,000 employees across the globe or lose its contract to operate out of San Francisco International Airport. In response, United—operating more than half of the flights and employing 18,000 people in the city—sued, claiming the city couldn't force it to follow the law, since the federal government, not local jurisdictions, regulates the airline. In April, U.S. district judge Claudia Wilkin ruled that San Francisco "reached beyond the limits of its power within the federal government." But the war isn't over: the city is now seeking to terminate United's leases for its flight kitchen and ground-maintenance facilities at the airport.

As Mayor Willie Brown's old-paradigm thinking tightens its grip on the city, it's only a matter of time before the apparently sizzling economy begins to fizzle and the tourism industry dwindles as crime and disorder increase. Yet Brown still stands a good chance of being reelected next year. His probable opponent will be political consultant and real estate magnate Clint Reilly, whom few consider a serious candidate. Brown may well take San Francisco into the new millennium, unless voters make the clear connection between the mayor's reign and the city's newly uncivil streets.

A few years ago, San Francisco seemed ready to abandon at least some of its antiquated ideals, tired of their disastrous real-world consequences. But with Willie Brown, San Francisco's past, like a scary acid flashback, has claimed it again.

—Autumn 1998

HEATHER MAC DONALD

Jerry Brown's No-Nonsense New Age for Oakland

ASK NINE PIERCED AND TATTOOED PUNKS what they think of former California governor, now Mayor, Jerry Brown and his effort to banish crime from Oakland, and you'll get an instant measure of how dramatically Brown has changed the city in his ten months in City Hall. "He's a f—k," announces Scrappy, a blue-haired 25-year-old with tongue rings, nose rings, and dagger-shaped earrings. "Oakland used to be a cool town, but now we can't hang out on the streets without someone saying you gotta go." Last time he wandered through downtown Oakland with his sleeping bag, Scrappy says, the police stopped him five times in seven blocks to ask about drugs. He shakes his head philosophically: "No, they don't like gutterpunks *at all* in Oakland."

Oakland used to be known as Baja Berkeley, but those days may be over. Brown, who won the mayoralty in a landslide in June 1998, carrying every district but two Hispanic ones, is on a fervent crusade to resuscitate this still-lovely city, long associated with urban failure. Should this most enigmatic of politicians succeed in his surprising new role, it will be a testament to an emerging national consensus regarding what cities need in order to flourish—public safety, order, decent schools, and a respect for private creativity.

Brown's election in this birthplace of the Black Panthers has a further significance: it may signal the waning of Oakland's counterproductive race politics. In voting for Brown, black Oaklanders decisively rejected a black political establishment they saw as arrogant and incompetent. Arising in its place is a new breed of black politician, personified by Oakland city manager Robert Bobb—passionate about results, indifferent to racial appeals, and determined to foster personal responsibility. Together Bobb and Brown are cleaning up a barnacle-encrusted city government and shaking off the failed orthodoxies of the Great Society.

Since taking office, Brown has relentlessly pursued four goals, ignoring backlash from disgruntled insiders and from anti-development community groups. He wants to bring 10,000 new residents to downtown Oakland by attracting unsubsidized, market-rate housing; to reduce crime 20 percent a year; to start charter schools; and to strengthen the arts. Sitting ramrod straight on the edge of a chair in a newly pressed white collarless shirt and dark jacket, his eyes downcast and his gravelly voice halting abruptly at the ends of phrases, Brown promoted his agenda at an East Oakland neighborhood meeting last August. Austere to the point of stiffness, rubbing his hands absentmindedly on his knees, Brown is an unlikely politician—but most of the group is eating it up. They ask hopefully about real estate values downtown, with the poignant yearning of Oaklanders to recover their city's vanished vitality.

A lesbian mother of two asks the inevitable, race-tinged question about "gentrification": "I'm concerned how you plan to maintain diversity over time downtown," she says piously. Brown squints at her from under his bushy eyebrows and shoots back: "There's no diversity there now. You have a homogenous population—the elderly, parolees, people in drug rehab, from mental hospitals, transients—concentrated, because people are working the system. This is not the vibrant civic culture some might have in mind."

This kind of talk is a far cry from Brown's rhetoric at the start of his campaign in early 1997. "I see Oakland as an 'ecopolis' of the future—a city that is both in harmony with the environment and in harmony with itself," he enthused then. Such language was right out of the obscure populist organization called "We the People" that he then headed from his $2 million loft building in the newly trendy Jack London area of waterfront Oakland. Having moved there from San Francisco not long after his disastrous 1992 run for president, Brown had continued to hammer away at his presidential campaign themes of corporate greed and political corruption, as well as to pursue the New Age interests he'd cultivated as California's "Governor Moonbeam" from 1974 to 1982: biodynamic gardening, yoga and meditation classes, and discussions on ecologically sensitive urban planning. His weekly talk show on far-left Pacifica radio featured various countercultural critics denouncing global capitalists, American inequality, and the "propaganda system of the so-called free world."

But once on the mayoral campaign trail, Brown noticed that Oaklanders cared more about crime, abysmal schools, and the continuing downtown economic vacuum than about environmental sustainability and social justice. He sagely jackknifed. Whereas as radio announcer he had mocked the war on crime as a media-driven "scam" serving only the interests of prison guards and "corporate criminals" (i.e., CEOs), as mayoral candidate he began speaking with ruthless honesty about Oakland's public safety problem. "Muggings, car break-ins, burglaries—this is real, no matter what anyone says," he declared a month before the election. "The city has to ensure your safety. Any administration that can coexist with an increasing number of people locked up in their own homes is not doing its job." Now that he's in office, the turnabout persists. As a talk-show Jeremiah, he had blasted welfare reform and argued that "crime in the suites" is more dangerous than "crime in the streets," yet now he is wooing large corporations to Oakland and complaining that welfare recipients are "working the system." On the radio, he complained of a "conspiracy" to lock people away, yet as mayor he plans to imprison as many of Oakland's criminals as he can get his hands on.

The truth is that, beneath his left-wing rhetoric, Brown has a realistic, even conservative streak, as he proved during his two terms as governor, when he held down state spending, called for mandatory prison sentences to increase the cost of crime, and announced the death of liberalism: "The fact that there's a problem does not mean that more government will make it better. It might make it worse."

Now that he's an elected official again, the realism is back. "If you countenance open drug markets, shoplifting, car thefts, you're not going to have a city," he says in his dark, high-ceilinged office, decorated with sixties classics like Paul Goodman's *Compulsory Miseducation*. Though he's not about to repudiate his recent left-leaning credos, he's not going to govern according to them, either. "You can look at the social dynamics [of crime] and realize what's caused this," Brown explains as he shifts back and forth between a modernist chair and a dark taupe couch. "But after you've looked at all that, now you're here, you're in the neighborhood. If someone's selling dope on the street—hey, you've got to get him out of there. It's that simple." He chooses his words carefully, gesturing expansively. "I want to deal with transforming the urban space. While I can give you an analysis of why this is from a global point of view, when it is time to effect improvement I'm going to use every lawful constitutional means to get those improvements within the time frame I set forth."

Watching Brown's ceaseless efforts to promote Oakland, residents are dropping their usual ironic defensiveness about their city and indulging in optimism. There is a palpable energy downtown, particularly noticeable among developers long-accustomed to bureaucratic inertia and crippling regulatory roadblocks. One morning last August, a beaming Ken Hofmann, co-owner of the Oakland A's, escorted an enthusiastic team of developers through City Hall's marble rotunda to tell Brown about their plans to convert an abandoned GM plant into lofts. Several weeks later, Brown repaid the courtesy by showing up at an East Oakland community meeting to support the project against the inevitable opposition, part of his ceaseless rounds of the city to encourage change.

Local real estate agent Dean Treadway marvels at Brown's determination to get things built. Treadway just brokered the sale of a $5.5 million property on Lake Merritt known as "Das Hole," named for the unfinished subterranean parking garage that has gaped at the site since the early 1980s. When the new owners announced plans to put up a 20-story condominium, neighbors strenuously objected that the project would cast shadows on the tiny downtown lake and disturb the ducks. "The opponents were nipped in the bud," marvels Treadway. "Brown doesn't put up with it. He just charges ahead, saying these projects will be good for the city." Indeed, Brown boasted of his unwillingness to brook opposition in his state-of-the-city address three months into his term. "Every single project that has surfaced in the first 100 days has been opposed," he said. "Many of these reasons are fine, but if we let them decide the day, we're moving back to stagnation."

Brown's market timing is excellent. Housing and office costs in San Francisco—just a few minutes across the bay from Oakland on the BART subway line—are astronomical; despite a 1 percent apartment-vacancy rate, anti-development forces there are crushing new construction and loft conversions. For the last several years, developers have been scouting out Oakland, attracted by its cheap land. San Francisco–based mega-developer Doug Shorenstein, for instance, delighted the city by buying the failed City Center downtown office and retail project at fire-sale prices several years ago, and polishing it to a fare-thee-well. Major tenants now include American President Lines, Deloitte & Touche, and Merrill Lynch.

Interest has heated up under Brown's 10,000-new-residents initiative; housing developers are flying in from across the country, drawn by Brown's determination to sell off all the city's big properties. Businesses are moving from San Francisco and Berkeley, too, drawn by 50 to 65 percent lower rents. "What continued to impress us was the city's very aggressive approach in getting major companies here," says Dick Partida, a vice president at Koret, a $300 million-a-year women's clothing manufacturer that left San Francisco for Oakland this year.

With an almost guileless personal directness coupled with intellectual intensity, Brown has won a following across all social classes. A table of off-duty cops at a bar in the Jack London district breaks into smiles when Brown walks in. "How's it goin', Mayor?" one officer happily asks him. Even Oakland's vagrants have caught the new civic spirit. Three men in various states of decay are playing dominoes in newly renovated, oak-shaded Lafayette Square behind Broadway, Oakland's main business thoroughfare. Condemning the city's new enforcement of quality-of-life laws, the men complain that the police harass them now for littering and open liquor containers. "How can you drink if it's not open?" jokes an older man encased in layers of filthy clothing. Yet a younger man in black overalls comes to Brown's defense. After scooting a crushed Budweiser can across the asphalt walk like a shuffleboard puck, he says: "I've seen a lot of good things Brown said he'd do in this park. He's made some excellent changes." He points with seeming pride to development on the periphery. "They're building new condos around here," he says, though he criticizes the lack of "affordable housing."

That even these citizens could find something to support in Brown's crusade shows how hungry Oaklanders are for a success story. For three decades, Oakland has been sold one massively subsidized development scheme after another—freeways, a West Oakland BART station that was supposed to ignite retail development, a convention center, government buildings, an abortive downtown shopping center, the Raiders' fiscally disastrous return, a soon-bankrupt ice-skating rink. All were supposed to bring the city back to life, but many projects only made things worse by tearing down existing buildings and leaving empty parking lots. And Oakland's once-proud history faded from memory, though it is still visible in the city's architecture.

Oakland sprang into existence during the California Gold Rush as a more bourgeois—as well as sunny—alternative to San Francisco's wild debauchery. It prospered for 100 years. By making it the terminus for the first intercontinental railroad in 1869, the Central Pacific cemented the city's role as the shipping hub for the entire West; two more national railroads followed suit. Oakland's waterfront, where numerous factories processed California's raw materials before sending them overseas or back east, quickly became "one vast workshop for the Pacific Ocean," as an 1877 real estate brochure boasted.

Oakland started gracing itself with grand public buildings at the turn of the century. Wealthy San Franciscans ferried across the bay to the imposing Hotel Oakland for sun and healthful air; today, in the arc typical of many cities, the hotel provides subsidized housing to senior citizens. As development moved uptown along Broadway and Telegraph Avenue, department stores and movie theaters erected fantastical Art-Deco temples, like the immense, maniacally ornate Paramount Theater. Smaller stores were no less sumptuous; today, these little jewel boxes, encased in jade or celadon tile, with gold-leaf acanthus moldings encircling doors and roofs, often are struggling to survive or standing vacant next to burned-out buildings.

In the first two decades of the twentieth century, Oakland embraced progressive reformist politics and City Beautiful urban design, by contrast with San Francisco's gritty political bossism. For a while after the 1906 San Francisco earthquake, it seemed possible that California's business nerve center might shift from San Francisco, nearly always visible under its fog canopy across the bay, to Oakland. But the construction of the Bay Bridge and Golden Gate Bridge in 1936 and 1937 ended that East Bay hope, by making San Francisco easier to reach and solidifying its status as the commercial and financial heart of the state.

World War II transformed Oakland. Along with nearby Richmond, the city boomed as the West Coast's largest shipbuilding center and the supply and distribution point for the Pacific war basin. Operating 24 hours a day, the shipyards drew in a flood of workers from across the country and rolled Liberty Ships into the Alameda Estuary after a mere three weeks in construction.

The city's population swelled by a third from 1940 to 1945, and a long demographic shift began: black residents grew from 3 percent of the population in 1940 to over 12 percent in 1950, nearly 23 percent in 1960, 34.5 percent in 1970, and 46.9 percent in 1980, making Oakland California's black capital. In the last decade, an influx of Mexicans, Chinese, and Filipinos has reduced the proportion of blacks in the 400,000-person city to around 40 percent, with whites at 30 percent.

Oakland's first blacks were proudly respectable "railroad men"—mostly Pullman porters, who settled into West Oakland around the train stations and shared the era's progressive beliefs. A 1913 editorial in the *Oakland Sunshine*, a black newspaper, typifies their civic-minded optimism: "What, I ask in all seriousness, with the advantages which our schools afford our young men, are their possibilities in the future? They are simply unbounded and indescribable." These old-timers were wary of the World War II migrants. Before the war, West Oakland had been relatively integrated and racially harmonious, but many of the new southern migrants brought with them the expectation of segregation and, old-timers grumbled, an inclination to public disorder. But they brought spending power, too. Hot West Oakland jazz clubs drew people from miles around (as did the new prostitution, bootlegging, and gambling operations); a black professional class grew up to serve the new workers. Today, many view West Oakland's thriving war years as the Harlem Renaissance of the West.

The war's end brought Oakland's boom to a halt, and in the fifties giant companies such as GM and GE moved their plants out to bigger suburban tracts. While Oakland's surrounding Alameda County gained over 10,000 manufacturing jobs between 1958 and 1966, Oakland itself lost nearly 10,000 jobs—and 23,000 residents between 1950 and 1970.

The War on Poverty filled the vacuum. After the Johnson administration deemed Oakland ripe for the next race riot—based on unemployment and racial tensions, underscored by one black leader's threat to a federal official that "we'll have a Watts here, and kill and bomb"—the feds rolled in a $23 million pilot jobs program in 1966, hoping to forestall trouble. Governor Edmund G. (Pat) Brown, Jerry's father, welcomed Washington's decision to "conduct in Oakland a massive experiment in solving the principal urban problem, unemployment." Though the result of the experiment was pitifully few new jobs, 140 non-military federal programs were spending $100 million a year in Oakland by 1967, close to twice the city's own budget. The city became a laboratory for government poverty fighting, closely studied by Berkeley urban-planning professors.

The War on Poverty didn't end Oakland's poverty, but it did trigger a momentous political upheaval. Oakland had always been a Republican town. Its twentieth-century patriarchs, Congressman Joseph Knowland and his son U.S. Senator William Knowland, led the national party's conservative wing and directed local politics from the turquoise and rose tower of the *Oakland Tribune*, which they owned from 1915 to 1977. "Kingmaker" Joseph Knowland pushed the careers of such Republican notables as Earl Warren, later U.S. Chief Justice, and Alameda Assistant D.A. Edwin Meese, later U.S. Attorney General; William ("Senator Formosa") Knowland, infuriated that opponents were recruiting Berkeley students to demonstrate against Barry Goldwater's nomination in 1964, set off the Free Speech Movement by pressuring the Berkeley chancellor to ban political organizing on campus. Oakland's City Council backed the Knowlands' conservative policies: it was committed to cutting taxes and skeptical of government's ability to solve social problems.

While Washington poured anti-poverty money into Oakland, the Black Panthers were on the rise there; Huey Newton had founded the violent black-power group in 1966, partly as a response to real and perceived police brutality. The Panthers glorified black criminality; they preached the murder of police officers and practiced what they preached. While wowing white radicals and the liberal establishment with their breakfast programs, free clinics, and Panther school, they were establishing a violent criminal empire in Oakland and pilfering from their community centers.

The Panthers co-opted a big slice of the anti-poverty effort, as their members took control of many community War on Poverty boards and doled out enough federal and state funds to make themselves formidable power brokers. By the 1970s, the Panthers had become an important force in Oakland politics and the state Democratic Party. Panther Bobby Seale made a credible run for mayor in 1973, and Panther Elaine Brown got 40 percent of the vote for a City Council seat in 1975, with the backing of Congressman Ron Dellums and organized labor. In 1976, Governor Jerry Brown appointed her as his delegate to the Democratic presidential convention.

The next year, Elaine Brown parlayed her new clout into a political revolution. With her assistance, Lionel Wilson, a former judge, became the city's first black mayor—and its first Democratic one. Though Panther power waned thereafter, the group had been key to making Oakland a black-controlled Democratic town, with black majorities on the City Council and the school board, and black chiefs of most city departments.

Like any political machine, the black Oakland machine viewed government as a jobs program. During a 1996 teachers' strike, school-board member Toni Cook rejected calls to cut the school bureaucracy on the grounds of racial solidarity. "I will not send people home without a job," she asserted— "and they look like me disproportionately." The city bureaucracy that grew up became legendary for haughtiness and intractability. When a big-money developer came to town to look at several city-owned properties, he arranged for the city development officer to show him around. As he waited for her outside one of the buildings, a sedan rolled past and slowed down; a set of keys came hurtling out the window. The development officer, late for another meeting, had simply thrown out the keys to the building and driven past.

Oakland has long harbored the full complement of urban ills. By 1990, 20 percent of the population was on welfare, and the poverty culture is still thriving. Crime spiked up in the 1970s, when brutal drug lord Felix Mitchell created the country's first large-scale, gang-controlled drug operation. Gangs still operate in the East Oakland housing projects where Mitchell reigned, contributing to a murder rate over twice that of San Francisco and New York. As in all western cities, appearances in the city's most dangerous areas are deceptive. Filled with Victorian cottages and 1930s bungalows rather than the oppressive brick projects of the East Coast, spread out horizontally under the huge sky rather than squeezed up vertically, East and West Oakland—in the flatlands between the estuary and the affluent foothills—retain some of their original charm during the day, despite the occasional stripped car, burned-out house, and trash-strewn vacant lot. "At night, it turns into something else," advises Archie, a recovering drug addict with a diamond stud in his ear and a big tattoo on his heavily muscled arm.

Despite missteps, Oakland has made some sensible efforts to fight its problems in the last decade, especially with its port initiative. Oakland's port was the first on the West Coast to reconfigure for containerized shipping, permanently squelching competition from San Francisco. Now it is further upgrading its facilities to best Los Angeles's and Portland's booming harbors. Nevertheless, frustration with the city's social and economic stagnation continued, leading to cracks in the black power structure well before Jerry Brown's candidacy. A white county-board member, Don Perata, won once-sacrosanct black seats first in the state assembly and then in the senate. An Asian developer launched a credible primary challenge to Mayor Elihu Harris in 1994. In 1996, a white progressive unseated an unresponsive black city councilwoman in West Oakland, the very heart of the black East Bay, to join a multi-ethnic council where blacks no longer hold the majority.

Most important, Oakland began sprouting a few highly articulate black critics of the status quo, led above all by Shannon Reeves, the dynamic young president of the local NAACP. In a typical sally, Reeves charged in 1997 that the school board was "absolutely riddled with nepotism, cronyism, and favoritism. The district spends $100,000 on a new logo, because they worry that the old one looks like broccoli. But they don't worry about whether kids can spell broccoli." Reeves's refusal to hold his fire against government incompetence even when black politicians face white challengers has left many an incumbent fuming.

But nothing shattered the old alliances more than Brown's run for the mayoralty. Gus Newport, Berkeley's radical black mayor from 1979 to 1986 and an East Bay patriarch, came out in support of Brown early on. "All of the black regulars had been in elected positions for ten to twenty years," he explained in an interview. "They fell into the same culture; they didn't know where to go to get professionals to crunch numbers. Oakland needed a severe leadership change," Newport concluded.

The old guard tried to concentrate its forces against Brown by persuading some of the many black mayoral contenders to drop out. None did, and Brown swept into office with more black votes than all the other candidates combined.

To Brown's good fortune, he found waiting for him in City Hall a new-generation black official, City Manager Robert Bobb, who is too busy cleaning up Oakland to worry about racial correctness. If Oakland does revive, it will be as much due to Bobb's management as to Jerry Brown's high-profile mayoralty.

Hired by the Council in 1997, Bobb roared into town from Richmond, Virginia, like a hurricane, vowing to drive criminals and inefficient bureaucrats out of town and to beautify the city. Tall and strongly built, with a taste for bright suspenders, flared pocket handkerchiefs, and well-tailored suits, the deceptively soft-spoken city manager immediately began an urban cleanliness program that could serve other cities as a model. At his urging, the Council passed a tough blight ordinance that heavily fines businesses for broken windows and graffiti, and home owners for couches dumped or laundry hung in their front yards. Trash detectives track down illegal dumpers and take them to court. Dilapidated houses now sport huge signs naming their often-absentee owners as public nuisances, and Bobb has demolished well over a hundred infamous properties that were blighting neighborhoods. Bobb wants to make all city employees ride along with street-sweeping crews to "start taking ownership for grime prevention," as his website announces. "I'm trying to instill a sense of pride," he explains in his large airy office overlooking City Hall Plaza. "In community meetings, I ask people who's been to Disneyland, and whether they put their hamburger wrappers on the street there. 'If you litter,' I tell them, 'it says it's okay to commit crime.'"

At the same time, Bobb turned to cleaning out the city workforce's deadwood. "We had assistants with an assistant," he recalls. He began by firing two black female department heads, igniting a firestorm among the black establishment that led to a City Council investigation—off limits to the public, for fear of publicizing the actual overrepresentation of blacks in managerial positions, according to a City Hall gadfly.

When Brown took office in January 1999, the housecleaning accelerated, for Brown shares Bobb's insistence on performance. "You have to be able to produce; this is what the world is about," Brown maintains. "That's what people in Oakland wanted." Bobb demoted four of ten department heads, 60 employees received "performance deficiency notices," and the rest of the city's 4,800 workers got warnings that unless their performance improved and they could demonstrate a contribution to Mayor Brown's blueprint for the city, they would be fired. The head of the municipal union cried that Bobb was creating a "climate of fear"; non-unionized city workers rushed to unionize.

The climax came when Brown and Bobb took on the city's first black police chief, Joseph Samuels. The mayor and the manager saw Oakland's reputation as a high-crime city as its biggest bar to renewal, and though crime had been falling at the national average, that wasn't good enough for them. The two flew east to study New York's innovative crime-fighting techniques and came back convinced that Oakland needed an explicit crime-reduction target and a plan for reaching it. "I kept waiting for the police chief to tell me his goal," Brown explains. "He never did, so I got myself a new police chief."

Blacks and white liberals throughout the city saw the firing of Samuels as an act of profound disrespect. A group of the city's black elite stormed City Hall, threatening civil disobedience and warning that the Black Panthers would return if Bobb and Brown instituted "Giuliani-style policing." The mayor and the city manager didn't flinch. "It was an intense evening, an interesting evening," Bobb now chuckles when asked about the confrontation. But he and Brown don't care whether the heads of city departments are popular, he says. "Rather, can they convince me that they are in touch with the nuts and bolts of their operation, and have a strategic vision?" The new top cop, a respected young black department veteran named Richard Word, has signed on to Brown's annual 20 percent crime-reduction goal, which he intends to meet by questioning criminals about other crimes they know of, finding the city's 750 lost parolees, serving 1,500 arrest warrants, and prosecuting gun violations in federal court.

Last November, five months after the mayoral election, a Brown-initiated ballot measure to replace Oakland's weak mayor–strong city manager form of government with its opposite passed by a whopping three-fourths majority—a sign of how high Oaklanders' hopes are for Brown. Though the measure transferred much of Bobb's power to Brown, the manager shows no sign of chagrin at his redefined role, nor does Brown evidence any desire to limit Bobb's de facto authority. The "Killer Bs," as the two are known, have been an unbeatable team, loping around the city, browbeating it into change.

Their toughest challenge will be the schools—the greatest casualty of Oakland's decades of race politics. Even today, though Oakland students have among California's lowest test scores, and an overwhelming majority of tenth-graders can't read at grade level, the school board and the teachers waste time in race baiting and radicalism. Last January, for instance, because "prison and the death penalty are poignantly real issues" for minority students, the teachers' union voted to hold a "teach-in" on cop killer Mumia Abu Jamal—on the same day as the funeral of a policeman murdered in cold blood by a young sniper.

This, after all, is the school system that in 1996 brought us "Ebonics," the school board–approved plan to "instruct African-American students in their primary language"—black English. No one talks about this civic embarrassment in Oakland these days, yet two members of the task force that proposed Ebonics have jobs in curriculum development today, and the city's teacher training now includes elements of the original plan, says former school-board member and Ebonics proponent Sylvester Hodges. Add to this foolishness a bureaucracy so incompetent that it loses applications from prospective teachers for months or years at a time, despite a claimed teacher-shortage emergency, and you have a recipe for disaster.

Though the mayor has no direct control over education, Brown has tried to shame the system into reform. "It's shocking beyond words," he said of the bureaucracy's attempts to defend its performance in the face of a 75 percent citywide reading-deficiency rate. "There is a pervasive denial of what is happening." When Superintendent Carole Quan pointed out that test scores had inched up recently, he mocked her "pathetically low expectations"—and then focused his guns on her. Though Asian, she was a 30-year insider and an ally of the black contingent in the school administration. No matter; in Brown's view, she was an obstacle to change. State Senator Don Perata backed up Brown's campaign against Quan with a bill promising a state takeover of the schools if the board did not fire her.

The counterattack followed the usual lines, with a member of the still-extant Ebonics task force charging that the fight over the schools was about "white and Jewish control." But Brown refused to get drawn into the race baiting. "Remember, this is a very powerful group of people who don't want to change, and they are fighting like mad to keep the status quo," he coolly responded. Two months after Police Chief Samuels departed, Superintendent Quan tearfully resigned. The Killer Bs named Bobb's deputy assistant as acting superintendent. Determined to force deeper change, Brown appointed a commission to develop alternative means of selecting the school board, including mayoral appointment.

Brown is also urging parents to form charter schools as part of his blueprint for Oakland; when the teachers' unions got a bill through the state assembly requiring such schools to unionize, the mayor used his hefty political clout to kill it. Charters appeal to Brown's populist, anti-authoritarian side; in an interview, he mischievously proposes as one possible model A. S. Neill's ruleless Summerhill, where class attendance was optional and the exit-exam failure rate by the school's untutored Noble Savages astronomical. Brown endorses the Romantic critique of traditional schooling as an assault on children's natural wisdom and creativity, which makes him unlikely to oppose the radical teaching theories that, no less than the stifling bureaucracy, are holding today's students back. Yet with his usual heterogeneity, he readily acknowledges that the Catholic education he received as a child and continued in a Jesuit seminary was pretty darn good training as well.

Expect Brown's realism to triumph yet again over his ideological commitments. Brown understands the all-importance of basic skills and has proposed a very un-Summerhill-like military academy and elite selective high school. His preference for private initiative over big government and his unflagging emphasis on results just might galvanize Oakland's schools out of their stupendous incompetence.

The Brown and Bobb era might turn out to be Oakland's fourth seismic shift, as momentous for the city as the Gold Rush, World War II, and the black revolution of the 1960s and 1970s. The March fury, when Brown and Bobb were facing down Police Chief Samuels and Superintendent Quan, has faded, and the relaxed race relations already visible on the street finally may be reaching the black political class, as well. Some of Brown's most strident black critics now concede that he may be just the man to shake up the city.

If he succeeds, it will be not just because of his star power. It will also be because, for all his far-left pronouncements, he understands cities' basic needs for order and private development, and he is willing to beat down all opposition to achieve them.

—Autumn 1999

JOEL KOTKIN

Why LA Is Bouncing Back

WHEN MAYOR RUDOLPH GIULIANI of New York announced that the 1997 Grammy Awards would take place at Madison Square Garden after being held for several years in Los Angeles, he seized the opportunity to demean the nation's second-largest city. New York, he declared, was "the real city," while Los Angeles merely existed "on tape." New York would now be not only the "capital of the world" but the "music capital of the world" as well.

Angelenos are used to such disparagement from New Yorkers, but perhaps it's time for Giuliani and other Gothamites to wake up and smell the cappuccino. In contrast to New York's weak economy, southern California's long-simmering economic resurgence is now truly building up steam after a half decade marred by the loss of over 100,000 aerospace jobs, a major riot, and a devastating earthquake, as well as assorted fires and floods. It is a recovery that holds vital lessons for cities—lessons about the critical importance of entrepreneurship, economic diversity, and decentralization to healthy urban economies.

The best evidence of the recovery lies in the job statistics. During 1995 Los Angeles County, the heart of urban southern California, created nearly 93,000 jobs—a hefty 2.5 percent increase in employment over the previous year, a rate roughly 50 percent above the national level. Suburban Orange, Riverside, San Bernardino, and Ventura counties enjoyed similar rates of growth, creating another 50,000 jobs.

By contrast, New York City over the same period could point to only 1,700 new jobs, according to the Bureau of Labor Statistics, many of them in government-funded social services; adding the immediate suburbs brings the total to barely 5,000. Indeed, since January 1994 urban Los Angeles County alone has produced more jobs than all of New York State, which has more than twice Los Angeles County's population.

True, southern California, which vied with New York for the nation's worst decline during the early 1990s, has not returned to the boom conditions of the late 1980s. Although employment is now back to or above pre-recession levels in outlying areas, most economists predict it will take another two years for L.A. County to recover all the jobs lost in the 1990–94 period. And the region, particularly the urban core, continues to be plagued by serious (albeit declining) levels of crime, weak schools, and troublesome racial politics. Yet L.A.'s economic future looks brighter than New York's. "Los Angeles has been beaten up a lot the last few years, and New York has been promoting itself," observes David Birch, president of Cognetics Inc., a Cambridge, Massachusetts, firm that tracks small-company growth. "But look at the numbers and the pattern is clear."

What's fueling the recovery? Above all, the existence of a vibrant entrepreneurial economy in the Los Angeles area. Take, for example, the comparative strength of Los Angeles on the *Inc. 500* roster of the nation's fastest-growing small private firms—precisely the companies creating most new jobs. In 1995 Los Angeles County had 15 companies on the list, compared with only three for New York City; the five-county Los Angeles region boasted 33, versus greater New York's 17. Of course, this is only the tip of the iceberg: along with these 33 of the fastest-growing are thousands of the merely fast-growing.

These small, fast-growing firms have become especially important to southern California in the wake of the defense industry's massive downsizing. Since 1979 the percentage of Californians who worked in companies with fewer than 100 employees grew from 42.1 percent to 51.5 percent of the workforce. Companies with over 1,000 employees lost more than 700,000 jobs, while the smallest firms—those with fewer than ten workers—gained well over 1 million. The statewide rate of new business incorporation rose 7 percent last year, far above the nation's 5 percent level.

The shift to smaller, newer companies was even more profound in Los Angeles itself. A 1993 study by economist David Friedman found that nearly 45 percent of all jobs in L.A. County were in companies under 15 years old. The growth of these firms through the recession rebuilt the southern California economy from the ground up.

Contrary to the rhetoric of conventional class-warfare politics, many of these jobs are in high-paying sectors. Last year Los Angeles County added some 20,000 jobs in motion picture and television production, compared with 3,200 in New York. Employment in engineering and management services, another key high-wage area, rose by roughly 18,000 jobs in the five-county L.A. area. At the same time, the long-battered industrial sector also began turning around, led by such small firms as apparel maker French Rags (with 92 employees) and credit-card producer Western Badge and Trophy (with 300 employees), as well as larger companies such as wheel manufacturer American Racing, part of a conglomerate that employs 2,000 people in Los Angeles. The growth of such firms has driven the county's industrial vacancy rates down to single digits.

L.A.'s entrepreneurial economy is largely the creation of immigrants. Southern California attracted 2 million immigrants in the 1980s, more than any other North American region and half a million more than New York. More important than their numbers has been the immigrants' work ethic and entrepreneurial culture. Asians and Latinos in California are, on average, one-fourth to one-third more likely to be self-employed than their counterparts in New York. Latino males have the highest labor participation rate of any ethnic group in the region, while poor Mexican immigrants have a rate of welfare recipiency one-third that of low-income Dominicans in New York.

Roughly two-thirds of all production workers in Los Angeles County are Latino; they are the linchpin of the local industrial economy, staffing everything from low-paid sewing shops to more upscale metal bending, electronics, and medical instruments firms. "People come here for a new life," observes Anthony Munoz, a native of Spanish Harlem and international sales manager for American Racing, 84 percent of whose 2,000 workers are Latino. "I find that the immigrants here are tremendously motivated and driven, and have an enormous pride in doing the job right," Munoz says.

Immigrants are reviving even parts of riot-torn south Los Angeles, now sprinkled with thriving businesses. This area, along with Compton and a string of industrial cities south of downtown, is home to an industrial economy that employs over 300,000 people, including 95,000 commuters—dwarfing the entire manufacturing sector in New York City. These are mostly smaller factories producing everything from textiles and garments to bicycle parts and biomedical and electronic goods. Food processing alone, a traditional Los Angeles industry, employs 30,000 workers in this region.

Though the riots were the last straw for many Anglo businessmen, immigrant entrepreneurs like Wesley Ru saw them as just another bump in the road. On the second day of rioting, Ru opened the doors early as usual at Western Badge and Trophy in the Pico-Union district. His workers arrived punctually as usual. But by 11 that morning, the madness was beginning to surge inexorably northward, toward Pico-Union. With several bus lines cut off, Ru began shuttling his workers by car. Then he returned to the factory with a handful of supervisors, ready for the worst. "We stood by and watched the street fill with people," the Taiwan-born Ru recalls. They were "rioting and looting. But we stood our ground." The angry mob simply passed them by.

Four years later Ru is still standing his ground—and then some. Western Badge and Trophy has spawned a series of related businesses, including the largest credit-card manufacturing business on the West Coast. The dying trophy company he bought in 1985 with $50,000 borrowed from relatives has blossomed into a small industrial powerhouse with 500 employees and clients that include Price Club, Coldwell Banker, and Walt Disney Studios.

Ru suggests that this immigrant-led recovery is invisible to many L.A. residents—including members of the Anglo establishment—who have not participated in it. "They don't drive through the stuff I see," Ru says. "There are thousands of Guatemalans, Salvadorans, and Koreans with small businesses. It's different, for sure, but it's the basis of something very vibrant."

The resurgent, immigrant-dominated industrial economy in south Los Angeles is sparking a renaissance in retailing throughout the area. For the past decade developer José de Jesus Legaspi has been bringing investors—from Latino, Asian, and Middle Eastern as well as Anglo backgrounds—into heavily Latino areas such as Huntington Park, a small industrial city abutting Los Angeles. Fifteen years ago Pacific Boulevard, Huntington Park's main street, was derelict, with vacancy rates as high as 50 percent. Today it competes with downtown's Broadway and Beverly Hills' Rodeo Drive for the region's highest sales volume per square foot.

As many older, Anglo-owned businesses and their owners have left town, immigrants have stepped into the breach. Over the past decade the number of Latino- and Asian-owned firms in Los Angeles has more than tripled. Some 1,200 Chinese electronics firms, most in the heavily Asian San Gabriel Valley, have created a local computer industry with over 5,000 employees and combined annual sales well in excess of $3 billion. Since 1993 Legaspi and a client, Iran native Darioush Khaledi, have opened 14 major supermarkets in largely Latino areas south of the Santa Monica Freeway. "These areas have been underserved for years," Legaspi says, inspecting a potential new supermarket site in a decrepit but busy strip mall on Long Beach Boulevard. "When a shopping center like this one is still successful, imagine what it could do if you fix it up."

L.A.'s immigrant-fueled vibrancy even extends to downtown. Get a few blocks away from the high-rise districts, where office vacancy rates remain in the low to mid-twenties, and you'll find a thriving industrial, warehouse, and distribution economy run by immigrants. "The people who own the high-rises haven't faced the music yet, but we are already developing new properties for where the future is," says Doug Hinchliffe of Lowe Development, a major builder now developing a 23-acre import/export center on downtown's Alameda Street. "It's the importers, the garment people, the immigrants, the Asian entrepreneurs who are driving things."

Perhaps the most influential of these new immigrant entrepreneurs is Hong Kong native Charlie Woo. Stricken by polio as a child, he walks with crutches as he surveys his empire. Taking advantage of cheap real estate and easy access to the Los Angeles harbor, Woo started a toy distribution business in the early 1980s in a largely abandoned warehouse district east of downtown. City planners, dreaming high-rise dreams, yawned. "They didn't understand what I was doing and didn't know why I wanted to be there," Woo recalls. "It was totally dead. No one wanted to be there."

The planners were wrong. Where they saw no future, Woo and a handful of other entrepreneurs envisioned a global center for the toy trade. Today the area is home to more than 500 toy distributors, employing 6,000 workers and boasting an estimated $1 billion in revenues. The success of Toytown, as the area is called, is also breeding new opportunities for local manufacturers and designers. Woo, for example, contracts out to local freelancers who design toys to be manufactured in China. And the Otis Art Institute, a division of Parsons School of Design, is starting a new program for toy designers in Los Angeles's Westchester district, near Mattel's facility in the city of El Segundo. Ten Otis graduates already work for Mattel, designing, among other things, fashions for the company's ageless icon, Barbie.

Buyers from around the world and from other parts of the U.S. crowd the area, looking for new products. "L.A. is becoming the ultimate middleman, not only for Asia but for Mexico, the Midwest, and the South," Woo says. He describes Los Angeles as "the new Hong Kong," with its scattered, dense, specialized commercial zones.

Downtown Los Angeles and the east-side warehouse district might be terra incognita for much of Anglo Los Angeles, but for Woo's customers, they are ideal locations. "If you say we're in downtown L.A., people from Mexico are comfortable," Woo says. "The same is true for people from China or Taiwan. All you say is, we're near Chinatown or Monterey Park—in these places you are really closer to the world. This is where the information comes together."

The resurgence epitomized by Toytown, the rapid growth in the entertainment industry, the continued vibrancy of the L.A. garment district, the new interest among developers in south Los Angeles: all these trends reflect the vibrant economic potential of central cities. Los Angeles's economic recovery makes clear that even poorer urban precincts possess enormous economic promise.

Surprisingly, a key factor promoting Los Angeles's recovery is southern California's polycentric, sprawling model of development, which has proved far more conducive to the emergence of small businesses than the old, heavily centralized model New York perfected. Though the Los Angeles area has long been derided as "suburbs in search of a city," this decentralized structure has proved a blessing.

Journalists, urban politicians, and planners tend to dislike polycentric cities—understandably—for their lack of focus and grandeur. With development dispersed throughout a region, such cities lack arresting skylines, spectacular entertainment districts, and throbbing train stations. In 1979, when sociologist John Kasarda of the University of North Carolina presented his findings on the advantages of polycentric cities to HUD officials in the Carter administration, he was, he says, virtually "booted out of town."

Yet here's the record since then: nearly all the fastest-growing metropolitan regions of the country—Atlanta, Charlotte, Dallas, Denver, Houston, Orlando, Phoenix—follow an essentially polycentric model, with the bulk of their economic activity scattered throughout different urban mini-centers and what author Joel Garreau calls "edge cities." In 1970 downtowns accounted for about 80 percent of all office space nationwide; today they account for roughly half that.

In many polycentric cities, downtowns are the weakest link in the regional economy: according to Garreau's newsletter, *Edge City News*, vacancy rates for the central districts in Atlanta, Cleveland, Dallas, Los Angeles, Miami, and San Diego are 5 or more percentage points higher than those in the surrounding office districts. Downtown L.A.'s vacancy rate is over 20 percent; the rate in most suburban areas ranges from 9 to 15 percent. Dallas has a 35 percent vacancy rate; the Dallas suburbs, only 13 percent.

Polycentric regions like L.A. are laboratories for discovering what kind of municipal policies work best to encourage economic growth. Around the central city, dozens of smaller municipalities have developed their own distinct styles of urban governance, some more successful at attracting and nourishing business than others. In L.A. County, strong pro-business administrations in cities like Burbank, Glendale, and Culver City have enabled businesses from financial services to costume-jewelry manufacturing to germinate, take root, and spread. All this clearly visible competition for business forces these smaller urban centers to stay friendly to entrepreneurship and resistant to the business-killing burdens imposed by an expanding municipal welfare state, excessive regulation, and politically powerful public-sector unions—burdens that all too visibly encumber the central city.

Consider in this regard the development of the L.A. region's entertainment industry. Roughly 90 percent of its expansion has occurred outside of Hollywood, the city of Los Angeles's historic movie district. This is not so much because the studios have moved as that more and more of the industry's workers are freelancers or are employees of firms with fewer than ten individuals, working under contract for the major studios. Most such firms prefer low-rise buildings in nondescript neighborhoods near one of the studios in municipalities that are less hostile to business than the city of Los Angeles.

Burbank, for example, is closer to downtown Los Angeles than are many parts of L.A. itself. But the Burbank city government charges developers of office space a maximum of $6.38 per square foot in fees, less than half of what Los Angeles charges. Burbank's benefits are greater still for companies that occupy existing space. For the average provider of business services using 30,000 square feet, fees in Burbank average around $12,000, compared with $116,000 in Los Angeles; an electrical-equipment manufacturer in Burbank must pay roughly $8,980 per year, his Los Angeles counterpart $23,860.

This disparity, suggests consultant Larry Kosmont of the L.A.-based consulting firm Kosmont and Associates, reflects the higher costs imposed by Los Angeles's expansive bureaucracy and larger welfare population. Equally important, says Kosmont, who has served as Burbank's director of community development and Bell Gardens' city manager, is that smaller cities have more responsive governments. No wonder, since most have populations under 100,000, compared with 3.5 million in L.A. proper. They don't suffer from the paralyzing balkanization that affects the Los Angeles city government, dominated by a 15-member city council whose constituents live in far-flung and wildly differing districts. Councilmen from the east and south sides of L.A., for example, oppose growth in the entertainment industry, since it doesn't directly benefit their districts. By contrast, Kosmont says, the councils in smaller cities, for obvious reasons, have "an easier time focusing on the whole picture."

As a result, cities like Burbank can accommodate relocating or expanding businesses with remarkable promptness. Decisions that take the L.A. bureaucracy years can be made by Burbank in weeks. "I have windows of opportunity that open and shut in a matter of weeks," explains one entertainment executive, who decided to move his 150-person firm from Los Angeles to Burbank. "I don't have time for L.A. city hall to make the deal."

These small cities constitute "urban villages"—dense agglomerations without big-city bureaucratic roadblocks. "This is small-town America in the middle of a big city," boasts Bob Tague, Burbank's present community development director. To preserve its small-town ambience, this predominantly middle-class city of 98,000 has worked to keep its streets clean, to wipe out graffiti, and to spruce up its once-desolate central area—the much-maligned "beautiful downtown Burbank"—into a pleasant, mildly busy shopping district. Tague and other city officials have worked closely with Burbank's two major anchors, Warner Brothers and Disney, each of which has added upward of half a million square feet of space, including Disney's new animation center. They have also lured hundreds of smaller specialty movie industry firms, particularly in multimedia and post-production (the editing and dubbing of completed films and television shows). Firms like these have occupied another 750,000 square feet of new space. Future plans call for as much as 6 million more square feet just from Disney and Warner. Largely as a result of this expansion, Burbank's unemployment rate—despite the loss of

Lockheed and 14,000 aerospace jobs since 1989—is just 5 percent, 2 to 3 points below the county average.

Because of all this growth, Burbank's revenues are surging, enabling it to begin keeping libraries open over the weekend, just as Los Angeles County is cutting back and contemplating closures. Burbank has also appropriated new funds to help fix schools, maintain roads, and finance other amenities crucial to media firms.

Other examples of booming urban villages abound. Nearby Glendale, which previously had almost no entertainment-industry presence, now counts entertainment and multimedia as the largest employers in this city of 198,000. That presence will soon swell with the opening of a new Dreamworks animation facility and the arrival of a large administrative unit of the Walt Disney Company, which will occupy seven floors of a 14-story tower. Demand for space is so strong that a Korean developer has announced plans to build a new 24-floor office tower in the city.

It's not just conservative middle-class urban centers that are showing renewed economic life, but also predominantly minority ones like Compton, Inglewood, and Southgate, which are far more business-friendly than Los Angeles. Even left-wing officials in cities like Santa Monica and West Hollywood realize that anti-business policies would drive out the firms that pay for such social programs as they have.

The success of these urban villages has spurred L.A. proper to try to improve its own business climate. "It really comes down to the competitive environment," observes Gary Mendoza, Los Angeles's deputy mayor of economic development. "Competition drives improvement in the private sector and also in the public sector." Mayor Richard Riordan formed the Los Angeles Business Team, a 15-person "strike force" that tries to identify and work with firms contemplating expanding or leaving the city. The team assigns an individual caseworker to a firm to help it get through the bureaucratic process—a matter of course in places like Burbank. The team has persuaded such firms as Brenda French, a West Los Angeles knitwear maker, and Carole Little, a major apparel firm near downtown, to stay in the city. "They helped us with the permits so everything could go very smoothly," says French, whose firm employs 92 people and has annual sales of $6 million. "And on top of it, they were very nice. It was not like working with the city."

More recently the city has begun reforming its fee structure—still the region's highest, usually by a large margin. The City Council has reduced utility taxes for telemarketing firms and has slashed sewer hookup fees—which can run into the millions of dollars—by two-thirds. In a move to stem the flight of businesses to Burbank and Glendale, the city this year approved a cap on business license fees at roughly $25,000 for entertainment-related companies in the adjacent, run-down North Hollywood area. Formerly these licenses could cost upward of $100,000.

Both Riordan and Mendoza admit that these changes have been far from sufficient to compete with the peripheral cities in terms of either amenities or taxes. But market conditions may soon give L.A. a boost. With soaring rental rates and tightening vacancies in the smaller cities, languishing districts like Hollywood—a neighborhood of Los Angeles, not a separate city—are becoming competitive again for the first time in decades. There are now 37 new projects and 27 expansions on tap for Hollywood, up from zero three years ago. These include upscale restaurants, office-building renovations, and two new entertainment-oriented museums on Hollywood Boulevard, both scheduled to open this fall.

Riordan's efforts to make L.A. competitive with the peripheral cities represent a break with the policies of his predecessor, Tom Bradley, who dreamed of transforming the long-declining downtown area into something more akin to midtown Manhattan. Bradley's expansive vision included a multi-billion-dollar subway system, new high-rises, and new cultural institutions. His plan couldn't stand up to the economic shocks of the early 1990s. Today, despite the recovery, downtown struggles with 20 percent or higher vacancy rates. The push to turn downtown into a bustling cultural center has failed; the subway has become a laughingstock.

Sensibly, Riordan has abandoned many of Bradley's grandiose centralized visions. The mayor's main goal now is finding ways—given a tight budget situation—to lighten the tax and regulatory burden for smaller firms. Major overhauls of the city's permitting and tax programs are expected later this year. "Everything is being reconsidered," Mendoza says. "We recognize that the L.A. economy is changing dramatically."

What can New York learn from Los Angeles? The two cities have much in common. They are America's premier centers for international trade, culture, communications, fashion, tourism, and business services. Each is in the midst of a radical demographic transformation, driven by an inflow of immigrants—roughly 100,000 annually in Los Angeles and 80,000 in New York—and by a record out-migration of native-born residents. Each suffers from high costs, an aging infrastructure, dysfunctional bureaucracies, and the usual array of urban social scourges.

Los Angeles is rebounding from the enormous setbacks of the past five years. New York could too—but its leaders need a change of attitude. Above all, they must stop looking at New York as simply Manhattan and start recognizing the enormous economic potential of the outer boroughs, with their concentrations of immigrants and entrepreneurs. Just as in Huntington Park and the San Gabriel Valley, immigrants are revitalizing neighborhoods like Astoria and Flushing in Queens.

But they, too, will flee New York unless the city drastically reduces the costs of doing business. Only by lightening the burdens of taxation and regulation that drive entrepreneurs away—as Burbank has done and Los Angeles is belatedly trying to do—can New York mount a real, lasting economic comeback. Such a step will require a change in New York's governmental culture. "New York has historically been oriented to the *Fortune* 500—it's a system set up for large companies and has disincentives for smaller companies," says John Kasarda of the University of North Carolina. "New York will offer $100 million for a large firm to be in Manhattan, but it maintains impossible regulatory and tax burdens on small companies. The orientation is to go for the trophy rather than to open to entrepreneurs."

Such an approach is profoundly misguided in today's economy: since 1980 the *Fortune* 500 have reduced employment by 5 million workers. Tax concessions to large companies force smaller firms to pick up more of the tax burden. Barring a cutback in the extravagant costs of city government, the breaks the Giuliani administration and its predecessors have given to large firms such as Condé Nast can be made up only by keeping taxes crushingly high for the smaller firms that in Los Angeles account for virtually all new employment gains.

Another important step in reviving New York would be to decentralize decision making. The city would have to devolve real power—over taxes, fees, and zoning—to officials elected at the borough or neighborhood level. A poorer neighborhood, for example, should have the freedom to adopt policies that would enhance its advantages as a location for warehousing or light distribution without imposing Manhattan-like costs on business. Under such a regime, parts of New York could see Burbank- or Glendale-style economic expansion.

New York's future lies not in boasting about being the "capital of the world" but in facing the economic challenges of an ever more competitive environment. That's a lesson Mayor Riordan is learning. "We are seeing a shift to a new wave of business leaders who are used to dealing with a different kind of economy," the Los Angeles mayor says. "L.A. has the best future of any major American city. It will be dominated by small companies, ethnic business, international trade. It will be very good—but also very different."

—Summer 1996

II

CRIME

The greatest domestic policy success of the last generation has been the slashing of the urban crime rate, led by the innovative policing tactics of New York City. Crime had been the Number One cause of urban decay, driving the law-abiding to the suburbs and causing businesses to flee. But then New York discovered that it could prevent crime rather than just trying to solve it after it had already occurred. In six years, crime fell by half, murder by nearly two-thirds, and as a result businesses began to flourish and dying neighborhoods, especially poor ones, sprang back to life as people stopped being afraid to go out. Police departments around the nation and the world have flocked to New York to learn how to do it. Here's how.

WILLIAM J. BRATTON AND WILLIAM ANDREWS
What We've Learned About Policing

EVERYONE KNOWS ABOUT New York's spectacular crime turnaround, with murder down 68 percent and overall felonies down 50 percent in the five years since 1993. But how we accomplished that turnaround—and what we've learned about how to police New York—isn't widely known or fully understood. It should be, because the New York story adds up to a textbook on how to police any big city.

Our success rested on two major changes. First, we had to remake the NYPD into an effective, focused organization. Second, we had to use this instrument actually to police the city by developing strategies and tactics that would prevent and uproot crime rather than just react to it. In practice, of course, these were parallel, often overlapping efforts. The re-engineering was more challenging than the strategizing; and if we hadn't changed the way the department did business, it wouldn't have mattered what field strategies we chose, because we wouldn't have been able to translate them into practice.

Professors of business administration and organizational management would have caught on to what we were doing right away, since it was no different from the restructuring and re-engineering that had transformed American business in the late 1980s and early 1990s. Like the corporate CEOs of that era, we began with a large, unfocused, inward-looking, bureaucratic organization, poor at internal communication or cooperation and chronically unresponsive to intelligence from the outer world. We reduced layers of management, drove responsibility down to the operating units, improved communication and data processing, tightened accountability, and rewarded results. In short order, we had the NYPD's bureaus and divisions competing with criminals, not with one another.

Police work is by nature decentralized and discretionary. The cop in the field, the front-line supervisor, the precinct commander—these are the real decision makers in day-to-day police work. The only way you can control a police department from headquarters is if your aim is to prevent police from doing anything, rather than to have them function effectively—and for many years that was precisely the aim of the NYPD. The organization didn't want high performance; it wanted to stay out of trouble, to avoid corruption scandals and conflicts in the community. For years, therefore, the key to career success in the NYPD, as in many bureaucratic leviathans, was to shun risk and avoid failure. Accordingly, cops became more cautious as they rose in rank, right up to the highest levels.

One anecdote that a deputy chief likes to tell perfectly captures how risk-averse the department had become. One weekend in the late eighties, when he was serving as duty captain in upper Manhattan, he arrived at a crime scene where cops had arrested two drug dealers, one of whom had tried to flee to an apartment. The deputy chief helped the cops secure search warrants for the apartment and a safe they found inside it—which contained drugs, cash, and weapons. The next day, the borough commander—"apoplectic with rage," the deputy chief recalls—called him in to yell at him for seeking a warrant. "It's people like you who cause problems in the department," the commander roared. If something like that happens again, the commander ordered, "you will walk away." Sums up the deputy chief: "I, as a captain, was not supposed to encourage these officers to do police work. My job was to stop them from doing police work." After all, something could go wrong.

As for its management philosophy, the NYPD combined the worst of both worlds: it was a micromanaged organization that was strategically adrift. "Cops felt," as one prosecutor remembers it, "as if the brass were checking up on them, not backing them up." Management consisted of sending sergeants around to make sure that patrolmen were at their assigned posts. Woe to the cop who wasn't there—even for a good reason—when the sergeant came at regular intervals to sign his memo book. The message: just sit there and get your ticket punched.

We had to change the department's methods and mind-set. The first step, when author Bratton became commissioner in 1994, was to draw as many people as possible into the planning process, especially the precinct and unit commanders, who corresponded to a corporation's middle managers, and the sergeants and lieutenants, who were, in effect, the front-line supervisors. "Bratton ran an organization that was open to talent," says Jack Maple, a former NYPD deputy commissioner for crime-control strategies. "It was an organization of inclusion, where people weren't afraid to come up with the wildest ideas." Maple himself was a prime case in point. When only a Transit Police lieutenant, he caught Bratton's attention with an idea-crammed memo on how to control robberies in the subway, and he rose rapidly thereafter.

We brought almost 500 people into the planning process, serving on 12 re-engineering teams that questioned everything in heated debate that sometimes escalated to a free-for-all. "An organization as big and as venerable as the NYPD accumulates a lot of bad habits," points out John Timoney, who was chief of department in 1994 and first deputy commissioner in 1995 and is now Philadelphia's police commissioner. "We did things a certain way because we had always done them that way. We had to banish the phrase, 'We have always' from our vocabularies. We had to start asking, 'How should we do it?' and 'How can we do it better?'"

Ideas and innovations bubbled up. The commissioner didn't originate most of the ideas that ended up transforming the way we did business; instead—and crucially—he created the atmosphere in which paradigm-breaking ideas could flourish. A December 1994 plan of action listed more than 600 recommendations, of which we adopted more than 400. We raised recruiting standards and improved training for the real world of police patrol. We redesigned the uniform with input from the officers who wear it, and, with the advice of the police unions, we revamped the archaic discipline system to make it swifter. We retooled our job-performance evaluation system. We even changed our super-secret internal-affairs process, bringing precinct commanders into internal investigations, which strengthened our capacity to prevent and detect police corruption and abuse. Formerly, only a half-dozen internal-affairs officials attempted to control misconduct in a 38,000-person department.

But the most important reform we made was decentralizing the department, devolving power to the precinct commanders and creating a career path for them to ascend. In the old NYPD, precinct commanders had little genuine authority. They couldn't conduct an anti-prostitution operation or use plainclothes officers in anti-drug operations; they couldn't secure search warrants and conduct searches. These constraints reflected a deep mistrust of the precincts, a fear that something could go terribly wrong out there that would embarrass the command staff. But as Robert Johnson, head of the private First Security Services and a member of Bratton's kitchen cabinet, puts it: "A management team that concentrates on preventing failure usually forecloses success. When you don't trust your basic resource, it's hard to perform your basic business."

The precincts are the primary unit of policing, and the precinct commanders are policing's equivalent of corporate line managers. It was just plain crazy to limit their options. Worse, the precinct commander's job was all downside risk in 1993, just before we arrived; there was no real way to succeed and a dozen ways to fail. An outstanding precinct commander's performance against crime would have gone largely unnoticed—nobody was monitoring that kind of success—but a corruption scandal or a mishandled community incident could set a career back years. No wonder that captains tried to hurry through their precinct commands and move on to less career-threatening assignments in the bureaucracy at 1 Police Plaza.

We gave precinct commanders—typically people with 15 years' experience, a college education, and a sophisticated knowledge of the city and the department—the authority to run what amounted to miniature police departments. John Timoney devised a new career ladder for these commanders, ascending from one of the 35 "C" precinct houses with moderate workloads to one of 31 higher-pressure "B" houses and ultimately to one of the 10 extremely busy "A" houses. As a commander rose through these steps, he could advance from captain to deputy inspector to inspector without ever leaving the precincts. A few battlefield promotions made it clear that precinct command was the place to shine in the NYPD.

The good commanders reveled in their new authority, and their precincts became natural arenas for team building. Their cops were energized. Cops like to do police work: stinging a drug dealer with a buy-and-bust operation, executing a search warrant at the apartment of a gun dealer, even catching someone blasting a car radio with a decibel meter—these are interesting jobs compared with regular patrol. They are also team activities that give the workers a shared sense of purpose and a renewed sense of energy.

Accountability goes hand in hand with decentralization; you can't give all that power away without a means of maintaining strategic oversight. The NYPD does that through its now-famous Compstat process, which uses computerized crime statistics, electronic crime maps, and intensive crime-control management meetings to guide and monitor the department's anti-crime strategies.

From the start, Jack Maple had insisted on timely weekly data about crime in the precincts, an approach completely foreign to the NYPD, where crime data typically lagged events by up to three months. Because we couldn't live with flying blind, not knowing what was actually happening precinct by precinct and week by week, Maple, Chief Louis Anemone, and Anemone's staff developed the basic format for the weekly report that the department has been using ever since. It showed weekly felony crime and arrest data for every precinct, comparing it with the totals for the previous week and the month- and year-to-date totals. Compstat was the computer-file name of this report, a contraction of "comparison statistics." Maple and Anemone began going over the new data at meetings with precinct personnel, quizzing commanders about crime in their precincts and what they were doing about it. Soon they were using pin maps and acetate overlays to display the patterns of criminal activity. They began calling in special unit commanders and narcotics commanders. The Compstat process was off and running.

As Compstat grew more sophisticated, we began computer mapping the crime patterns and displaying the maps on large overhead screens. We could identify local crime increases almost immediately and respond to them rapidly with effective measures before they could add up to a big, city-wide crime spike. You could see the clusters of shootings, robberies, burglaries, and car thefts. We mapped arrest and patrol activity and compared crime incidents with police response. If the two didn't match up, you knew you were doing something wrong. We compared our deployment patterns with time-of-day graphs that showed when crime spikes were occurring. Compstat's maps helped make sure that we were putting our resources where the problems were, and when they were happening. We could quickly assess whether new strategies and tactics worked or failed.

Compstat enforced cooperation among the department's many bureaus and units. Every week, a different group of commanders from a particular part of the city stands up at the podium to get grilled about crime and prevention in their precincts, but every other relevant special unit and task force commander for that area of the city is also present and must be prepared to respond. Just having them all in one room instantly cut the bureaucratic Gordian knot. Chief Anemone and Deputy Commissioner Maple could broker solutions to current problems on the spot. Was drug dealing causing an increase in shootings? Narcotics enforcement could be called in swiftly. Were burglaries on the rise in a community? The warrant division could search for wanted burglars in the area. Were auto thieves following a certain route to a nearby highway? Highway units could set up a checkpoint.

Above all, as John Timoney puts it, "Compstat is the greatest accountability tool ever." It's an instrument for holding precinct commanders responsible for crime in their areas, rewarding them if they push crime down and removing them if they don't come up with plans to do so. In addition, it gets the whole department, top brass included, involved in thinking about how to push back crime, and it lets precinct commanders know, on a weekly basis, that their bosses support their efforts. Eventually, we used Compstat to manage everything from civilian complaints to overtime to police auto accidents.

It's not too strong a statement to say that we reinvented police strategy in 1994. Before then, the prevailing criminological wisdom held that the police couldn't do much about crime and that police strategies and tactics didn't really matter. In that spirit, the NYPD and most other police departments spent almost no time thinking about anti-crime strategies. Police brass lurched from emergency to emergency, with no one looking at the overall picture.

Strategy is a way of seeing things whole, of focusing on the entire system of crime and how it operates. Since 1994, the NYPD hasn't just been solving crimes; it has been dismantling criminal enterprises and support systems. It has been taking away the things that criminals need to function: their guns, their fences, their chop shops and auto exporters, their drug-buying and prostitution customers, their buildings and apartments, their cars, and the unpoliced sectors of the city where crime used to thrive.

In early 1994, the department developed strategies on guns, drugs, youth crime, domestic violence, and quality of life. Though much has been made of quality-of-life enforcement as key to the overall New York strategy, it was hardly the whole story. To say that "zero tolerance" policing turned New York around, as if driving away squeegee men and panhandlers could by itself cut the robbery and burglary rates, is a gross oversimplification. To succeed, we had to employ the quality-of-life strategy in concert with a range of strategies targeting felony crime.

But quality-of-life enforcement is important for three reasons. First, most neighborhoods are usually more concerned about prostitution, low-level drug dealing, excessive noise, underage drinking, and other minor offenses than major crimes. Citizens want the police to do something about these highly visible disturbances. Second, as George Kelling has persuasively argued in the pages of *City Journal*, disorderly environments breed both crime and fear. Third, criminals who commit serious crimes frequently commit minor violations as well; quality-of-life enforcement lets cops intervene with this population and sometimes prevent serious crimes before they happen.

In 1994, we took quality-of-life enforcement to the streets. Author Bratton had pioneered this style of policing in Boston in the 1970s. He imported it to New York when he became chief of the Transit Police in 1990, and it had transformed the subway from a place where young thugs thought they could get away with anything into a place where they felt they could get away with nothing, with a steep drop in crime as a result. So, too, with the city as a whole: as Kelling has observed, New York City had "depoliced" its streets in the quarter-century prior to 1994. Police officers were walking by disorderly conditions and letting them fester. They were openly giving freedom of the streets to the drug dealers, the gangs, the prostitutes, the drinkers, and the radio blasters. A sense of fear and anarchy pervaded many neighborhoods. The traditional order-keeping forces, the responsible adults in these communities, played less of a role as their own fear and uncertainty grew. They—along with the wrongdoers—had gotten the message that even the cops didn't care, and they were understandably hesitant to put themselves on the line.

The newly empowered precinct commanders targeted prostitution, public drinking and underage drinking, street drug dealing, and excessive noise. They instructed patrol officers to intervene in street disorder and to try to restore a sense of civility and safety to neighborhoods. "We had always been telling the cops what *not* to do in street situations," says Michael Julian, formerly chief of personnel and now a private security executive. "They needed training in what they *could* do."

As part of the quality-of-life initiative, the police checked identification of people stopped for minor offenses. When the checks turned up a wanted person, a parole violator, or a repeat offender, cops arrested and searched him, instead of letting him off with a relatively toothless desk-appearance ticket, as is usual with minor offenders.

This intensified police presence had an almost immediate impact on illegal guns. We flooded shooting hot spots, identified through the Compstat maps, with both uniformed and plainclothes enforcement teams. People carrying illegal guns quickly realized that they risked gun charges after being arrested for minor crimes. After rising briefly in 1994, gun apprehensions then began to fall; the gunslingers were leaving their weapons at home. With far fewer guns on the street, far fewer people were shot and far fewer were killed. In month-to-month comparisons from 1993 to 1994, homicide was down 32 percent in September 1994, 46 percent in October, 28 percent in November, and 34 percent in December.

At the same time, we brought the department's detectives more forcefully into play. We told them to make shootings a priority and to investigate every one as if it were a murder. "There was no good reason why the detective response to a killing was always so much greater than to a shooting," says John Timoney. "An aggravated-assault victim is just a lucky homicide victim whose assailant missed." To keep on top of the issue, Jack Maple had the operations center beep him every time a shooting occurred. In 1994, he got beeped nearly 4,500 times, day and night.

We enlisted detectives in an anti-gun offensive, instructing them to grill anyone arrested in a shooting or on gun charges about how and where he had acquired his weapon. The murderer who fired on Jewish students in a van on the approach ramp to the Brooklyn Bridge, killing one boy, was in custody within a few days; within a week, so was the gun dealer from whom he had purchased his weapon. By the end of 1994, the NYPD had arrested more than 200 gun dealers and confiscated their supply of weapons. Between 1993 and the end of 1995, handgun homicides declined by 40 percent, and shootings declined by more than 2,000 cases.

We fed information about gun trafficking from the precinct interrogations to the NYPD's joint task force with the federal Bureau of Alcohol, Tobacco, and Firearms, which in turn used this intelligence to make arrests for illegal gun trafficking in the main states that supply weapons to New York City. The task force also began closely scrutinizing applicants for federal firearms-dealing licenses, in the belief that some dealers would use the right to buy guns in quantity to sell them illegally to unlicensed New Yorkers. In the first years of the program, 92 percent of applicants for new licenses and for license renewals either failed to win approval or—once they knew the police were watching them—withdrew their applications.

Precinct detective squads adopted a new intelligence-gathering strategy. They began to question all arrestees not only about crimes that they might have committed themselves but also about any other crimes that they knew anything about. Detectives asked arrestees about open homicides, about robbery and burglary patterns, and about where drugs or firearms were for sale. Some talked in return for a promise of more lenient treatment, but many were willing to talk gratis, swelling the NYPD's supply of criminal intelligence and case leads. A car thief turned in a fence, who turned in a father-and-son gun-dealing team. A gun-crime debriefing in the 46th Precinct in the Bronx led to several arrests in a year-old murder case and to arrests for a recent stabbing and a carjacking in the neighboring 43rd Precinct.

Detectives began using the department's improved intelligence to identify robbery patterns more quickly and to apprehend the robbers on the second or third crime of the pattern rather than the ninth or tenth. Identifying a pattern early, staking out the locale, and catching the guy can prevent 20, 30, or even 50 robberies a year. We also told detectives to pursue *all* accomplices in any robbery, instead of playing the old detective game of building clearance rates by closing cases with just one arrest. Our goal was preventing crime, not closing cases. Robbery fell by more than 26,000 incidents, or 31 percent, in 1994 and 1995. By 1998, it was down 55 percent from its 1993 level.

The Detective Bureau also placed a new emphasis on warrants and on finding wanted fugitives, since warrant absconders who fail to show up for their court appearances are frequently recidivists who will continue to commit crimes for as long as they are free. We expanded the warrant division and doubled warrant apprehensions between 1993 and 1995. Detective Bureau arrests of all kinds, including warrant apprehensions, are up about 138 percent since 1993.

To control burglaries and thefts of car radios, we went after fences who traffic in stolen goods, another thing that the NYPD had never bothered to do. Early on, police used sting operations to nail two major fences in Brooklyn, recovering enough stolen merchandise to fill a warehouse. Eventually, the fences helped identify a who's who of Brooklyn burglars; one fence even had security videotape showing many of the burglars' faces. Even when it doesn't lead directly to mass burglary arrests, as this operation did, shutting down local fences can have a dramatic impact on neighborhood burglary rates. It may take burglars a while to find another outlet for their stolen goods, and they can't go back to work until they can move the hot merchandise. Burglary was down 25,000 incidents in 1994 and 1995, or 25 percent. By 1998, it was down 53 percent.

When we arrived, New York City, and especially the borough of Queens, looked like the car-theft capital of the world, with more than 112,000 cars, worth about $400 million, stolen in 1993. Organized-crime groups stole an estimated 70 percent of them, for parts and for export. Using the same logic that we had applied to burglary, we went after chop shops and auto exporters. In 1995, we set up more than 30 phony fencing operations to catch car thieves, and we conducted more than 60 operations in which undercover officers offered supposedly stolen parts to dealers. We also used stings to make cases against exporters of stolen cars to Russia, the Dominican Republic, Saudi Arabia, Nigeria, and Colombia. We requested district attorneys in Queens and Brooklyn to prosecute auto thieves routinely and send them to jail. Car theft plummeted by more than 40,000 cases in 1994 and 1995, or 36 percent. By 1998, it was down 61 percent.

We knew, as Michael Julian puts it, that "drugs were causing probably half of the crime and a lot of the fights and gunplay." There was no way to reduce crime without going after narcotics. But the department had long been combating drugs in the wrong way, arresting street dealers and seizing drugs—commodities that were expendable, and almost infinitely renewable, as far the drug gangs were concerned. We believed that we had to concentrate on the local drug gangs and dismantle them. These are the critical middlemen between the street dealers and the international drug importers.

Narcotics Division commander Pat Harnett developed a new strategy in 1995 and 1996: he established turf-based drug units that would concentrate on reclaiming individual neighborhoods, investigating and dismantling the drug gangs operating in an area, however long it took. They made drug buys, infiltrated organizations, cultivated informants, planted wiretaps, investigated bank accounts, and built solid cases against all the participants in a gang or group of gangs. When a case was ready, they would roll up 20 or 30 members of a gang in a single day. The department supplemented these investigations with civil actions and eviction proceedings against drug dealers' buildings and apartments. It also sent out uniformed patrolmen in force, to hold the gains and discourage drug buyers from reentering the neighborhood. Everywhere the drug initiatives have gone, they have driven down murders, shootings, and street crime.

All these strategies—and a host of other ones targeting youth crime or family violence, for example, or using civil lawsuits to hamstring criminal enterprises—send one clear message to the criminal population of New York: "It's not your street," as one cop put it. "This street belongs to the people of New York. We are going to take it back."

Many criminologists, as you'd expect, are sticking to their guns and insisting that nothing we have done had the slightest effect on New York's crime drop. Crime fell not just in New York but nationwide, they say, proving that some impersonal force much bigger than the NYPD has come to bear on all of urban America. In truth, however, in 1994 and 1995, the drop in New York crime accounted for *more than half* of the crime decline in the entire country: we weren't *part* of the national trend; we *drove* the trend.

But what reasons do the experts proffer to explain the drop in crime? The crime-prone youth population shrank, they argue, and employment expanded. In New York, however, the teenage population was stable in the early 1990s, not declining, and the minority teenage population was actually on the rise. Between 1990 and 1994, New York City public high school enrollments were up 12 percent. Throughout the period of steep crime decline, moreover, New York had an unemployment rate of between 8 and 10 percent, just about double the national rate. According to the demographic and economic theories, crime should have been raging out of control instead of falling off the charts.

"The experts will never forgive Bratton and Giuliani for proving them wrong," says Tom Repetto of the Citizens' Crime Commission. "They want to believe that crime can only be reduced by sweeping social change. But they do have a fallback position: if the police *did* reduce crime, they did it by illegitimate means."

The claim of "illegitimate means" is growing more insistent, accompanied by accusations that the NYPD routinely uses unconstitutional searches and "Gestapo tactics." Policing in New York, critics charge, has been "militarized," as if SWAT teams were roving around the city on search-and-destroy missions. The tragic shooting of Amadou Diallo in February and the outrageous abuse of Abner Louima in 1997 have fanned this talk significantly. Many who claim to speak for minority communities say that they now fear the police more than they fear the criminals.

The fear may be understandable, but the problem has been overdrawn. The NYPD is not a racist or brutal department. It won its gains against crime not by abusing citizens but by strategically managing and focusing its resources. Its problem is a problem of attitude: cops need to be more respectful in their encounters with the public. With crime under control, we have the breathing space to provide much better training in the human side of policing and to build trusting relationships in every neighborhood in the city. The

NYPD rose to the challenge of crime in the mid-1990s; it certainly can rise to this challenge now.

Though the department can do much more to win the confidence of minority communities, it has already done the most important thing: today, those communities receive the level of police protection and service they deserve. They aren't written off as unimportant and unpoliceable. The Compstat revolution had the effect of allocating resources to the neighborhoods that needed the help most. "All the dots representing crime on Compstat maps are the same size, whether the victim is Leonardo DiCaprio or Fred Mertz," says Jack Maple. "The resources go where the problems are." As a result, minority neighborhoods like East New York and Washington Heights have seen huge crime drops. Kids can play on the street again; they don't go to bed to the sound of gunfire anymore.

What we learned above all from the New York experience is that police can control and manage virtually every type of crime in virtually every neighborhood. No place is unpoliceable; no crime is immune to better enforcement efforts. Though underachieving in the past, American police departments can take the lead in restoring safety and order to communities all over the country. After a generation of police executives who were convinced that cops couldn't cut crime, a new group of leaders is following the New York example and sending the message that police can make a difference. These leaders are junking the old reactive model, in which police responded to crimes and filed reports, in favor of a new strategic policing that gets criminals on the run and keeps them running. American police departments are beginning to live up to the boast posted by an anonymous officer in the NYPD Command Center in 1995: "We're not report takers," it read. "We're the police."

—*Spring 1999*

PETER REINHARZ

Why Teen Thugs Get Away with Murder

THE HARDEST PART OF MY JOB as a prosecutor is facing victims or their relatives after the perpetrator has figuratively—and sometimes literally—gotten away with murder. Take what happened to John B., 28, in a relatively empty car on the Number One subway train shortly before Christmas a few years ago. As the train rumbled south from 34th Street to 28th Street, the door between the cars banged open and in swaggered every New Yorker's nightmare—four teen hoodlums in army-style parkas, stocking caps, baggy pants, and unlaced, steel-tipped boots. As the four hooted and jumped around the car, the passengers pretended not to notice, terrified of making eye contact. Then the hoodlums surrounded John and his date, Loretta W., 27, and each in turn put his hand on her handbag and then let go, teasing their victims and delighting in the show of control. Suddenly, one youth yelled, "Let's do it!" They threw John to the floor and began kicking and punching him. He covered his head with his arms, but just as he raised it to beg them to stop, the leader of the wolf pack, Tarion W., 15, jumped onto a seat, grabbed the overhead strap, and swung forward, driving his steel-tipped boot through John's glasses and sending shards into his eye. The boys jumped off the train at 28th Street, laughing and high-fiving. The attack wasn't about money; it was sport.

A transit cop nabbed the wolf pack on the platform, and Tarion ended up in Family Court, charged with felony assault. His punishment: 18 months—the maximum he could get.

Eighteen *months*? In a camp-like residential facility? For a violent, unprovoked assault of such ferocity? Loretta shook her head incredulously. "Is that all he gets? It can't be true," she said to me. But however unbelievable, that really is the maximum period of incarceration that New York's juvenile justice code allows for most crimes—including many crimes of violence—committed by 13- to 15-year-olds and for any crime, including murder, committed by a 12-year-old. True, the authorities of the residential facility can extend the term if they can prove a need for continued confinement, but they rarely do. Even for the hardest-core juveniles, the average stay is a mere ten months. As for the nonviolent teen felons—the car thieves and the pick-pockets—though they are liable for the same 18-month maximum as kids who've committed reckless manslaughter or robbery in a wolf pack, the over-whelming majority get off with nothing more than probation. It's not quite a no-fault system, but New York's legislature, which passed and preserves the Family Court Act that governs the administration of juvenile justice in the state, has made sure that a New York crime victim's suffering comes cheap.

Little wonder that teen crime in New York City is soaring, even while crime overall has dramatically declined. In the decade from 1986 to 1995, robbery cases referred for prosecution in the New York City Family Court tripled, increasing over 30 percent from 1993 to 1994 alone, and an additional 11 percent from 1994 to 1995. Felony assaults (often referred to as aggravated assaults) were up 30 percent from 1994 to 1995. Not just the amount but the severity of juvenile crime in New York has grown hugely. Ten years ago the majority of juveniles prosecuted in the Family Courts of New York City were arrested for misdemeanor offenses. In 1995 all but 6 percent of the crimes referred for prosecution were felonies, and 86 percent were crimes of violence or major narcotics offenses. Possession of a loaded gun—often considered a direct link to the number of homicides—more than quadrupled among juveniles arrested in New York City during the early 1990s, at the very moment when the Giuliani administration's aggressive enforcement policy was reducing illegal gun possession in the city overall.

Everything in the juvenile justice system is designed to relieve teen malefactors of responsibility for their criminal acts. Start with the system's euphemistic language, which defines deviancy down in a way that approaches Orwellian newspeak. Under the Family Court Act, gun-toting teen muggers are not criminals but juvenile "delinquents," and they have not committed crimes but rather "acts which if committed by an adult would be a crime." As they haven't committed crimes, it follows that they acquire no criminal record. They are charged in Family Court as "respondents," not as defendants. They are not indicted but "charged in a petition." They don't go to trial but appear at a "fact-finding hearing," where they are "adjudicated" rather than convicted, and they go to "disposition" rather than being sentenced. For a felony assault that results in a mangled face and a punctured eye, the architects of New York's juvenile justice system do not want to punish the offender; they seek his rehabilitation through treatment.

But first you have to catch a teen criminal—and the Family Court Act makes that even harder to do than catching adult criminals. The Family Court has no power to issue search warrants. The only way within New York's present juvenile justice system to enter an apartment to retrieve, say, a gun brandished by a 15-year-old mugger is to rely on the good faith of the perpetrator or the cooperation and consent of one of his parents. If the police do retrieve the gun without a search warrant, lawyers for the offender—usually from New York City's largest criminal-defense office, the Legal Aid Society—would seek suppression of the weapon as evidence on the grounds that police acted outside the Constitution, which requires a search warrant. Of course, the Legal Aid Society has repeatedly opposed giving the Family Court the authority to issue search warrants, assuring their armed clients the protection of a legal Catch-22: no search warrant authority for the court, but an absolute requirement for a search warrant in order to seize evidence without fear of suppression.

Family Court judges also lack the authority to issue arrest warrants, although the U.S. Supreme Court requires their use in juvenile delinquency proceedings. Exceptions to this constitutional standard exist: in the case of emergencies, for example, or hot pursuit. But when an offender is named by witnesses, police may not take him into custody while he is in his home without an arrest warrant. If police do enter the home without a warrant, the custody of the offender is deemed illegal, and all evidence flowing from that arrest will be suppressed. Again, the Family Court Act, with the full support of the State Assembly, has created an unworkable situation for police, who must expend limited resources waiting outside a perpetrator's house until he emerges, use a ruse to lure him out, or ask him and a parent to come voluntarily to the precinct house to be questioned or arrested.

When the State Legislature enacted the Family Court Act in 1962, such omissions were understandable. Who could have foreseen the explosion in the 1980s and 1990s of gun and narcotics crimes among teenagers— crimes that police can't combat without being able to find the contraband or weapon or to apprehend the suspect? Back in the sixties, young offenders were a tamer lot. But under today's radically different circumstances, the Assembly's leadership has pushed aside repeated requests from city officials and, more recently, from Governor Pataki, for the statutory authority to issue search and arrest warrants. Why? Some legislators believe these warrants would be a pretext to search and harass the parents of young offenders.

While the Legislature was establishing all these protections to insulate juvenile offenders from the consequences of their actions, the federal courts were adding safeguards of their own. In the 1960s the U.S. Supreme Court extended to juvenile delinquents all the procedural rights applicable to adult criminal defendants, with the sole exception of trial by jury. *Miranda* warnings, the exclusionary rule, proof beyond a reasonable doubt, and the other trappings of criminal justice became a constitutional requirement in juvenile proceedings. Violent young offenders got the right to court-appointed counsel, along with the right to suppress any evidence obtained without a search warrant or any statements made to police without a lawyer present or without the proper *Miranda* warning. It did not matter that the alleged purpose of the system was rehabilitation, not criminal sanction. Rehabilitation could begin only after the juvenile predator had taken advantage of all the criminal protections. The child advocates succeeded in developing a system that lets offenders reap benefits both ways: they may not be charged or convicted of criminal conduct, but they enjoy almost all the rights afforded under the criminal justice system.

In New York, the state courts have been every bit as generous with the rights of violent young felons. For instance, the right to a speedy trial in New York's Family Court has been interpreted by New York's highest court almost to guarantee the right to a trial within 90 days. Even when the defense causes the delays—or when the youth fails to show up in court—the clock keeps ticking against the prosecution. In effect, the youth who skips court may help engineer the dismissal of the charges against him. Sometimes, when the prosecution fails to start a trial as few as three days after arraignment, the court dismisses the case for failure to meet speedy trial guidelines. As if such safeguards *within* the juvenile justice system were not enough, the state courts now seem determined to shield juveniles with the Constitution's Fourth Amendment procedural rights even in matters of school discipline. In September a state appellate court threw out the suspension from high school of a Bronx student whose loaded gun was discovered by a school security guard in a patdown conducted without, the court said, "reasonable suspicion."

New York, it is often said, is tough on teen criminals: after all, once they turn 16, it tries them not in Family Court but in the adult criminal courts. Many other states don't send them to adult courts until they reach 17 or 18. New York even sends 14- and 15-year-olds to the adult courts for rape or armed robbery or for an assault with a deadly weapon that leaves the victim crippled for life. This toughness, though, is usually mere illusion. For New York has still another cloak of protection to throw over these criminals: the Youthful Offender (YO) law.

A judge can choose to grant YO status to a teen thug at the time of sentencing, and the promise of it is often part of a plea bargain in felonies involving 16-, 17-, and 18-year-old defendants (along with 14- and 15-year-old offenders tried in adult court). YO status confers several advantages. First, it automatically reduces the sentence the offender faces—from a maximum of 5 to 15 years for a second-degree robbery, say, to a mere 1½ to 4 years. In practice, however, most YOs get nothing more than 5 years of probation—an even *lighter* sentence than the paltry 18 months they might have gotten in Family Court.

Second, this section of the Criminal Procedure Law allows the courts to transform a criminal *conviction* into a non-criminal *adjudication*. All criminal aspects of the case—including the criminal record—disappear, in the hope that the offender's misdeed was an isolated error of youth. The case record is sealed and remains unavailable for public inspection or even for use in future sentencing. Result: if a violent YO robber, free on probation, commits another violent robbery, the court must consider him a first-time offender. So instead of facing a much stiffer penalty as a second-time felony robber, he will just be sentenced as an adult first-timer.

Surely it would be wiser to grant YO status conditionally rather than conferring it irrevocably at the moment of sentencing. Under such a revised system, a version of which Governor Pataki unsuccessfully pushed this year, a court could revoke the YO status of a youth who fails to meet his conditions of sentence—by, say, failing to report to his probation officer—and could resentence him accordingly, giving him (for instance) the 5- to 15-year maximum that an adult would get for second-degree robbery. Further, if the offender committed another crime while on probation, this change would allow the first crime to serve as a "predicate offense," meaning that it could be used to enhance his sentence. As it exists, the YO scheme merely extends the lenient terms of the Family Court Act: minimum sanctions for maximum crime.

The philosophy behind the state's no-fault juvenile justice system might have made sense in the days when juvenile offenders stole apples and picked pockets, often driven by poverty. Such acts really might have been isolated errors of youth, so the law gave these kids another chance, saving them from the lifelong stigma of their isolated mistakes and treating them not as criminals but as children in need of the paternal care of the state. But are the teen criminals in court today, almost nine out of ten of whom are violent felons, really juvenile delinquents rather than criminals?

Does it make sense to think in such terms about chronic malefactors like Keith A., who was prosecuted along with several accomplices for savagely beating a drunk in upper Manhattan's Mount Morris Park and then dousing him with lighter fluid, as he screamed and begged, and burning him so badly that his charred corpse was scarcely recognizable? Keith, a couple of weeks shy of his 13th birthday (though a burly 15-year-old in appearance), then went home and had a snack: indifference to human life doesn't come much more depraved. Keith's neighbors knew he was trouble and crossed the street to avoid him; he'd beaten up drunks before, with bloodthirsty zeal, and he was on probation for grabbing and groping a girl at a swimming pool. Does it make sense to think that the 18-month sentence he received for the murder will bring him to his senses and set him on the straight and narrow?

And what about the fundamental assumption that underlies the whole philosophy of New York's juvenile justice system—the idea that the system's principal purpose is rehabilitation? Is there the ghost of a chance that the 36-month sentence handed out to 15-year-old Stacy L. will send him back to society rehabilitated? Two 13-year-old boys were walking together one morning near Lincoln Center when one of them accidentally bumped into Stacy. Both kept walking when he demanded an apology. Enraged, he spat out a few anti-white epithets and then kicked and stomped the two boys, knocking one unconscious and severing the ligaments in the other's wrist, so that even after many operations he will never regain full use of it. The unconscious boy was left with blurred vision and memory loss. But as Stacy told the court psychologist, he "likes to hurt people." Fond of guns, which he often carries, he had a robbery charge pending at the time of the attack. The psychologist concluded that he had an explosive personality, with a tendency toward violence, and ought to be removed from the community. But Stacy will almost certainly be back in our midst in about two years—bigger, stronger, unrehabilitated.

The truth is, we have had very little success rehabilitating violent teens. We've tried counseling and family preservation, prevention programs and community-based services—all with no discernible result. Boot camps, the most promising recent rehabilitation scheme, have just been shown to be a failure by a National Institute of Justice study. All the programs in the study exhibited "high attrition rates for non-compliance, absenteeism, and new arrests." Even during their time in boot camp, offenders committed assaults against inmates and staff; some escaped. Those offenders who graduated and went into a follow-up program were arrested at rates of up to 70 percent before they had even finished the program.

Even if experts knew how to rehabilitate violent youths, it's hard to imagine that the 18 months, or even 36 months, that young offenders spend in confinement is long enough to untangle a twisted character, to undo 14 or 15 years of bad influences and bad habits. Rehabilitation is an inner transformation, requiring the offender's deepest engagement and assent; it isn't something done from outside, like an engine tune-up, and it's certainly something no government has ever proved itself able to effect, notwithstanding the claims of China's Cultural Revolutionaries. The Division for Youth residential facilities to which teen malefactors in New York are sent haven't found the secret. When these facilities release offenders, it's not because they've been rehabilitated (and usually not even because they've served out their sentences) but rather because bed space for new arrivals has become scarce. A *Daily News* reporter once dryly observed to counselors at a facility that the youth they were releasing for lack of room was likely to re-offend. One counselor replied, with world-weary, cynical realism, that the teen's release was appropriate because "he's as good as he's gonna get." Such is the system's own view of the possibility of rehabilitation. And in the juvenile justice system of Family Court, no parole board exists to consider what effect the teen offender's release will have on the community or to oversee his conduct once he is free, or even to tell his victim or the prosecutor that he's again on the loose.

In 1976, after a decade in which juvenile crime had exploded both in quantity and severity, the Legislature changed the Family Court Act to require the courts to consider the protection of the community as well as the needs of the youth. Unfortunately, the Family Courts did not take the message to heart, and teen crime continued to grow, and grow more implacably violent. Yet however incapable we may be of routinely rehabilitating juvenile offenders, we know very well how to protect the community against the Tarions, Keiths, and Stacys in our midst. What works is incarceration.

Some 70 years' worth of data from the FBI's Uniform Crime Reports— which break down crime in the U.S. by age, gender, race, and crime type (among other factors)—show why incarceration works for teen criminals in particular. According to these reports, the likelihood of violent criminal activity increases as youths go from their early to their late teens: 17- and 18-year-olds are more likely to be arrested for violent crimes than 15- and 16-year-olds. When young offenders are released at 18 or 19, they are at the peak age for violent crimes like robbery and assault. And indeed, most of them do get re-arrested: a 1993 audit of juvenile justice facilities by then-state comptroller Ned Regan found that about nine out of 10 offenders committed further serious crimes after being released.

In addition, the criminologists who compile the data have recognized for years that when offenders reach their early to mid-twenties, violent activity starts to level off. Among those age 25 or so, the number of arrests for violent crimes drops precipitously, and for those approaching age 30 the rate of felonious activity drops faster and faster. To be sure, the entire population does not "age out" of violent crime past age 35. But in 1993 the number of 15-year-olds arrested for robbery was more than double the number of the entire group of those 40 to 44.

Juvenile justice philosophy runs counter to the criminological data. Simple logic suggests that violent young offenders who presently suffer little or no incarceration ought to be held for far longer terms. What purpose is served by setting the periods of incarceration for armed juvenile felons at only a few months, or giving them probation in a YO plea deal, when the statistics tell us that they are likely to commit more, and worse, crimes when released? Were the juvenile courts to sentence them to terms of six or seven or eight years, the total amount of crime would drop precipitously. Even if juveniles had to spend three or four years in confinement between crimes, the total amount of crime would shrink drastically. The sad truth about the juvenile justice system in New York is that it does little to interfere with young criminal careers.

Not only has it largely done away with the best means of preventing crime—locking up criminals—but it also fails to send the message that society takes crime seriously enough to hold criminals responsible and punish them severely. In every way, it has blunted the natural consequences of criminal actions. Indeed, the architects of the juvenile justice process have worked hard to create a system and a euphemistic language that deflect individual responsibility and remove all stigma and shame from the process. But these powerful sentiments are society's best deterrent to antisocial behavior; virtually doing away with them ensures recidivism.

Calls for juvenile justice reform have echoed round the country for a decade, with mayors, governors, prosecutors, and state and federal legislators swelling the chorus. In most of the nation, the cries are beginning to be heard and acted upon, especially since legislators know the demographic data that show a big rise in the number of teens over the next 15 years. The U.S. Senate, for example, is looking to divert some of the $150 million a year that the Department of Justice's Office of Juvenile Justice and Delinquency Prevention spends on teen crime-prevention programs into prevention by means of tougher law enforcement. More than half the states either have modified or are now modifying their juvenile justice codes to lengthen sentences and to try violent teens in the criminal courts at younger ages. The Democratic Party platform endorses such measures. Even the president has looked at the exploding juvenile crime statistics and called for consideration of curfews in America's largest cities and for monitoring every juvenile arrest involving a firearm. And these measures have begun to show encouraging results: in 1995 juvenile crime decreased 2.9 percent nationwide.

But not in New York. Though the New York State District Attorneys' Association, the New York Law Enforcement Council, Mayors Koch, Dinkins, and Giuliani, Congressman Charles Schumer, Attorney General Dennis Vacco, Governor Pataki—even Governor Cuomo, hardly a law-and-order politician—have all pressed for reforms, the New York State Assembly has shot them down year after year. It has rejected lengthening sentences, giving prosecutors the power to seek arrest and search warrants, moving some violent juvenile offenders into the adult prison system, and permitting extensive recordkeeping and sharing of data on teen criminals. It has allowed the number of residential-facility beds in the juvenile justice system to remain constant at just over 2,000 during the 1980s, while teen crime soared and the number of adult prison beds tripled. (In 1995 New York City's Family Court ordered more placements than there were available beds in the whole system, which handles youth for the entire state, not just the city.) The one reform the Assembly did pass, after 13 years of pressure from Brooklyn as-

semblyman Daniel Feldman, is the limited fingerprinting and photograph-
ing of juvenile felons, which, when it goes into effect in November, will give
police and courts important new tools against repeat offenders.

But the big reform that the Democratic Assembly leadership put forth
in 1994 went in the opposite direction: it sought, unsuccessfully, to have all
first-time arrestees for many classes of robbery, assault, burglary, even criminally negligent homicide diverted from the courts entirely and sent by the
Probation Department directly to counseling or community service. This
suggests a legislature living in an intellectual time warp, wedded to theories
of juvenile justice that the rest of the nation discarded long ago. Unfortunately for New Yorkers, these are theories with the gravest real-world consequences for ordinary, law-abiding citizens.

Surely it's time for our Assembly leadership to get mugged by reality, as
the expression goes, before the rest of us all get mugged in earnest.

—Autumn 1996

PATRICK J. HARNETT AND WILLIAM ANDREWS
How New York Is Winning the Drug War

WHO SAYS the war on drugs is unwinnable? From 1995 to 1999, we have been winning it in New York. Using an innovative strategy that author Harnett put in place when he became head of the New York Police Department's Narcotics Division, the NYPD has dismantled some 900 drug gangs citywide, crippling the street drug trade. And the strategy has helped fuel New York's overall crime decline, as well. From 1996 through 1998, it accounted for nearly a third of Gotham's homicide decline.

Up till now, narcotics cops across the nation have been fighting the war on drugs on the wrong ground. They have been playing a numbers game, measuring success by how many street dealers they arrested and how much dope they seized, chasing the ever-elusive Kilo Fairy. But no one can ever win the war that way: the street dealer is the most easily replaceable commodity in the entire drug trade, and the major drug organizations simply factor even the largest local drug seizures into their cost of doing business. No matter how many street dealers the cops arrest, no matter how much dope they seize, drug-afflicted neighborhoods are bound to continue their downward spiral, ravaged by drug-gang turf wars and the other violent crimes that drug-dealing areas breed, along with the constant threat to children and the disorder that addled addicts create.

Based on this frustrating experience, little wonder that police brass have pessimistically concluded that they'll never be able to uproot the drug trade—contain it perhaps; but drive it out of neighborhoods, no. And with the front-line experts so gloomy, no wonder that responsible thinkers from all over the political spectrum have assumed that the drug war was lost and that the legalization and controlled distribution of narcotics was the only viable course.

But in the years since 1995, New York City has shown that, with a major shift in our narcotics-enforcement strategy, we can uproot the drug trade, restore safety to neighborhoods, and drive down overall crime. We can win the drug war by shifting the ground on which we fight from entire boroughs or a whole city to individual neighborhoods and even individual streets.

The drug war isn't a conventional military campaign against a unified enemy. In reality, it is a neighborhood-by-neighborhood effort to disrupt and dismantle the business activities of dozens of decentralized local gangs. It requires narcotics investigators to pay extremely close attention to the particular conditions in specific neighborhoods and to the personnel and structure of the individual gangs controlling the local trade. After every victory, it also entails working closely with the community to prevent the dealers from coming back.

Working under this novel theory, Harnett assigned narcotics units to specific geographical areas and to the drug gangs active there. Their job wasn't merely to bust street dealers or confiscate product but—more important—to analyze, penetrate, and eventually eliminate the local drug gangs operating in their areas. They were to knock out the critical intermediary organizations that connect the street dealers with major drug distributors and importers. Street dealers are expendable, and product is replaceable, but the drug-gang infrastructure that hires the dealers and supplies the product is not so easy to rebuild, especially if narcotics investigators continue to work an area. In other words, since the local drug trade is rooted in local drug gangs, to uproot the trade, you have to uproot the gangs.

In the 43rd Precinct in the Bronx, about two blocks from where Amadou Diallo was shot, is a place once known as "the Hole." When Harnett was the precinct commander in 1990 and 1991, the Hole—literally, a hole in the wall of an abandoned building—was a notorious drug-dealing spot. A dealer would sit looking out of it, selling drugs like a pharmacist in a dispensary. Early on, Harnett had led a couple of raids on the Hole, but he soon learned that arresting the dealer—a pathetic junkie who sampled the product when he wasn't selling it—accomplished little. Arrest him, and there was someone else sitting in the Hole the next day, equally pathetic, equally expendable. Year in and year out, the Hole remained a fixture in the Four-Three.

For Harnett, it came to symbolize the frustration he felt as commander of a precinct with a tough drug problem. He had almost no power to do anything himself about the drug gang supplying the Hole. True, he could establish a Street Narcotics Enforcement Unit (SNEU) made up of precinct personnel, but headquarters gave very little encouragement to do so, warning that it was more trouble than it was worth. Still, Harnett persisted, but he found his SNEU tied down, like Gulliver, by petty constraints. SNEUs had to operate in uniform, and they could target only outdoor locations. Unfortunately, in a bright blue uniform it's not easy to make observations of drug activity without being observed yourself, and once dealers figured out that SNEUs worked only out of doors, they began steering clients to hallways and vestibules, where SNEUs couldn't go. So SNEUs caught only guppies, not the bigger fish—and only guppies too dumb to adjust to the SNEUs' tactics. It wasn't quite what Harnett had in mind.

Trying to get outside help was equally frustrating. By 1990, when the crack epidemic had pushed violent crime to unheard-of levels, including two drug-related murders of cops on a single night in October 1988, the NYPD had doubled its Narcotics Division's ranks to 1,600 (still only 4 percent of all cops). These trained investigators worked in eight-man teams under the tight supervision of a sergeant, to guard against the notorious corruption that had riddled the Narcotics Division in the sixties and early seventies. Half the teams, each covering several precincts, were supposed to work on precinct drug problems, investigate drug complaints, and maintain contact with precinct commanders.

In reality, however, these teams were too few to cover their territory, and they tended to "chase the case," going wherever their informants and other evidence led them. Investigators officially assigned to the Bronx might end up doing most of their work in Manhattan. As for investigating citizen complaints, the teams did so only haphazardly, for they were swamped by the huge volume of complaints that the crack epidemic generated—61,000 in 1987. At best, they might close a complaint by arresting a dealer in the general vicinity, who didn't fit the complainant's description at all. More often, they ignored complaints altogether, dismissing them as "kites," a term of obscure derivation, which seemed to imply that if you let a complaint go, it would fly away by itself. So though in theory Harnett should have been able to get help from one of these teams, in practice he had almost no contact with the sergeant of the team officially assigned to his and two other precincts.

The best hope for a commander with a drug problem in his precinct was that a contingent of the Tactical Narcotics Teams (TNTs) that made up the other half of the Narcotics Division would come to his precinct, but Harnett had no way of knowing when the brass would grant his request for TNT reinforcements. Nor could he be sure that the TNT, which provided intensive anti-narcotics enforcement in a precinct for 90 days before moving on to the next troubled precinct, would succeed once it did arrive. After all, Harnett knew, TNTs focused almost entirely on arresting street dealers in "buy and bust" operations. As a result, they could suppress street-narcotics conditions for a while but couldn't permanently uproot them. Their 90-day limit was also self-defeating. Dealers caught on, lay low for three months, and came back when the TNT was gone.

When a TNT finally arrived in the 43rd Precinct, Harnett told the team's captain about the Hole. If someone is still in the Hole after 90 days, he remarked, then this whole thing will have been a failure. The TNT made its arrests for the next three months, then picked up stakes and moved on. A street dealer popped back up in the Hole as if TNT had never been there. And this was only one of the 12,500 or so drug locations that flourished in New York City in the mid-nineties.

By the time Harnett took over the Narcotics Division, Commissioner William Bratton and his deputies had already made major changes in the NYPD and its strategies, and they understood clearly that attacking the drug trade would keep overall crime headed down, since a quarter of the city's homicides from 1989 to 1993 were drug-related.

Harnett's shrewd predecessor, Chief Martin O'Boyle, had shaken up the division, requiring investigators to work nights and weekends and imparting a new energy and purpose to drug enforcement. The department had also begun to encourage precincts to establish Street Narcotics Enforcement Units, even allowing SNEU observation officers to work in plainclothes and supplying them with binoculars, night-vision devices, and nondescript vehicles, so that they could watch drug operations closely without being observed themselves.

Remembering the 43rd Precinct and the Hole, Harnett came into the Narcotics Division determined to redefine its entire mission. He abolished the TNTs and their 90-day sweeps. Instead, the division would pit its turf-based narcotics teams against the turf-based drug gangs and keep the teams in place until the gangs were out of business. The teams would work closely with precinct commanders, detectives, and SNEUs and share information freely. In fact, their first task wasn't to arrest the gangs in their areas but to analyze them, learning who controlled which streets and who worked for whom.

"We changed our pattern from buy and bust to making cases against drug gangs, and we finally saw results," says Lieutenant Jay Rivera, one of the first supervisors to apply the new model. "For me, the old way was very frustrating. If something came our way—if we had an informant—we would go with it. But as far as, 'Tony is running this operation; let's get Tony,' we didn't do that. It was just buy and bust, get the numbers, and move on."

Between 1995 and 1998, Harnett's troops dramatically doubled, from 1,600 to 3,200 officers. In 1996, he began to send big contingents of investigators into the Lower East Side, the Bronx, and Brooklyn North, all neighborhoods overwhelmed by the sheer numbers of gangs. The investigators, experienced cops who knew how to talk to people, started working their neighborhoods, meeting community activists, doormen, superintendents, and store owners, tracking 911 calls, and investigating drug complaints. They quickly identified the gangs they were targeting. "Once I started working in one precinct, within eight weeks, I knew all the organizations, what they were doing, and how they were doing it," Rivera recalls.

With the gangs identified, the work of meticulously gathering evidence began. Instead of just arresting street dealers, the investigators would "buy up" into the organization, purchasing increasingly large amounts and winning the confidence of gang leaders. If undercover officers couldn't penetrate the gang, they'd use informants to make controlled buys and to gather evidence. Sometimes they would arrest gang members for the large sales they had made to undercovers and "flip" them—that is, turn them into informants—offering to help get their sentences reduced. Surveillance, to identify gang members and document their lawbreaking, was also key. And though it was no longer their primary measure of success, the turf-based teams made increasing numbers of arrests to help develop information about drug-gang leaders. They also executed a flurry of search warrants, seizing ever more drugs and guns.

Harnett, an ex-detective, required the teams to investigate citizen complaints methodically, like detectives investigating a serious crime, and to report on their response to each one. Investigators grumbled but soon found that even anonymous "kites" were flying straight to the target. Two investigators checking out an anonymous complaint in the 44th Precinct in the Bronx found a long line of drug buyers stretching down a building hallway and heard the mad scramble inside an apartment as dealers opened windows and pitched drugs out. Not surprisingly, the victims of drug crime in the community knew a great deal about where, when, and how narcotics trafficking was taking place.

The capture of Hector Santiago, a canny drug dealer who for years controlled East 7th Street between Avenues B and C, perfectly illustrates the new strategy. Officer Jimmy Mantone, the narcotics investigator who finally arrested Santiago, remembers hearing about him when he first joined the police force as a uniformed cop back in 1982. Over the years Santiago and his operation had effortlessly weathered every police-enforcement effort. "The word on the street was that Santiago was tough to get to," Mantone says. "He didn't deal with anyone he didn't know and was extremely methodical in his operation."

A martial artist and a tough guy, Santiago had the whole block terrorized. His minions deployed with almost military precision—a lookout at each end of the block, a kid on a bicycle riding up and down, and a rooftop lookout with a walkie-talkie to spot police observation posts, since Santiago knew that SNEU officers often used rooftops to observe drug deals without being seen. Gang members challenged strangers on the block, asking what their business was and intimidating them if they tried to park their cars there. The sellers wore ski masks and maintained strict discipline among their buyers; police observers once even saw a seller whacking buyers into line with a stick. Santiago also continued to pay his employees if they were arrested, as long as they didn't squeal.

For three months in the spring of 1996, Mantone and his team worked every angle against the Santiago organization. Three undercovers established themselves as buyers and bought repeatedly from the gang's ski-masked street sellers, eventually learning their names and building solid cases against them. Mantone had a confidential informant who had known Santiago for years and who agreed to make buys from him directly in increasingly large amounts. (Investigators develop a stable of such informants, who are sometimes paid but more often are "working off the case," that is, trying to earn a lighter sentence for their own drug-dealing activities.)

From an apartment on East 9th Street, which had an unobstructed view of East 7th Street across an empty lot, Mantone and his team videotaped Santiago's entire operation, documenting the role of each seller and lookout. They repeatedly watched Santiago crossing the street at the same time each night, going from the apartment where he lived to the "stash" apartment where he kept his drugs, to pick up the day's receipts. His minions would stop the traffic as he came back with the cash, and he would hurry across.

When Mantone's team had assembled their evidence, they swept down on Santiago one night in June as he crossed the street carrying drugs and cash. Mantone remembers with relish the astonished look on Santiago's face, after having operated with impunity for at least 14 years. He also remembers people on the street applauding and cheering as cops led Santiago and his gang away in handcuffs.

Faced with the massively documented case against him, Santiago pled guilty and is serving a 12-year term. The entire gang pled guilty also, with some members providing evidence against their boss. Exit a supposedly untouchable dealer and his entire entrenched gang.

This same drama took place again and again over next three years on the Lower East Side, in the West Bronx, and in Brooklyn North, and then in northern Manhattan, southeast Queens, and the East Bronx, as the drug initiatives spread there. Narcotics investigators built case after case and took down gang after gang. Sometimes a handful of arrests would close down a small operation; sometimes investigators would round up as many as 40 people in a single day, uprooting an entire gang infrastructure from a housing project. Gang investigations became the primary work of the narcotics teams, and drug dealers who had been too clever to be caught by an SNEU or a TNT, and too small to concern major case units or federal agencies, suddenly found themselves under extremely thorough and persevering scrutiny. Between 1996 and 1999, the turf-based teams have dismantled nearly 900 New York City drug gangs. In Harnett's old precinct, 15 drug teams now work 24 hours a day, seven days a week. They have closed the Hole, by the way, and the building has been reclaimed for residential apartments.

For the first time, the NYPD structured itself to fight drug-related violent crime. Narcotics lieutenants began appearing before the department's Compstat meetings, the now-famous strategy sessions where top managers grill precinct commanders and detective squad commanders about crime and tactics in their precincts. Precinct commanders in turn convened their own weekly drug-control meetings of narcotics team commanders, detective squad commanders, and SNEU supervisors, so that enforcement units that had previously ignored one another could exchange information and work together to solve drug-related homicides and clear out drug-related crime hot spots.

Young, reckless, and well armed, small-time drug dealers could cause big-time violence. The investigation of a grisly double homicide in a stairwell of the Lehman Houses at Madison Avenue and 109th Street in Manhattan's 23rd Precinct illustrates how the drug teams helped stop the killing. The victims were a street dealer and his female customer, both shot in the head. Lieutenant George Poggioli, in charge of drug investigations in the Two-Three, was at the crime scene at noon, along with ten police cars, three TV news crews, and about 100 spectators milling on the other side of the street. Suddenly, someone committed a third murder in the crowd, shooting a man walking a pit bull in the chest. Allegedly, the third killing was a payback for the first two, committed by a drug gang so brazen that they didn't even wait until the police had left the scene. The leader of the gang was Jermaine Carter—"Hootie"—a powerfully built, 280-pound 25-year-old who liked to terrorize those around him to show his power.

Hootie ran the drugs on Madison Avenue from 106th to 108th Streets. He was muscling in on the Lehman Houses at 109th Street, the territory of two 19-year-old dealers named Mike Peck and Luke Williams, who were, says Poggioli, "like kings in that housing project." To protect his turf, Peck had killed Hootie's dealer and his female customer in the stairwell. Hootie's gang allegedly struck back by killing one of Peck's friends in the crowd.

The narcotics team and the precinct detectives joined forces to bring the murderers down. They couldn't find a confidential informant who knew someone in Peck and Williams's little gang, so an undercover officer went in cold. He went back multiple times to make buys on high floors in four different buildings, risking his life, hanging out with the volatile Peck and Williams, winning their confidence, and ultimately buying $1,500 worth of crack from them in one transaction. Based on his evidence, the narcotics team executed five search warrants and arrested 11 people, including Peck and Williams. In addition to weapons and narcotics, the police seized six rottweilers and five pit bulls belonging to the gang. Williams ultimately gave up Peck as the shooter in the stairwell killings.

Then it was Hootie's turn. This time a confidential informant introduced another undercover to Hootie's people. The undercover went back seven times, buying from Hootie's dealers and asking for more each trip, until he ultimately asked for an ounce of crack. This time, the underlings brought him to an apartment to see Hootie. "Hootie being Hootie, he took the undercover's money and gave him just a quarter ounce," says Poggioli. But that was enough evidence to make the case. The police executed two search warrants and arrested 16 people, but Hootie got away. So the police staked out the apartments of Hootie's girlfriend and his mother, tracked his other known associates, and finally arrested him in New Brunswick, New Jersey. Some very nasty people were off the streets.

Other innovative tactics subverted the drug gangs from a variety of unexpected directions. Police-department lawyers in the Civil Enforcement Unit, for example, used the nuisance-abatement law to shut down storefronts and even entire buildings where the drug trade took place. Narcotics investigators gathered the evidence needed to make the civil case — usually three or four documented drug-dealing incidents to establish the presence of a nuisance. Unscrupulous landlords who had rented repeatedly to drug dealers had their buildings padlocked and shuttered, unable to reopen them without the NYPD's approval of future tenants. Between 1996 and 1998, Civil Enforcement shut down 1,941 locations.

In another innovation, the Trespass Affidavit program, landlords of buildings where drug dealing was taking place signed affidavits allowing police to patrol their buildings, and they posted "no trespassing" signs in their hallways. Police could then target drug customers who had no legitimate reason to be present in the buildings and arrest them for criminal trespass and, if they had purchased drugs, for possession. These buyers often provided the evidence for search warrants to raid the "work" apartments, so that investigators could arrest the dealers who packaged and sold the drugs.

Commissioner Howard Safir has added a new strategy to the drug initiatives — the active participation of the federal Drug Enforcement Administration, the FBI, the Immigration and Naturalization Service, the IRS, the Secret Service, the U.S. Customs Service, the U.S. Marshal's Service, and the New York State Police. This idea of coordinating drug enforcement at every level of government is still in its infancy, but its potential is enormous. Imagine the day when the Compstat model for fixing accountability and evaluating results might be applied to federal agencies as well. At "Fedstat" meetings in every major metropolitan area, local police chiefs, the U.S. attorney, the district attorneys, and the special agents in charge of the district offices of each federal agency could work together to focus and coordinate the attack on local drug gangs. In the best of worlds, we would come at the drug gangs from every direction—taking out the gang personnel, confiscating product and cash, closing locations, cutting off sources of supply, tracking fugitives and illegal aliens in the drug business, clamping down on money laundering, and squelching demand—all at once. We would be dismantling the drug trade's entire infrastructure.

Commissioner Safir has also sponsored the development of the next logical step in turf-based drug enforcement at the local level: the model block program, the brainchild of 33rd Precinct commander Garry McCarthy. Controlled by an entrenched drug gang, 163rd Street between Broadway and Amsterdam Avenue was the crime hot spot of the Three-Three. According to local lore, it was actually the place where the drug trade had begun in Washington Heights—the Northeast's drug-dealing capital—back in the 1940s, when Irish gangs held sway. After a months-long investigation, turf-based narcotics units arrested 40 people and eliminated the drug gang that had controlled the block. McCarthy and his precinct team decided to press further: to try to keep the block drug-free and allow the social order to reknit there. "The model block grows out of turf-based enforcement," says McCarthy. "At 163rd Street, we were taking back a particular piece of turf."

"As long as there is demand, supply will eventually come back," McCarthy observes, "but most of the drug buyers in Washington Heights weren't from the community, so we could deter demand." For a seven-week period beginning in August 1997, McCarthy closed the block to through traffic and had uniformed police officers challenge cars seeking to enter, turning away those with no legitimate purpose on the block. Police also explained to pedestrians how they were working to discourage drug buyers. They couldn't deny pedestrians access to the block, of course, but their very presence was enough to deter would-be drug buyers, especially suburban customers.

The precinct team enrolled every building on the block in the Trespass Affidavit program, so that police could patrol building hallways and make arrests for criminal trespass. McCarthy and his supervisors themselves worked the block often during the seven weeks, explaining what was going on and urging residents to cooperate. At first, McCarthy wasn't sure that he could win their confidence. But when he called a community meeting in early September, 300 enthusiastic people showed up, ready to reclaim their street. "It was simply electric," he says of the meeting. "They embraced the idea, and they are running with it."

To help reknit the social fabric, McCarthy enlisted the aid of five city agencies to clean the street, fill potholes, repair streetlights, replace street signs, tow abandoned vehicles, and exterminate rodents. Residents and cops painted over graffiti. With police guidance, landlords took steps to make their buildings more secure. The police helped residents establish a block association, tenant associations in each building, a youth council, and citizen patrols. As precinct teams completed narcotics investigations on 161st Street and 162nd Street, the model block spread there, too.

Even when McCarthy gradually cut the police presence to a single patrol officer on each of the blocks, the program's full impact remained. Fear of the drug dealers and possible reprisals had faded, while confidence in the police—and in the community's own innate strength—had grown. On 163rd Street, violent crime plummeted from 23 incidents in the year before the model block to only one incident in the year after it. People who had lived as virtual hostages in their own homes felt free of the terror and tyranny of the drug gangs. Where gunshots and shootings were once common, children now played ball and rode bicycles. McCarthy argues that the Police Department "literally changed the social conditions" on the model blocks, promoting a vibrant and resurgent community. Commissioner Safir adopted the model block program citywide and oversaw its implementation in 20 other locations.

One day last April, Lieutenant Rivera took a walk down Avenue D on the Lower East Side, where he had served as an undercover and investigator in the 1980s and where he helped implement turf-based narcotics enforcement in the 1990s. He remembers the haunted landscape back in the eighties—the rundown buildings, the dangerous-looking people, the menace in the air.

"What a difference from the old days," he says. "Seeing people outside, the mothers with their kids in the park, you could just sense it—that this was not the place it used to be. There wasn't a single shooting in the 9th Precinct in the first four months of 1999. That's incredible. When I was an undercover, you wouldn't walk down those streets. Now, to see the restaurants and the clubs and the renovated buildings, it made me feel really good. And I thought to myself, 'I was part of that.'"

That's what winning the war is all about.

—*Summer 1999*

PAUL E. O'CONNELL AND FRANK STRAUB

Why the Jails Didn't Explode

FIVE YEARS AGO, Gotham's jails looked like they were ready to explode with violence. At Rikers Island—the democratic world's largest penal complex, with ten facilities sprawling across 490 acres of concrete and razor ribbon—"a full-scale riot [was] . . . only one dis, one argument, one short-tempered outburst away," as *New York* magazine then put it. And then, as Mayor Giuliani got tough on crime, even more prisoners crowded into the already-packed jails; the 110,410 inmates who went through the system in 1994 increased 20 percent, to 133,000 today. But even with combustible prisoners jammed in ever more tightly, the Attica-like conflagration never ignited. On the contrary, the threat dissipated, violence plummeted to negligible levels, the jails became clean, quiet, and orderly. How that happened is an unsung triumph of institutional leadership and organizational reform, well worth studying and emulating.

Once you've seen the orderliness of today's facilities, it's hard to imagine the mayhem that prevailed only a few years ago. A particularly bloody two-month period in the summer of 1994 captures the flavor: Rikers Island, with its seething population of 16,000 prisoners, chalked up 176 slashings or stabbings—one for every 90 inmates—usually carried out with smuggled razors or makeshift shivs. In those days, the system as a whole averaged more than 1,000 violent acts yearly.

The assailants typically were gang members, whom authorities allowed to advertise their affiliation with color-coded beads—black and white for the Nietas; black and yellow for the Latin Kings—or such other gang paraphernalia as red "do-rags" for the Bloods. Gang members proudly marked out their turf with signature graffiti "tags" on the jail walls, and they flaunted their criminal conduct, from extortion to drug running, within the jail itself. Rikers had become a hoodlum counter-city within the city, where gang rivalry raged anarchically, to the ceaseless din of transistor radios.

Even jail employees were in danger. Some years ago, Jorge Ocasio, then a young captain and now deputy warden in command at Rikers, had transferred a dangerous inmate from one section of the jail to another, to the inmate's displeasure. "Back then," Ocasio says, "inmates had no regard for staff and would challenge us to fight and threaten us, as this prisoner did to me." In due course, the disgruntled inmate staged a fight between two jail mates as a distraction while Ocasio did his rounds. As Ocasio struggled to separate them, the inmate jumped him, stabbed him in the back twice with a nail, and brained him with a telephone. Ocasio missed six weeks of work.

The sequel, though, was worse. Consistent with jail policy of punishing inmate wrongdoing—if at all—with loss of privileges rather than with criminal prosecution, the assailant wasn't charged. "Had he attacked a cop on the street, he would have been prosecuted for attempted murder and probably served 25 years," Ocasio ruminates. "So who was running the jail?" he asks. Here was a powerful message for inmates and staff: once you set foot in New York's jails, civilized laws no longer applied.

No wonder that Department of Correction employees hated their jobs. Recalls Emmanuel Bailey, a 14-year DOC veteran and now assistant deputy warden: "It was rare you would have a quiet day. Seeing that kind of gore every day was depressing. These guys always cut each other on the face, to leave a 'telephone' on someone—a life mark." Another veteran, Anthony Serra, commanding officer of both the department's Emergency Services Unit and its special gang unit, agrees. "Imagine coming to work every day and knowing that you're going to have to deal with some kind of violence," he says grimly. "Morally and physically, that starts to grind you down."

The menacing atmosphere took its toll on job performance. Correction officers routinely worked overtime, whether they wanted to or not, to fill posts left vacant by fellow officers who used sick time to avoid coming to work they feared and disliked. DOC staff averaged 21 sick days a year, the highest absentee rate of any city agency. "Sometimes," Serra recalls, "you'd have to do four straight 16-hour days—it was an unhealthy, unsafe environment with a lot of stress." Budget cuts reduced correction officers from 10,700 in 1992 to 9,800 in 1994, worsening the problem. In a sad but predictable irony, overtime costs spun out of control—$2.2 million a week during the first three months of 1994 alone—rendering the cuts futile.

The disorder at Rikers Island and throughout the city's jails—one warden called it "a system of organized chaos"—went against everything Mayor Giuliani was trying to do to slash Gotham's crime rate and restore the city's quality of life. If the mayor had an overriding message, it was that tolerating even minor transgressions, such as public drunkenness or aggressive panhandling, rapidly leads to more serious crimes, as potential lawbreakers realize that the authorities are no longer in charge. Yet here, at the very heart of the city's criminal justice system—teeming with precisely the bad guys who most urgently need to learn that the authorities won't tolerate disorder and crime—even major crimes went unpunished, and illegality and chaos reigned, sending exactly the wrong message and emboldening criminals.

City jails—jails, incidentally, are short-term county or municipal detention facilities in which the average stay is less than a year—fanned the crime problem in another way, too, since incarcerated gang leaders freely enlisted new recruits, who would return to crime on the streets strengthened by now belonging to a gang organization.

Seeing that the DOC was a mess, in January 1995 Mayor Giuliani appointed the cerebral Michael Jacobson, a former commissioner of probation with a Ph.D. in sociology, as acting DOC commissioner, promoting him to commissioner in March 1996. He also named the vivid, take-charge Bernard Kerik, formerly a Passaic county jail warden and New York City narcotics detective, as well as a military security specialist and martial arts expert, as first deputy commissioner, elevating him to commissioner in late 1997, when Jacobson returned to academe. Giuliani gave them a clear mandate: stop the violence and take back the jails.

They did exactly that. Under their regime, inmate violence fell 90 percent in four years. Only 229 violent incidents occurred during the last fiscal year, and just 54 during the first six months of fiscal 1999, even though the number of inmates passing through the DOC continues to rise. Morale has shot up. Overtime costs have shrunk by half, and sick leave is down 25 percent as employee enthusiasm strengthens.

How did Jacobson and Kerik bring about this seemingly miraculous transformation? They began by tightening up DOC's absurdly lax management culture, a change that Kerik orchestrated. On his first day on the job, he gathered all the wardens and chiefs on Rikers Island and asked each one: "What's your inmate count?" Some didn't know, and Kerik blew up. At the end of the day, he called them back and asked them again. A few *still* didn't know. Incensed, Kerik docked them a day's pay, sending a crystal-clear message: get with the program or suffer the consequences.

"Early on," Kerik notes, "I established a very simple rule: produce and work, and I'll support you, you'll have your job, you'll have your career; do not produce, do not work, and you'll have to go." Using attrition and demotion—upper-level DOC positions are commissioner appointments, unprotected by civil service safeguards—Kerik determinedly seized control of his own organization.

He had his work cut out for him. In the old days, sartorially resplendent wardens left the real work to their staff. As deputy warden Ocasio sarcastically put it, "The warden was like a king: he just sat in his office while everybody else worked." Kerik is more scathing: "Five years ago, the wardens had no idea who were in their jails; they weren't managing at all."

Nor did they take responsibility for anything that occurred in the jails. "'Shit happens'—that was their attitude," Kerik contemptuously recalls. "I said: 'You make $120,000 for *what*? What do you *do*?'" Things changed in a hurry. "Today, I'd put my managers up against any managers in New York City, and I'll bet you my people know more about their jobs," Kerik confidently asserts. Now wardens are accountable for all phases of their facilities' operations, and Kerik encourages them to talk regularly with subordinates, collect information, and identify and correct problems before they get out of hand. Ocasio captures the new spirit: "If there's an incident at 3 PM in my jail, and you call me at 8 PM, I'll explain to you what happened."

Kerik himself exemplifies the attitude he demands from his staff. Veteran correction officer Serra notes that "Kerik is the kind of person who'll pull up on Rikers and notice a light bulb burnt out on a lamp, or a patch on a department vehicle with the old logo on it—he's in tune." Thomas Antenen, the agency's deputy commissioner of public relations, praises his boss in the same terms: "He'll show up at Rikers unannounced at 11 PM, and if he sees a dirty floor, someone's going to have a problem. Accountability with a capital A," says Antenen —"that's what he's all about."

Kerik found the key to establishing accountability in the New York Police Department's now famous Compstat meetings, which use crime and arrest statistics to plan and evaluate crime-reduction efforts, to figure out what might be going wrong, to deploy resources effectively, and to make everyone in the organization answerable for how he does his job. In late 1995, Kerik persuaded Jacobson to set up a version of Compstat on Rikers Island. The DOC uses its version—called Teams, for Total Efficiency Accountability Management System—to survey every aspect of the department's work. In former commissioner Jacobson's words, "the Teams meetings keep everyone focused on the data and on performance."

Here's how Teams works. Every month, Deputy Commissioner Deborah Kurtz, Captain Frank Ciaccio, and their staff put together a report of 90 or so significant "performance indicators"—the number is expanding all the time. Of course, jail security is pivotal. Each month, Kurtz and company look at the number of inmate acts of violence, the number of times the staff used force or sprayed mace, the number of searches and arrests of inmates. But they also track inmate library use, attendance at religious services, and use of health-care services to make sure these services are running efficiently. They watch overtime spending and sick leave, jail cleanliness, and an array of other indicators, always seeking to expand the DOC's institutional knowledge.

The statistical report forms the basis for the monthly Teams meetings on Rikers Island. About 100 people attend these highly charged sessions, which the commissioner runs from a dais, flanked by his deputy commissioners and uniformed chiefs on either side of the room. Four jails make presentations each month from a central podium, as large video screens display each facility's statistics overhead. Commissioner Kerik will ask a warden:

"Who is your top Latin King, and where is he?" The warden had better know the answer, since the commissioner will check on the spot. Kerik might quiz the warden about the number of Bloods under his jurisdiction, or why his cells have graffiti on them, or what he's doing to minimize overtime costs. Nobody is confused about what the commissioner wants and expects.

Prior to Teams, each of New York City's 16 jails, 4 hospital prison wards, and 15 court holding facilities operated largely as a separate entity, and intra-agency communication was minimal. Today, Teams quickly disseminates whatever one jail learns throughout the system. As Serra nicely puts it: "Teams opens everyone's eyes—from all the facilities—to see if they're having similar problems; if something works, everybody gets enlightened." A Teams meeting we visited focused on several scalpels seized from inmates on Rikers Island. The Teams session figured out where and how inmates had acquired the scalpels and devised new department-wide inventory control measures to prevent it from happening again.

Teams also has helped Kerik spot talent and reward it. The recently appointed chief of operations, William Fraser, a 21-year veteran whose career had stalled out, is a perfect example: in 18 months after Kerik's arrival, he scaled the ranks from warden to the highest uniformed position in the department. As warden, he found a way of combating extortion. Plunderers chronically bullied weaker inmates into surrendering their commissary purchases (usually cigarettes), which the extortionist could then use to buy favors, like extra phone calls, from other inmates. Fraser launched early-morning cell searches; if he found that an inmate had more cigarette packs than commissary records said he should, he seized the extras. After a while, the bullies got the message and stopped extorting. Kerik, deeply impressed at a Teams meeting with Fraser's initiative, instituted the pre-dawn searches throughout the system—and promoted Fraser. Says Fraser: "This man has made all the difference. He certainly revitalized my career."

Jacobson and Kerik's first and biggest job was to carry out their original mandate from Mayor Giuliani: to control inmate violence and criminality. "Violence had to be reduced and a safe and secure work and living environment created," says Kerik, "before any other operational issues could be addressed."

With that aim in mind, Kerik quickly made sure that Gotham's jails were clean and brightly lit, since he intuited that dark, grungy jails proclaimed that nobody cared, encouraging inmates to act up. "In the old days, graffiti was all over everything, and the floor looked like you were growing penicillin on it," recalls assistant deputy warden Bailey. Today, says Bailey, it's another world: "No more 'Nietas Rule!' everywhere: this place is immaculate." Chief of operations Fraser is equally enthusiastic: "I challenge you to find a hospital as clean as our oldest building here, the North Infirmary, which was built in 1933." New lighting and new fans keep halls bright and air circulating. Floors are high-buffed. The tidy look bespeaks professionalism and order, proclaiming that someone is in charge.

As part of his effort to cut violence, Kerik early on established a red I.D. card system to brand, as with a scarlet letter, inmates caught in the jail with weapons. As one correction officer described it: "The I.D.s tell everybody— the inmates, the officers, the civilians—that you're a potential threat." Since correction officers search red I.D. bearers far more frequently than they search other inmates, the system serves as a strong deterrent to smuggled and makeshift weapons.

Early on, too, Kerik spied a significant weakness in controlling jail crime and violence. The department's emergency services division—which tackles unusual and dangerous situations, from mass transfers of prisoners to riots—employed only 18 people, none of whom worked nights or weekends. "What happens if a housing area acts up at 9 PM or on a Sunday and needs physical support?" the commissioner asked. Kerik went to the mayor for additional resources, and now the Emergency Services Unit has 150 permanent members and a team available 24 hours a day, every day. It doesn't just react to emergencies but also does random searches in the jails. At Jacobson's prompting, the mayor restored all agency staffing to pre-budget-cut levels: 10,700 correction officers and 2,300 civilian employees. The agency's 1998 budget totaled $792 million.

Arrests are a powerful new weapon in the DOC's campaign against crime and violence in the jails. Though this may seem an obvious technique, remember that before Jacobson and Kerik arrived in 1995, inmates who committed crimes in jail, even violent assaults, at most might have privileges suspended (no more going to the commissary for cigarettes) or might be transferred to a disciplinary unit. Unless they killed someone, real punishment was rare. You expect savage behavior in a jail, former DOC officials rationalized, so why waste dollars going after guys already behind bars? It was bad enough that this laxity let anarchy rage in the jails. But equally important, if lawful order doesn't exist where the criminal justice system supposedly has the most authority, what does that say about order in society at large? As Emmanuel Bailey stresses, "These guys were violating jail rules, but more importantly they were violating *society's* rules." An inmate was likely to leave correction emboldened, not chastened.

Kerik and then-chief of department Eric Taylor put a brusque halt to tolerating inmate crime. "The only reason inmates were expected to act violently in the past is that we let them do it," the commissioner says. Now, the DOC prosecutes inmate crimes within the jails as vigorously as if they had been committed outside.

Raymond Rojas's case is typical of hundreds of similar department prosecutions. Rojas entered Rikers in August 1997 on weapons charges. In February 1998, awaiting the outcome of his case, Rojas set his mattress on fire, creating a smoke hazard and causing serious burns to the two officers who snuffed out the blaze. Two weeks later, Rojas received a one-year sentence on his weapons case, most of which he had now served. In times past, Rojas soon would be back on the streets, his arson shrugged off as understandable misbehavior in anarchic Rikers. No more: the DOC arrested, prosecuted, and convicted Rojas for torching his mattress, and he received a multiple-year prison sentence.

Bailey enunciates the new regime's bottom line: "You touch an officer, we will prosecute you. You cut someone, we'll prosecute you. You burn something, we'll prosecute you. It's that simple." Arrests have skyrocketed from a half-dozen or so a month to over 100. According to correction personnel, the word is out among the inmates: "They know that they no longer run anything in here," an officer proudly asserts.

Most arrests within Gotham's jail system are the responsibility of the Gang Intelligence Unit, perhaps the most successful of all of Jacobson and Kerik's Teams-forged reforms. Formed three years ago, the 36-member "Gang Intel," as correction officials call it, has become the troublemaking inmate's nemesis. "When inmates commit a criminal act," says Gang Intel's commanding officer, Anthony Serra, referring to the elite unit's trademark jackets, "they know that a short time later the guys in the windbreakers will come running."

Gang Intel's sole task is to investigate and crack down on gangs in New York's jails. It's a big responsibility, because gang members—some 12 percent of the department's inmates—have been responsible for a disproportionate amount of jail violence. Using a sophisticated computer "super base," Gang Intel tracks 55 different "serious risk groups" in city jails and maintains a database on some 12,000 gang members who've passed through DOC. The four most widely represented gangs are the formerly L.A.-based Bloods (600 in jail today), the Latin Kings (358), the Nietas (288), and the quasi-Muslim Five Percenters (114). But from the Aryan Nation to the Zulu Nation, Gang Intel keeps an eye on a wide assortment of other unsavory groups.

Shortly after Jacobson and Kerik arrived, the DOC obtained a court order allowing it to ban all gang paraphernalia, making it harder for members to identify one another. But it's not easy for correction officers to pick out gang members, either—especially since the department scatters them throughout the jails, to diminish gang strength. Gang Intel has accordingly established a database for gang tattoos. Assistant deputy warden Bailey, the executive officer of Gang Intel, says the tattoos are crucial: "We look constantly for body markings. We make these guys undress; we take photos. The gang members can't wear their beads anymore, so tattoos help mark out what group they belong to, and I make sure all my men can recognize them." NYPD gang intelligence regularly briefs Gang Intel, too, and police officers routinely ask arrestees if they belong to gangs. Most important, Bailey says, Gang Intel encourages gang members to come forward with information: "When the inmate cuts ties with the outside world, he often wants to tell, and I'll help him tell the DA, the FBI, overseas—anywhere."

Gang Intel's information-sharing relationship with New York City cops—and with the FBI, the DEA, with police and fire departments across the country, even with an agency associated with Interpol—is another new departure. It was Kerik's brainchild. "There's no reason, I thought, that the DOC shouldn't be the premier gang-tracking database for the East Coast of the United States," he says. "We know who they are, just as we know their associates, their customs, their secret identities, their hand signals. We have more access to gangs than anybody."

The inter-agency cooperation has developed into an extremely effective gang-fighting tool. In an as yet unconcluded case, the Latin Kings had reorganized on Rikers Island, creating the "Inner-Island Council." The council appointed a leader for each of the ten jails on Rikers. Gang Intel began to monitor the leaders closely and came across information that helped identify the entire gang leadership in New York City. Operation Crown—a joint effort with the FBI—led to the arrest of more than 100 members of the Latin Kings hierarchy in the city's five boroughs. "We dismantled the Latin King Nation, and they're still having a hard time restructuring," declares deputy commissioner Antenen. Gang Intel, by deciphering secret gang street codes, also played a focal role in a joint New York–North Carolina case that busted the ruthless North Carolina gang Sex, Money, and Murder, Inc. In Gotham, the unit led to RICO indictments against the Bloods. Three years ago, Gang Intel didn't exist; now it is, in the words of one cop, "the Harvard University of hoodlum information."

Gang Intel's participation in these joint efforts has hugely boosted DOC pride. By conducting criminal investigations and making arrests, correction officers make clear that correction is no longer the dead end of the criminal justice system. "Commissioner Kerik has put a new twist on being a correction officer," asserts Bailey. "We're *peace officers*, and we're not second class to *anyone* now. I had an officer go to Florida recently to follow up on a lead—our people never thought they would be working on this level." Serra calls Gang Intel "the diamond of the department." Says he: "I've had great assignments, but I've never been so excited as I am as commanding officer of Gang Intel. It's a resource with unlimited potential."

Kerik has introduced an array of state-of-the-art technology into the DOC, beyond the sophisticated computer that Teams uses. Members of the

Emergency Services Unit, for example, brandish the "stun shield," which looks like gear Robocop might carry. It makes restraining out-of-control inmates much safer, for correction officers and inmates alike. Previously, it took five baton-wielding ESU officers to restrain a combative inmate. Lacerations, broken teeth, and broken bones commonly ensued. Now, when an officer pulls a trigger in back of the stun shield, a six-second burst of electricity — 50,000 volts of it — gets released. If the energized shield touches a rowdy inmate, his muscles contract from the charge; when the electricity shuts off, his muscles relax, turning his limbs to jelly and immobilizing him. Serra calls it "a perfect tool — an alternative to physical force." Though it sounds painful, it's relatively harmless, and every time officers use it, a supervisor watches and videotapes roll to ensure compliance with all departmental procedures.

Another new device Kerik introduced is the "Boss Chair" — the body-orifice scanning system. Inmates often hide a razor blade in their rectum, their foreskin, or their mouth. Before, body-orifice searches were one of the more unpleasant — and sometimes violent — features of daily life in correction. With the Boss Chair, however, the prisoner sits, while a metal-detecting magnetic scanner built into the chair silently searches. If the chair's red light blinks on, the inmate remains isolated until he relinquishes the weapon. Like the stun shield, the Boss Chair makes physical force less necessary.

Other technological advances include portable fluoroscope machines to check packages and inmate cells for contraband, "tube mitts" that restrain dangerous inmates' hands, improved body armor for correction officers, and chemical agents, like mace, that make quelling disturbances less risky. Kerik carefully monitors and evaluates the effectiveness of all of the new devices during Teams sessions. Teams ensures, too, that personnel know how to use the new technology correctly.

Kerik's changes have boosted DOC employees' morale dramatically. "Most of the staff is excited by the changes," says Emmanuel Bailey, "and I'm grinning from ear to ear." Gotham's jails are changed places for inmates, too. As Bailey puts it: "It's no longer a place where you come to learn to be a better criminal. These days, you might come back a better citizen."

—*Spring 1999*

III

EDUCATION

*For generations, urban schools were the route into
mainstream America for poor children, especially the
children of immigrants. But the failure of today's big-city
schools to educate the poor is notorious. The problem isn't
lack of resources; Catholic schools successfully educate
the very same kids for a small fraction of the public
schools' per-pupil cost. The culprit is a rigid public school
monopoly that puts teachers' interests before those of kids.
What's needed, new urban thinkers agree, is competition
from outside the system from private and parochial
schools supported by publicly funded vouchers. The goal
is not to replace the public school system but to force it to
adapt and become effective in order to stay in business, as
is happening in the few cities where experimental voucher
programs are under way.*

SOL STERN

How Teachers' Unions Handcuff Schools

WHEN TRACEY BAILEY received the National Teacher of the Year Award from President Clinton in a festive Rose Garden ceremony in 1993, American Federation of Teachers chief Albert Shanker called to say how pleased he was that a union member had won this prestigious honor. But Bailey, a high school science teacher from Florida, is an AFT member no more. Today he believes that the big teachers' unions are a key reason for the failure of American public education, part of the problem rather than the solution. The unions, he thinks, are just "special interests protecting the status quo," pillars of "a system that too often rewards mediocrity and incompetence." Such a system, he says, "can't succeed."

Bailey is right. In the final analysis, no school reform can accomplish much if it does not focus on the quality of the basic unit of education—that human interaction between an adult and a group of children that we call teaching. The big teachers' unions, through the straitjacket of work rules that their contracts impose, inexorably subvert that fundamental encounter. These contracts structure the individual teacher's job in ways that offer him or her no incentives for excellence in the classroom—indeed, that perversely reward failure.

So as Tracey Bailey and many other dedicated teachers have learned, schools can't improve until reformers confront the deadly consequences of the power that teachers' unions wield over a monopolistic industry, not only through contracts but also through the unions' influence on the elected officials who regulate the education industry. Until then, any reform—whether more money for the schools or smaller classes or high national standards or charter schools—will get short-circuited from the very outset.

Trade unionism is a recent development in public education. During the first 100 years of taxpayer-funded public schools, teachers had no collective bargaining rights, though many enjoyed civil service protection. While the public schools made steady progress during those years, it's indisputable that teachers were underpaid and often were moved around like interchangeable parts in a one-size-fits-all system. Many teachers, along with principals and other administrators, belonged to a staid professional organization called the National Education Association, to which the words "unionism" and "strike" were anathema.

Inevitably, teachers working in a factory-style system figured they might as well organize themselves into factory-style unions. The big breakthrough came in New York City in 1961, when the United Federation of Teachers (UFT), led by a charismatic high school math teacher named Albert Shanker—whose recent death deprived the teachers' unions of one of the towering figures in the American labor movement—went on strike and won the right to bargain for all city teachers. Though Shanker insisted that the struggle was about more than mere bread-and-butter issues—that it was also about improving the quality of public education and strengthening democracy—the contract the UFT signed with the New York City Board of Education nevertheless reflected the traditional industrial model. It set up uniform pay scales and seniority rights for teachers, limited their classroom hours, and required new teachers to be automatically enrolled in the union and have their dues deducted from their paychecks.

Following this example, the once conservative NEA also veered toward militant trade unionism. By the mid-seventies it had a majority of the nation's teachers covered by collective bargaining agreements. Now the NEA and the AFT, the national parent body of New York's UFT, together represent more than 3 million school employees, including 80 percent of the nation's 3 million public school teachers. The two unions and their state and local affiliates take in $1.3 billion each year from dues and employ 6,000 full-time staff members.

Today the two national unions cast a giant shadow over not just American public education but also Democratic Party politics. As a California judge recently found, that state's NEA affiliate spent only half of its dues income on activities related to collective bargaining and used the other half for electoral politics, lobbying, and general advocacy for social, educational, and political causes. Nationally, in the 1996 election, the teachers' unions contributed more than $9 million directly to Bill Clinton and other Democratic candidates through political action committees. But the PACs were just the visible tip of a vast iceberg of soft money, independent media buys, thousands of full-time campaign workers paid with union dues, and in-kind services such as phone banks and direct mail advertising. Myron Lieberman, author of a forthcoming book on teachers' unions, estimates that the NEA and AFT together spent at least $50 million for the campaign compared with the $35 million that the AFL-CIO spent. And at last summer's Democratic convention, the teachers' union caucus constituted 11 percent of all delegates—a bigger share than the delegation from California.

These political investments have paid off. In the Clinton Department of Education, former NEA issues director Sharon Robinson is assistant secretary for research and educational improvement, shaping the national education debate with her office's research reports and assessments of student performance. And when the Republican Congress was on the verge of passing legislation last year to rescue a few thousand poor students from Washington, D.C.'s hopelessly broken public school system by offering them private school scholarships, the NEA, fearful that these vouchers might encourage similar legislation in the states, furiously lobbied the White House. President Clinton, who had first indicated that he would sign the bill, backtracked and said he would veto it.

The teachers' unions spend millions each year on advertising to convince the American people that when they flex their political muscle in cases like this, more often on the state than on the national level, they are working for the benefit of the nation's schoolchildren. Their pitch goes something like this: in driving up wages and improving working conditions, the unions have made the teaching profession far more attractive to qualified young people. PAC activities and political lobbying help pressure elected officials to finance education adequately, so that school boards can pay teachers the salaries they deserve, hire more teachers and reduce class size, provide staff development, and purchase books. Result: better schools and improved student performance.

There's some truth in these claims. The rise in the sixties and seventies of powerful teachers' unions with exclusive bargaining rights *did* lead to a huge jump in public school funding: between 1965 and 1990, average spending per pupil nationwide increased from $2,402 to $5,582 in inflation-adjusted dollars. The average pupil-teacher ratio dropped from 24.1 to 17.3. The percentage of teachers with master's degrees increased from 23.2 to 52.6. The median years of experience for teachers went from eight to 15. Between 1979 and 1989 average teacher salaries rose 20 percent in real dollars. Salaries for new public school teachers during that period rose 13 percent, compared with a mere 3.5 percent increase for all other college graduates taking entry-level positions.

Unfortunately for America's children, the rest of the unions' argument doesn't stand up. The extra money didn't improve student performance. To the contrary, during that same period average SAT scores for public school students declined by 10 percent, dropout rates in urban school systems increased, and American students scored at or near the bottom in comparisons with the other industrialized nations. After years of examining the data, the nation's leading education economist, Eric Hanushek of the University of Rochester, concluded: "There appears to be no strong or systematic relationship between school expenditures and student performance."

So why did the bottom drop out of American public education just as per-pupil spending soared? Basic economics provides a compelling answer, though countless blue-ribbon commissions, and indeed much of the present national dialogue about school reform, have failed to acknowledge it: the $250 billion public education industry behaves precisely like any other publicly protected monopoly. Union negotiators in the *private* sector know that if they insist on protecting incompetent workers and cling to outdated work rules, especially in the global economy of the nineties, the company will begin losing market share, and union members will lose their jobs. In public education, by contrast, collective bargaining takes place without the constraining discipline of the market. When school board representatives sit down with union officials to negotiate a labor contract, neither party is under pressure to pay attention to worker productivity or the system's overall competitiveness: if the contract allows some teachers to be paid for hardly working at all, and others to perform incompetently without penalty, there is no real economic danger for either side. After all, most of the monopoly's customers, the schoolchildren, have nowhere else to go. Historically, tax revenues have continued to flow into the schools no matter how poorly they perform. Newark's public schools, for instance, have performed worse and worse in recent years, but per-pupil annual expenditure there is now almost $10,000, 50 percent above the U.S. average.

"Let's roll up our sleeves . . . and work together to give our children the schools they deserve," read the full-page *New York Times* ad taken out by New York City's United Federation of Teachers early this year. "We've tried everything else; now let's try what works," said a second UFT ad a few days later. These were the opening salvos of a major media blitz laying out the UFT's program for "turning our schools around." The nearly $1 million print, radio, and TV ad campaign was needed, UFT president Sandra Feldman told her members, because "often the union is erroneously looked at as an impediment to school reform, and it's time to set the record straight."

The UFT has good reason to be concerned. In a colossal understatement, one of the ads acknowledged that "recent school report cards show that students in our city are losing ground." Actually, what the State Education Department's recently released school performance reports show is a near meltdown of what was once the nation's premier urban school system.

Third-grade reading scores are among the most useful benchmarks for judging any school system's performance. Children who can't read in third grade are likely to fall even further behind in the later grades. And schools that can't manage to get children reading after nearly four years in the classroom are not likely to do very well in other areas. So it is stunning to discover that only 30.2 percent of New York City's third-graders are reading at grade level, compared with 62.2 percent in the rest of the state, and that the reading scores are dismal not only in schools with high numbers of poor, minority children but in many middle-class schools, in districts that have "choice" programs and districts that have resisted reform, in schools that favor "progressive" teaching styles and more traditional schools. For example, at predominantly middle-class P.S. 87, one of the city's "hot" schools and a bastion of progressive "child-centered" teaching methods, close to half the school's third-graders read below grade level. At the Mohegan School in District 12 in the Bronx, which has a very poor, all-minority student population and follows the more traditional "core knowledge" philosophy of scholar E. D. Hirsch, only 19 percent of the third-graders read at grade level.

In the 35 years since Albert Shanker and his followers took to the streets, the UFT has become the richest and most powerful teachers' union local in the country. It represents 95,000 school employees, including 60,000 classroom teachers, from whom it collects $60 million in annual dues. School chancellors come and go, but the UFT endures—a perennial power at the Board of Education and in the State Legislature, which regulates the city's schools. It has played a pivotal role in electing (and defeating) mayors and governors and has often exercised virtual veto power over the selection of school chancellors. In 1993 the UFT punished Mayor David Dinkins for not giving in to its contract demands by running a $1 million ad campaign against him at the beginning of the mayoral campaign and withholding the phone banks that were an essential part of Dinkins's successful campaign in 1989.

The UFT, together with New York State United Teachers, the state AFT affiliate, is easily the most powerful special-interest lobby in Albany. In the first six months of 1996 alone, the New York teachers' unions' PAC reported $900,000 in lobbying expenses and political contributions to legislators—three times as much as the next highest group, the state medical societies. The teachers' unions make their contributions to those legislators who are most likely to help them, regardless of party—to the majority Democrats in the Assembly and the majority Republicans in the Senate.

In return, the teachers' unions get to set the limits of permissible education debate in the Legislature. Debra Mazzarelli, the mother of two public school children and a parent activist, learned that lesson after she was elected to the State Assembly from Patchogue, Long Island, two years ago on a platform calling for ending automatic tenure protection for public school teachers. "I was just fed up that we were paying teachers $80,000 a year but couldn't hold them accountable and certainly couldn't fire them if they were incompetent," she said. Her bill to end teacher tenure won support from the New York State School Boards Association, which held hearings around the state. But in typical Albany fashion, the Assembly education committee, led by Steven Sanders, a leading recipient of teachers' union PAC money, won't even schedule a discussion in committee on the proposed legislation. Meanwhile, New York continues to have one of the most restrictive state laws for initiating disciplinary proceedings against incompetent teachers. Largely the work of the teachers' unions, it passed without public hearings and almost guarantees that no tenured teachers are ever fired.

After a recent public conference on the prospects of getting charter school legislation passed in Albany (26 states now have such laws, but not New York), Beth Lief, executive director of a reform organization called New Visions for Public Schools and one of the conference conveners, told a *New York Times* reporter that one group would ultimately decide the fate of the proposal. "There is no piece of education legislation in this state that passes without the UFT," the *Times* quoted her as saying. UFT president Sandra Feldman, standing next to Lief, didn't blink when she heard this assessment of her union's power. Indeed, the UFT leadership seems to enjoy reminding its members of its political clout. The union newspaper recently excerpted without comment an item from *Crain's New York Business* describing Feldman as someone who "wields more control over the education of New York City children than any mayor."

Several former Board of Education officials have told me that the chancellors they worked for would never make a high-level management appointment over the objection of the UFT. Chancellors accommodate the union for two very important reasons: they know that the UFT could have blocked their own appointments, and they realize that they need the union's lobbying power to help wring needed measures and funds from the State Legislature and City Council. As a result of this political alliance of necessity, the UFT has become part of the permanent government at 110 Livingston Street. The same former Board officials told me that UFT vice president David Sherman has had the run of Board headquarters for years and frequently participates in high-level policy meetings.

New teachers quickly learn how central the union is to the system's governance. A senior union official always directs the orientation at 110 Livingston Street for their first assignments. And when new teachers get their first paychecks, they discover that $630 of their yearly wages of $29,000 will be deducted for union dues.

The current contract between the Board of Education and the UFT can best be described as a "we-don't-do-windows" document. Among the tasks that principals are forbidden to require of teachers under the contract: attending more than one staff meeting per month after school hours, walking the children to a school bus, patrolling the hallways or the lunchroom or the schoolyard, covering an extra class in an emergency, attending a lunchtime staff meeting, or coming in a few days prior to the opening of school each September to do some planning.

The contract undermines teacher professionalism, excellence, and hard work in other ways. In all but a handful of the city's schools, principals must fill many of their teacher vacancies according to seniority rather than merit. J. Cozzi Perullo, principal of the elite Stuyvesant High School, has complained that she has no control over who is hired for half of the school's posted vacancies. And when a teacher does transfer from one city school to another, the principal of the new school can't even get the previous principal's written comments on the transferring teacher's personnel file.

The contract makes it almost insurmountably difficult for a principal even to begin the process of charging a teacher with incompetence under the union-written state education law. Every time the principal wants to record a negative evaluation in the teacher's personnel file, the teacher can contest that single entry through three separate grievance procedures, leading all the way up to the Board of Education. Even after the Board has upheld the principal, the teacher, with the help of the union, can go to arbitration to contest the single negative entry. The process is so tortuous that most principals don't even bother trying; they accept it as a fact of school life that a certain number of incompetent teachers must be carried on the payroll.

Jorge Izquierdo of P.S. 163 in Manhattan is one of the rare principals who have not only tried to purge incompetent teachers but are willing to speak publicly about the issue. He told me that in the case of one totally dysfunctional teacher, he has spent close to 100 hours out of the building over the past two years in grievance sessions at the district office, at the Board of Education, and at arbitration sessions. Although every one of his negative evaluations has eventually been upheld, he still must go through the process for another year before this one employee might have to face formal disciplinary charges—a process that could take several more years. "I am like the CEO of a little corporation," says Izquierdo. "I am judged by whether or not I achieve the equivalent of a profit—how much the children gain in learning. But unlike any other CEO, I can't hire the people who work here or fire them when they're incompetent."

What is most revealing about the UFT contract, however, is what it does not say. In its 200 pages of text, this labor agreement breathes not a word about how many hours teachers must work. Article six stipulates only that "the school day . . . shall be 6 hours and 20 minutes" and that the school year lasts from the Tuesday after Labor Day until June 26. School principals may not require teachers to be in the building one day before that Tuesday, one minute before the students arrive each day, or one minute after the students leave.

The number of hours teachers work is not a trivial issue. Teaching is a labor-intensive occupation. At the elementary and secondary school level, teachers get results not necessarily because they are brilliant or attended elite education schools but because of the hours they spend with students in and after school, the hours they devote to reviewing students' work, and the hours they spend speaking with parents.

So how many hours do union teachers really work? According to a survey by the U.S. Department of Education, public school teachers put in an average of 45 hours per week, including time in the classroom, work with students outside the classroom, preparation time in the school building, and work done at home. But since the survey is based wholly on teacher self-reporting, any bias is likely to be in favor of reporting too many hours worked rather than too few.

Doubtless, many public school teachers in New York do work 45 hours a week or more—at least during the 36 weeks that school is in session. One of the dirty little secrets of the system, however, is that there are many others who work close to, or exactly at, the contractual minimum. In the three different schools my children have attended, they have had several teachers who took the words in the contract about the length of the school day as gospel. Arriving in school just a few minutes before the children every morning, these teachers were usually out the door exactly at dismissal time. They rarely took any work home, grading at school the homework that they sporadically assigned. Assuming the teachers worked during all ten of the preparation periods provided for in the contract, and if we deduct their 50-minute "duty-free" lunch periods, I estimate that they worked a maximum of 28 hours per week, or about 1,000 hours per year. Some had enough seniority and graduate-school credits to put them at the top of the salary scale (presently $60,000, soon to be $70,000), so that they were earning a wage, not including benefits, of somewhere between $60 and $70 per hour. That's higher than the rate earned by employees with the city's top civil service titles.

I don't know if 5 percent or 50 percent of the city's teachers work to the contractual minimum. And—scandalously—the Board of Education and city hall are also in the dark about the productivity of the system's teachers. In the past, the Board's labor negotiators tried to raise the issue of monitoring the number of hours teachers work. "The union never wanted to discuss it," one former Board official recalls. "They said their teachers were professionals and it would be an insult."

It's unthinkable that managers of the city's police, fire, sanitation, or transportation agencies could do their job of trying to improve services without data on worker productivity. In public education, however, the city has agreed to ignore such basic management information. Worse, it doesn't matter, since all teachers get the same base salary, no matter how many hours they work or how effective they are in the classroom. Teachers get raises merely for showing up for another school year or for accumulating more education course credits, not for working hard and doing well.

This pervasive culture of mediocrity and time-serving takes a devastating toll on more ambitious teachers. Five years ago, journalist Samuel Freedman published *Small Victories*, a book about an extraordinary New York City teacher named Jessica Siegel. Following Siegel around for an entire year at Seward Park High School on the Lower East Side, Freedman was able to demonstrate just how much one teacher can accomplish with disadvantaged minority students through sheer hard work and determination. Freedman's reporting suggests that Siegel probably worked more than 60 hours per week, despite being at the low end of the salary scale. The book also makes clear that the system's bureaucracy and the UFT not only did not encourage Siegel but were obstacles she had to struggle to overcome. The union chapter chairperson at the school had a cushy assignment that put her in a classroom for no more than 90 minutes a day—after which she did everything she could to stifle Siegel's creative proposals to improve the school's performance. "The UFT did not exactly run the city school system," Freedman wrote, "but the system could not function without the union's assent."

By the time Freedman's book came out, Jessica Siegel had bailed out of teaching, having lasted ten years. The UFT, of course, is still present in every school, making sure that the city is never allowed to distinguish between teachers like her and my children's work-to-the-contract teachers. Instead of allowing a system of incentives that would encourage more Jessica Siegels to enter the classroom and stay in teaching, the union has been investing its energies in building its political power to ensure that won't happen.

Last July over 10,000 public school employees from every state in the union descended on Washington for the NEA's 75th annual representative assembly. I spent hours in the cafeterias and lounges speaking with delegates from places like Cedar Rapids, Iowa; Birmingham, Alabama; Billings, Montana; Honolulu, Hawaii; Denver, Colorado; and Storrs, Connecticut. Many were longtime union activists who had been coming to the conventions for years, with their very wealthy union paying their expenses.

All believed passionately that public education was under siege by the political right and profit-hungry corporations. One morning over coffee, a delegate from Connecticut told me that his school board was considering contracting with a private vendor to provide food services for the district's schools. His NEA local was mobilizing to fight this proposal, the delegate approvingly reported, because it was a step on the road toward privatizing all the school district's education services.

The NEA wants public education preserved as an enterprise-free zone. Jersey City is a case in point. Last year, Mayor Brett Schundler came up with a plan to give some poor students trapped in failing public schools tax-funded scholarships. When the state blocked Schundler's initiative, a local Pepsico distributor offered to pay for some of the scholarships. The New Jersey NEA affiliate immediately organized a boycott of Pepsi products, and the company quickly backed down. Speakers at the NEA convention threatened similar dire consequences, including more boycotts, for any company that dared to poach on the union's preserve.

It was hardly surprising that the delegates would be preoccupied with the specter of privatization and vouchers. But what was astonishing is that this once conservative organization now favors a political and cultural agenda not only to the left of the national political mainstream but also far to the left of the Democratic Party. It was as if the veterans of the Berkeley Free Speech Movement had taken off their tie-dyed T-shirts, cut their hair, put on 30 pounds, and taken over the Rotary Club.

Besides electing new officers and listening to a lot of speeches, the delegates spent their days at the convention passing resolutions on almost every issue under the sun—from federal housing and immigration policy to nuclear testing and the World Court to support for the special rights of every aggrieved racial, ethnic, gender, sexual-preference, and "otherwise-abled" group, subgroup, and tribe in America. The NEA believes that America faces no Social Security crisis and wants to lower the retirement age and repeal all taxes on Social Security payments. It also doesn't believe Medicare is in trouble and opposes any premium increases. It favors a national single-payer health plan supported entirely by tax revenues, full funding for Head Start programs, and a huge increase in federal spending on education—especially for "disadvantaged students," immigrant and American Indian students, and students with disabilities.

It would be an understatement to say that the NEA favors an expansion of the welfare state. Its economic program more closely resembles the most radical of the European socialist parties. John Berthoud, a senior fellow of the Alexis de Tocqueville Institution, has calculated that if Congress passed all the NEA's legislative proposals, the annual additional charge to the federal treasury would be $800 billion, requiring an average tax increase of $10,000 for a family of four.

The debate on education policy during last year's presidential election made much of the potential fragmenting effects on our civic culture of proposals like school choice or vouchers. Opponents of these experiments argued they would undermine the public schools, society's only means for inculcating children in our common civic heritage. They conjured up all sorts of imaginary horribles, including the specter that families would use vouchers to enroll their children in "David Duke schools," black nationalist schools, even schools that taught witchcraft. As *New Republic* editor Michael Kelly has summed up the case: "Public money is shared money, and it is to be used for the furtherance of shared values, in the interests of *e pluribus unum*. Charter schools and their like . . . take from the *pluribus* to destroy the *unum*."

Welcome to the NEA convention, Mr. Kelly. No charter schools or vouchers allowed, but not much *unum* either. This assembly of 10,000 public school employees celebrated not our common heritage but rather the disuniting of America. A standing convention resolution requires a set-aside of 20 percent of the convention seats for certain designated minorities. The NEA also officially recognizes numerous caucuses of the fragmented and oppressed and encourages delegates to join one or another, from the African American caucus, Hispanic caucus, American Indian and Alaska Native caucus, or Asian and Pacific Islander caucus, to the women's caucus or the gay and lesbian caucus. Each of these splinter groups proposes resolutions (almost never opposed by any other group) demanding special consideration in education and other domains for their particular ethnic, racial, or gender group. The resolutions add up to a massive assault on precisely those common ideals that the unions always insist are transmitted exclusively by the public schools.

For example, the NEA supports the "movement toward self-determination by American Indians/Alaska Natives" and believes these designated victim groups should control their own education. It supports "the infusion of Black studies and/or Afrocentric curricula into the curriculum." It strongly supports bilingual education for Hispanic students and opposes efforts to legislate English as the nation's official language. It believes that all schools should designate separate months to celebrate Black History, Hispanic Heritage, Native American Indian/Alaska Native Heritage, Asian/Pacific Heritage, Women's History, Lesbian and Gay History—which pretty well takes up the entire school calendar, leaving scant time for plain old American history.

It would be wrong to dismiss NEA convention debates as the adult equivalent of a high school model congress. The NEA's permanent bureaucracy takes the resolutions very seriously. Through its 1,300 field representatives assigned to state and local affiliates and through its permanent Capitol Hill lobbying staff, it works hard to get the convention agenda implemented by Congress and state legislatures and infused into the culture of the schools. The results include everything from distributing a classroom guidebook on sexual harassment by militant feminist Nan Stein of the Wellesley College

Woman's Center, to "urg[ing] the appropriate government agencies to provide all materials and instruments necessary for left-handed students to achieve on an equal basis with their right-handed counterparts."

No matter that the voters don't support NEA's diversity and affirmative-action agenda: this is America, where you can go straight to the courts. The NEA budgets $23 million a year for its legal arm, headed by a brilliant Washington lawyer named Robert Chanin. Chanin's primary mission, naturally, is to throw up legal challenges to every piece of legislation passed by democratically elected bodies that might free some children from the monopolistic public education system. But in addition, he intervenes in major court battles involving the pet issues of the Left. At the convention, Chanin spoke to the delegates about the NEA's amicus briefs on behalf of gay rights in Colorado, sexual integration of the all-male Citadel, and racial preferences in admissions at the University of Texas Law School. The NEA position had prevailed only in the first two cases, he reported, but racial quotas in the Lone Star State might fare better on appeal.

After the presidential election and the 1997 State of the Union address, with all its emoting about education, the two national teachers' unions may seem more powerful than ever. And with the NEA and the AFT seriously pursuing merger negotiations, a single national union might soon represent 3 million public school employees. It would be the biggest union not just in America but in the world.

Nevertheless, the teachers' unions may not be quite as unassailable as they appear. Despite the millions of dollars they spend on public relations every year, they have been unable to convince the American people that their children's schools and classrooms are in good hands. In a recent book, *Is There a Public for Public Schools?*, former Ford administration secretary of HEW David Mathews underlines the unions' dilemma when he writes that "Americans today seem to be halfway out the schoolhouse door."

Not only are the NEA and AFT clearly out of touch politically with the majority of the American people, but they have also positioned themselves far to the left of their own members. A 1995 NEA convention resolution calling for programs to train teachers to give "accurate portrayals of the roles and contributions of gay, lesbian, and bi-sexual people throughout history," for example, produced a ferocious backlash within the NEA's own membership, particularly in the South. When union teachers began turning in their membership cards and NEA locals faced losing their designation as exclusive bargaining agent, union leaders had to retreat.

The last reliable measures of the voting behavior and political allegiances of the nation's teachers were the CBS/*New York Times* exit polls during the 1980 and 1984 presidential elections. They showed that teachers, far from being way out on the left with their union leaders, were right in the

American mainstream. In 1980, 46 percent of them voted for Ronald Reagan, 41 percent for Jimmy Carter, and 10 percent for John Anderson. By comparison, non-teachers went 51 percent for Reagan, 40 percent for Carter, and 6 percent for Anderson. Some 45 percent of teachers identified themselves as Democrats, 28 percent as Republicans, and 26 percent as independents—almost exactly mirroring the rest of the voting population. The 1984 exit polling produced very similar numbers.

The difference in political outlook between the teachers themselves and their union leaders has given rise to some upstart organizations that, though still small, represent a serious enough challenge to the big unions' monopoly to make them uneasy. National Teacher of the Year Award winner Tracey Bailey is now on the board of one such alternative group, the Association of American Educators. When he speaks to teachers, he tells them that they don't actually have to pay dues to a union that seems more interested in gay rights than in getting children to read, that instead they can be members of professional teacher organizations that focus on educating children and still provide such necessities as insurance.

In "right-to-work" states such as Georgia and Texas, where teachers are not coerced into joining unions, independent teachers' groups now have more members than either the NEA or AFT. Even in "union shop" states, many teachers chafe at the unions' political monopoly. In California last year, the Individual Rights Foundation used federal labor law to represent 700 teachers who resigned from the union and were able to get 50 percent of their dues refunded (approximately $300 per teacher) because it was spent on political and social advocacy rather than collective bargaining. And now many of those same teachers have formed their own independent professional organization, the Professional Educators Group of California. The foundation expects the number of teachers defecting from the NEA to climb into the thousands next year.

Altogether the various independent teachers' organizations around the country now have close to 200,000 members. This ferment may lead the way to thoroughgoing teachers' union reform. What this budding movement needs in order to flower is a massive public information campaign. Teachers presently forced to pay dues to the NEA or AFT need to know what the unions are saying in their name and what rights they have to opt out. Parents and taxpayers need to learn more about teachers' union contracts and political lobbying, teacher productivity and credentialing, and even the $100,000-plus salaries of legions of teachers' union employees. It seems safe to say that if the American people merely knew about the resolutions passed at NEA conventions, the exodus "out the schoolhouse door" would accelerate.

The simple act of getting accurate information to the public about teachers' unions can greatly help the cause of school reform. Last year a good-government group called the Philadelphia Campaign for Public Education decided to butt into a nasty battle between the reform-minded superintendent of schools, David Hornbeck, and the Philadelphia Federation of Teachers over the next labor contract. Hornbeck had demanded that, in exchange for a wage increase, teachers should have to report to the schools a half hour earlier than the students and stay in the buildings a little after dismissal time. He also proposed that teachers who receive an unsatisfactory rating from their principals be denied automatic longevity raises. For Hornbeck's effrontery in suggesting that pay be tied to performance, the teachers' union (an AFT affiliate) launched a massive advertising campaign against him, calling him—what else—a "teacher basher."

That's when the Campaign for Public Education decided that the public needed some accurate information about Philadelphia's unionized teachers. The foundation-funded group began publishing a series of colorful newsletters with charts and graphs containing some amazing data about the existing union contract. One of these "School Updates" carried a headline that said "[Philadelphia] teachers enjoy one of the shortest school days in the nation—and Philadelphia's schoolchildren lose." Next to the text was a bar graph showing the number of minutes spent at school by high school teachers in the 21 largest urban school districts in the country. Philadelphia had the shortest bar (followed by New York City). Another newsletter highlighted some of the contract's work rules, including the fact that "open positions in schools are filled according to a pecking order that favors [seniority] over all other factors."

The union's response was first outrage (including an attempt to prevent the newsletters from being printed), then embarrassment, and finally a more accommodating position in the negotiations. The new labor agreement signed last fall contained the provision that teachers who receive an unsatisfactory rating will lose their automatic pay increase—a provision that seems utterly unexceptionable to a normal person but is revolutionary in the context of teacher unionism.

Imagine that there were similar citizen groups in other large city school districts, continuously channeling information to the public about the myriad ways that teachers' union contracts affect the operation and performance of the schools and how teachers' union politics subvert the common culture that the public schools are supposed to transmit. Imagine further that the same citizen groups communicated with teachers over the heads of their NEA and AFT leaders, informing them that they are entitled to resign from the union and receive a refund of that portion of their dues used for purposes other than collective bargaining. Suppose that in New York City, every time the UFT ran one of its full-page ads boasting that it was working to improve the schools, it was followed by another ad by a citizen group describing in simple, factual terms how many hours teachers work under the union contract, how difficult it is to fire incompetent union teachers, how principals are forced to hire teachers on the basis of seniority.

What I have described is not fanciful. It is occurring in fits and starts all over the country and is bound to grow. The only thing that can prevent the teachers' union reform movement from expanding is the one thing the teachers' unions can't seem to deliver—a public school system that works.

—Spring 1997

HEATHER MAC DONALD

Why Johnny's Teacher Can't Teach

AMERICANS' NEARLY LAST-PLACE FINISH in the Third International Mathematics and Sciences Study of student achievement caused widespread consternation this February, except in the one place it should have mattered most: the nation's teacher education schools. Those schools have far more important things to do than worrying about test scores—things like stamping out racism in aspiring teachers. "Let's be honest," darkly commanded Professor Valerie Henning-Piedmont to a lecture hall of education students at Columbia University's Teachers College last February. "What labels do you place on young people based on your biases?" It would be difficult to imagine a less likely group of bigots than these idealistic young people, happily toting around their *Handbooks of Multicultural Education* and their exposés of sexism in the classroom. But Teachers College knows better. It knows that most of its students, by virtue of being white, are complicitous in an unjust power structure.

The crusade against racism is just the latest irrelevancy to seize the nation's teacher education schools. For over 80 years, teacher education in America has been in the grip of an immutable dogma, responsible for endless educational nonsense. That dogma may be summed up in the phrase: Anything But Knowledge. Schools are about many things, teacher educators say (depending on the decade)—self-actualization, following one's joy, social adjustment, or multicultural sensitivity—but the one thing they are not about is knowledge. Oh sure, educators will occasionally allow the word to pass their lips, but it is always in a compromised position, as in "constructing one's own knowledge," or "contextualized knowledge." Plain old knowledge, the kind passed down in books, the kind for which Faust sold his soul, *that* is out.

The education profession currently stands ready to tighten its already vise-like grip on teacher credentialing, persuading both the federal government and the states to "professionalize" teaching further. In New York, as elsewhere, that means closing off any routes to the classroom that do not pass through an education school. But before caving in to the educrats' pressure, we had better take a hard look at what education schools actually teach.

The course "Curriculum and Teaching in Elementary Education" that Professor Anne Nelson (a pseudonym) teaches at the City College of New York is a good place to start. Dressed in a tailored brown suit with close-cropped hair, Nelson is a charismatic teacher, with a commanding repertoire of voices and personae. And yet, for all her obvious experience and common sense, her course is a remarkable exercise in vacuousness.

As with most education classes, the title of Professor Nelson's course doesn't give a clear sense of what it is about. Unfortunately, Professor Nelson doesn't, either. The semester began, she said in a pre-class interview, by "building a community, rich of talk, in which students look at what they themselves are doing by in-class writing." On this, the third meeting of the semester, Professor Nelson said that she would be "getting the students to develop the subtext of what they're doing." I would soon discover why Professor Nelson was so vague.

"Developing the subtext" turns out to involve a chain reaction of solipsistic moments. After taking attendance and—most admirably—quickly checking the students' weekly handwriting practice, Professor Nelson begins the main work of the day: generating featherlight "texts," both written and oral, for immediate group analysis. She asks the students to write for seven minutes on each of three questions: "What excites me about teaching?" "What concerns me about teaching?" and then, the moment that brands this class as hopelessly steeped in the Anything But Knowledge credo: "What was it like to do this writing?"

This last question triggers a quickening volley of self-reflexive turns. After the students read aloud their predictable reflections on teaching, Professor Nelson asks: "What are you hearing?" A young man states the obvious: "Everyone seems to be reflecting on what their anxieties are." This is too straightforward an answer. Professor Nelson translates into ed-speak: "So writing gave you permission to think on paper about what's there." Ed-speak dresses up the most mundane processes in dramatic terminology—one doesn't just write, one is "given permission to think on the paper"; one doesn't converse, one "negotiates meaning." Then, like a champion tennis player finishing off a set, Nelson reaches for the ultimate level of self-reflexivity and drives it home: "What was it like to listen to each other's responses?"

The self-reflection isn't over yet, however. The class next moves into small groups—along with in-class writing, the most pervasive gimmick in progressive classrooms today—to discuss a set of student-teaching guidelines. After ten minutes, Nelson interrupts the by-now lively and largely off-topic conversations, and asks: "Let's talk about how you felt in these small groups." The students are picking up ed-speak. "It shifted the comfort zone," reveals one. "It was just acceptance; I felt the vibe going through the group." Another adds: "I felt really comfortable; I had trust there." Nelson senses a "teachable moment." "Let's talk about that," she interjects. "We are building trust in this class; we are learning how to work with each other."

Now, let us note what this class was not: it was not about how to keep the attention of eight-year-olds or plan a lesson or make the Pilgrims real to first-graders. It did not, in other words, contain any material (with the exception of the student-teacher guidelines) from the outside world. Instead, it continuously spun its own subject matter out of itself. Like a relationship that consists of obsessively analyzing the relationship, the only content of the course was the course itself.

How did such navel gazing come to be central to teacher education? It is the almost inevitable consequence of the Anything But Knowledge doctrine, born in a burst of quintessentially American anti-intellectual fervor in the wake of World War I. Educators within the federal government and at Columbia's Teachers College issued a clarion call to schools: cast off the traditional academic curriculum and start preparing young people for the demands of modern life. America is a forward-looking country, they boasted; what need have we for such impractical disciplines as Greek, Latin, and higher math? Instead, let the students then flooding the schools take such useful courses as family membership, hygiene, and the worthy use of leisure time. "Life adjustment," not wisdom or learning, was to be the goal of education.

The early decades of this century forged the central educational fallacy of our time: that one can think without having anything to think about. Knowledge is changing too fast to be transmitted usefully to students, argued William Heard Kilpatrick of Teachers College, the most influential American educator of the century; instead of teaching children dead facts and figures, schools should teach them "critical thinking," he wrote in 1925. What matters is not what you know, but whether you know how to look it up, so that you can be a "lifelong learner."

Two final doctrines rounded out the indelible legacy of progressivism. First, Harold Rugg's *The Child-Centered School* (1928) shifted the locus of power in the classroom from the teacher to the student. In a child-centered class, the child determines what he wants to learn. Forcing children into an existing curriculum inhibits their self-actualization, Rugg argued, just as forcing them into neat rows of chairs and desks inhibits their creativity. The teacher becomes an enabler, an advisor; not, heaven forbid, the transmitter of a preexisting body of ideas, texts, or, worst of all, facts. In today's jargon, the child should "construct" his own knowledge rather than passively receive it. By the late 1920s, students were moving their chairs around to form groups of "active learners" pursuing their own individual interests, and, instead of a curriculum, the student-centered classroom followed just one principle: "activity leading to further activity without badness," in Kilpatrick's words. Today's educators still present these seven-decade-old practices as cutting-edge.

As E. D. Hirsch observes, the child-centered doctrine grew out of the romantic idealization of children. If the child was, in Wordsworth's words, a "Mighty Prophet! Seer Blest!" then who needs teachers? But the Mighty Prophet emerged from student-centered schools ever more ignorant and incurious as the schools became more vacuous. By the 1940s and 1950s, schools were offering classes in how to put on nail polish and how to act on a date. The notion that learning should push students out of their narrow world had been lost.

The final cornerstone of progressive theory was the disdain for report cards and objective tests of knowledge. These inhibit authentic learning, Kilpatrick argued; and he carried the day, to the eternal joy of students everywhere.

The foregoing doctrines are complete bunk, but bunk that has survived virtually unchanged to the present. The notion that one can teach "metacognitive" thinking in the abstract is senseless. Students need to learn *something* to learn how to learn at all. The claim that prior knowledge is superfluous because one can always look it up, preferably on the Internet, is equally senseless. Effective research depends on preexisting knowledge. Moreover, if you don't know in what century the atomic bomb was dropped without rushing to an encyclopedia, you cannot fully participate in society. Lastly, Kilpatrick's influential assertion that knowledge was changing too fast to be taught presupposes a blinkered definition of knowledge that excludes the great works and enterprises of the past.

The rejection of testing rests on premises as flawed as the push for "critical thinking skills." Progressives argue that if tests exist, then teachers will "teach to the test"—a bad thing, in their view. But why would "teaching to a test" that asked for, say, the causes of the Civil War be bad for students? Additionally, progressives complain that testing provokes rote memorization—again, a bad thing. One of the most tragically influential education professors today, Columbia's Linda Darling-Hammond, director of the National Commission on Teaching and America's Future, an advocacy group for increased teacher "professionalization," gives a telling example of what she considers a criminally bad test in her hackneyed 1997 brief for progressive education, *The Right to Learn*. She points disdainfully to the following question from the 1995 New York State Regents Exam in biology (required for high school graduation) as "a rote recall of isolated facts and vocabulary terms": "The tissue which conducts organic food through a vascular plant is composed of: (1) Cambium cells; (2) Xylem cells; (3) Phloem cells; (4) Epidermal cells."

Only a know-nothing could be offended by so innocent a question. It never occurs to Darling-Hammond that there may be a joy in mastering the parts of a plant or the organelles of a cell, and that such memorization constitutes learning. Moreover, when, in the progressives' view, will a student ever be held accountable for such knowledge? Does Darling-Hammond believe that a student can pursue a career in, say, molecular biology or in medicine without it? And how else will that learning be demonstrated, if not in a test? But of course such testing will produce unequal results, and that is the real target of Darling-Hammond's animus.

Once you dismiss real knowledge as the goal of education, you have to find something else to do. That's why the Anything But Knowledge doctrine leads directly to Professor Nelson's odd course. In thousands of education schools across the country, teachers are generating little moments of meaning, which they then subject to instant replay. Educators call this "constructing knowledge," a fatuous label for something that is neither construction nor knowledge but mere game playing. Teacher educators, though, possess a primitive relationship to words. They believe that if they just label something "critical thinking" or "community-building," these activities will magically occur.

For all the ed school talk of freedom from the past, teacher education in this century has been more unchanging than Miss Havisham. Like aging vestal virgins, today's schools lovingly guard the ancient flame of progressivism. Since the 1920s they have not had a single new idea; they have merely gussied up old concepts in new rhetoric, most recently in the jargon of minority empowerment. To enter an education classroom, therefore, is to witness a timeless ritual, embedded in an authority structure of unions and state education departments as rigid as the Vatican.

It is a didactic ritual as well. The education professor's credo is: As I do unto you, so shall you do unto your students. The education professor "models" how she wants her students to teach by her own classroom methods. Such a practice is based on a glaring fallacy—that methods that work passably well with committed 22-year-olds, paying $1,800 a course for your wisdom, will translate seamlessly to a class of seven- or 12-year-olds.

The Anything But Knowledge credo leaves education professors and their acolytes free to concentrate on far more pressing matters than how to teach the facts of history or the rules of sentence construction. "Community-building" is one of their most urgent concerns. Teacher educators conceive of their classes as sites of profound political engagement, out of which the new egalitarian order will emerge. A case in point is Columbia's required class "Teaching English in Diverse Social and Cultural Contexts," taught by Professor Barbara Tenney (a pseudonym). "I want to work at a very conscious level with you to build community in this class," Tenney tells her attentive students on the first day of the semester this spring. "You can do it consciously, and you ought to do it in your own classes." Community-building starts by making nameplates for our desks. Then we all find a partner to interview about each other's "identity." Over the course of the semester, each student will conduct two more "identity" interviews with different partners. After the interview, the inevitable self-reflexive moment arrives, when Tenney asks: "How did it work?" This is a sign that we are on our way to "constructing knowledge."

A hallmark of community-building is its overheated rhetoric. The education professor acts as if she were facing a pack of snarling Serbs and Croats, rather than a bunch of well-mannered young ladies (the vast majority of education students), hoping for a good grade. So the community-building assignments attack nonexistent problems of conflict. Tenney, sporting a black leather miniskirt and a cascade of blond curls, hands out a sheet of paper and asks us to respond to the questions: "What climate would allow you to do your best work? How should a class act to encourage open and honest and critical dialogue?" We write for a while, then read our response to our interview partner.

Now is this question really necessary, especially for a group of college graduates? Good classroom etiquette is hardly a mystery. In the evil traditional classroom, and probably also at Teachers College, if a student calls another a fathead, thus discouraging "open and honest and critical dialogue," the teacher would simply reprimand him, and everyone would understand perfectly well what just happened and why. Consensus already exists on civil behavior. But the education classroom, lacking a pressing agenda in concrete knowledge, has to "problematize" the most automatic social routines.

Of course, no amount of writing about the conditions for "open dialogue" can change the fact that discussion is not open on many issues at Teachers College and other progressive bastions. "If you don't demonstrate the correct point of view," says a student, "people are hostile. There's a herd mentality here." A former student of Tenney's describes the difficulties of dissent from the party line on racism: "There's nothing to be gained from challenging it. If you deny that the system inherently privileges whites, you're 'not taking responsibility for your position in racism.'" Doubtless, it would never occur to Professor Tenney that the problem this student describes impedes community-building.

All this artificial "community-building," however gratifying to the professors, has nothing to do with learning. Learning is ultimately a solitary activity: we have only one brain, and at some point we must exercise it in private. One could learn an immense amount about Schubert's lieder or calculus without ever knowing the name of one's seatmate. Such a view is heresy to the education establishment, determined, as Rita Kramer has noted, to eradicate any opportunity for individual accomplishment, with its sinister risk of superior achievement. For the educrats, the group is the irreducible unit of learning. Fueling this principle is the gap in achievement between whites and Asians, on the one hand, and other minorities on the other. Unwilling to adopt the discipline and teaching practices that would help reduce that gap, the education establishment tries to conceal it under group projects.

And so the ultimate community-building mechanism is the ubiquitous "collaborative group." No activity is too solitary to escape assignment to a group: writing, reading, researching, thinking—all are better done with many partners, according to educational dogma. If you see an ed school class sitting up in straight rows, call a doctor, because it means the professor has had a heart attack and couldn't arrange the class into groups.

For all their "progressive" sympathies, not all ed students like this regime. "I'm a socialist at heart," says one of Tenney's students, establishing her bona fides, "but some tasks, like writing, are not collaborative. It's hard when someone loses their voice." Another Columbia student in the Education Administration program complains that "teachers here let the group projects run wild." At $1,800 a course, it's frustrating "when the last four sessions of a class are group projects that are all garbage." Lastly, small group discussions have a habit of careening off the assigned topic. The professors rarely intervene, however, says a Teachers College student, "because they don't want to interfere with the interaction."

The elevation of the group entails the demotion of teachers—yet another plank in the Anything But Knowledge platform. To accord teachers any superior role in the classroom would be to acknowledge an elite hierarchy of knowledge, possessed by some but not all, at least without effort. Teachers traditionally represent elitism, learning, authority—everything that progressivism scorns—and so they must be relegated to the role of mere facilitators for the all-important group.

Linda Darling-Hammond's description of collaborative learning perfectly captures how inextricable the political is from the educational in progressive theory. "Whereas traditional classrooms tend to be still but for the sound of teacher talking, learning-centered classrooms feature student talk and collective action." (The "learning-centered classroom" is Darling-Hammond's jargon for a student-centered classroom.) "Collective action"—how exciting! But though lots of undirected "student talk" hardly seems conducive to learning, progressives abhor quiet. David Schaafsma, one of Columbia's more politicized teachers, told his English Methods class of visiting a quiet third-grade class in the Bronx, explaining: "It terrifies me when kids are really really still. They've got to move." It never occurs to these apostles of the Free Self that for many inner-city children, reaching a state of calm attention is a wonderful achievement.

Collaborative learning leads naturally to another tic of the progressive classroom: "brainstorming." Rather than lecture to a class, the teacher asks the class its opinion about something and lists the responses on the blackboard. Nothing much happens after that; brainstorming, like various forms of community-building, appears to be an end in itself. Hunter College professor Faith DiCaprio (a pseudonym) recently used two levels of brainstorming—whole group and small group—with her "Language and Literacy in Early Childhood" class. The class had just read *Wally's Stories* by Vivian Paley, essentially a transcript of freewheeling discussions among kindergartners in a progressive classroom. First, DiCaprio asked her students what they liked about the book. As students called out their responses—"I liked how she didn't correct the students," "She reminded us why a child-centered room is so necessary: she didn't intrude on their conversation"—DiCaprio writes their responses in abbreviated ed-speak on big posted sheets of paper: "Tolerance: they negotiated meaning" and "Created safe arena."

After DiCaprio fills up the posted pages, nothing happens. Nothing needs to happen, for the lists of responses are visible proof of how much the class already knows. We have just "constructed knowledge." On to the next brainstorming exercise. This time, it's a twofer—brainstorming plus collaborative learning. DiCaprio breaks the class into small groups. Their assignment: list and categorize the topics discussed by the kindergartners in *Wally's Stories*. So the students dutifully make lists of fairies, food, plants, witches, and other meaty matters. One outspoken girl enthuses to her group: "And the kids were smart, they were like, 'The turnips push up with the roots,' and I was like, 'How'd they know that?'" After the groups complete their lists, they read them to the rest of the class. Learning tally? Almost zero.

The consequences of the Anything But Knowledge credo for intellectual standards have been dire. Education professors are remarkably casual when it comes to determining whether their students actually know anything, rarely asking them, for example, what can you tell us about the American Revolution? The ed schools incorrectly presume that the students will have learned everything they need to know in their other or previous college courses, and that the teacher certification exams will screen out people who didn't.

Even if college education were reliably rigorous and comprehensive, education majors aren't the students most likely to profit from it. Nationally, undergraduate education majors have lower SAT and ACT scores than students in any other program of study. Only 16 percent of education majors scored in the top quartile of 1992–93 graduates, compared with 33 percent of humanities majors. Education majors were overrepresented in the bottom quartile, at 30 percent. In New York City, many education majors have an uncertain command of English—I saw one education student at City College repeatedly write "choce" for "choice"—and appear altogether ill at ease in a classroom. To presume *anything* about this population without a rigorous content exit exam is unwarranted.

The laissez-faire attitude toward student knowledge rests on "principled" grounds, as well as on see-no-evil inertia. Many education professors embrace the facile post-structuralist view that knowledge is always political. "An education program can't have content [knowledge] specifics," explains Migdalia Romero, chair of Hunter College's Department of Curriculum and Teaching, "because then you have a point of view. Once you define exactly what finite knowledge is, it becomes a perspective." The notion that a culture could possess a pre-political common store of texts and ideas is anathema to the modern academic.

The most powerful dodge regurgitates William Heard Kilpatrick's classic "critical thinking" scam. Asked whether a future teacher should know the date of the 1812 war, Professor Romero replied: "Teaching and learning is not about dates, facts, and figures, but about developing critical thinking." When pressed if there were not *some* core facts that a teacher or student should know, she valiantly held her ground. "There are two ways of looking at teaching and learning," she replied. "Either you are imparting knowledge, giving an absolute knowledge base, or teaching and learning is about dialogue, a dialogue that helps to internalize and to raise questions." Though she offered the disclaimer "of course you need both," Romero added that teachers don't have to know everything, because they can always look things up.

Romero's tolerance of potential teacher ignorance perfectly reflects New York State's official policy on learning, a sellout to progressivism in its preference for "concepts" and "critical thinking" over measurable knowledge. The Regents' much-vaunted 1996 "student learning standards" are vacuous evasions of facts and knowledge, containing not a single book or document or historical fact that students should know. Literature? The word isn't mentioned. Instead, proclaim the standards in classic educationese, "students will listen, speak, read, and write for literary response and expression"—literally a meaningless statement, matched in its meaninglessness only by the next "English Language Arts" standard: "Students will listen, speak, read, and write for social interaction." Teachers need to get hold of the third level of documentation accompanying the standards to find any specific historical figures or events or books, but there, excessive detail and gaseous generalization will overwhelm them.

But what New York State expects of its students is a model of rigor compared to what it formally expects of its teachers. The State Teacher Certification Exams are a complete abdication of the state's responsibility for ensuring an educated teaching force. If any teachers in the state know anything about American history, English literature, or chemistry, it is a complete accident, for the state's highest education authorities have not the slightest interest in finding out. The Liberal Arts and Sciences Test, the ticket to a teacher's first five years in a classroom, contains absolutely no substance; at most, it tests reading skills. The test preparation booklet is a classic of educationese. The exam section on "Historical and Social Scientific Awareness" (note: not "knowledge"), for example, tests teachers' "understanding [of] the interrelatedness of historical, geographic, cultural, economic, political and social issues and factors."

Now, by loading on the different types of "issues and factors" that prospective teachers are supposed to understand, the exam ensures that they need know nothing in particular. The only thing that test takers do have to know is the multicultural dogma that there is no history, only "multiple perspectives" on history. The certification exam asks prospective teachers to "analyze multiple perspectives within U.S. society regarding major historical and contemporary issues"—not history, but "historical *issues*," and not even "historical issues," but "multiple perspectives" on "historical issues." Such a demand is ripe for spouting off, say, on the "Native American perspective" on the Western expansion, without having the slightest idea what fueled that expansion, when and where it occurred, who peopled it, and what its consequences were. In fairness, the Content Specialty Tests teachers must take for permanent certification are much more substantive, especially in science and math, but only one-third of the teachers seeking provisional certification ever make it that far.

The pedagogy portion of the Liberal Arts and Sciences certification exam resembles a catechism more than an exam. "Multiple perspectives" are clearly not acceptable in answering such loaded questions as: "Analyze how classroom environments that respect diversity foster positive student experiences," or, "Analyze how schoolwide structures (i.e., tracking) and classroom factors (e.g., homogeneous versus heterogeneous grouping [presumably by ability], student-teacher interactions) may affect students' self-concepts and learning." Will a would-be teacher who answers that classrooms should stress a common culture or that ability-grouping promotes excellence remain just a would-be teacher? One hopes not.

The exams echo with characteristic ed school verbiage. The student doesn't learn, he achieves "learning processes and outcomes"; the teacher doesn't teach, she "applies strategies for facilitating learning in instructional situations." Disregard for language runs deep in the teacher education profession, so much so that ed school professors tolerate glaring language deficiencies in schoolchildren. Last January, Manhattan's Park West High School shut down for a day, so that its faculty could bone up on progressive pedagogy. One of the more popular staff development seminars was "Using Journals and Learning Logs." The presenters—two Park West teachers and a representative from the New York City Writing Project, an anti-grammar initiative run by Lehman College's Education School—proudly passed around their students' journal writing, including the following representative entry on "Matriarchys v. pratiarchys [sic]": "The different between Matriarchys and patriarchys is that when the mother is in charge of the house. sometime the children do whatever they want. But sometimes the mother can do both roll as a mother and as a father too and they can do it very good." A more personal entry described how the author met her boyfriend: "He said you are so kind I said you noticed and then he hit me on my head. I made-believe I was crying and when he came naire me I slaped him right in his head and than I ran . . . to my grandparients home and he was right behind me. Thats when he asked did I have a boyfriend."

The ubiquitous journal-writing cult holds that such writing should go uncorrected. Fortunately, some Park West teachers bridled at the notion. "At some point, the students go into the job market, and they're not being judged 'holistically,'" protested a black teacher, responding to the invocation of the state's "holistic" model for grading writing. Another teacher bemoaned the Board of Ed's failure to provide guidance on teaching grammar. "My kids are graduating without skills," he lamented.

Such views, however, were decidedly in the minority. "Grammar is related to purpose," soothed the Lehman College representative, educrat code for the proposition that asking students to write grammatically on topics they are not personally "invested in" is unrealistic. A Park West presenter burst out with a more direct explanation for his chilling indifference to student incompetence: "I'm not going to spend my life doing error diagnosis! I'm not going to spend my weekend on that!" Correcting papers used to be part of the necessary drudgery of a teacher's job. No more, with the advent of enlightened views about "self-expression" and "writing with intentionality."

However easygoing the education establishment is regarding future teachers' knowledge of history, literature, and science, there is one topic that it assiduously monitors: their awareness of racism. To many teacher educators, such an awareness is the most important tool a young teacher can bring to the classroom. It cannot be developed too early. Rosa, a bouncy and enthusiastic junior at Hunter College, has completed only her first semester of education courses, but already she has mastered the most important lesson: America is a racist, imperialist country, most like, say, Nazi Germany. "We are lied to by the very institutions we have come to trust," she recalls from her first-semester reading. "It's all government that's inventing these lies, such as Western heritage."

The source of Rosa's newfound wisdom, Donaldo Macedo's *Literacies of Power: What Americans Are Not Allowed to Know*, is an execrable book by any measure. But given its target audience—impressionable education students—it comes close to being a crime. Widely assigned at Hunter, and in use in approximately 150 education schools nationally, it is an illiterate, barbarically ignorant Marxist-inspired screed against America. Macedo opens his first chapter, "Literacy for Stupidification: The Pedagogy of Big Lies," with a quote from Hitler and quickly segues to Ronald Reagan: "While busily calling out slogans from their patriotic vocabulary memory warehouse, these same Americans dutifully vote . . . for Ronald Reagan, giving him a landslide victory. . . . These same voters ascended [*sic*] to Bush's morally high-minded call to apply international laws against Saddam Hussein's tyranny and his invasion of Kuwait." Standing against this wave of ignorance and imperialism is a lone 12-year-old from Boston, whom Macedo celebrates for his courageous refusal to recite the Pledge of Allegiance.

What does any of this have to do with teaching? Everything, it turns out. In the 1960s, educational progressivism took on an explicitly political cast: schools were to fight institutional racism and redistribute power. Today, Columbia's Teachers College holds workshops on cultural and political "oppression," in which students role-play ways to "usurp the existing power structure," and the New York State Regents happily call teachers the "ultimate change agents." To be a change agent, one must first learn to "critique" the existing social structure. Hence, the assignment of such propaganda as Macedo's book.

But however bad the influence of Macedo's puerile politics on future teachers, it pales compared to the model set by his writing style. A typical sentence: "This inability to link the reading of the word with the world, if not combated, will further exacerbate already feeble democratic institutions [*sic*] and the unjust, asymmetrical power relations that characterize the hypocritical nature of contemporary democracies." Anyone who dares criticize Macedo for his prose is merely trying to "suffocate discourses," he says, with the "blind and facile call for clarity." That Hunter College could assign this gross betrayal of the English language to future teachers is a sufficient reason for closing its education program down. Rosa's control of English is shaky enough as it is; to fill her ears with such subliterate writing represents professional malpractice.

But Macedo is just one of the political tracts that Hunter force-fed the innocent Rosa in her first semester. She also learned about the evils of traditional children's stories from education radical Herbert Kohl. In *Should We Burn Babar?* Kohl weighs the case for and against the dearly beloved children's classic *Babar the Elephant*, noting in passing that it prevented him from "question[ing] the patriarchy earlier." He decides—but let Rosa expound the message of Kohl's book: "[*Babar*]'s like a children's book, right? [But] there's an underlying meaning about colonialism, about like colonialism, and is it OK, it's really like it's OK, but it's like really offensive to these people." Better burn *Babar* now!

In New York, as in almost every state, the focus on diversity and antiracism indoctrination comes with the highest imprimatur. The State Board of Regents requires all prospective teachers to have at least one course in "diversity"; many local ed schools pride themselves on weaving "diversity" into all their courses. The nation's most influential education school, Teachers College, promotes the most extreme race consciousness in its mandated diversity program. In her large lecture course, Professor Valerie Henning-Piedmont sneered at "liberal correctness," which she defined as "I don't see the color of my students." Such misguided color blindness, she said, equals: "I don't see the students."

Expect the folly only to grow worse. A draft report from the Regents Task Force on Teaching, grousing that future teachers lack sufficient grounding in diversity, calls for special training in such challenges as "teaching both sexes," thus further legitimizing the ludicrous proposition that schools mistreat girls. The Regents also make recruiting a more "diverse" teaching force a top priority, based on the assumption that minority students learn best from minority teachers. Currently, 34 percent of teachers in New York City, and 15 percent statewide, are minorities, compared with a student population that is 83 percent minority in New York City and 43 percent statewide. Asked what evidence the Regents have for the proposition that the color of the teaching force correlates with achievement, Doris T. Garner, staff coordinator for the Task Force, admitted, "I don't think hard evidence exists that would say that." If black students should be taught by black teachers, should white students be taught by white teachers? "I would not recommend that," replied Garner, fearless of illogic.

Since the Regents are making teacher diversity a top priority, something is going to have to give. Currently, blacks fail the content-free Liberal Arts and Sciences Test of provisional certification at a rate five times that of whites. But that's just a temporary obstacle, because the test-bias hounds may be already closing in for the kill: the discovery that the exam discriminates against minorities. The Regents' most recent paper on teacher training warned that the certification exam "must exclude language that would jeopardize candidates, and include language and content that reflects diversity." Now, the only candidates who would be jeopardized by the exam's language are those, of any color, who are deeply troubled by hot air. As for "cultural bias," at present the exam is a rainbow of multicultural examples and propaganda—one sample question, for example, features a fawning review of a "multicultural dance work that is truly representative of the diversity of New York." Don't be surprised if the complete absence of any "bias" in the exam, however, fails to prevent a concerted, taxpayer-funded effort to redraft it so as to guarantee an equal pass rate among all groups of takers.

Though the current diversity battle cry is "All students can learn," the educationists continually lower expectations of what they should learn. No longer are students expected to learn all their multiplication tables in the third grade, as has been traditional. But while American educators come up with various theories about fixed cognitive phases to explain why our children should go slow, other nationalities trounce us. Sometimes, we're trounced in our own backyards, causing cognitive dissonance in local teachers.

A young student at Teachers College named Susan describes incredulously a Korean-run preschool in Queens. To her horror, the school, the Holy Mountain School, violates every progressive tenet: rather than being "student-centered" and allowing each child to do whatever he chooses, the school imposes a curriculum on the children, based on the alphabet. "Each week, the children got a different letter," Susan recalls grimly. Such an approach violates "whole language" doctrine, which holds that students can't "grasp the [alphabetic] symbols without the whole word or the meaning or any context in their lives," in Susan's words. Holy Mountain's further infractions include teaching its wildly international students only in English and failing to provide an "anti-bias multicultural curriculum." The result? By the end of preschool the students learn English and are writing words. Here is true belief in the ability of all children to learn, for it is backed up by action.

Across the city, young teachers are dumping progressive theories faster than Indonesian currency. For all the unctuous talk of diversity, many progressive tenets are dangerously ill-adapted to inner-city classrooms. "They don't say 'boo' about this population," scoffs Samantha, a recent Hunter graduate now teaching in Brooklyn's Bedford-Stuyvesant section. "My course in multiculturalism had zero to do with the classroom."

A former dancer, Samantha was an open receptacle for progressive ideas. But her early efforts to follow the model have left her stranded. Her fourth-grade class is out of control. "I didn't set it up in a strict manner at the beginning," she laments. "I gave them too many choices; I did a lot of things wrong." Collaborative learning? Forget about it. "My kids resort to fighting immediately if I put them in groups." Samantha tried to use groups to make a poster on electricity. "It was mayhem; they couldn't stay quiet," she recalls.

The student-centered classroom is equally a fraud. "You can't give them choices," Samantha asserts flatly. Next year, with a new class, she will do things differently. "I will have everything set up to the last detail—their names on the desks, which notebooks to buy, how to label them. They need to know what hook to hang their coat on and where to go from there. Every minute of the day has to be scripted. You can't just say: 'Line up!' because they'll fight. Instead, you have to say: 'Boys, stand up, push in your chairs, and here are your line spots.'"

As for "metacognition," that is out as well. "My kids need the rote; they can't do half of six or four divided by two." Samantha is using the most un-holy of unholies to teach her children to read—a basal reader, derided by the education establishment as spirit-killing. But the reader gives her specific skill sets to work on—above all, phonics and grammar. "My kids don't hear the correct sound of words at home, such as 'th' or the ending of words, so teaching reading is harder."

Journals, whole language, and "portfolio assessment" became more casualties of the real world at the Holy Cross School in the Bronx. The school recently hired a Teachers College graduate who arrived fired up with those student-centered methods. No more. Now she is working very hard on grammar, according to assistant principal William Kurtz. "Those [progressive] tools don't necessarily work for kids who can't read or tell you what a noun or a verb is," he says. In his own history class, Kurtz has discovered that he needs to be as explicit about study habits and research methods as Samantha is about classroom behavior. "When I give an essay question, I have to be very structured about going to the library and what resources to use. If you don't do that, they look up nothing."

The education establishment would be unfazed by these stories. Samantha and William, it would say, are still prisoners of the "deficit model." All these two benighted teachers can see is what their kids don't know, instead of building on their strengths. If those strengths are hip-hop music, for example, focus on that. But for heaven's sake, don't deny the children the benefits of a child-centered classroom.

In fact, the strict environment that Samantha plans is the best thing that could happen to her pupils. It is perhaps the only place they will meet order and civility. Samantha's children are "surrounded by violence," she says. Many are not interested in learning, because at home, "everyone is dissing everybody, or staying up late to get high. My kids are so emotionally beat up, they don't even know when they're out of their seats." A structured classroom is their only hope to learn the rules that the rest of society lives by. To eliminate structure for kids who have none in their lives is to guarantee failure.

Given progressive education's dismal record, all New Yorkers should tremble at what the Regents have in store for the state. The state's teacher education establishment, led by Columbia's Linda Darling-Hammond, has persuaded the Regents to make its monopoly on teacher credentialing total. Starting in 2003, according to a Regents plan steaming inexorably toward adoption, all teacher candidates must pass through an education school to be admitted to a classroom. We know, alas, what will happen to them there.

This power grab will be a disaster for children. By making ed school inescapable, the Regents will drive away every last educated adult who may not be willing to sit still for its foolishness but who could bring to the classroom unusual knowledge or experience. The nation's elite private schools are full of such people, and parents eagerly proffer tens of thousands of dollars to give their children the benefit of such skill and wisdom.

Amazingly, even the Regents, among the nation's most addled education bodies, sporadically acknowledge what works in the classroom. A Task Force on Teaching paper cites some of the factors that allow other countries to wallop us routinely in international tests: a high amount of lesson content (in other words, teacher-centered, not student-centered, learning), individual tracking of students, and a coherent curriculum. The state should cling steadfastly to its momentary insight, at odds with its usual policies, and discard its foolhardy plan to enshrine Anything But Knowledge as its sole education dogma. Instead of permanently establishing the teacher education status quo, it should search tirelessly for alternatives and for potential teachers with a firm grasp of subject matter and basic skills. Otherwise ed school claptrap will continue to stunt the intellectual growth of the Empire State's children.

—Spring 1998

SOL STERN

The Invisible Miracle of Catholic Schools

OVER THE PAST SEVERAL YEARS, Cardinal John J. O'Connor has repeatedly made New York City an extraordinary offer: send me the lowest-performing 5 percent of children presently in the public schools, and I will put them in Catholic schools—where they will succeed. Last August the cardinal sweetened the offer. He invited city officials to come study the Catholic school system, "to make available to public schools whatever of worth in our Catholic schools is constitutionally usable. The doors are open. Our books are open. Our hearts are open. No charge."

The city's response: almost total silence.

In a more rational world, city officials would have jumped at the cardinal's invitation. It might, first of all, have been a huge financial plus for the city. The annual per-pupil cost of Catholic elementary schools is $2,500 per year, about a third of what taxpayers now spend for the city's public schools. Assuming that the Catholic schools really did absorb 50,000 more students (roughly 5 percent of the 1 million now enrolled in public schools), the city might save over a quarter billion dollars a year.

But the city would gain a still greater benefit from having thousands more of its disadvantaged children finish school and become productive citizens, for O'Connor's claim that Catholic schools would do a better job than public schools is no idle boast. Catholic schools are already transforming the lives of thousands of poor black and Hispanic children, many of whom are not Catholic. Unlike the public schools, which have trivialized their curriculum and abandoned their standards in the name of multiculturalism, Catholic educators have remained committed to the ideal that minority children can share in, and master, our civilization's intellectual and spiritual heritage. Indeed, Catholic schools are among the last bastions in American education of the idea of a common civic culture.

This makes for a supreme historical irony. When America erected the "iron wall" of separation between church schools and government schools more than a century ago, the public school system seemed the best instrument for educating poor immigrants and assimilating them into the nation's mainstream culture and shared civic ideals. The separatist Catholic schools, on the other hand, saw themselves as a bulwark against an attempt by the public schools to impose first Protestantism and, later, secularism on Catholic children.

But beginning in the 1970s, as public schools were deteriorating, urban parish schools, inspired by Vatican II's universalism and by its call for an end to racism and social injustice, opened their doors to the new poor, mostly minority and non-Catholic. Minority enrollment in New York State's Catholic schools shot up—from 12 percent in 1970 to 36 percent in 1991. In New York City the figure is almost 60 percent; in Manhattan and the Bronx, 85 percent.

It turned out that Catholic schools were superb at this new mission. Mountains of data make the case conclusively. A landmark 1982 study by education scholars James Coleman, Thomas Hoffer, and Sally Kilgore, for instance, demonstrated that Catholic school students were one grade level ahead of their public school counterparts in mathematics, reading, and vocabulary. A study by Andrew Greeley revealed that the differences between Catholic school and public school performance were greatest among students from the most disadvantaged backgrounds.

The early scholarship attributed Catholic schools' superior performance to their more rigorous academic curriculum and their greater degree of discipline. Researchers also credited the distinctive organization of Catholic schools. Free from the central bureaucratic controls that weigh down public schools, they seemed more like autonomous communities, yet were accountable to their students' families. Coleman observed that whereas the public school system had become an arena for the clash of political and economic interests, Catholic schools were infused with an atmosphere of trust and cooperation between teachers, administrators, and parents, based on a shared moral vision.

During the next decade, a growing body of research confirmed the Catholic schools' advantage. In 1990 the RAND Corporation compared the performance of children from New York City's public and Catholic high schools. Only 25 percent of the public school students graduated at all, and only 16 percent took the Scholastic Aptitude Test. By contrast, over 95 percent of the Catholic school students graduated, and 75 percent took the SAT. Catholic school students scored an average of 815 on the SAT. By shameful contrast, the small "elite" of public school students who graduated and took the SAT averaged only 642 for those in neighborhood schools and

715 for those in magnet schools. The national average, heavily dominated by white middle-class pupils, is 900.

A 1993 New York State Department of Education report compared New York City schools with the highest levels of minority enrollment. The conclusions were striking: "Catholic schools with 81 to 100 percent minority composition outscored New York City public schools with the same percentage of minority enrollment in Grade 3 reading (+17 percent), Grade 3 mathematics (+10 percent), Grade 5 writing (+6 percent), Grade 6 reading (+10 percent), and Grade 6 mathematics (+11 percent)." And a seminal study by Anthony Bryk, Valerie Lee, and Peter Holland, based on a national database of student performance, found that Catholic schools succeed in reducing—by almost half—the impact of a student's minority background on academic achievement.

Public education interest groups—of which the most powerful by far are the teachers' unions—argue that both a "creaming" and a "self-selection" bias distort the survey data. While public schools must take all children, they claim, Catholic schools allegedly can screen out those from troubled backgrounds. What's more, the poor minority children whose parents choose to pay Catholic school tuition are more motivated.

Yet the 1993 State Education Department study found that Catholic and public schools had similar percentages of students from troubled families with low incomes, while Bryk, Lee, and Holland report that Catholic schools expel far fewer children than public schools. And the experience of a wealthy New Yorker named Charles Benenson dramatically demonstrates how negligible a part self-selection plays in Catholic schools' success with inner-city pupils.

As part of the "I Have a Dream program," which pays college tuition for minority children who finish high school, Benenson adopted several classes at P.S. 44 in the South Bronx. Disappointed by how few students even made it through high school, Benenson began offering to pay the tuition for any of the eighth-graders who wished to attend Catholic high schools. Results for his first adopted graduating class: of the 38 students who stayed in public high schools, only two made it to college; of the 22 who attended Catholic high schools, only two failed to go to college.

"They were the same kids from the same families and the same housing projects," says Benenson, a non-Catholic. "In fact, sometimes one child went to public school and a sibling went to Catholic school. We even gave money to the public school kids for tutoring and after-school programs. It's just that the Catholic schools worked, and the others didn't."

Most of New York's elite is resolutely uninterested in the Catholic schools' success. Last August, when Mayor Giuliani extolled the Catholic schools for their success in educating minority children and suggested that they held important lessons for public schools, most of the city's education reporters were mystified. Catholic schools? They wouldn't have known where to find one. The *New York Times* carried extensive quotes from public-school teachers and principals angry at the mayor's comparison. The *Times* editorialized that "the two systems are simply not comparable," repeating the old canard about self-selection. The paper didn't publish a word about the large body of scholarly literature on Catholic schools' success.

Mayor Giuliani was right: educating the public about how consistently well Catholic schools have done with New York's inner-city pupils would help pave the way for the kind of radical reforms public schools desperately need. Such kids are eminently educable, Catholic schools show—and here's how to educate them, for a mere third of the public schools' per-pupil cost. In the face of this fine performance, public schools can have no excuse for not doing as well. Nor can the public schools claim that lack of money accounts for their dismal record: as the Catholic schools show, something other than money is the key to success.

Consider Manhattan's Community School District 3, where my own children have gone to school. In some respects this district, which includes most of the Upper West Side and a large chunk of Central Harlem, typifies the city school system. At its southern end it serves a racially mixed, largely middle-class student population. In Harlem, a broad swath of schools with 100 percent minority enrollment have remained dismal failures.

During the past decade, the district has been a laboratory for each new trend in public-school reform. After taking root in East Harlem's District 4, a program of choice was instituted for our district's middle schools. Parents can select among the various schools in the district, instead of having their child automatically assigned to the nearest one, on the theory that the need to compete for pupils will force individual schools to improve. At the same time, some of the existing large schools were reconfigured into smaller, supposedly more autonomous, units. All of our schools have planning councils of parents and teachers.

The total impact of these reforms has been negligible. Overall student performance hasn't improved. And although choice is supposed to be for everyone, middle-class students always somehow find their way into the limited number of academically acceptable schools. Some of these schools are performing well, but it could just be that they're getting the best, most motivated students. Sound familiar? It's called "self-selection." For the poor black and Hispanic children trapped in the northern part of the district, the reforms have been irrelevant.

Even the best public schools remain in the stranglehold of the system's special interests. There is not a "choice" school, an "alternative" school, or a "new vision" school that doesn't continue to suffer from incompetent and nonperforming teachers who can't be fired, whose principal isn't hamstrung by union work rules, where learning doesn't suffer from onerous regulations and mindless bureaucracy.

But if the public schools in our district are not yet free from these imprisoning fetters, the Catholic schools are.

Free Catholic schools? Isn't that an oxymoron? Complacent behind the iron wall of separation, enlightened West Siders know that Catholic schools are run by a rigid, regressive church hierarchy.

I have been walking past some of those Catholic schools for the past ten years. One of New York City's 325 such schools, which serve a total of 150,000 pupils, is Saint Gregory the Great, an elementary school on West 90th Street. Every morning, as I accompanied my children to their public school, I couldn't help noticing the well-behaved black and Hispanic children in their neat uniforms entering the drab-looking parish building. Yet my curiosity never led me past the imposing crucifix looking down from the roof, which evoked childhood images of Catholic anti-Semitism and clerical obscurantism. Finally, earlier this year, I visited this underfunded Catholic school and learned why it outperforms many of the public schools in our very progressive district.

Not one of Saint Gregory's 280 students is white, almost all are poor, and some come to school from Harlem and Washington Heights. If Saint Gregory's didn't exist, they would likely be attending failing public schools like P.S. 180 or P.S. 76. Year after year, education officials put these two Harlem elementary schools on notice that they are performing below the minimum academic standard. In 1995, for example, only 33 percent of P.S. 180's third-graders scored above the state's minimum standard in reading; 69 percent in mathematics. P.S. 76's scores were even worse: 18 percent and 58 percent, respectively. By contrast, 62 percent of Saint Gregory's third-graders were reading above the minimum standard, and 92 percent were above the standard in math.

In fact, Saint Gregory's holds its own even when compared with some of District 3's more middle-class schools. P.S. 75, five blocks north of Saint Gregory's, has received considerable media attention as an innovative school. Incorporating all the new reforms, and with a dynamic new principal, active parents, and a student body more than 40 percent white, P.S. 75 was only six percentage points higher than Saint Gregory's in reading, and five points below the Catholic school in math.

When I finally stepped inside the parish doors, I realized that Saint Gregory's resembles an education reform many of us have been calling for in New York—the charter school. Public charter schools, now legal in 21 states, receive varying degrees of relief from constricting regulations and teacher contract rules. The group holding the charter—it may be a consortium of parents or a university or a nonprofit organization—is accountable for the school's performance: if a school fails, it can be closed. In theory, such freedom will lead to better performance.

That's almost exactly what's been happening in Catholic schools like Saint Gregory's. Four years ago it was in dire financial straits, with enrollment down to 209 from a high of over 300 a decade ago. The archdiocese was getting ready to close it down. In a last-ditch effort to save the school, the parish hired a determined African-American woman named Deborah Hurd as the new principal.

Hurd exemplifies the new generation of lay educators replacing the priests and nuns who used to staff Catholic schools. Herself a Catholic-school graduate, Hurd had no intention of pursuing a teaching career: she took her first job, as a substitute teacher in a Catholic school, while attending business college. But one day she got a desperate call from a nun at the Saint Joseph's school in Harlem. "I didn't want to teach," recalls Hurd, "but she kept asking me to 'just take this class.'" That was more than a quarter century ago. She remains in the system because she believes in the moral and academic structure that Catholic schools provide.

Hurd's own seven-year-old daughter is a case in point. "I had her in a progressive kindergarten run by the Quakers, but she was floundering. So I moved her to Saint Gregory's. Now she's learning how to study and concentrate. What we do in first grade is set the tone. The children learn to sit in a chair, to put their coats away, to raise their hand when they want to be called on, to understand when an assignment begins and ends. These things, and the uniforms they wear: they are all signs—and our kids are decoding them. So right from the start they are learning structure and skills."

When Hurd became principal of Saint Gregory's, the parish gave her five years to turn the school around. She did it in less then three. Taking charge right away, she did some fund-raising and found a few patrons who helped her add new programs, including preschool and kindergarten classes. To build enrollment to its current 280, she advertised in local newspapers.

During her first summer, Hurd had the school painted and the rest rooms renovated. She cut the auditorium in half to make space for more classrooms. Unlike a public school principal, she didn't have to wait years for a central building maintenance office to approve her renovation requests. "I just went out and found a contractor and a plumber who gave me a good price," she says. "There's no magic to it. It can all be done if you have half a brain and you don't have a bureaucracy breathing down your neck."

The school must pass the test of the market: it will survive only if it meets the needs of its students, whose parents pay up to $1,700 in tuition. (The rest of the school's $2,500 per-pupil budget comes from the archdiocese, private donors, and government grants for books, transportation, and school lunches.) Catholic schools are "called into being by the community," as principal Pat Kelley of Saint Angela Morrici School in the South Bronx puts it. "The community comes. The community pays. And the school goes. If the people didn't want to come, it would be closed." In return for the $100 per-pupil subsidy Saint Gregory's receives from the archdiocese's scholarship fund, the only requirements are that all students study religion for one period a day (though non-Catholics aren't required to perform the sacraments) and that the school follow a standard curriculum, which parallels the state curriculum.

But Catholic schools succeed where state schools fail because they have virtually no central-office bureaucrats telling principals how to do their jobs. In public schools teachers almost automatically get tenure—a lifetime job guarantee—after three years. Most Catholic schools around the country have no tenure system whatsoever, though in New York City, where the teachers are represented by a union, many do get tenure after three years of successful teaching. But it is the principal who grants tenure, not some distant bureaucrat. And unlike in the public schools, tenured teachers have no claim on job openings in other schools. The labor contract imposes no work rules that tie a principal's hands in the area of teacher hiring and assignments. Even tenured teachers can be fired for incompetence or nonperformance far more easily than in the public schools. And there is no rigid credentialing system: principals can select teachers for their talent and commitment.

Consider how Hurd hired Susan Viti, Saint Gregory's fourth-grade teacher. Viti had been a public school teacher near Chicago when her fiancé was transferred to New York. The young couple found an apartment a few blocks from Saint Gregory's. While trying to decide what she wanted to do in New York, Viti befriended some of Saint Gregory's students, who played in a small playground next to the school. One day, on a whim, she walked in off the street in her tennis clothes to meet Deborah Hurd. Hurd was impressed, and when a position opened up just before the first day of school, she offered it to Viti.

Only nominally Catholic, Viti took the job because she believed she could make a difference in the lives of some of the children she had met. She could not have been hired in a public school, for she lacked a city teaching credential, and, in any case, the central bureaucracy moves at a glacial pace. But at Saint Gregory's, Viti was in front of the classroom a few days after being offered the job.

Viti's fourth-grade classroom is nicely decorated with students' artwork and writing samples. On one of the walls hangs a poster:

CLASSROOM RULES

1. Follow directions.
2. Be prepared for class.
3. Respect others and their property.
4. Be a good citizen.

CONSEQUENCES

1. Name written down.
2. No recess.
3. Discuss with parent.
4. A meeting with principal.

Viti's students, all black and Hispanic, project an admirable tone of civility and seriousness. The boys are dressed in gray slacks, light blue shirts, and ties; the girls all wear the same plaid jumpers and blue shirts. They sit in matched pairs of desks, their books and notebooks stacked under their chairs. It's a far cry from the worst public schools, where disorder prevails. Catholic schools, after all, never went through the rights revolution of the 1960s, which eroded the order-keeping authority of schools and discouraged teachers and principals from disciplining disruptive students by elaborate due-process procedures.

When Viti asks a question, hands shoot up enthusiastically. When she returns graded assignments, each child says, "Thank you, Miss Viti." "You're welcome, darling," she answers cheerfully. I sat in as Viti conducted a review lesson on the geography of the western United States. All the children were completely engaged and had obviously done their homework. They were able to answer each of her questions about the principal cities and capitals of the western states—some of which I couldn't name—and the topography and natural resources of the region.

"Why do the Rocky Mountains have lower temperatures?" she asked. One of the children explained the relationship between altitude and temperatures.

"Which minerals would be found in the Rocky Mountains?" Eager hands shot up; Viti called on several children, each of whom contributed an answer. She used the lesson to expand the students' vocabulary and understanding of concepts such as the differences between crops and minerals. When the children wrote things down, she insisted on proper grammar and spelling.

Without pausing for a break, Viti moved on to the day's math lesson. She had the children go to the blackboard in teams to do multiplication problems with fractions and decimals. She praised the students who solved the problems and gently corrected mistakes.

As I sat in that classroom, I found myself wishing that my own son's fourth-grade teachers at P.S. 87, reputedly one of the best public schools in the city, were anywhere near as productive and as focused on basic skills as Viti. Both my boys' teachers have wasted an enormous amount of their time with empty verbiage about the evils of racism and sexism. By contrast, in Viti's class and in all the other Catholic school classes I visited, it was taken for granted that a real education is the best antidote to prejudice.

I was amazed at the children's ability to endure more than two hours of learning without losing their concentration. The students at Saint Gregory's, as at most Catholic schools, have very few breaks. Saint Gregory's cannot afford art and music classes, and offers only one gym period per week. From first grade on, children are expected to sit quietly and learn for most of the day.

Viti, too, has few breaks. On some days, other than a lunch period, she is on her feet in front of her class for almost six hours. Because she assigns considerable homework, Viti does a lot of grading at home. She is constantly on the phone or writing notes to parents. Four days a week she stays after school to do remedial work with some of her struggling students; twice a week she gives up her lunch hour to do extra work with her more advanced math students. On weekends she sometimes drops in on students' Little League games.

She earns just $21,000 a year, $8,000 less than a first-year teacher in a public school. "I've taught in an all-white, affluent suburban school, where I made over $40,000," she says. "This time I wanted to do something good for society, and I am lucky enough to be able to afford to do it. I am trying to instill in my students that whatever their life situation is now, they can succeed if they work hard and study. I involve the parents, and they know that I am serious about holding their children to a high standard." Saint Angela Morrici principal Pat Kelley echoes this sentiment: "Those of us who are doing the work do it not only for a paycheck. We're doing it because we get to practice a profession that we love."

Of course not all Catholic school teachers are as impressive as Viti. I visited some classes where the teachers overemphasized rote learning and focused too narrowly on the textbook. But in every classroom I visited, the teachers were deeply, personally engaged with their students. They were on top of them constantly, refusing to let them fall behind. It was inconceivable that I would see what I and other parents have witnessed in several junior high schools in our district: children literally asleep in the classroom. I was reminded of an epigram of Bryk, Lee, and Holland: Catholic schools take the position that "no one who works hard will fail," whereas the prevailing approach in too many public schools is that "no one who shows up will fail."

On Amsterdam Avenue, six blocks north of Saint Gregory's, sits the Holy Name of Jesus Elementary School. It began serving the neighborhood's Irish and Italian immigrants almost 100 years ago; today 99.5 percent of its 600 students are black or Hispanic. Thirty percent of the children are on welfare, 40 percent are from single-parent families, and 98 percent are poor enough to qualify for the federally funded school-lunch program.

Holy Name's principal is Brother Richard Griecko of the De La Salle Christian Brothers, one of the Catholic Church's teaching orders. Griecko has managed to create a technological wonderland that would be the envy of the city's best high schools—and on a budget of less than $1.5 million per year, or just $2,500 per student. The school has two computer labs, each with 30 state-of-the-art computers. Each classroom is also equipped with two computers, one for the students and one on the teacher's desk. A satellite dish on the roof receives interactive programming: the seventh-grade English class can turn on the TV and receive a live lesson in poetry from a poet in Boston.

Some public schools have modern computer labs where the students play games while their teacher gets a period off. At Holy Name, by constrast, the computers are an integral part of the curriculum. Students use them to write journals and reports, work with special educational programs, and learn computer languages. When I visited the school, I saw first-graders in the lab intently working on an IBM phonetics program called "Writing to Read."

Some came from homes where no English was spoken. Unlike in the public schools, there's no bilingual program here. "We believe it's important to have the children reading and speaking English as soon as possible," Brother Griecko says. "Sometimes we take children from public school. The parents put them here because they want them finally to learn English."

Sitting in an office cluttered with videotapes and papers, soft jazz playing in the background, Griecko explains how he managed to acquire the elaborate technology on a shoestring budget. "Its pretty simple: I have the freedom to control the budget and how our money is spent. I can see areas where we underspend, and I can transfer funds to another project—such as the computers." He also applies for private grants. Griecko estimates that the technology cost about $250,000 over eight years. He was able to squirrel away $30,000 each year for his dream project—proving again that when educators with a vision have freedom and the support of a community of parents and teachers, anything becomes possible.

Like Hurd, Greicko is grateful for his freedom from bureaucratic regulation in the selection of staff. "Some of my best teachers don't have an education degree, but they happen to be born teachers," he says. "Then you have teachers with all the credentials, but they can't manage a group of kids. Our curriculum is not that difficult to pick up. What can't be learned is self-assurance and classroom management."

One of the uncredentialed teachers Brother Griecko hired was Frances O'Shea, a striking young blonde woman born and raised in Limerick, Ireland. She arrived in America four years ago with a liberal arts degree from Dublin's University College. In O'Shea's seventh-grade life-science class, I observed the same combination of academic rigor and personal engagement I had seen in Viti's classes at Saint Gregory's. Addressing the students in her rich brogue, O'Shea held forth on topics ranging from white and red blood cells to bacteria and infectious diseases. Her sense of humor livened up the proceedings: when a student got an answer completely wrong, she gently said, "Well, Steven, you are way out in the Wild West."

A slightly built black boy named Jonathan read a report he had researched on cystic fibrosis. O'Shea frequently asked him to stop while she made sure the students understood such concepts as the difference between malignant and benign tumors. At one point the coed class had a mature and unembarrassed discussion of the female reproductive system.

Yudelka Martinez, a divorced mother raising four children on her wages as a day-care worker, enrolled her son Andres at Holy Name because he was learning very little in public school. "He couldn't understand the teacher, and the teacher would say, 'I don't have time for him; there are too many children.'" In contrast, O'Shea made her son work very hard, and at the beginning of the year called her several times a week. Martinez struggles to come up with $150 a month for Andres's tuition, but she is determined to keep doing it: "I have to make the best for my son."

O'Shea told me that even if she had the credentials, she wouldn't consider teaching in a public school. "I just can't accept the lack of discipline. I am a believer in structure and self-control. The idea of a 14-year-old wielding weapons—I just can't adapt to something like that. We have the same children. They are very poor and their parents are scrimping. But we think they will overcome their bad surroundings. In the public schools little is expected of the children, and they sense that."

The success of schools like Holy Name and Saint Gregory's, despite their penury, is no miracle. It's a matter of doing the right thing, the human thing: hiring teachers because they can teach, rather than for their credentials. It's also a matter of simple common sense. Catholic schools' strong discipline rests not on an authoritarian ideology, but rather on an age-old, well-tested understanding of human nature. "The discipline in our school comes down to one word: respect," says Brother Griecko. "It is respect by students for teachers and teachers for students. We expect the students to listen and be respectful in class, and if they can't do it we will call in the parents. And it really works."

What is common sense in a Catholic school is almost unthinkable in the public school system, with its crushing bureaucracy on one hand and its exaggerated ideology of individual rights on the other. Catholic schools have all the freedom they need to keep things simple, to focus on the human encounter called teaching and learning. "We are here to educate and empower these kids, to do two things with them," says principal Pat Kelley. "One is to make sure that they learn how to read, write, and do math—every day. The other is to form their character. We believe in the divinity of being; we believe in the holiness of our existence. That infuses the culture we're in."

You might expect that liberals, self-styled champions of disadvantaged children, would applaud the commitment and sacrifice of educators like Deborah Hurd, Richard Griecko, Susan Viti, Frances O'Shea, and Pat Kelley. You might even expect them to look for ways of getting government money to these underfunded schools. Instead, they have done their best to make sure the wall of separation between church and state remains impenetrable. Liberal child-advocacy groups tout an endless array of "prevention programs" that are supposed to inoculate inner-city children against delinquency, dropping out of school, and teen pregnancy—yet they consistently ignore Catholic schools, which nearly always succeed in preventing these pathologies.

Read the chapter on education in Hillary Clinton's *It Takes a Village*. The First Lady advocates an alphabet soup of education programs for poor children. She favors charter schools, public school choice, and of course her husband's Goals 2000 legislation. But she says not one word about Catholic schools. Similarly, in his books on education and inner-city ghettos, Jonathan Kozol offers vivid tours of decrepit public schools in places like the South Bronx, but he never stops at the many Catholic schools that are succeeding a few blocks away.

Why are Catholic schools taboo among those who talk loudest about compassion for the downtrodden? Certainly, the religious tradition of the Catholic schools stands against the liberal agenda on issues like abortion, feminism, and gay rights. And many liberal commentators may sincerely believe that the Constitution requires maintaining the "iron wall" of separation between religious schools and government. Yet these explanations seem inadequate to explain the total silence, the refusal even to admit that something worthwhile is going on behind the parochial school gates, from which we can at least learn.

It's hard to escape the conclusion that one of the most powerful reasons liberal opinion makers and policy makers ignore Catholic schools—and oppose government aid to them—is their alliance with the teachers' unions, which have poured hundreds of millions of dollars into the campaign coffers of liberal candidates around the country. Before the rise of the teachers' unions to political power, it was not unusual to see urban Democrats such as Hugh Carey and Daniel Patrick Moynihan support government aid to Catholic schools. Mario Cuomo once supported it too, and his flip-flop on this issue makes especially clear that the teachers' unions, rather than legal or philosophical objections, have been the chief barrier to government aid to Catholic schools.

In 1974, when he first ran for public office, Cuomo wrote a letter to potential supporters: "I've spent more than 15 years . . . arguing for aid to private schools," he said. "Unfortunately, although there are millions of people in this nation who agree with this position, they've been outmuscled politically to the point where the Supreme Court of the United States was persuaded in a series of cases to take hard positions against various forms of aid. This is regrettable but it's no reason to surrender. . . . If you believe aid is a good thing, then you are the good people. If you believe it, then it's your moral obligation, as it is my own, to do something about it. . . . Let's try tax-credit plans and anything else that offers any help."

Cuomo soon learned his lesson. In his published diaries he wrote: "Teachers are perhaps the most effective of all the state's unions. If they go all-out, it will mean telephones and vigorous statewide support. It will also mean some money. I would have had them in 1977 [in his losing race for mayor] if it had not been for a clumsy meeting I had with [union leader Albert] Shanker. I must see that I don't make that same mistake again."

He didn't. In his 1982 campaign for governor, Cuomo gave a speech trumpeting the primacy of public education and the rights of teachers. He won the union's enthusiastic endorsement against Ed Koch in the Democratic primary. Over the next 12 years, in private meetings with Catholic leaders, Governor Cuomo would declare that he still supported tax relief for parochial school parents. Then he would take a completely different position in public. For example, in 1984 he acknowledged that giving tax credits for parochial school tuition "is now clearly constitutional" under a recent Supreme Court decision—but he refused to support such a plan.

To take Catholic schools' success seriously is to expose the fatal moral flaw at the heart of public school reform efforts. Reformers in Albany and New York City talk as if all that's needed is a change in the balance of interests among those who control the school system. Some call for more mayoral power. Others draw up plans for school-based councils, assigning a prescribed number of seats to the various constituencies at the school—parents, teachers, supervisors, other school workers.

These plans miss the point. In all the Catholic schools I visited, there was a greater sense of community, of collaboration between teachers and parents, than in any public school I know of. Yet Saint Gregory's and Holy Name have no official school council or even a parents' association. What they have instead is a shared commitment that no interests matter but the children's. The idea that the interests of other "stakeholders" can supersede those of children—plainly immoral when stated so bluntly—has no force in these schools.

Catholic schools work because they focus on the basic human encounter that is at the heart of all good education. Says principal Pat Kelley: "Parents walk into my office once a week, twice a week, and I know they pay my salary. They say, 'I want to know why Junior failed this test. I want to know why Junior has detention.' So I spend a lot of time dealing with families, who are the backbone of the school. The school exists for their kids. There's no other reason this school exists. None."

Politically controlled schools are unlikely to improve much without strong pressure from outside. Thus the case for government aid to Catholic schools is now more compelling than ever, if only to provide the competitive pressure to force state schools to change. And the conventional wisdom that government is constitutionally prohibited from aiding Catholic schools has been undermined by Supreme Court decisions such as *Mueller v. Allen,* which approved tax deductions for tuition and other expenses in parochial schools, and *Witters v. Washington Department of Services for the Blind,* approving public financial assistance to a blind student in divinity school.

Since the powerful teachers' unions vehemently oppose any form of government aid to Catholic schools, reformers are often skittish about advocating vouchers or tuition tax credits, fearing that will end the public school reform conversation before it begins. But trying to placate the unions is futile. When a New York City Council committee held a hearing recently on charter schools and other public school reforms, the United Federation of Teachers dispatched five people to rail against reform. Union officials said they were "troubled and disturbed that the hearing was held at all." So much for meaningful dialogue.

To abandon the idea of aid to Catholic schools in the name of public school reform is a sucker's trap. We have ended up with no aid to Catholic schools and no real public school reform either. Thus it's time to tear down the wall of separation, to accept Cardinal O'Connor's offer, and to help Catholic schools benefit as many of New York's children as possible. Government must rescue poor children from failing public schools. It can do so in a variety of ways: providing a targeted student population with vouchers that can be used in Catholic schools, allowing tuition tax credits for both secular and religious schools, establishing cooperative ventures between public and parochial schools, and encouraging more private money to flow to Catholic schools.

Catholic schools are a valuable public resource not merely because they so profoundly benefit the children who enroll in them. They also challenge the public school monopoly, constantly reminding us that the neediest kids are educable and that spending extravagant sums of money isn't the answer. No one who cares about reviving our failing public schools can afford to ignore this inspiring laboratory of reform.

—Summer 1996

SOL STERN

The School Reform That Dares Not Speak Its Name

IN THE SUMMER of 1991, alarm bells went off at the governor's mansion in Albany. The New York State Board of Regents was about to consider a proposal to liberate 5,000 poor and minority students trapped in the state's worst public schools: under a pilot program, the children would have received tuition vouchers worth $2,500, usable at any private or parochial school. Mario Cuomo, without a flicker of his fabled indecision, swung into action. This shall not pass, he determined. Not on his watch.

Earlier regents' deliberations about such hotly contested issues as condom distribution and multiculturalism had never aroused Governor Cuomo's ire. He had remained silent when the regents appointed racial strife sower Leonard Jeffries to head a curriculum commission to detect bias against minorities. Yet when he heard the dreaded word "vouchers," the governor leaped immediately into the fray. At a private meeting, he tried to convince the regents that the proposal shouldn't even be on the board's agenda, that it was a dagger aimed at the heart of public education. In public, he called the limited voucher plan a form of "malign neglect."

Despite the governor's pleading, the regents went ahead and debated the voucher proposal at their next scheduled public meeting. After a spirited discussion in front of an overflow audience, the board rejected the program by an eight-to-six vote (one regent was absent and another abstained).

The mere fact that the state's highest education authority would consider tuition vouchers, let alone come within two votes of approving them, sent a tremor through the public education community. Leaders of the education establishment thought they had killed the voucher idea when it was first floated two years earlier in a preliminary draft of the "New Compact for Learning," a document of proposed reforms prepared for the regents by State Education Commissioner Thomas Sobol. In a recent interview Sobol said that he had included vouchers because he thought that when the state had tried everything to improve its nonperforming schools, and the children were still not learning, "why not at that point step outside the traditional public school system and try the private schools? . . . Under New York's Constitution, the state has a duty to educate the children. It is not a constitutional duty to protect the system."

Sobol learned soon enough that the rest of the education establishment did not agree with his reading of the state Constitution. "The teachers' unions and the school board associations and the PTAs were up in arms," he recalled. "They basically told us they were out to kill everything if we persisted with the voucher proposal. The message was, 'If you do this, nothing else will be done, and your agency will go nowhere.' I pulled the private school proposal off the board. It was a political decision. I said to the regents, in effect, 'Ladies and gentlemen, this reform agenda will not go anywhere as long as vouchers are on the table. The opposition is just too strong.'"

To Commissioner Sobol, a Cuomo appointee with impeccable liberal credentials and a staunch partisan of public education, the intensity of the reaction came as a shock. After all, the voucher program would have affected only a few thousand out of the 2.7 million students in the state. The children selected would all be poor, mostly minority, and they would be leaving schools where no learning was going on anyway. And if the experiment didn't work, it could be shut down after three years. Why the panic?

In retrospect, one can see that the interest groups that helped kill the voucher plan had a much clearer understanding of what was at stake than its proponents did.

Public education is New York State's largest government enterprise. It is a $25 billion monopoly industry that doesn't compete for its customers and is rarely even required to answer to its presumed shareholders—the taxpayers. The monopoly's business practices are largely shaped by its employees, by way of the political lobbying and collective bargaining power of the teachers' and supervisors' unions. In 1993–94, New York State United Teachers spent $3.3 million on lobbying and campaign contributions—more than three times as much as the next-highest group. The political clout these millions buy the unions in Albany and New York City allows them a key role in writing the rules governing the licensing, credentialing, and hiring of teachers, the terms under which they can be fired, and how they are deployed in a school. The industry's first priority is the job security and well-being of the more than 250,000 people who make their livelihoods from it. The children are an afterthought.

That is why it is incorrect to view voucher programs as merely one among many other possible reform options. In fact, it is the only reform that fundamentally challenges the monopoly system of public education from the outside. If the regents' voucher proposal had been implemented, it would have begun transforming poor families from a coercive system's cannon fodder into consumers with real choices. And then, if kids began leaving the public schools and parents were happy with the results, the program would have put a harsh spotlight on the public education industry's monopolistic practices.

Of course, if the monopoly were doing its job — providing a quality education to all the state's children — there would be no education crisis, and the voucher alternative would be purely academic. Parents are so passionate about their children's schooling that if they were getting decent results, they wouldn't be especially disturbed about the public dollars the monopoly soaks up.

But it is now an open secret that in many areas of the state, the taxpayers' money is going straight down the drain. If Governor Cuomo could characterize a never-tried, experimental voucher program as an example of "malign neglect," how does one evaluate the non-voucherized public education system's record during the 12 years Cuomo spent in Albany? It was during his tenure that the Empire State achieved the rare distinction of being the third-most-generous state in the country in per-pupil expenditure (currently a little less than $10,000 per year) while simultaneously ranking near the bottom in student performance measured by average SAT scores and high school graduation rates.

Not even the regents who were moved by Governor Cuomo's entreaties and voted against vouchers believed that the public schools were doing well. They didn't defend the status quo as much as they pleaded for more time and effort, so that other, more acceptable public school reforms could have a chance to succeed. New York City Regent Mimi Lieber, who voted against the 1991 proposal because she believed it would take resources from the public schools, told me that "our kids don't have good schools to go to," and she even blamed her own board for not doing enough to improve the non-performing public schools. Or, as a *New York Times* editorial put this sentiment: "Vouchers become a copout for a system that has not tried hard enough to make itself work properly."

Voucher opponents — at least many of them — sincerely believe in the mission of the public schools. What they don't see is that a targeted and limited program of vouchers, by challenging the system from the outside, has the potential of actually making the public schools work better.

Consider the problem of failing schools. When schools in the private sector fail, dissatisfied parents take their tuition money to another school, and the failing school must respond either by improving itself or shutting its doors. In the public school sector, however, failure has its perverse rewards. Not only is no one ever fired and no school ever closed, but failure creates a rationale for even more jobs for the industry.

The State Education Department's main remedy for failing public schools has been to assign the very worst to a special category called "Schools Under Registration Review," or SURR schools (pronounced "sir"). Creating this blacklist of the damned has become the bureaucracy's way of saying, "We take this problem seriously, we'll provide additional resources, and if those schools still don't shape up, we'll do something drastic." Thus the State Education Department maintains an office in New York City that does nothing but monitor and minister to the SURR schools. More than 100 people are employed in this effort.

There are 90 official SURR schools in the city, but 300 more could easily be on the list, if the cutoff point used in the state's performance standards weren't so unrealistically low. The failing schools are spread out in clusters throughout every poor neighborhood in the city. A few have been reorganized, but almost none have been closed.

Year after year, hundreds of thousands of poor and minority children are sentenced to this archipelago of failure and despair. When the children emerge, either as dropouts or with worthless high school diplomas, most have neither the skills nor the knowledge to compete in the complex, information-based local economy. The failure of these schools to educate so many of the city's poorest children endangers New York's economic future.

Every other year, the city installs at 110 Livingston Street a new chancellor who says all the right things—how intolerable it is that we have allowed such institutional failure to continue, how no effort will be spared to whip the SURR schools into shape at last. The city's newest education leader, Rudy Crew, is even more determined than his predecessors. Within weeks of his arrival in the city, he vowed to take over some of the SURR schools and rehabilitate them by sending in SWAT teams of new administrators and other remedial experts.

But if money, resources, and advice dispatched from 110 Livingston Street or Albany could make the difference for these schools, they would have been fixed long ago. During the 1980s, the city's per-pupil expenditures in constant dollars went up dramatically. All the extra money couldn't help the children in the SURR schools, because central bureaucracies don't know how to make good schools out of bad ones.

The illusion of reform from the center, however, does justify more dollars, more experts, and more bureaucrats. Thus the teachers' unions' favorite reform, staff development, is touted as one of the best cures for bad schools and their incompetent teachers. The basic idea is, don't fire the incompetents; use still more teachers to "staff develop" them and thus create more jobs for the union.

Another in-system reform many public school educators have touted during the past decade has been school-based management. After developing it in Dade County, Florida, Joseph Fernandez brought the concept to

New York City with great fanfare when he became schools chancellor in 1990. The idea behind school-based management is that individual schools will do better if parents are "empowered" and work collaboratively with the teachers and the principal, within a school council that might make decisions on everything from allocating resources to staffing to curriculum issues. But a critical report by John Fager of the citywide Parents Coalition for Education revealed that 110 Livingston Street had subverted this reform by giving teachers the majority in the school councils, effectively giving the union control over the councils' decisions. Parents received only token representation.

Imagine, though, if in 1991 Governor Cuomo had been sufficiently embarrassed by the state's education record and had signaled the regents that a voucher program for poor children in failing schools was at least worth trying. Imagine further that with the governor's support, the program had been approved by the Legislature and that each year since then, several thousand students had left those 90 SURR schools to enroll at private and parochial schools. Suppose, too, that most of the students and their families were happy with their new schools, that the students' academic performance had improved even marginally, and that there was a long waiting list of parents who wanted one of those vouchers. Now suppose that thousands of low-income parents in all the other awful schools in the city started clamoring for a pass out of the system for their own children. With the prospect of more children coming into the private sector, backed by public dollars, new private secular schools would begin to open. Parents dissatisfied with the public system would then have an even greater variety of schools to choose from.

If anything like this happened, new constituencies would develop with a stake in challenging the prerogatives of the education interest groups. If the voucher program managed to survive, producing a steady stream of children moving from the monopoly education system to a broader system of choice, parents and voters would take note of the differences between the two systems. In the one system, incompetent teachers are protected; in the other, they are held to account and even occasionally fired. In one system, many teachers work to the rules, refusing to put in one minute more than the contractually sanctioned six-hour day, refusing to attend more than a prescribed number of staff meetings, refusing to walk the kids out to the school bus. In the other, even though they make lower salaries, teachers do whatever has to be done to make the school work. There would then be irresistible pressure for major changes within the public school system.

Is this scenario too implausible, too utopian, for New York, with its ingrained statist political culture? Perhaps. But something like this has begun to happen in Milwaukee, the nation's 15th-largest school district. A pilot voucher program started there at about the same time that the New York regents were voting down vouchers. It came about because of a struggle led by Polly Williams, a state legislator and the former director of Jesse Jackson's presidential campaign in the state, and Howard Fuller, an educator and policy analyst—and something of a black nationalist.

With deep-seated resentment building up in Milwaukee's black community over the abject condition of the schools, Williams was able to win support in the Wisconsin State Legislature for a limited voucher plan for 1,500 students, but only for non-parochial private schools. The program quickly became very popular in the black community. A recent poll of Milwaukee's black residents found that 95 percent supported vouchers and 70 percent favored the inclusion of Catholic schools.

The Legislature responded to the community's will and expanded the program to 7,000 vouchers in 1995, with 15,000 slated to be offered in 1996. This time the plan included parochial schools. Once again, low-income black Milwaukee parents quickly grabbed up the vouchers.

At that point, the state teachers' union fought back in the courts, arguing that the program violated the constitutional separation of church and state. Backed by the ACLU, which has a long-standing opposition to any program that provides public funds for religious institutions, the teachers' union was able to get a temporary injunction stopping the voucher payments while the case winds its way through appeals and possibly to the U.S. Supreme Court. But so popular had the program become in the community, and so many allies in the business community had it won, that private groups, led by the Bradley Foundation, quickly raised enough money to pay the children's tuition in the Catholic schools.

Howard Fuller eventually became Milwaukee schools superintendent and fought the teachers' union for most of his term, until he resigned early last year. "I am not supporting vouchers because I just want to let a small number of kids escape lousy public schools," says Fuller. "I believe this is a strategy that will create opportunities for all the kids, because even in the public school system people will begin to make demands. They will begin to ask why can't this happen in the public schools if it is happening outside the system. It will create an entirely new dynamic."

Something like that does seem to be happening in Wisconsin. For example, the Milwaukee School Board recently announced an expansion of the public school choices available to parents, and the State Legislature has voted to allow school districts to contract out educational services to private companies at some public schools.

Williams and Fuller, despite their radical backgrounds, were able to make common cause with Republican Governor Tommy Thompson, elements in the business community, and "new Democrats" such as Milwaukee mayor John Norquist. Similar crossover alliances of black community leaders and Republican elected officials were behind new voucher initiatives in other cities and states. In June 1995 the Ohio Legislature, with the enthusiastic support of Republican Governor George Voinovich, passed a voucher bill almost identical to the proposal the New York regents debated in 1991. Slated to begin in September 1996, the program will provide 2,000 low-income families in Cleveland with tuition vouchers worth $2,500, usable at private or parochial schools. In Jersey City, GOP Mayor Brett Schundler, who received 40 percent of the black vote, has pushed for a similar program, presently under study by a commission appointed by Governor Christie Whitman. In the meantime, when Pepsico managers offered to fund a version of the program, union opposition and threats of a statewide Pepsi boycott quickly cowed the company into changing its mind.

In November the House of Representatives, for the first time ever, approved voucher legislation for the District of Columbia. The bill was sponsored by Republican Congressman Steve Gunderson of Wisconsin and supported by the black superintendent of schools, Franklin Smith. As part of the District of Columbia appropriations bill, an unlimited number of tuition vouchers worth $3,000 would be available for all Washington, D.C., children below the poverty line. The vouchers could be used in any private or parochial school in the District or in surrounding counties. Unless held up in the courts, the program would start this year.

What is missing so far in New York is anything resembling that crossover alliance between reform-minded Republicans and leaders from those communities most victimized by the condition of the public schools. Indeed, in the Empire State, Republican and Democratic officeholders seem to compete with one another in currying favor with the teachers' unions.

After his victory over Mario Cuomo, George Pataki selected Diane Ravitch as co-chairman (along with investment banker and Catholic schools advocate Peter Flanigan) of his transition committee on elementary and high school education. This was a hopeful sign because Ravitch, the noted historian and former assistant secretary of education, has been one of the few prominent education reformers in the state who have dared to speak out for a package of system-challenging reforms—including giving poor children trapped in failing schools the choice of escaping to private or parochial schools.

The transition committee report supported vouchers (which it called "scholarships") and also recommended legislation that would allow individual school districts to contract for instructional services with private companies in schools that were failing. Ravitch says she knew that Mario Cuomo would never cross the teachers' unions, but she thought it was possible that Pataki would do the right thing.

Anything is possible, of course. Governor Pataki could wake up one morning and declare himself a bold education reformer, tapping the support for vouchers in the minority community and taking on the teachers' unions—just as his Republican colleagues, Governors Thompson of Wisconsin and Voinovich of Ohio, have done. So far, however, it appears that the governor has no definable education agenda. Indeed, no one in the administration seems able to locate a copy of the transition committee's report.

Even in New York's city hall, movement toward education reform seems stalled—or worse. From the moment he took office, Rudolph Giuliani demanded mayoral control over the education system, promising that if he were in charge, the central bureaucracy would be "smashed" and more decisions over budgets and hiring would be made at the individual school level. But last fall, presumably bowing to the intimidating power the teachers' unions exercise over the political process, the mayor negotiated a contract with the city teachers' union that would have moved the education system in precisely the opposite direction. When the rank and file, overreaching themselves, rejected the contract, commentators focused on money considerations rather than on the more important issue of the contract's implications for the mayor's reform agenda.

Diane Ravitch has described the city's public school system as a nineteenth-century structure designed to "replicate a factory-style assembly line." The mayor's proposed contract would have locked the city into that nineteenth-century system of hierarchical, bureaucratic work rules until the beginning of the twenty-first century. Centralized, one-size-fits-all rules and regulations would continue to be imposed on almost all of the city's more than 1,000 schools.

A year ago the mayor stood up to the custodians' union and the Board of Education and insisted on a contract that for the first time obtained a degree of accountability from one of the system's special interests. By allowing the city to privatize custodial services at individual schools, the contract put competitive pressure on the remaining union custodians.

By contrast, the mayor proposed a teachers' contract that would have protected all the teachers' perks, including the notoriously wasteful sabbaticals and the extra winter holiday period negotiated in the last contract, but in return would have given the city no greater ability to hold teachers accountable for their performance.

The contract would have done nothing to help individual schools break free of the central bureaucracy's rules and regulations or develop their own workplace ethos and teaching strategies best suited to their students. It would have left in place the present byzantine work rules: the principal can't ask teachers to hold a staff meeting during a lunch period, can't hold more than a prescribed number of after-school staff meetings, can't ask teachers to walk the children to the corner on dismissal, and must make many in-school assignments based on seniority and an arbitrary credentialing system. Indeed, the proposed contract added a new restriction: principals would no longer be able to ask teachers to cover lunchrooms or patrol the hallways.

Claiming that it had at least done *something* for school-based reform, the mayor's office insisted that the contract would for the first time allow principals to fill teacher vacancies with the most qualified candidate rather than on the basis of seniority. But teachers' union president Sandra Feldman immediately went public to dispute City Hall's interpretation. She pointed out, quite correctly, that a mere 25 percent of the teachers in a school would still be able to block it from changing the current seniority system for filling school vacancies. She reassured her members that even in those schools that vote for the new hiring procedures, teachers would dominate the personnel committees. The committees, in turn, "must award the position to the most experienced qualified applicant unless someone else possesses extraordinary qualifications," according to the union. And unsuccessful candidates could always appeal. In other words, the contract would have guaranteed continued seniority protection and still more bureaucracy. Innovation, creativity, and autonomy at schools would continue to be undermined, while centralized bureaucratic enforcement of the work rules was strengthened.

The teachers' rejection of the contract on Pearl Harbor Day sent shock waves through City Hall. But the impasse gives the mayor a second chance to re-establish his credentials as an education reformer. He might consider whether the best approach to so obstructionist a force as the union is accommodation—or confrontation. Indeed, he might even start thinking the unthinkable—a voucher proposal.

The mayor's willingness to accept the retrograde work rules in the proposed contract ought to give the public school reform coalition some pause. The reform movement's strategy is to create a liberated zone of small, autonomous schools—on the school-based management model, or the public school choice model, or the charter school model—and then gradually to expand that liberated zone until it reaches critical mass and creates irresistible pressure that tips the rest of the system toward school autonomy. But the proposed teachers' contract raises the question of whether the system of central regulations and work rules is more likely to subvert the autonomous schools movement rather than the other way around.

This is precisely the problem anticipated by John Chubb and Terry Moe in their 1990 book, *Politics, Markets and America's Schools.* Chubb and Moe argued that although public school choice is better than no choice, school-based management better than centralized management, and small alternative schools better than traditional schools, these reforms could accomplish only so much. In Chubb and Moe's formulation, they were all "system-preserving reforms."

That's why a more radical reform like vouchers, coming from outside the system and directly challenging its most fundamental assumptions and settled arrangements, is essential to force change on an establishment that has resisted it with every fiber of its being and dollar of its lobbying fund. For the present moment, however, vouchers remain the reform that dares not speak its name. The New York Democratic Party in control of the Assembly, once the party of urban ethnics that supported tuition tax credits for parochial schools, has been captured by the teachers' unions and the public education industry. But since the Republican governor and his legislative allies seem to have abdicated, it is the Democrats who will give us an education bill next spring. It is likely to make some changes in the governance of the system but will essentially keep the monopoly in place. Which means moving the deck chairs around on the *Titanic*.

The public, on the other hand, is way ahead of the politicians. The Empire State Survey on Education (a joint project of the Empire Foundation and the Lehrman Institute) asked New York City residents whether they agreed that "district school boards should be abolished and control of schools placed in the hands of parent-teacher councils in the schools." This is a very strong version of school-based management, one of the pillars of the public school reform coalition's strategy. Yet it was supported by only a narrow 46 to 40 percent margin.

The more radical idea of vouchers does much better with the public. In July 1995, the same survey organization conducted a statewide opinion poll using a randomly selected sample of 1,218 residents. By a majority of 54 to 42 percent, New Yorkers favored a program that "would allow parents to send their children to the public, parochial, or private school of their choice and use state and local tax dollars to pay for all or part of it." Amazingly, the support for private school choice was higher in liberal New York City (60 to 37 percent) than in the state overall. Parents with children in the public schools supported vouchers by 57 to 40 percent; blacks supported it by 61 to 32 percent—almost two-to-one. Moreover, 60 percent of state residents and 63 percent of city residents agreed with the statement that tuition voucher plans "would improve the quality of the education children receive in this country."

In other words, parents prefer vouchers to public school reforms such as school-based management and parent-teacher councils. Their first priority is good schools for their children, and they apparently believe that the best way to achieve that is to give education consumers real choices.

Having that right to choose is, of course, an issue of fairness and equity.

It is simply wrong to trap poor children in failing schools when there are good alternatives just a few blocks away, and when families with money are able to exercise that choice. Commissioner Sobol had it right four years ago in insisting that legally and ethically, the state Constitution requires educating children by any means necessary, rather than protecting the monopoly system of public education.

Beyond the issue of equity is a practical and political consideration. It is clear that in New York City a strategy of school improvement that merely relies on a combination of inside-the-system reforms such as small schools, public school choice, school-based management, and decentralization will come up short. Under the pervasive influence of the teachers' unions and other special interests, the system has shown its ability to eat up these reforms. Paradoxically, then, it may be that only voucher programs, with the imminent prospect of freeing the monopoly system's captive children, could persuade the interests to stop sabotaging improvement.

But no matter which reforms we support, we should agree that employees who provide a government service, paid from taxpayer funds, should not be able to exercise veto power over how that service is delivered. Americans would not tolerate a situation in which social workers employed by the government set the limits of welfare reform. Just as surely, New Yorkers and all Americans will someday refuse to allow the teachers we hire to dictate what kinds of schools we make for our children.

—*Winter 1996*

SOL STERN

The Schools That Vouchers Built

RECENTLY I went to Milwaukee and Cleveland, the only two cities in the country with publicly funded school voucher programs, to visit four (among the more than 100) schools that have accepted voucher students. School voucher proponents—myself included—have argued that providing tax-funded scholarships for low-income pupils to use in any private or religious school would rescue thousands, perhaps millions, of children presently trapped in failing inner-city public schools and would lead to the creation of thousands of innovative new schools. In addition, competition from voucher-supported schools would challenge the public education system from the outside, forcing it to reconsider its own hidebound ways. That's the theory: now that these two cities had made it possible, I could hardly wait to see what actually happens in practice.

What I saw was exhilarating. No one who has spent any time at these schools could fail to be impressed by their orderly, energetic atmosphere and solid academic achievement—all the more impressive when compared with the violent, dysfunctional inner-city public schools that were the alternative for these children. Moreover, the schools I saw couldn't have been more different from one another: they ran the gamut from an evangelical Christian academy and an independent Catholic high school to a secular elementary school with a Hispanic cultural theme and a secular school with a strong focus on computer technology.

What these inspiring schools had in common was that, at their creation, their founders and many of their staff did not qualify as professional educators. They did not have degrees from the education monopoly's prescribed ed schools or credentials issued by government education boards, and they certainly did not belong to the monopoly system's teachers' unions. Yet every one of these outsiders had all they needed to educate and inspire children— a sense of mission, a willingness to work long hours for little pay, and common sense about the discipline and the core knowledge that inner-city children need in order to succeed. Unconstrained by the official school system's suffocating bureaucratic regulations, they were able to develop an entrepreneurial, problem-solving approach that helped overcome hurdles likely to sink any rule-driven public school.

The education establishment is as frightened by these schools as I was impressed. No wonder.

Look first at the Believers in Christ Christian Academy, which lights up a desolate, predominantly black Milwaukee neighborhood. At this school, everyone arrives very early and stays very late. By 8 AM, the children, staff, and many parents have filled the basement auditorium's plain folding chairs for an assembly that is part gospel-singing prayer meeting and part academic pep rally. Up on the stage, three parents form a makeshift orchestra that accompanies the hymn singing on two pianos and a tambourine, while at the lectern, swaying to the hymns and exhorting the children to work hard in their classrooms that day, is the school's founder, a tall, attractive, African-American woman named Cheryl Brown. Invoking the Scriptures, she reminds the children, all of them black and from the city's worst neighborhoods, that they were made in God's image. "No matter what anyone tells you and no matter what messages you hear from society, you can each achieve great things," she exhorts them. "But you have to work for it. Are you going to work hard in your classes today?" she demands. "Yes!" the children shout back in unison. "No excuses," she intones again and again.

Cheryl Brown's school is the teachers' unions' worst nightmare. According to the union-led anti-school-choice coalition, the problem with vouchers is that they are likely to cream off the best and brightest kids presently attending inner-city public schools, leaving only the most disadvantaged and academically unprepared children. Yet almost in the same breath, opponents of vouchers contend that those "cream of the crop" children and their parents are too stupid to avoid being victimized by educational charlatans. Dire warnings about "witchcraft" schools, "Farrakhan" schools, and "creationist" schools greedily waiting to get their hands on voucher money have been stock features in the teachers' union propaganda.

Well, Believers in Christ is a "creationist" school. The people running it believe in the literalness of the Scriptures, and they don't separate their faith from their role as educators. Bedecking the hallways and every classroom are posters that proclaim such inspirational messages as "I can do all things through Christ" and "God gave me a brain." Many teachers expound the biblical story of creation in the classroom. Cheryl Brown herself teaches biology, and in that class, she told me, she offers her students a perfectly mainstream scientific account of DNA and RNA, while also telling them: "God created everything; it all began with him. Science can't contradict that. Science can explain how everything works physically in relation to everything else." I watched Reginald Johnson, a young African-American with a degree in physics from Xavier University, teach seventh-graders a fairly sophisticated lesson on black holes. Later I asked Johnson, who is an evangelical Christian, whether he also teaches the children the biblical version of creation. "Sure," he said. "I don't see it as a conflict. It's going to make them stronger adults. When they get to college and all through life, they will have to reconcile their faith with science."

"We absolutely believe in our faith," Cheryl Brown explains, "but we also believe that there is a body of knowledge that our children must know in order to survive in the real world." Brown is adamant that if the condition of receiving voucher students were that she had to separate Believers in Christ's religious teachings from the rest of the school's educational mission, she would instantly forgo the vouchers. "This is who we are," she said.

The teachers' unions believe that giving poor kids tax money to go to Cheryl Brown's school is a stain on the Republic. Never mind that her kids are learning something, that they might actually stay in school. Never mind too that nothing in the school's curriculum has been imposed on the parents—unlike the public school parents who have had graphic and inappropriate sex education lessons or texts such as *Heather Has Two Mommies* inflicted on their children against their will.

Cheryl Brown never recruited any unsuspecting children into her school. Rather, the school was called into existence by the community—by minority parents who felt that the public schools were trashing their most cherished values as well as their children's futures. Eight years ago, Brown was a director of nursing at Milwaukee County Hospital. At the time, she was also a lay pastor for Believers in Christ, an independent evangelical congregation started as a Bible study group a few years earlier. For two years, Brown had been running a six-week summer school for the children of the congregants and other poor families in the neighborhood. So successful was the summer program—and so dysfunctional were the regular Milwaukee public schools the children would have to return to in the fall—that many parents told Brown that they were determined not to send their children back. They begged her to start a year-round school. She agreed to give it a try. Within a year she had resigned her job at the hospital and was embarked on her new career as an educator.

It was a rocky start. Space wasn't a problem, because the ministry had already leased an abandoned Catholic school from a nearby parish for a modest rent. But there was almost no money for books or teachers' salaries. Brown recruited parents as volunteer teachers, and she herself took no salary the first few years, subsisting on savings and offerings from the church. Most of the parents were too poor to pay more than $50 a month in tuition.

"We felt it was our mission, our personal responsibility," Brown told me.

"We just trusted that somehow our needs would be met." One of the parents explained further: "We stuck it out because we felt our children would escape the violence and lack of religious values" of the Milwaukee public schools. When this parent mentioned religious values, I took her to mean something that went beyond religion, too. She also meant, as I understood her, that the public schools had abandoned the most rudimentary values of them all: the very idea of a shared civility and reverence for higher aspirations that all parents, secular ones included, should be able to endorse.

As Brown had trusted, the school's needs were met. In 1990, the Wisconsin State Legislature passed the Milwaukee Parental Choice Program, the first publicly funded voucher program in the country. The lawmakers initially restricted the program to 1,000 low-income Milwaukee public school students, who could use the vouchers only at non-religious private schools—which didn't include Believers in Christ. But the new legislation prompted an organization of philanthropists called Partners Advancing Values in Education (PAVE) to launch a private voucher program that poor children could use in religious schools, enabling Believers in Christ to get, for the first time, a number of customers paying something like full tuition. Then, three years ago, the Wisconsin Legislature expanded the Milwaukee voucher program to include up to 15,000 students and allowed them to take their tuition vouchers to religious schools. This year, half of Believers in Christ's 250 students are carrying public vouchers worth $4,900 or the per-pupil cost of the school (whichever is lower), and a couple of dozen still have PAVE vouchers. That allowed Cheryl Brown to begin to pay her teachers and herself real salaries and meet some of the school's other basic financial needs.

Even so, Brown still hires her staff not on the basis of state credentials or education courses but on other vital qualifications. "We want people who are committed to children and to values," she explains. "We want staff here who view this school as a mission in life. I believe that if you are committed to children and love them, they will respond and learn anything."

All the classes I visited kept a sharp focus on a traditional, skills-based curriculum. The fifth-grade class I watched was typical. The children were working over a map of the United States with the place names removed. They eagerly showed off their knowledge of the states and their principal cities. Each of the 20-odd children was engaged, polite, enthusiastic, and informed. Unremarkable, you might say; isn't this what schoolrooms are supposed to look like? But anyone who has been in an inner-city school in the past generation knows how exceptional, and precious, such a scene really is.

These children are much more likely to become productive citizens than if they had remained in the public schools. Reams of social science research demonstrate that children involved in faith-based institutions are less likely to drop out of school, to end up as teenage parents, and to get caught up in the criminal justice system. Four of the first five graduates of Believers in Christ have already gone on to college. Considering the staggering 80 percent dropout rate among black males in the Milwaukee public schools, who can say that these parents made anything but an excellent choice for their children?

Just as Cheryl Brown was called into urban education by poor, minority parents desperate to save their children so too was Brother Bob Smith. When Smith, an African-American, took his vows as a Capuchin friar almost 20 years ago, the last thing he ever thought he'd be doing was running an inner-city high school. After graduating from Wayne State University in Detroit with a degree in criminal justice, he did his first service for his order as a youth worker and then taught social studies and economics in a Catholic high school. He arrived in Milwaukee in 1984, just when an inner-city Catholic archdiocesan high school named Messmer was going through a crisis. Its run-down neighborhood abandoned by the white ethnic former parishioners, Messmer now had a predominantly black, largely non-Catholic student population, whose parents had difficulty paying the tuition.

With almost no warning to parents and staff, the Milwaukee Archdiocese abruptly decided to stop making up Messmer's growing deficits, and, right in the middle of the spring 1984 semester, it closed the school. Determined not to send their children to public schools, many parents refused to take no for an answer. They organized a Save Messmer committee. After surveying the available talent, the parents' committee turned to Smith to lead the efforts to save the school and to become its new principal. Then all of 27 years old, he had offered Messmer his services as a teacher, but he had zero experience as a school administrator.

When I met him, still only 41, he reminisced about his 14 years of successful struggle to rebuild Messmer into one of the Milwaukee area's premier high schools. "For years, we just lived hand-to-mouth," he recalled. "The parents worked as volunteers in the business office, in the cafeteria, all around the school. Some of them even took out second mortgages to help cover the payroll. At one point we were half a million dollars in debt." With a trace of bitterness, he remembered that the Milwaukee Archdiocese not only refused to offer any help in getting Messmer on its feet again but denied it the right to advertise itself as a Catholic school.

All around Smith's office are testimonials to Messmer's resurrection— plaques honoring students for outstanding academic performance, photographs of such visiting notables as William Bennett and George Will, and copies of laudatory newspaper articles about the school. But the acknowledgment that Smith cherishes most is the Milwaukee Archdiocese's April 1998 decree recognizing Messmer once again as a Catholic school. The signer of the decree: the same Archbishop Rembert G. Weakland who had ordered Messmer closed in 1984.

Smith rebuilt Messmer on a foundation of excellence and accountability, for students as well as staff. He took no student solely because he or she could pay or came with a scholarship, and he turned away no student solely for lack of funds. Every student he accepted had to make a firm commitment to strive for academic excellence and to complete the school's very demanding curriculum, which requires every student to take many more courses in math, science, and foreign languages than most of Wisconsin's affluent suburban high schools require. As for the teachers, says Smith, "We looked for people we considered the best, the most knowledgeable, the most committed, whether they had state teaching credentials or not."

One of those teachers is 32-year-old Jeff Monday, another first-class educator hired without any graduate education-school training. "Jeff is the only person I ever hired on the spot," Smith says. "There were people with teaching credentials and more experience, but I have never met anyone with a greater sense of mission." Eight years ago, Smith decided to groom the young math teacher to become Messmer's next principal, so that he himself could focus on fund-raising. Two years ago, Monday took over as principal, and Smith became Messmer's president. Since then, Smith recounts, Monday has been recognized as one of the most talented high school principals in the state and has turned down high-paying offers from other private schools.

Monday's starting salary as a math teacher was $13,000. As principal, he still makes far less than the top salary paid to teachers in the Milwaukee public schools. He routinely puts in 70- to 80-hour weeks. Monday's own Catholic education is part of the reason that he is making the financial sacrifice. "What also inspired me about Messmer," he says, "is the sense of mission here, of working with poor students yet holding them accountable and helping them strive for excellence. We are not in the business of making excuses or allowing the kids to make excuses for themselves."

You can see evidence of the school's sense of decorum and seriousness everywhere throughout the ornate building—even in the cafeteria. Look at a typical inner-city public school cafeteria, and you will see everything that's wrong with the system. The room is generally the noisiest, tensest place in the school building. To keep the students from erupting into violence, burly security guards and a platoon of other teachers and aides are usually on patrol. Central school district employees serve the unappetizing meals mess-hall style. At Messmer, by contrast, a variety of outside vendors, including Pizza Hut, have set up several food stations. The students—from very tough, very violent neighborhoods—line up quietly and pick their favorite foods. Students working part-time are behind the counters or manning the cash register. Not a single security guard or faculty member is in the cafeteria to enforce order—an amazing sight to a regular visitor to urban public schools.

The secret is the inculcation of a culture of civility, through sensible rules enforced fairly and consistently—no hats in school, for instance, no lying, immediate expulsion for violence. I sat at a table with two seniors, Jennifer Vega and Shalonda Greer. They told me that the existence of those rules was the major difference they perceived between Messmer and the public schools that some of their friends attended. "They are very tough here," Jennifer said. "You can't break any rule without being punished. And you have to work hard to stay in the school. In the public schools, there's a lot of violence, and you don't have to work hard."

Messmer's per-pupil cost is $4,600, compared with the public schools' $7,200. No Messmer student pays more than $2,800, however, and no student who keeps up his grades is ever turned away for inability to pay. The biggest current sources of income to make up the difference are 40 private PAVE scholarships at $1,500 per student and the 150 students who carry state-supported vouchers valued at $4,900 each.

Clearly the taxpayers are getting their money's worth. With a student body that is 85 percent black and 10 percent Hispanic, with 60 percent of the children from single-parent families and a similar number below the poverty line, Messmer manages to get academic results more characteristic of middle-class, suburban high schools. Its graduation rate is over 95 percent, and almost all the graduates go on to college—the favorite selections being Notre Dame, Marquette, the University of Wisconsin at Madison, and a number of black colleges, such as Howard and Spelman. Those who don't go on to college go either into the military or straight into the workforce. "I have been here 12 years, and I have never had a kid on graduation day say, 'I don't know what I am going to do,'" says Smith.

Needless to say, Smith is a big enthusiast for vouchers, not only for helping his school achieve its goals but also for what they might accomplish for the pupils in the public schools. "The Milwaukee public schools started out hating vouchers," he says, "but it was a real wake-up call for them. They have created a lot of new schools in the last few years, and every one of them has a big banner over the front of the building that says, 'High standards begin here.' The superintendent now says, 'We ought not to be fighting with the choice schools; we should be working with them.' I want to see the public schools learn the lesson that when they stop making excuses about having to work with poor, minority kids, they will improve."

While some Milwaukee parents have chosen to take their vouchers to religious schools such as Believers in Christ Christian Academy and Messmer High School, others have chosen to use them in private secular schools. On the city's Hispanic Near South Side—across town from the neighborhood where Messmer and Believers in Christ stand some 12 blocks from each other—a school called Bruce-Guadalupe has enrolled some 200 to 300 voucher recipients among its 500 students for several years. Once part of the Catholic archdiocese, it is now a secular private school owned by the United Community Center.

The school is the brainchild of the center's executive director, Argentine-born Walter Sava, 54, a gray-haired, former sixties student activist at the University of Wisconsin at Madison. After taking a Ph.D. in romance languages at Wisconsin and teaching at Carroll College, Sava took over the reins of the United Community Center ten years ago. In those days, the center had little more than a gymnasium, an after-school program for children, and a drug-prevention program for adults. Since then, Sava has been able to raise several million dollars (from the Bradley Foundation and a long list of major corporations) to build two new buildings and expand the range of the center's activities. By far his biggest innovation has been to bring the Bruce-Guadalupe K–8 elementary school in under the wing of the center. Combining schools with adult community centers, Sava believes, is a dramatically efficient use of space, since the building and facilities are in use when school is not in session.

A brand-new addition to the main community-center building houses the school. Strikingly beautiful, it has a Spanish architectural flavor, with a pyramidal front entrance that evokes Mayan culture, and traditional Mexican murals and mosaics decorating the corridors. The school and community center share many facilities, including the gym, a health clinic, dance studios, and a large performance auditorium. The center houses a popular, handsomely decorated Hispanic restaurant, which also cooks the meals for the school's cafeteria. This combining of facilities not only makes for efficient usage of space and economic efficiency, but also provides a sense of shared community and civility. Parents and grandparents mingle with the children, since they often come to the center to attend English classes, visit the health clinic, or eat at the restaurant.

What is immediately striking about the school is that it is multicultural in the best sense of the word. The second- and third-grade classes I visited were full of Hispanic children, many of them recent immigrants, with varying degrees of limited English-language proficiency. In public schools in Milwaukee (and indeed, in most parts of the country), many of these children would have been shunted into bilingual-ed classes. Here, though, I witnessed teachers drilling the students in the English alphabet and sounding out words in English. The reading lessons were clearly based on traditional phonics, not on the faddish and ineffective whole-language method.

This approach largely reflects the educational philosophy of Walter Sava, who, of course, is not a "professional educator." "People think that because this is a school in the barrio, we are only interested in preserving our culture and our language," he told me. "Of course we are, but we are also eager to see to it that our kids become proficient in the English language. They are learning to read through phonics. The curriculum is knowledge-based, with clear benchmarks that the teachers can't deviate from very much. At the end of each grade, there are certain things they have to know and are tested on." In addition to the full traditional curriculum, the children get plenty of extra work in Hispanic history and literature.

Despite a per-pupil expenditure of $4,200 that is still far less than the $7,200 the city's public schools spend, Bruce-Guadalupe caps its classes at about 25 students and offers its pupils an amazing range of services—sports programs, a full arts program, and a health clinic with a full-time nurse. This cornucopia of resources results partly from the sharing of facilities with the community center and partly from the administrative and budgetary flexibility Sava enjoys by not being burdened with either a centralized school bureaucracy or a teachers' union contract.

With its required uniforms and its strict disciplinary code, the school has the feel of an orderly Catholic school stressing character and values. The results in academic performance have been striking. Eighty-one percent of Bruce-Guadalupe's third-graders scored at or above grade level on the state's standardized test last year—not only a better outcome than most Milwaukee public schools but close to what some of the suburban Wisconsin schools achieve. These results are all the more remarkable when you consider that 100 percent of Bruce-Guadalupe's students had to take the test, whereas public schools often excuse students with English-language deficiencies from taking it.

The success of Bruce-Guadalupe has been so universally recognized in Milwaukee that the public school district decided to get on the bandwagon this year and make some money in the bargain. In a unique arrangement, the district contracted with Sava to count all his students as public school students. (There is a certain sleight-of-hand in this arrangement, which claims to be analogous to a public school system's counting as its own students the disabled kids it contracts to send off to private schools equipped to educate them.) The public school district gave Bruce-Guadalupe $4,800 per pupil from the district, while charging the state $6,000 for each of those same students and pocketing the $1,200-per-kid difference.

Even the Milwaukee Education Association would have supported this arrangement, had Sava allowed the union to come in and try to organize his teachers. He refused. Although he's paying his beginning teachers the same rates as the public school system, he regards the union culture as the kiss of death. Without the constraints of the Milwaukee teachers' union contract, for example, he is able to have his teachers come into the school for two weeks or more before the opening of the school year for staff training sessions. He is also able to offer a longer school day and to assure parents that if their children should somehow wind up with an incompetent teacher, that teacher can be fired.

Sava has nothing against the public schools. Indeed, he persuaded a retired Milwaukee public school principal, Allan Nuhlicek, to be Bruce-Guadalupe's principal for its first two years. "Being a public school person," Nuhlicek told me, "I wasn't for vouchers for private schools when I came here. I didn't like to see money drained off from the public schools—until I saw what you can accomplish with half of the per-pupil costs of the public schools." Nuhlicek also told me that in 12 years as a Milwaukee public school principal, he had been able to hire only two teachers that he had personally selected; all the rest were forced on him because of the union contract. "Now I'm for schools like this," he concluded, "to give the union some competition."

If school choice spreads to more cities and states, David Brennan—a colorful, cowboy-hat-wearing, 68-year-old resident of Akron, Ohio—should write the book on how to get new schools up and running in a hurry. Brennan, a wealthy industrialist, has long fretted about the poor education of many applicants for jobs at his companies, and he has concluded that the public schools, without competition from outside, will never produce the literate, numerate workers the twenty-first-century economy will need. As a prominent Republican fund-raiser, he played a key role in persuading Ohio governor George Voinovich to support the legislation that resulted in Cleveland's voucher program for 2,000 low-income students.

When the state officially announced the voucher program in April 1996, Brennan was on the spot to make sure that all the children who opted for the program actually had a school to attend. After all the spaces in the existing private schools were filled, 300 or so students were left over, and they enrolled in the two new secular schools that Brennan promised to open. He called them the Hope Academies.

But when the teachers' union challenged the program's constitutionality, vouchers were put on hold, pending a ruling from the Ohio courts. The green light didn't come until mid-August. At that point, 300 students had signed up for a school that didn't yet exist. If Brennan hadn't been able to get his schools opened by September 1, those students would have been forced back into the public schools they thought they had escaped.

Until there was a favorable court decision, however, Brennan couldn't enter into contracts with principals, teachers, and support staff. The only thing he had in hand was an abandoned Catholic school building, leased to him for $1 a year by a friendly bishop. In the 15 frantic days after the August ruling, he and his associates hired principals and teachers for the two schools and bought desks, chairs, and computers. Miraculously, on the official September 1 opening of the two Hope Academies, over 300 poor, mostly minority children, whose parents had fled in desperation from their previous public schools, found reasonably competent teachers in each fully furnished classroom. A few teachers were defectors from the public schools; some were substitute teachers who didn't have regular, full-time licenses; some were completely unlicensed recent college graduates, who just wanted a chance to teach young children.

Nothing came easy for the rest of that first year. Unaccustomed to a demanding workload, none of the former regular public school teachers lasted till summer vacation. Even the most dedicated teachers found themselves challenged by the job of taking public school children with poor work habits and inculcating them with a disciplined approach to academic work. "I was shocked to find that many of my third-graders couldn't spell their names, couldn't add four plus three, couldn't even sit still," recalled teacher Wynne Udovich, a veteran of the school's first year.

Nevertheless, the school survived. Under tough, battlefield conditions, David Brennan was able to offer a real-life demonstration of his theory that open markets and freedom from bureaucratic constraint will work wonders in education. At the beginning and at the end of the first year, all the Hope students in the third grade took standardized achievement tests in reading and math. According to an analysis by respected scholars from Harvard, Stanford, and the University of Texas, the students scored, on average, 5.4 percentile points higher at the end of the year on the reading test and 15 percentile points higher on the math test. Noting, correctly, that "many of the poorest and most educationally disadvantaged [of the voucher] students went to the Hope schools," the three scholars concluded that these students nevertheless appeared to be "learning at a faster rate" than their counterparts in other public schools.

A recent analysis by Indiana University professors showed some slippage on the test for the next group of third-graders. David Brennan doesn't dispute the findings; he attributes them to some unprepared teachers, since departed, and promises that the school will remedy the situation. But while one appropriate yardstick of the voucher schools' success is standardized test scores, an equally important evaluation is the one that parents deliver. Even more than whether their children score a few points higher on a standardized test, what they want to know is whether their kids are in a safe environment, and whether they are being taught good study habits and appropriate moral lessons.

When I visited the Hope Central Academy, I could easily see why most of the parents were satisfied with their choice. The school is located in a formerly Polish and Czech neighborhood in southeast Cleveland. It doesn't need security guards or metal detectors. Dressed in their blue-and-white school uniforms, the children move through the hallways quietly and civilly. In every classroom I visited, the children were deeply engrossed in serious academic work. Each of the rooms had its own computer area, with five or six workstations. In a second-grade classroom, children sat at each of the terminals, working on a math program coordinated with a standardized achievement test. All the other children were quietly writing in their workbooks, under the no-nonsense supervision of their teacher, Kay Linear.

Like the other voucher schools I visited, Hope Central Academy was living proof that professional education certification and graduate education degrees are not synonymous with better educators. Kay Linear is a case in point: a middle-aged black woman, she had had a successful career in business and then had decided to go into teaching, without an ed-school degree, after her own children had grown up. The school's dynamic computer director and fifth-grade teacher, 27-year-old Stacie Morris, is another case in point. A former public school teacher from upstate New York, she moved to the Cleveland area when her husband got transferred, and she discovered that her New York State teaching license wasn't valid in the Cleveland public schools. So she went to work at Hope Central, which, unhampered by the public school system's bureaucratic regulations, hired her with enthusiasm. "I've been thrilled to work here," she told me. "My colleagues are really committed; everyone works very hard, and we have the flexibility to do things that couldn't be done in the public schools."

Similarly, the principal of the school is Linas Vysnionis, now 35, a tall, bearded lawyer who had his own law practice and did some college teaching before deciding that he wanted to teach young children. He taught fourth grade at Hope Central before becoming principal last year. "I'd be the first to admit that I have a lot more to learn," says Vysnionis, "but I think I'm given the freedom and discretion to get things done that I wouldn't get in a public school. And a lot of what I do is simple common sense: you let the teachers do their jobs, and you back them up."

Part of the commonsense approach is that the school spends very little for administration. Vysnionis has an office staff of three: a secretary, an admissions secretary, and a bookkeeper. The only expenditures for security are the closed-circuit cameras near the front door and the buzzer system for letting visitors in. The school is able to direct almost all its financial resources to the classroom, so it can keep class size under 30 and can afford computers and educational software for the classrooms.

David Brennan, the man who hired Vysnionis and brought Hope Central into existence, is probably the most optimistic and visionary voucher advocate in the country. He sees his two Cleveland schools as prototypes for a revolutionary approach to education. He has already surveyed his hometown, Akron, and discovered that the city has enough room in existing churches and community centers to create new schools for all the city's public school students if, as is highly unlikely, a voucher program should impel them to abandon the existing public schools *en masse*. And he is certain that more school choice will bring more, and more creative, Americans into education. "I know that when choice becomes universal, there are 1 million people out there who are smarter than we are, who are going to solve all these problems of inner-city education," he says, with infectious enthusiasm. "There is nothing more impressive than American innovation. Let's give it a chance."

Cheryl Brown, a black evangelical Christian; Brother Bob Smith, a black Capuchin friar; Walter Sava, a Hispanic community activist; and David Brennan, a millionaire white industrialist—here is a taste of what American diversity at its best can achieve. What these four exemplary Americans have accomplished is to kindle some of those "thousand points of light" that one of our ex-presidents liked to talk about. In their schools, they are giving thousands of disadvantaged children the best possible opportunity to grow up to be productive adults. They do this not by portraying the children as victims needing special privileges but by holding them to one common standard of excellence and hard work.

But these four individuals are also accomplishing something else of significance. In their separate ways, they are demystifying schooling by disproving the widely accepted dogma that only government-certified education professionals know what and how to teach children. This myth has spawned a vast, interlocking industry of education schools, certification boards, teachers' unions, and school board officials, and it has certainly boosted the material interests of those certified professionals. But the dogma has done little for America's schoolchildren. The four educators profiled here, and hundreds of others like them, are showing us a different—and better—way. Clearly, it's in our interest to make sure that they are able to continue.

—*Winter 1999*

RICHARD E. MORGAN

Yes, Vouchers Are Constitutional

IT HAS BECOME an American reflex over the past generation for advocates who lose in the political arena to try to kill in the courts what they can no longer defeat in the legislature. That is happening with the school voucher issue today. A recent national poll shows parents in favor of vouchers 82 to 13 percent: the majority of Americans with children in school seem to understand that only competition from outside the dysfunctional, union-dominated public school system can bring about the sweeping educational reforms the nation needs. Black parents, whose children are disproportionally stuck in educationally bankrupt inner-city schools, support vouchers even more strongly, with 84 percent in favor. But teachers' unions and their political allies, as they see their support ebb away, reply: Too bad; school vouchers are unconstitutional, so the issue is moot. Since many families would use them to send their children to Catholic and other church-related schools, vouchers violate the "separation of church and state."

Are these opponents of vouchers correct? Is there anything in the Constitution of the United States, or in the constitutions of the several states, that forbids such programs?

At the level of the federal Constitution, the answer should certainly be no. The phrase "separation of church and state" does not occur in the document (or in any of the 13 original state constitutions). The clause of the federal Constitution that is widely, but incorrectly, held to mandate "separation" is that part of Amendment One that forbids Congress to make any law "respecting an establishment of religion." The original proposal, introduced by James Madison, simply provided that a "national religion" not be "established." While the documentary record of the First Congress is too fragmentary to allow us to know precisely what the amendment's authors intended by the change they wrought in Madison's language, it is safe to say that the prohibition against laws "respecting an establishment of religion" embodied Madison's original aim (with which no one really disagreed) of forbidding Congress from establishing a national religion or granting any sect or denomination preferences that might tend in that direction.

One other thing is known for sure: the provision as finally proposed by Congress and ratified by the states was intended to prevent the central government from interfering in the arrangements worked out within the several states with respect to religion and the public order. After all, the primary reason the First Congress was proposing amendments was to satisfy the large multitude who worried that the new Constitution left the states too exposed to central government meddling. And, of course, half the states had some form of religious establishment in 1790—and their congressmen and senators were determined to protect those practices.

Connecticut congressman Benjamin Huntington, for instance, was quick to remind the House that in most of New England the support of ministers and the "expense of building meeting houses" were "things regulated bye laws." And while Huntington understood that the "gentleman from Virginia" did not intend the proposed amendment to preclude such arrangements, he was worried that "others might find it convenient to put another construction on it," and he wanted it clear that the provision was not meant to satisfy "those who professed no religion at all."

In sum, the establishment clause was meant to allow the states to continue to chart their own courses in church-state relations. At the national level, it precluded both an established church and sectarian favoritism, but it did not embody a policy of indifference or hostility to religion, much less a ban on all cooperative arrangements between the central government and religious institutions. As Robert A. Goldwin puts it in his new study of the framing of the amendments that became the Bill of Rights: "There is solid evidence that this Congress looked favorably on a general sort of government aid to religion, so long as it was not preferential or discriminatory."

Of course, there were those in the early Republic who did favor radical separation. In 1802 Thomas Jefferson broke with the practice of issuing Thanksgiving Day proclamations, which Washington had established and which Jefferson's successors immediately resumed. A small storm of criticism of Jefferson's administration resulted, and in a scramble to establish some cover, the president addressed a letter to the Danbury, Connecticut, Baptist Association, arguing that his action was not purely personal but was compelled by the Constitution. It was here he hatched his ill-founded metaphor asserting that the First Amendment erected a "wall of separation" between church and state. Along similar lines, in the 1830s, Kentucky senator Richard ("Rumpsey-Dumpsey") Johnson led a quixotic crusade seeking Sunday mail delivery on the grounds that its omission constituted an establishment of religion.

But such radically separationist ideas were never mainstream. For over a century and half after the ratification of the First Amendment, the states charted their own courses with respect to religion and the public order. During the nineteenth century, those with established churches gradually disestablished them, though as late as 1902 New Hampshire's Constitution empowered the Legislature to authorize towns to provide "public Protestant teachers of piety, religion and morality." As established churches receded into the past, a variety of cooperative, non-preferential arrangements between state and local governments and religious institutions flourished. In New York, for instance, the Children's Law of 1875 welcomed sectarian child-care institutions as part of a state-funded system of institutional care. In some poor, predominantly Catholic, school districts from Maine to Missouri (where supporting a separate public school for the few non-Catholic children would have been impractical), parochial schools eliminated religious instruction during most of the school day, accepted all children from the community without regard to religion, and received some public support for maintenance and for teachers' compensation. In New York, this arrangement, called the Poughkeepsie Plan, persisted until it was targeted for elimination by politically powerful nativist forces late in the nineteenth century.

At the national level, wherever the federal government directly provided for local governance and social services—in the territories, the military, the Indian reservations, and the District of Columbia—it followed a similar course without constitutional embarrassment. For example, the same Congress that proposed the First Amendment to the states reenacted the Northwest Ordinance, which provided not only for freedom of religion in the territories but also for the "encouragement of religion, and education, and schools," by (among other things) setting land aside "for the purposes of religion." And in 1899 the Supreme Court approved a congressional appropriation to pay for an addition to a Roman Catholic hospital in Washington.

So where does the constitutional argument against voucher plans come from? The short answer is that, as with so much contemporary mischief, it comes from the Supreme Court—and especially, the Warren Court of the 1960s.

The developments of the sixties and seventies have their prelude in a famous 1947 Supreme Court decision called *Everson v. Board of Education of Ewing, New Jersey*. New Jersey had authorized local school boards to reimburse parents for the fares their children paid on regular bus lines getting to and from school—whether public or parochial school. One Arch A. Everson challenged the expenditure as violating the establishment clause. Everson was a member of the Order of United American Mechanics, a nativist organization dating from the Know-Nothing movement of the 1850s and dedicated to the exclusion of Roman Catholic institutions from American public life. The Order filed an *amicus curiae* brief in support of Everson's position.

Justice Hugo Black wrote the opinion of the Court, and from the vantage point of 50 years later, it stands out as a shockingly poor piece of work.

The most fundamental issue the case presented was one of federalism, and here, it might have seemed, Everson faced an insurmountable barrier. For the Court to find in his favor, it would have to undo a century and a half of precedent and hold that the establishment clause applied to acts of the states. On what argument could the Court do that? Justice Black solved this problem by ignoring it; without any argument at all, he simply asserted that the states were bound by the prohibition against Congress making laws "respecting an establishment of religion."

It is difficult to overstate the seriousness of this blunder. A constitutional provision intended, in large measure, to shield the states from federal meddling with the choices they made about relations between government and religious institutions was turned into a potential engine of federal power against them. Black could do this because he did not understand the establishment clause, as both its framers and modern scholarship understand it, as serving multiple but limited purposes, one of which was to protect the federal structure of the American union. He saw it, rather, as a blunt mandate of strict separation, and he apparently concluded that, if it was important enough to have been put in the Bill of Rights as a rule for the national government, it was important enough to impose on the states as part of that "due process of law" required by the Fourteenth Amendment. His opinion contains no references to the framing or ratification of the First Amendment or to how the establishment clause was understood by any of the great nineteenth-century constitutional commentators. In 1833, for example, Justice Joseph Story had written that "the whole power over the subject of religion is left entirely to the state governments," and in 1883, Judge Thomas Cooley had explained that "a law respecting an establishment of religion," as the First Amendment puts it, would be one that would "effect a union of Church and State, or . . . establish preferences in law in favor of any one religious persuasion or mode of worship."

Instead of resting upon long-settled legal understandings, Black's opinion pivoted on Jefferson's idiosyncratic letter to the Danbury Baptists, with its naked assertion that the establishment clause had "erected a wall of separation between church and state"—a metaphor that misrepresented our constitutional history but captured perfectly the separationist fundamentalism to which the justice had been exposed in his youth in Alabama, as a member of another nativist organization—the Ku Klux Klan.

Though Black's mangling of the establishment clause would draw plenty of fire in the future, it drew little at the time, probably because Black emerged from the *Everson* case looking like a moderate. For all his primitive separationism, he upheld the New Jersey law: he simply did not see returning the nickels and dimes to New Jersey parents as aid to the parochial schools. In his view, the state was aiding the schoolchildren themselves, providing for their safety—just as it did in providing smallpox vaccinations, which no one doubted could go to parochial as well as public school pupils.

In the wake of *Everson*, those favoring the traditional American policy of accommodation and cooperation between government and church-related institutions hoped that the actual, commonsensical result Black had reached might prove more important than the radically separationist part of his opinion. Perhaps as long as government programs were intended to aid students, and benefited schools only incidentally, the states might retain some flexibility. And indeed, through the decade of the 1950s it remained unclear the extent to which Justice Black's strict separationism had become the official doctrine of the Supreme Court. Decisions pointed in different directions.

But hopes for judicial moderation proved illusory. In the early 1960s, the Court, under Earl Warren, returned with a vengeance to Black's broad-brush separationism in decisions striking down school prayer and otherwise commanding a thoroughgoing secularization of the American public square.

What Black had launched in *Everson* was a myth—the myth of a strict separationist American past. The sixties saw the rise of a militant secularism—a mind-set Justice Anthony Kennedy later described as "an unjustified hostility toward religion"—and the carriers of this militant secularism were precisely the liberal elites who dominated the country's intellectual and political life in that period. Black's myth was tailor-made for them, regarding religion and religious institutions, as they did, as forces of reaction and obscurantism standing in the way of secular progress—forces from which schoolchildren, in particular, needed protection. The liberals then dominating the Supreme Court faithfully reflected this attitude. Sometimes the opinion was by Black himself, sometimes by Tom Clark or Abe Fortas. The effect was to lock strict separationism tightly into constitutional law.

Surprisingly, with the arrival of Chief Justice Warren Burger in the 1970s, things got even worse. In a series of cases, beginning with *Lemon v. Kurtzman* in 1971, the Court struck down state efforts to include religious-school students in general programs of educational enrichment, and it evolved a new test, the "Lemon test," to be used to determine whether a public program complied with the establishment clause. The requirement was threefold: the program must have been enacted to serve a secular legislative purpose; the program's "primary effect" must neither advance nor inhibit religion; and the operation of the program must not involve government in "excessive entanglement" with church-related institutions. Any program that significantly benefited a religious school, even incidentally, the Court held, would have the "primary effect of advancing religion." Armed with this rigid formulation ("the fruit of the Lemon tree," one commentator called it), the separationist block on the Court, led by Justice William Brennan, continued to scythe down most programs that aided church-related schools into the early 1980s.

This militant judicial separationism reached its zenith in Brennan's majority opinion in *Aguilar v. Felton* in 1985. New York City, using federal funds under Title 1 of the Elementary and Secondary Education Act of 1965, provided services to educationally deprived children in low-income areas by allowing public school teachers to go into church-related schools to teach math and reading and to provide guidance counseling. The schools removed religious symbols from classrooms during the public school teachers' visits, and city education officials kept watch to ensure that the publicly provided instruction really was kept separate from programs of religious instruction. Brennan pounced on this monitoring, declaring that it constituted "excessive entanglement." The city was reduced to buying trailers (with scarce educational dollars) and parking them at the curbside outside schools, so the children could troop out to receive the services.

But even as Brennan triumphed in *Aguilar*, an intellectual counterattack against the strict separationist misreading of the establishment clause was finally gaining traction and undercutting the shallow historical foundation on which the Court's separationism rested. Among the most important examples of the new scholarship, Walter Berns's *The First Amendment and the Future of American Democracy* had appeared in 1976, followed by Michael Malbin's *Religion and Politics: The Intentions of the Authors of the First Amendment* in 1978 and Robert Cord's *Separation of Church and State* in 1982. Carefully and persistently, these authors exploded the separationist myth that Black had conjured up in 1947. Even within the legal academy (where strict separationism had been credulously accepted in the 1960s), the Lemon test was coming under criticism from such figures as Professors Philip Kurland and Michael McConnell of the University of Chicago Law School and Mary Ann Glendon of the Harvard Law School as a wooden and unwieldy instrument for dealing with contemporary America's multiplicity of differently nuanced church-state issues.

All this ferment came to a head in a lengthy, impassioned dissenting opinion by then-justice Rehnquist in a case called *Wallace v. Jaffree*, decided a few weeks after *Aguilar* in the spring of 1985. Here the Brennan bloc struck down a state law providing for a moment of silence as part of the opening of the public school day. The majority insisted this was a backdoor encouragement of prayer by the state. Incredible as it now appears, Rehnquist's dissent contained the first full review of the historical evidence on the framing and original meaning of the establishment clause by any member of the Court, and his conclusion was devastating: "The Establishment Clause did not require government neutrality between religion and irreligion nor did it prohibit the federal government from providing non-discriminatory aid to religion. There is simply no historical foundation for the position that the Framers intended to build the 'wall of separation' that was constitutionalized in *Everson*."

Things have never been the same for radical separationism; it has been on the intellectual defensive ever since, with major scholarship adding to its discomfort year by year, and new members of the Court distancing themselves from the doctrine. Despite labored attempts by Justice David Souter and by a few die-hard professors, the intellectual dominance of Warren-era separationism cannot be restored either within the judiciary or the academy.

Does this mean the battle to reclaim the constitutional law of church and state has been won and the future of vouchers is assured? No; but the outlook is brighter than ever before. Two justices, Clarence Thomas and Antonin Scalia, are in full agreement with Rehnquist's traditionalist reading of the establishment clause. Two others, Anthony Kennedy and Sandra Day O'Connor, are not prepared to turn their backs on *Everson*, but they have both been critical of what they see as mechanical applications of the Lemon test and have shown some flexibility on church-state issues. Four justices continue to constitute a strict separationist bloc—John Paul Stevens, David Souter, Ruth Bader Ginsburg, and Stephen Breyer—but even here some observers suspect, based on hints buried in earlier decisions, that one or more of them might support vouchers. Professor Laurence Tribe, Harvard's left-leaning legal guru (who personally thinks vouchers are a "lousy idea"), is also a very shrewd Court watcher, and he predicts that six or seven justices might vote to sustain them.

Furthermore, the Court has already made some significant breaks with its separationist past in its case law—notably, its reversal, in the spring of 1997, of *Aguilar v. Felton*. Invoking a little-used Supreme Court rule that allows one of the original parties to a case to move to reopen it if subsequent decisions of the Court have "eroded" the foundation of the original decision, New York City persuaded the Court to reopen—and overturn—*Aguilar*. Justice O'Connor, writing for the majority, held that recent decisions of the Court had modified the Lemon test: no longer would incidental benefits to religious institutions be held to have the effect of "advancing religion," and no longer would it be presumed that public employees functioning in sectarian institutional settings would require the kind of government monitoring that would create "excessive entanglement." As a result, the Board of Education teachers could go back into the parochial schools, and the trailers could be hauled away.

This new decision, *Agostini v. Felton,* had an almost immediate salutary effect in the legal battle over vouchers. The Milwaukee Parental Choice

Program, one of the nation's most promising voucher experiments, had been tied up in a legal challenge for years and was before the Wisconsin Supreme Court when *Agostini* came down. Last June, in a 4–2 decision, that court sustained the program against both state and federal constitutional challenges. The impact of Justice O'Connor's opinion in the New York case was evident throughout Judge Donald W. Steinmetz's majority opinion in Wisconsin. While dutifully noting that on the federal establishment clause issue he was required to follow *Lemon*, Steinmetz noted that its "continued authority . . . is uncertain," and he treated it as a general guide with plenty of play at the joints.

Various parties to the Wisconsin suit have filed petitions asking the U.S. Supreme Court to review the decision, and we should know within the next few months whether the justices will agree to do so. But even should the Court decline to take the Wisconsin case, there are enough others moving forward around the country (including cases from Ohio, Vermont, and Maine) to make a Supreme Court resolution of the matter likely sooner rather than later.

But even if things are looking up for vouchers at the federal constitutional level, what about the state constitutions? Many of them, including New York's, contain a "Blaine amendment"—a provision that specifically prohibits state support of religious schools. It is often argued that in these states, at least, voucher plans are unconstitutional, whatever the U.S. Supreme Court decides. This argument is just as wrongheaded as arguments relying on the federal establishment clause.

Seeing why requires a brief historical detour. The mid-1870s saw the first of three major surges of bitterly anti-Catholic and anti-immigrant nativist sentiment that disfigured post–Civil War America. (The second, particularly relevant to New York, was in the mid-1890s, and the third in the early 1920s.) In 1875 the faltering Grant administration, stained by scandal and casting about for a way to revive Republican prospects before the election of 1876, moved to exploit this resurgent anti-Catholicism. Grant himself delivered a tub-thumping speech before the veterans of the Army of the Tennessee, urging them to see that "not one dollar appropriated" for education be spent to support any but "free"—that is, government-run—schools.

At this point, that prince of political opportunists, James G. Blaine, the Maine Republican who was minority leader of the House of Representatives, took the lead (it would be in Blaine's 1884 presidential campaign that the Democrats would find themselves branded as the party of "Rum, Romanism, and Rebellion"). He introduced the following amendment to the U.S. Constitution: "No state shall make any law respecting an establishment of religion or prohibiting the free exercise thereof; and no money raised by taxation in any state for the support of the public schools . . . shall ever be under the control of any religious sect." Blaine's amendment passed the House 180 to 7, but with 98 members not voting. In the Senate, a weaker version fell short of the necessary two-thirds vote.

But thereafter, the idea of writing into state constitutions an explicit provision guaranteeing that Catholic parochial schools would never receive a share of the common school fund become a leading item on the agenda of nativist thought and agitation. It received strong support from such benighted and intolerant groups as the American Protective Association, which spearheaded the anti-Catholic insurgency of the mid-1890s, and the revived Ku Klux Klan, the most powerful organization in the nativist outbreak of the 1920s. Responding to these pressures, a number of states added these provisions to their constitutions.

New York's Blaine amendment (actually Article XI, Section 3, of the state Constitution) provides that "neither the state nor any subdivision thereof shall use its property, directly or indirectly, in aid or maintenance . . . of any school or institution of learning wholly or in part under the control or direction of any religious denomination, or in which any denominational tenet or doctrine is taught."

New York framed its present Constitution in 1894, at the peak of that decade's anti-Catholic furor. The American Protective Association was a major political force upstate that year, purporting to defend "true Americanism" against the "subjects of an un-American ecclesiastical institution" and retailing bogus papal encyclicals calling on Catholics to "exterminate all heretics." A more genteel (but even more effective) nativist formation, centered in the city and the southern counties, styled itself the National League for the Protection of American Institutions. Historians disagree as to the relative degrees of influence these groups exercised over the leadership of the Republican Party that controlled the Constitutional Convention, but all concur that, in winning the inclusion of the school provision, nativist influence was decisive. The tone was set by John Jay, urbane great-grandson of the Founding Father and a leading New York City anti-Catholic, who denounced "the Roman hierarchy, with whose widely organized and relentless hostility to American schools and American principles our people . . . are fast becoming familiar." (The nativists failed in their effort to include in the Constitution a ban on state support of religiously affiliated hospitals and orphanages, principally because the Jewish community maintained a number of these, and the combined strength of Jewish and Catholic agitation was enough to determine the issue.)

Those who would today resort to New York's Blaine amendment (or to similar provisions in other states) to attack voucher programs ought to be ashamed of themselves. Wherever adopted, such provisions were the handiwork of men whose vision of America was anything but pluralistic; they are part of the darker side of our history. It is a bitter irony that some of the groups now most ready to go to court on the basis of Blaine provisions—the American Civil Liberties Union, for instance, and the Anti-Defamation League—were originally organized to combat nativism and the kind of One-Hundred-Percent-Americanism that sought to marginalize non-WASP newcomers. And why in heaven's name should the NAACP be poised to defend the handiwork of groups, including the Klan, that were uniformly hostile to the aspirations of America's black people? Moreover, viewing religious schools, and post–Vatican II Roman Catholic schools in particular, as dangerous threats to American liberty is, to say the least, atavistic.

Aside from their unsavory origins, Blaine amendments are not, as a legal matter, fatal to school choice plans that include religious schools. What is forbidden by New York's Article XI, Section 3, for instance, is "aid," and there is no reason—historical, logical, or legal—to understand this term as encompassing any and all monies that might flow to church-related schools as a result of some governmental program. In affirming the Milwaukee Parental Choice Program, the Wisconsin Supreme Court had to deal with an objection based on a Blaine-type provision in the Wisconsin Constitution. In response, Judge Steinmetz and his colleagues relied on an earlier Wisconsin decision in a case upholding tuition payments for veterans at religiously affiliated high schools and colleges: "The contention that financial benefit accrues to religion from [this program] is . . . untenable. Only the increased cost to such schools occasioned by the attendance of beneficiaries is to be reimbursed. They are not enriched by the service they render. Mere reimbursement is not aid."

And this was exactly the position the New York State Court of Appeals took on the last occasion it was asked to construe Article XI, Section 3. The decision was in 1967, upholding an early Rockefeller program that lent publicly purchased textbooks to independent schools, including those with religious affiliations. With respect to the Blaine objection, Judge John F. Scileppi wrote: "Since there is no intention to assist parochial schools as such, any benefit accruing to those schools is a collateral effect of the statute, and, therefore, cannot be properly classified as the giving of aid directly or indirectly." Thus, the seemingly ferocious ban in New York's Blaine amendment against giving aid to church-related schools either "directly or indirectly" collapses in the case of vouchers, once it is understood that, absent an "intention to assist," no aid is involved at all.

After all, what the original backers of Blaine amendments were aiming at was the proposal, made by certain adventurous Catholic spokesmen in the late nineteenth and early twentieth centuries, that parochial schools should receive equal government funding with the public schools. Such a general governmental underwriting of a religious school system, to which church authorities exhorted Catholic parents to send their children, is altogether different from what happens under a voucher plan. Here public funds are placed at the disposal of parents in a program that is neutral among various kinds of schools—the voucher might be used at a better public school in another district or even another town; it might be used at a charter school; or it might be used at a private school, either religious or non-religious. The independent decisions of non-governmental third parties guide the transmission of funds. Constitutional language designed a century ago to preclude the complete funding of a sectarian school system cannot be stretched to apply to vouchers today.

The constitutional assault on vouchers is as perverse at the state level as it is at the federal. After all, for many years vouchers have been acceptable at religiously affiliated colleges and universities and at preschool and day-care facilities. Why should K-through-12 be different? The traditional American understanding of the separation of church and state is one of pragmatic flexibility, open to accommodations between religion and the public order so long as these are non-discriminatory and not coercive of conscience. The strict separationism of the old nativists, and of Justice Black and the Warren Court, were aberrations.

Of course, defenders of the discredited views still control many commanding heights in the media, the universities, and the legal profession. Justice Black's *Everson* version of separation held sway for almost half a century, taught from middle school to law school. Many judges still accept it uncritically. The liberal establishment is determined to protect it and extend it into a new century: "Breaching the Church-State Wall," the *New York Times* cried in alarm, in response to the Wisconsin voucher decision.

The accumulated result of years of separationist bullying was hilariously revealed a few years ago when former president George Bush was asked to recall his thoughts as a young naval aviator, shot down and pitched into the waters of the South Pacific. "What sustains you in times like that?" he said. "Well, you go back to fundamental values. I thought about Mother and Dad and the strength I got from them, and God, and faith—and the separation of church and state." Now, we are not really to suppose that, as he frantically paddled that "little yellow raft off the coast of an enemy-held island," Lieutenant Bush was reflecting on Jefferson's letter to the Danbury Baptists. What was operating was the reflex of an experienced, late-twentieth-century American politician: better not invoke the Deity, even in such a profoundly personal context, without immediately appeasing the strict separationists.

It is time to put an end to such nonsense.

—Autumn 1998

IV
WELFARE

Cities and states have been at the forefront of welfare reform, forging the policies that cut welfare rolls in half nationwide as the twentieth century closed, with no discernible rise in homelessness or distress. For all the good intentions that accompanied its founding during the New Deal and its vast expansion during the 1960s, welfare allowed dependency to become an intergenerational way of life for millions of inner-city residents—a consequence unforeseen and unintended by the welfare system's architects. Worse, the children whose welfare the system was designed to ensure too often ended up being harmed by it, unable to take advantage of opportunity and spreading disorder throughout the cities.

As welfare reform puts mothers back to work, the unanswered questions remain: What about illegitimacy? What about the kids?

HEATHER MAC DONALD
Compassion Gone Mad

IN 1984 the New York Legislature passed the Teenage Services Act (TASA), targeted at teen mothers on welfare. It is the perfect expression of New York City and State's failed war against social disintegration.

The city and state already spend millions on pregnancy prevention, pre- and neonatal care, day care, welfare, parenting classes, and drug abuse prevention and treatment—none of which has had the slightest impact on spiraling teen pregnancy and its accompanying social pathologies. So who needs another program? But TASA is cleverly premised on that very glut of services. It creates a new category of social worker, whose sole purpose is to shepherd teen mothers through the maze of existing social workers and services.

TASA, one might say, is a rational response to an irrational situation. Over the last 30 years, New York City and State have devoted an increasing share of their revenues to the most dysfunctional members of society, and now social service spending constitutes the largest share of both city and state budgets. Yet as spending grew, so did the social problems that spending was supposed to solve. The government responded by adding more programs. The result is a tangle of entitlements and services so complex as to require a guide service like TASA and many similar programs.

All you need is the evidence of your senses to know that New York City's enormous commitment to social welfare spending has not stemmed social breakdown. The question is: has it made things worse? The answer is yes—on two counts. Social service spending has sucked out of the private economy capital that could have been used to create jobs, the best mechanism for ending poverty. But in response to inner-city poverty, welfare advocates call for *further* social service spending, thereby accelerating the flight of business from the city. This vicious circle characterizes welfare's impact on the family as well. The two-parent family is all but extinct in some neighborhoods, rendered superfluous by welfare's subsidy for illegitimacy. The resulting increase in juvenile delinquency, truancy, and teen pregnancy brings in more social services, which in turn further erode the incentives for personal responsibility.

The message social service programs convey is all too often the polar opposite of what the inner-city poor need. Typically, such programs reward dysfunctional behavior and subordinate the well-being of children to dubious ideology—such as the belief that even a flamboyantly neglectful single-parent household, riven by drugs, possesses basic strength and goodness. Above all, the basic purpose of these services to provide the spiritual and material benefits of a stable two-parent family is largely futile. Families create sound individuals by imposing discipline and moral values on children. Even if a government program could do this, these programs don't: for years, imposing values has been anathema to social workers, who studiously avoid making judgments about the "life-style choices" of their clients.

The best way to see the social service apparatus whole is to trace the life cycle of a family moving through it. Each stage has its appropriate service; the city even envisions "transitional services" in one program to ease a child's passage from children's to adult services.

Start with a woman below the poverty line, pregnant with an illegitimate child. Aid to Families with Dependent Children (AFDC) benefits begin in her sixth month of pregnancy. She can also get free or low-cost medical care from the city's clinics, as well as a host of "preventive" services, such as Healthy Start, a nationwide effort to reduce infant mortality.

In Healthy Start, which pumps $8 million of additional federal aid a year into nonprofit social service agencies in Mott Haven, Bedford-Stuyvesant, and Central Harlem, we can see the outlines of many services to come. Like TASA, it is a "case management" program, a hot social service trend. Case management takes a "case"—that is, an individual who has made some very bad decisions—and "manages" it by directing the individual to *other* services, above all to various entitlements for which the client may have failed to apply. Healthy Start directs clients to pre- and neonatal medical care, for example, and to such welfare benefits as Medicaid and the Women, Infants and Children food program. "Case management is a real scam," judges University of Massachusetts sociologist Peter Rossi. It's a "marvelous way to keep social workers from dealing with clients. All they do is deal with the 'case' and talk to each other as to how to manage it."

Healthy Start employs an extremely fuzzy definition of infant-mortality prevention. It funds programs that train tenant organizers, that encourage teens to pursue careers in health and social services (thus perpetuating the life of the social service establishment, if not of infants), and that deliver "life skills" and self-esteem training for teens. The link between any of these services and the prevention of infant mortality is remote.

But in today's social service programs, nearly any service can count as "prevention" of nearly any social pathology. The same nonprofit agencies, such as the ubiquitous Puerto Rican Family Institute or Victim Services,

Inc., are under contract with a variety of government agencies, including juvenile justice, child welfare, youth services, and mental health, to provide the identical set of services, appropriately repackaged as "pregnancy prevention," "delinquency prevention," "truancy prevention," or "child-abuse prevention." While the logic of prevention may sound convincing—it's cheaper to intervene early to prevent social problems than to respond after the fact—there is little evidence that prevention programs make a difference.

Imagine the baby who's had this supposed "healthy start" a few years later. Assume his mother's parenting class didn't take, as parenting classes so often don't. The child, or children by now, start asking neighbors for food and appear unwashed and ill-clothed. A neighbor calls the Child Welfare Agency (CWA) to report neglect. A CWA caseworker investigates the home and finds the children sleeping on the floor, no food in the refrigerator, and a filthy kitchen and bathroom. Just as the birth of illegitimate children provided the mother with an income, so will deplorable child-rearing bring her a benefit. The CWA worker might conclude that the mother is overwhelmed with being a parent and assign her a homemaker to help with her chores. The caseworker might also order still more parenting classes. Meanwhile, the neighbors next door, a poor working couple struggling to provide a decent home for their child, are left to scrub their own floors.

If the maltreatment is serious enough to warrant placing a child into foster care—the temporary custody arrangement for victims of parental abuse or neglect—the CWA may decide to provide the mother with "family preservation" instead. A relatively late arrival on the social service scene, dating from the 1980s, family preservation is its current queen. It is prototypical in its confusion of moral deficit with material need.

Family preservation works as follows: for six to eight weeks, an abusive or neglectful parent gets several visits a week from a social worker, who is on call 24 hours a day. The social worker provides home-based therapy to the family on such topics as "anger management" and "rational-emotive control." Equally important, the social worker provides a host of material services: she may buy groceries for the family, pay any outstanding rent arrears, drive the mother to medical or other appointments, help with home repair, or buy furniture, all at taxpayer expense. Meanwhile, the working couple next door, who also could use new furniture, is again out of luck.

Family preservation presupposes that many families "at risk" of losing a child to foster care are in a short-term crisis. Give them the psychological skills and financial assistance to weather the storm, the theory goes, and the risk of foster-care placement will recede. But many target parents suffer from problems too deep for a short-term fix. A drug-addicted teen dropout who happens to have gotten pregnant in all likelihood lacks the maturity to raise children; propping her "family" up with an array of services will never make it whole.

The animating philosophy of family preservation—that all "families," however dysfunctional or fragmentary, deserve respect—epitomizes contemporary social work's refusal to make moral judgments. To family preservationists, a single mother on crack who neglects her children is equal to a family of two working parents who can't afford day care. This ideology has profoundly affected child-welfare agencies nationwide, making them see their dominant mission as "keeping families together" rather than protecting children.

Even in those cases when the city must conclude that preventive services haven't worked, that doesn't dampen social workers' zeal for keeping deeply troubled families together. Under an arrangement known as kinship foster care, the city pays relatives—usually grandmothers—to care for their kin's children. It's a lucrative arrangement: the monthly foster-care payment ranges from $400 to $1,000 a head, depending on the children's "special needs"—far more than they are worth living with their mother.

Not only parents are eligible for family preservation. The practice has spawned several clones directed at the children of troubled families, with the same aim of preserving the often toxic family unit. Imagine a 12-year-old boy—"Johnnie" (a composite based on interviews with dozens of social service providers)—whose drug-addicted mother has already received various "preventive" services, maybe even full-blown family preservation. His chaotic home life starts erupting at school. He fights with fellow students and falls ever further behind in reading. The system will start prescribing services. His school is likely to conclude that he suffers from a "behavioral disorder" and a learning disability. It will put him in the special-education program and give him his own social worker as part of his special-education School-Based Support Team.

Nevertheless, Johnnie grows increasingly unruly and agitated. One day he threatens his teacher with a box cutter. His school psychologist recommends that he be temporarily hospitalized. But the emergency-room doctor feels that hospitalization can be averted by providing the family with—no surprise—social services. He refers Johnnie to the Home-Based Crisis Intervention Program, overseen by the state's Office of Mental Health but run by community-based nonprofits. A social worker from a nonprofit, on call 24 hours a day, will provide six to eight weeks of intensive "anger management" and "problem solving" training for the family in its home. The caseworker might teach Johnnie's mother how to budget or how to help her children with their homework. The worker will also meet with Johnnie's teachers and develop a "service plan" with them.

Sound familiar? It should. Home-Based Crisis Intervention is the brain-child of the same Washington-based organization—the Behavioral Sciences Institute—that developed family preservation. The program models are identical.

The families in Home-Based Crisis Intervention are, with few exceptions, from the most dysfunctional subset of the welfare population. This subset consumes a disproportionate share of service spending and has become so embedded in various service systems that "caseworkers from different agencies are tripping over each other," says Anita Appel, who oversees Crisis Intervention. Such families' entry into the social service universe is a foregone conclusion; the only mystery is the exact point of entry. "The typical scenario is a mother on crack who has lost custody of her mentally disabled child to CWA," explains Denise Arieli of the city's Department of Mental Health. "If the child's point of entry is mental retardation, and in the mental program he sets a fire, he becomes a mental-health child. If he happens to set the fire first, however, he will be a juvenile-justice child. The kids touch multiple systems, and the larger system struggles hard with where they should go."

The system is certain, however, that kids should *not* go to an institution. The clumsy dance of social workers serving the same family grows out of the social service system's commitment to "community care," closely linked with the philosophy of "keeping families together." Rather than taking children or adults away from destructive environments, the reigning service ethic dictates that they remain "in the community" and "in the family" for treatment. This ethic, born in the 1960s, when "community" was a code word for minority "empowerment," is based on a romanticized view of both underclass communities and the troubled families they produce. "We don't listen to families enough," says Anita Appel of the Office of Mental Health, in defense of her agency's various community-based programs.

The greatest fallacy of community-based treatment is that usually there is no real community to go back to. Treating a juvenile delinquent in the war-torn environment that produced him does not look like a recipe for success. Some observers also question the worth of the community-based organizations. "The staff is usually one baby step above their clients in pathology," observes a teacher who works with disturbed children. "They're from the same population, without education."

As a child placed in special education or in the Home-Based Crisis Intervention program progresses deeper into the social service world, one pattern will become dominant: the transfer of parental functions to his social workers, themselves often very ill-qualified to be parental surrogates. For example, in the Intensive Case Management program, which often follows the Crisis Intervention program, "the intensive case manager is just like family," explains Jeffrey Holliman of the city's Department of Mental Health. The manager will sit in on planning sessions at the child's school to develop a service plan for him and will try to line up yet more services for the family to ensure that the child stays at home, rather than in an institution such as foster care, a psychiatric hospital, or a juvenile detention center.

The children in any of the city's social services could just as easily have landed in its criminal system. Many ultimately do. Family Court, which adjudicates juvenile crime along with foster-care proceedings, is the very vortex of the social service system. All social problems that haven't been solved by other agencies end up there only to meet the usual services.

Imagine that Johnnie, at age 15, pulls a gun on a grocery clerk but runs away when he sees a guard coming. At his arraignment for attempted robbery and assault, the judge may order him into the Probation Department's Alternative to Detention (ATD) program, a pre-trial probation program for chronically truant kids. It is the most desperate of the city's social services: faced with the obvious failure of every other institution in a child's life, it tries to do everything that those other institutions did not. "Because we have a captive population, once we're monitoring a child, we want to address as much as we can for the time we have them—reading, writing, literacy, math issues, drug counseling," explains Michael P. Jacobson, commissioner of probation. ATD places kids in a small school-like setting during the day and offers them schooling, individual and group therapy, and field trips. If a child does not show up one day, a social worker will try to find him.

After three months in ATD, Johnnie's case comes to trial. Johnnie admits to the attempted robbery. But rather than sending him upstate to prison, the judge orders him into Family Ties, the most remarkable offshoot of family preservation yet. Run out of the city's Department of Juvenile Justice, Family Ties gives convicted juvenile delinquents and their families eight weeks of the usual litany: cognitive restructuring, behavioral modification, anger management, and rational-emotive therapy. Then the Family Ties worker recommends a sentence—usually probation—to the judge. If the original idea of family preservation—that six to eight weeks of intensive counseling and material aid could cure child abuse and neglect—seems fanciful at best, the claim that short-term therapy can overcome the 13-odd years of lack of socialization that produces juvenile delinquency seems preposterous.

From this point, Johnnie's future is hazy. He may go straight, finish school, and stay out of trouble. But if he doesn't—if he ends up homeless or on drugs or HIV-positive or in and out of prison—the city will have social services for him at every stage.

Many social programs treat as short-term crises what are in fact unsustainable ways of life. The city's huge "homelessness prevention" efforts are typical. Consider a family living in an apartment that costs nearly twice as much as its welfare housing grant. The rent is far in arrears and the landlord is threatening eviction. The mother's social worker advises a trip to the Homeless Prevention Unit in her local welfare office.

The obvious thing to do would be to talk to the mother about finding a cheaper apartment. But the city's welfare agencies seldom do the obvious. "The overriding policy in the Human Resources Administration is to prevent the loss of accommodations at all costs," explains HRA spokesman David Ortiz. After paying the back rent to forestall eviction, the homelessness-prevention worker decides to go for the gold: a "Jiggetts" supplement.

Named after a lawsuit filed by homeless advocates, Jiggetts supplements pay the difference between a client's monthly welfare shelter allowance and her actual rent—forever. The monthly shelter allowance for a three-person family is $286 a month; Jiggetts will double that to $572. Brokers and landlords frequently game the system, striking agreements to rent welfare clients apartments well beyond their means, and to forgo a few months' rent, with the understanding that the client will apply for a Jiggetts grant once she faces eviction.

The Jiggetts program exudes misguided beneficence. While the average rent in New York City is, in fact, well above the welfare shelter grant, Jiggetts money anchors indigents to a locale they can't afford, instead of leaving them to migrate to places with lower costs of living or better job prospects, as the poor have traditionally done. Further, tenants often face eviction because of personal irresponsibility, such as a drug habit that consumes the rent money. Propping them up only abets their underlying problem.

If homelessness prevention fails, more social services beckon. Thanks to court cases that gave the homeless the unconditional right to emergency shelter on demand, the city now operates the nation's largest, most expensive shelter system. All told, the city's expenditures on the homeless amount to an estimated $790 million a year, exclusive of medical costs, or $39,500 per homeless person, which includes transportation to visit renovated apartments, moving expenses, furniture allowances, and payments to landlords for renting to homeless families.

Homeless families, as distinct from homeless single individuals, get the most elaborate services. Visit, for example, the Westside Intergenerational Residence, a clean, orderly family shelter in an apartment building on Manhattan's staid West End Avenue. The shelter assigns each resident, almost always a single mother with one child, a social worker and a preventive services worker, who provide entitlement advocacy, counseling, referrals, and parenting-skills training. The residence requires enrollment in an educational program—though self-esteem and parenting-skills classes will sometimes suffice—and it provides *two* on-site day-care programs for its mothers.

According to administrators, the residence's GED program uses an "unconventional" approach to teaching, emphasizing such activities as journal writing, along with academic subjects. "Our ladies won't come in just for reading and writing; getting up to go to math is very boring," explains director Linda Sergeant. And if a mother's attendance record is spotty, her social workers, instead of asking *her* to change, will create a less structured and less demanding program for her.

The residence has an informal program to help its mothers write to their political representatives in support of welfare, Medicaid, and child care. The residence's program isn't unique: students in a city high school for teen mothers recently traveled to Washington, at taxpayer expense, to lobby against welfare cuts. Such a program sends precisely the wrong message to homeless mothers: that more government spending can rebuild their lives. What that spending *can* do, of course, is preserve the jobs of the social service workers who assist their clients' lobbying efforts.

The social service imperative not to make moral judgments has a corollary: a social worker's job is to shield clients from the consequences of self-destructive behavior. This philosophy ends up normalizing bad behavior, nowhere more than in the city's response to teen pregnancy. The Board of Education has five high schools for pregnant and "parenting" teens, which supplement the regular curriculum with parenting classes. That's not all: the school system's Living for the Young Family in Education (LYFE) program operates highly enriched day-care centers in 35 regular schools and in several homeless shelters, at an annual cost of $7.6 million, or $12,666 per teen mother. Its purpose is to increase the chances that a teen mother will graduate from school by removing the burden of travel to an off-site day-care center. And LYFE is just one leg of the city's day-care empire, which cost $557 million in fiscal 1995.

The LYFE program epitomizes the way social services can feed the very problems they're supposed to cure. The program responds to the argument of necessity: ignoring the baby won't make it go away, so now we have to make the best of a bad situation. This argument is a powerful one. It motivates program after program intended to sop up the mess caused by socially destructive behavior. But the inevitable result is to legitimate that behavior. Day-care centers in schools cannot avoid sending the pernicious message that society not only tolerates but *expects* teens to have babies. By removing the pain from very bad decisions, such programs simply enable further bad behavior.

The LYFE program goes out of its way to insulate teens from the consequences of bearing illegitimate children. Teen mothers don't even have to visit the day-care center to feed their babies during the lunch period. "Lunch is the only time they get to hang out with their friends," explains Joan Davis, assistant principal of the program. "The hardest thing about being a teen mom is not being able to be a teen."

This is "compassion" gone mad. The last thing a child needs is a parent who acts like an adolescent. Yet with an unfailing instinct for doing the wrong thing, the social service establishment has made preserving adolescence a goal of the statewide Teenage Services Act for teen mothers on welfare. Director Harriet Nieves explains the TASA philosophy: "We try to give them support so that they can have some of the immaturity and giddiness of being a teen, yet still say to them: 'You have a child.'" TASA nurtures adolescent "giddiness," Nieves explains, by helping teens to "negotiate the school system and the dating scene," and to develop such crucial life skills as "how to budget and go to fashion stores."

The numbers show how dismally the whole social service effort has flopped. While city and state spending to fight poverty in New York City totaled between $100 billion and $150 billion between 1970 and 1990, the city's poverty rate increased from 15 to 19 percent in the same period. In 1970, 15 percent of poor households in the city were single-parent families; in 1990, 25 percent. The dependency rate in the city—defined as the percentage of the total population receiving means-tested public assistance, medical assistance, or Supplemental Security Income—is 19 percent. In Brooklyn it is 22 percent, in Manhattan close to 30 percent, and in the Bronx 30 percent.

The city's vast array of "preventive" services hasn't prevented much. Despite widespread sex education and pregnancy-prevention programs, teen birthrates rose 15 percent between 1986 and 1989. Drug-abuse prevention programs notwithstanding, 62 percent of preschool children in foster care in 1991 were at risk of serious health problems because of prenatal drug exposure, more than double the rate in 1986. And countless violence prevention initiatives haven't made inner-city life more civil.

The cost of all this is mind-boggling. New York City spends over one-fifth of all local social service dollars *in the nation*. Local governments— cities and counties—spend an average of $6.74 on social services for every $1,000 of personal income within their jurisdictions; New York City spends nearly $40, though $11 of that pays for the New York City Medicaid contribution, a mandate on localities nearly unique to New York State. Largely because of its huge social service commitment, the city collected twice as much in taxes in 1992 per $1,000 of personal income as the national local government average and had a total budget that in 1994 was larger than 46 *state* budgets.

Profoundly undemocratic, New York's social service industry consumes billions of tax dollars but is largely unaccountable to taxpayers. No one even knows exactly how much, in total, government spends on social services in New York City. All existing estimates are incomplete, since they don't include the vast social service operations tucked away in a host of city agencies, from the Board of Education to the Health Department to the Parks Department. The city comptroller's Comprehensive Annual Financial Report for fiscal year 1994, for example, put social service spending at $8 billion, or 26 percent of the city's budget—the largest share of city spending. The Board of Education was the next-largest share, consuming $7.15 billion, or 25 percent of the budget—but that includes school-based social services and massive spending on special education. The comptroller's estimate of social service spending includes only four agencies and excludes state and federal Medicaid spending.

No budget anywhere in the city lays out every social service program and its costs. Though the nine-volume city budget breaks down costs in infinitesimal detail, it doesn't link them to recognizable programs. The comptroller's annual financial report, considered the city's most accessible budget document, divides agency spending into two vast, murky categories: personnel spending and "other than personnel spending." Again, it doesn't break down spending by particular programs.

At the state level, the budget consists of five separate documents, once again lacking complete programmatic analysis. "People have worked hard for many years to make sure the budget is difficult to understand," explains Tim Murphy, director of fiscal research in the state comptroller's office. "It means nothing to say that an agency spent $21 billion. The question is, on what?"

The best rough estimate of spending in the city is the state Department of Social Services total expenditures within the five boroughs—$19.5 billion in 1993. This represents the total federal, state, and city spending on the anti-poverty programs DSS administers—though it excludes spending by city agencies such as the Board of Education and the Department of Homeless Services.

On the basis of the 1993 DSS figures, one can make certain broad observations about the city's social service spending. The lion's share goes to Medicaid ($11.4 billion, of which the city contributed $2.2 billion), followed by welfare "income maintenance" programs ($2.7 million total; city share, $924 million). The city's almost unique jurisdictional structure explains part of this huge cost. Unlike most cities, New York has no county government to share the burden of local welfare spending. Moreover, New York State requires localities to pay a greater share of non-federal welfare spending than any other state. New York is one of only two states—the other is North Carolina—that require a full 50-50 split for the non-federal share of

AFDC. California, by contrast, picks up 90 percent of the non-federal share; New Jersey, 75 percent; 43 states require no local matching at all. Even fewer states require local matching of Medicaid spending.

The city has no direct control over most of its welfare spending, concentrated in programs for which Albany sets the benefit levels and eligibility criteria. Whenever the state increases spending, the city must pay. Rudolph Giuliani seems to be the first mayor to have understood this: he made history in 1995 by asking the state to *reduce* its welfare budget. The city's social service establishment, however, has considerable muscle in the State Legislature, which ultimately determines such matters.

But don't conclude that New York City bears little responsibility for the making of this vast municipal welfare state. Though recent mayors have chafed under the burden of state social service mandates, the city was an enthusiastic co-conspirator in the creation of the welfare establishment. During the New Deal, the city, regarding itself as more progressive than the state, seized control over new federally established welfare programs by volunteering to assume fiscal responsibility for them. Albany happily gave the city, much richer than the rest of the state, free rein in developing programs.

The other turning point came in 1966, the year John Lindsay was elected mayor. Lindsay came into office criticizing his predecessor, Robert Wagner, for his lukewarm embrace of the War on Poverty, which the new mayor, red-hot, had helped plan as a congressman. Convinced that social welfare programs would bring blacks and Puerto Ricans into the mainstream, Lindsay took the mandate in federal poverty initiatives for the "maximum feasible participation" of the poor quite literally. He devolved all authority for anti-poverty programs onto community groups, so that within a few years no one knew what programs or groups were out there or what their spiraling budgets were.

Just then, too, the welfare-rights movement, led by Frances Fox Piven and Richard Cloward of Columbia University, sought to sign up every eligible person for welfare, to hike grant levels sharply, and to remove "demeaning" conditions on the receipt of aid. In an influential 1966 article in *The Nation*, Piven and Cloward had advocated mass protest and the disruption of welfare offices as a means of forcing these changes. Welfare clients obediently stormed the city's welfare centers, terrifying workers.

In response, the city boosted welfare grants and made procedural changes that proved costly. No longer would social workers visit applicants at home to confirm eligibility; the system would be based on trust. Welfare-rights attorneys won the right to a hearing before the termination of welfare eligibility; the U.S. Supreme Court would later adopt the ruling.

The movement's impact on New York City was jolting: welfare caseloads, already climbing 12 percent a year in the early sixties, rose by 50 percent during Lindsay's first two years; spending doubled. By the end of Lind-say's first term, welfare costs had reached $1 billion; the new Medicaid pro-gram cost another $1 billion.

The welfare-rights movement failed in its ultimate goal of overwhelm-ing the welfare system and forcing a national guaranteed minimum income to take its place. But it succeeded in greatly weakening the stigma attached to welfare, in teaching the poor to view welfare as a right, and consequently in vastly increasing the rolls. The city had 150,000 welfare cases in 1960; a decade later it had 1.5 million.

The procedural changes of the 1960s, meanwhile, turned welfare into a check-writing system and took social workers out of the business of influenc-ing their clients' behavior. Ironically, that suited the once-radical welfare workers just fine. Though many had entered the profession in the 1960s out of sympathy for the poor, years of harassment had taken their toll. By 1970 the caseworkers "were thoroughly in terror of the clients: they didn't want to go near them," says Charles Morris, who became Lindsay's welfare chief in 1971.

For Lindsay, too, the bloom had come off the welfare clientele. By his second term, he "hated welfare recipients," says Morris. "He had done all these good things for them, and they had fucked him. My job was to cut them." The public, once almost universally pro-welfare in the 1960s, was growing wary as well; good intentions seemed to have created a monster. Even liberal Governor Nelson Rockefeller warned in 1971 that, without re-form, "the welfare system will eventually overload and break down our soci-ety."

Modest reform did come a few years later. In 1975, New York City—with the highest AFDC grant and the highest Medicaid costs per recipient in the country, the largest drug-addiction and methadone programs in the world—was bankrupt, and the state nearly so. Hugh Carey, the new gover-nor, introduced anti-fraud measures in welfare and started to reform Medi-caid. He slowed the rate of new program creation and kept spending growth below inflation.

But with the 1980s economic boom and the administration of Mario Cuomo, the growth of the welfare state barreled full-speed ahead once more. New initiatives rolled out of Albany, designed to capture ever more federal matching dollars. State government spending rose at twice the rate of infla-tion; welfare rolls increased 24.5 percent statewide during Cuomo's three terms. In the city the same spirit of profligacy reigned. "The attitude was," says former city human-resources chief William Grinker, " 'We have the money; let's spend it.' "

Today, with the city's fiscal condition parlous and its economic growth anemic, with the federal government shifting responsibility for welfare spending back to the states, Governor Pataki and Mayor Giuliani have wisely begun to challenge the welfare establishment. Both leaders stress personal accountability. Giuliani has implemented the nation's most comprehensive fraud detection program for Home Relief recipients, producing an astounding drop in the rolls. He is rigorously enforcing the work requirement for able-bodied recipients. Pataki has introduced commonsense regulations requiring homeless shelter clients to refrain from violence and drug use, as well as to contribute a portion of their welfare check to their rent. He has persuaded the Legislature to enact a fingerprinting requirement and more rigorous work demands for Home Relief recipients; he also won a measure to dock welfare mothers if their elementary school-age children are truant. But Assembly Democrats shot down Pataki's proposal for time limits on Home Relief. In December, Pataki announced a set of more dramatic reforms that would bring New York's AFDC payment into line with New Jersey's, impose a five-year lifetime limit on AFDC and Home Relief, and allow localities to test welfare recipients for drugs and to require those with positive results to participate in treatment as a precondition of receiving benefits.

The fate of Pataki's reforms in the Legislature is uncertain. But their passage is crucial, for New Jersey and Connecticut remain way ahead of New York in reform. New Jersey has implemented a "family cap," so that a client's AFDC grant doesn't go up when she has additional children; Connecticut has enacted strict time limits for AFDC as well as for Home Relief. These changes make New York's more generous system all the more attractive to would-be migrants.

New York needs to challenge foursquare the credo that has guided social work for too long: "Thou shalt not judge." Lacking any moral compass for determining who is most deserving of help, the city has, perversely, spent most on those who act the most destructively, because by definition they have the worst problems. The evolution in the city's day-care programs is a case in point. Fifteen years ago most parents using city day care worked, according to Rhonda Carlos-Smith of Child Care, Inc., an advocacy group. Now working parents are at the bottom of the priority list. At the top are parents who have abused or neglected their children. Between 1989 and 1994, the number of teen parents using day care increased by 94 percent, and the number of homeless families by 21 percent.

It's time for New York to junk the demonstrably false shibboleths of social services as well: the reflexive worship of "community care" or "family preservation." With no real community to go back to, no real family to preserve, community-based drug treatment, pregnancy prevention, family preservation, foster care, and juvenile rehabilitation can do little other than to enrich the coffers of the nonprofits. In an extraordinary development, some juvenile delinquents are now refusing probation and requesting incarceration upstate, recognizing that they need the structure provided by an institution and fearing the mayhem on the streets.

The city ought to restore the distinction between the deserving and undeserving poor. For the poor who do deserve and can benefit from help, especially children, the state and city should consider the use of boarding school–like institutions outside the city. But those who behave the most irresponsibly should no longer have the greatest claim on city revenues. And for the most part, the city should get out of the business of social uplift, which three decades' experience has proved is beyond the capacity of municipal government to accomplish.

—Winter 1996

HEATHER MAC DONALD
Welfare Reform Discoveries

IF THE ARCHITECTS of welfare reform ever harbor doubts about the future success of their plans, people like Lisa and Rhafel McElrath must haunt their dreams. Will the new federal law that makes welfare recipients work for their checks reverse the passivity and degradation the old system has entrenched over the last 30 years? It's much too soon to know. But couples like the McElraths suggest how monumental the task of reclamation will be.

Late last October, Rhafel, 33, fidgeted in the hallway of a New York City Parks Department building in East Harlem while Lisa received her orientation for the city's workfare program. Tall and well built, sporting a trendy Tommy Hilfiger Collection sweatshirt and a gold earring, Rhafel quickly changes the subject when I ask why Lisa, not he, will start working for the couple's welfare check tomorrow. Pressed further, he takes his stand on principle: "I'll have to like the job I'm doing. And I won't work for less than minimum wage."

Lisa and Rhafel are the end products of one of the more perverse schemes for social improvement designed by man. They live on Home Relief, a state- and city-funded program for able-bodied childless adults that is virtually identical in both its benefit levels and its destructive consequences to Aid to Families with Dependent Children (AFDC), the main federal welfare program. Devoid of personal initiative, they define their lives wholly by the welfare entitlements that surround them. Move to another state? Only if the welfare system there will support them. Look for work? Sorry, not compatible with their gypsy life in the city's homeless shelter system, which requires them to move every month. While in some respects easy, such an existence is by no means simple. They are at the mercy of faulty computers, incompetent bureaucrats, arbitrary rules, and periodic changes in their welfare case that they may or may not deserve but almost never comprehend. "I'm getting very sick of this," Rhafel petulantly says, as if he has no other choices.

As we wait for Lisa, Rhafel fills in some details of their lives. They consume just about every social service the city offers, from shelter to corrections. About six months ago, they were burned out of their apartment, in a fire that neighbors blame on Rhafel. Since then, they have been navigating the city's archipelago of homeless hotels while they wait for the magic day in November when they become eligible, as six-month veterans of the homeless system, for federal Section 8 housing vouchers.

The clean and orderly hotel where they now live on a tree-shaded block of West 22nd Street supplies them with soap, toilet paper, fresh linen, and a refrigerator; on-site social workers provide directions to food pantries and clothing giveaways. A manager of the hotel, a dapper African named Mr. Diop, expresses pessimism about the current welfare reforms: "I sit here five years and observe these people," he says. "They never should have put able-bodied people in this mess. At least the criminal lives for crime, but these people have lost all their motivation."

In fact, Rhafel is no stranger to crime, having been on Rikers Island three times for selling drugs. He admits he steals. His "wife" Lisa—they purport to be married, though they can't find their marriage license and the city does not recognize them as such—has been in jail, too.

Rhafel says he could find employment—albeit off the books—in a week. Relatively well-spoken and affable, he recounts that the longest he ever held a job, as a kitchen aide, was eight months; his last job, working as a low-paid messenger four years ago, lasted three days. "That job sucked," he says. "I told myself: 'This is not the way.'" Instead of looking for work, Rhafel intends to apply for his own food stamps. "Let them pay my rent," he asserts defiantly. "I'm going for every dime I can get out of them." He adds one caveat: "If they make you work, I'm not doing it."

Fortunately for Rhafel, Lisa doesn't take quite so principled a stand against working for welfare. Rhafel takes pride in his willingness to let Lisa be the breadwinner of the family. "She's the case head, and I don't want to touch that," he says. "She feels more comfortable that way. I try to make her happy, which is not an easy task."

Finally Lisa emerges from her workfare orientation, complaining loudly. Wearing a nose-ring, high-heeled leather boots, and an American Express T-shirt over an extremely full figure, she has only two remaining teeth protruding from her upper jaw. "I told them: 'I'm homeless; I can't be doing all this traveling,'" she sputters. Lisa insists that she has been assigned to a Brooklyn park, though her assignment clearly states that she will be working in lower Manhattan. This will be her fourth placement in the city's workfare program; she went AWOL from each of her previous assignments. The couple's explanation of why she quit her last placement lacks all connection with reality. "They took her computer away," says Rhafel. "I don't know why." The likelihood that Lisa, who claims to be learning disabled and is at the very least a challenged reader, was ever given a computer workfare assignment is zero. But people caught in the welfare system typically develop just such fanciful explanations for why things happen to them.

Twenty-eight now, Lisa has worked only once—14 years ago in a summer youth job. She doesn't get along well with people, she explains; also, she has hypertension and takes medication for a mental disorder. As we leave the Parks building and her partner disappears to do an errand, Lisa explains why she, not Rhafel, will be working tomorrow: "Because he's lazy," she says decisively. But why not make him head of the welfare case, so he has to do the workfare program? She taps her head meaningfully: "I may be slow, but I'm not stupid." Like many underclass women, she has opted for the security of welfare over the sure disaster of a shiftless man—a shiftlessness that the welfare ethic is at least partly responsible for perpetuating.

When Congress voted last July to abolish AFDC, it hoped to smash the dependency culture that defines Rhafel and Lisa McElrath's lives. It ended the entitlement status of federal welfare programs, meaning that the federal government will no longer guarantee assistance to everyone who meets its criteria for neediness. No provision struck greater fear and loathing into the hearts of poverty lobbyists, for they realized its potential to shift the ground of all social policy from a rights-based system of claims on government to one of mutual obligation: to get a government benefit, you now must do something in return. Equally abhorrent to the advocate bloc is the moral message of abolishing AFDC: you have no unconditional claim on your neighbors' support if you have an illegitimate child.

In lieu of automatic federal welfare payments, Congress created a system of block grants to the states. States will now determine who should receive aid and for how long, using the federal money to supplement their own programs. For now, state definitions of welfare eligibility aren't likely to change markedly, but over the long run states may decide that teen mothers, say, are not eligible for cash assistance, or may require them to live in group homes to get benefits.

Two aspects of the new law will have an immediate impact, however: its work requirements and time limits on federal aid.

The work requirement is hardly new in America. For two centuries before the activism of welfare-rights advocacy and the explosive growth of AFDC distorted the system, the able-bodied had to work in exchange for aid. The new law reinstates the requirement, penalizing states financially if they don't put a rising portion of their welfare recipients to work. The new law won't require welfare grantees to work right away; it allows a two-year period of idleness (which states may override) and gives states a six-year grace period until they have to put just half their caseload to work.

The most controversial aspect of the bill is its five-year lifetime limit on federal aid for any given family. An exemption of 20 percent of a state's caseload, a percentage roughly equal to the irremediably dysfunctional population, softens the federal limit, and states remain free to use their own money for support beyond the five years. Nevertheless, the time limit is crucial: today, across the entire national welfare caseload, the average cumulative length of stay is 13 years, with plenty of 15- and 20-year spells on the rolls. The time limit, more than anything else, should push states to move recipients aggressively toward independence.

The law will spark change on an unprecedented scale, but local welfare reform efforts make it possible to predict some likely results. The centerpiece of reform thus far has been workfare, and two places—New York City and the state of Wisconsin—have led the national effort to put welfare recipients to work. New York's is a largely untold story, while Wisconsin, which organizes workfare very differently, has become a symbol of aggressive reform. Taken together, both stories demonstrate the strengths and limitations of workfare. While putting people to work is a necessary prerequisite to rebuilding character, it only *begins* the moral reconstruction of the inner city.

New York City is the sleeper of welfare reform. Despite its well-earned reputation as the nation's dependency capital, it is actually making giant changes in its fossilized welfare culture. It is putting into practice key lessons learned 20 years ago in the aftermath of the welfare-rights revolution. Following the advocacy-inspired surge in the welfare rolls in the seventies, the state and city imposed stricter welfare eligibility tests and work requirements. Officials discovered that for every trivial hurdle put between a recipient and his welfare check, a very non-trivial portion of the caseload simply disappears. Pick up your welfare check in person? Too much trouble. In the late seventies, welfare commissioner Blanche Bernstein ordered individuals on Home Relief to participate in government-operated workfare. The refusal rate ranged from 21 percent to 40 percent, demonstrating that many welfare recipients already work and cannot be in two places at once.

These lessons were quickly suppressed, however, and by the nineties New York's welfare caseload had skyrocketed to well over a million individuals. Welfare advocates had long since regained control over local policy; Mayor David Dinkins's welfare commissioner, Barbara Sabol, engaged in what a former welfare official dubs "pizza policy making": invite all the advocates in at 6 PM, order pizza, and figure out what to do next to help poor people.

The Giuliani administration has reversed that approach. If welfare officials once seemed embarrassed to inquire too closely into a recipient's eligibility, the Giuliani administration, by contrast, has taken to heart Blanche Bernstein's admonition that "there is no reason to believe that the poor are less adept at manipulating welfare than the rich are at manipulating the income tax system." In 1995 the city began verifying eligibility with home visits and finger imaging: the rejection rate for Home Relief applicants tripled; for AFDC applicants, it doubled. From March 1995 (when the city began its eligibility reviews and workfare program) to November 1996, the rolls dropped from 1.16 million to 951,263—a decrease of 18 percent. If you look only at the Home Relief population, the initial target of reform, the results are even more dramatic: a drop of 35 percent in 20 months. The combined Home Relief and AFDC rolls are now dropping by 10,000 a month.

The centerpiece of the administration's welfare reform effort is its huge workfare program, called the Work Experience Program, or WEP. It is unique among the nation's current workfare experiments in its massive creation of public sector jobs: 35,000 welfare recipients, consisting of all new applicants and an increasing proportion of existing cases, the great majority on Home Relief, are currently sweeping the city's streets, cleaning its courthouses, and tending its parks. City Hall will have to increase that number to approximately 60,000 by 1997 to meet the requirements of the new federal welfare bill—a daunting task. One thing that immediately strikes a visitor to the city's WEP sites is that the program is not make-work. WEP workers are doing desperately needed maintenance tasks. They are cleaning jury rooms neglected for years, painting and repairing broken park furniture, and removing great swaths of graffiti. Street cleanliness ratings are setting records.

It has fallen to city employees to try to instill the work ethic in people who either have long since lost it or, like the McElraths, never had it. Reggie Washington, a WEP supervisor in Central Park, is just about ideal for that task. Small, round-faced, and wearing a diamond stud in one ear, he acquired his views on work and welfare from his feverishly disciplined Cuban mother and his travels abroad. "In Africa," he says, "if you don't work, you don't eat. These people here don't know how good they've got it." He cites the contents of the current welfare package—free phone installation, food stamps, a housing allowance, and Medicaid—in wonder. "I've got a guy who got out of prison after ten years, and now he's getting benefits," he muses incredulously.

One cold October morning, Washington herds a group of WEP workers into a green Parks Department van and rumbles off with them to Fifth Avenue and 60th Street. There the workers tumble out, seize their tools, and immediately start raking and bagging leaves and trash. The alacrity and efficiency with which they begin working is the fruit of three weeks of training. For many, this is their first socialization to work. "Sometimes I have to send people home for bad language or street habits," Washington says. "This is work; I'm not going to tolerate that." Workers sent home have to make up the time. WEP sites try to maintain strict lateness policies and to enforce a modest dress code as well. Workers with unexcused absences get cut from the program and may lose their grants for a period of time.

The crew itself is a key source of socialization. Washington recalls that one crew threatened to beat up a fellow worker who was so lazy that he was holding it back. The women on Washington's current crew recently had a "little talk" with an extraordinarily hostile fellow worker about her attitude — she had screamed at me, for example, that workfare was "indentured servitude." Now she has settled down and become a good worker.

For many welfare recipients, the demands of the WEP program, including simply getting to work on time, are impossible to meet. The attrition rate is high. Up to 50 percent of recipients never show up for their first WEP orientation; after that, many supervisors lose 10 to 15 percent of their workers every two weeks.

Malik Medora, a slight, pale 19-year-old with a few bristles on his chin, is one of those who didn't make it. Raised in Children's Village, a large foster home in Dobbs Ferry, Medora is a homeless orphan, his mother having died of drug use and his father of drug-related AIDS. He spent his teens in the Coxsackie detention center near the Catskills for robbery, burglary, assaulting a police officer, and resisting arrest. Most of his brothers and sisters ended up in jail as well. He is currently trying to assemble a wardrobe, in part by theft. The possibility of getting caught holds no terrors for him: "At least if I go to jail, I'll have three meals a day," he sighs during a break from his park WEP job. A ninth-grade dropout, Medora has been filling out job applications, but he has no address or phone number to give employers.

When I spoke to him in October, Medora expressed gratitude for the WEP program. "This is constructive," he said. "It gets me experience." Less than two weeks later, he went AWOL. When welfare advocates insist that the city should be investing huge additional sums in job training for welfare recipients, it is well to bear in mind that many of the trainees, like Medora, are so far from job-ready that the investment will go down the drain. Medora needs help, to be sure, but job training doesn't address his problems.

For those many other WEP workers ready for work—estimates range from a quarter to a third of the caseload—the program offers a small but real step into the job market. Supervisors quickly learn the work habits of their workers, and many go out of their way to provide some additional training, as well as job references, for the good workers. Omar Williams, a slender, remarkably polite 32-year-old, went from Reggie Washington's WEP crew to a maintenance job with the Central Park Conservancy. "It was a great experience," Williams says of the WEP program.

His enthusiasm is not an aberration. Many WEP workers appreciate the chance to do something useful. An older woman on Home Relief for the first time told me, "They shoulda done this long ago. It's a fair deal and valuable work. Some people sit there and do nothing and take advantage of the system." Some WEPs volunteer extra hours and take pride in their work, especially if they are stationed close to home and neighbors can see the results of their efforts.

Other WEP workers, however, seethe with indignation. Unlike other cities' workfare programs, WEP makes little attempt to place people according to their skills, and recipients with work histories often feel insulted by being asked to clean streets. The city should be finding them jobs, they say, not "exploiting" their labor.

Unfortunately, New York's welfare bureaucrats themselves sometimes disseminate the exploitation charge. I attended several WEP orientations that sent a decidedly mixed message, playing upon the resentment of recipients, even as the leaders stressed that the reforms are real. On the positive side, one director said: "They're not playing around this time. They're terminating people's grants." And many leaders also drive home the urgency of getting a job: "Take a minimum-wage job," exclaimed a vivacious young trainer named Alison Williams to incoming WEPs at the Department of Citywide Administrative Services. "If I were you, I would be flipping hamburgers so fast they would give me two spatulas." Yet the message to get a job is laced with resentment against the program. "The welfare system is using you," said Williams, questioning the legitimacy of the reforms and encouraging the hope that they can be repealed. "I hope you vote in November," Williams counseled. "We should've left Dinkins in office: we'd be okay." One life-skills trainer for the Department of Citywide Administrative Services directed me to an organization she has joined, the Welfare Reform Network, a coalition of left-wing Manhattan advocacy groups protesting and litigating against the reforms. Converting the bureaucracy to avoid such internal resistance is one of the biggest challenges of big-city welfare reform.

Thoughtful critics question whether workfare should take the form of a vast government jobs program. Many welfare experts, for instance, argue that large public employment programs like WEP are impossibly expensive. For the moment, though, New York makes a plausible case that the program is cost-effective. The city calculates that its net savings in fiscal 1995 were $175 million—the decreased benefit payouts minus the costs of administering WEP and the city's intensive eligibility screening. That figure is expected to rise to a whopping $250 million during the current fiscal year. Moreover, the city is gaining extra labor that would cost $600 million if performed by unionized workers. Though individual city agencies initially hesitated before accepting the WEP program, since they received no extra funding for operating it, they have now embraced the idea. For an additional several thousand dollars in salaries for supervisors, who come from the ranks of city workers, an agency gets a dozen or more workers, who individually may not be as reliable as regular employees but en masse constitute serious additional help.

Other critics cite the risk that government workfare jobs will become an entitlement, "just another form of welfare," in Wisconsin governor Tommy Thompson's phrase. People doing workfare, these critics say, can grow satisfied with their duties and feel little imperative to find private work. This charge has real bite. WEP supervisors already notice a tendency among good workers who enjoy their jobs to settle in for the long haul. The threat of time limits may, in the future, change that, but the city will also have to step up its nascent efforts to push people into the private sector.

If New York does increase its job placement efforts, according to another set of skeptics, it might well find that public sector workfare is dead-end work, offering no bridge to the private economy. How many employers are looking for street cleaners or snow shovelers? But this criticism misses the point. Specific job skills are not the issue; socialization and discipline are.

Given the vastness of New York's welfare population and the less-than-robust local economy, the public workfare program may be not only the best response to a very difficult situation but a unique opportunity to accomplish essential work that unionization and civil service rules have priced out of reach. Of course, a program of this size has widespread problems of implementation: faulty record keeping, arbitrary terminations, an inadequate number of supervisors, inept assignments—such as placing non-English-speakers in clerical jobs—and, in office jobs, a growing risk of worker over-saturation and make-work. A vaunted requirement that recipients look for jobs before starting their workfare assignments remains largely unenforced. These problems need quick solutions, before the administration expands WEP. And City Hall can expect growing political problems, especially from municipal unions. The city maintains that it is not using welfare workers as a substitute for city labor, but WEP workers already outnumber city workers two to one in some buildings, and as the WEP population grows, that assertion may be harder to maintain. An effort is under way, abetted by some city unions, to organize the WEPs and demand city jobs. But the WEP concept is a legitimate one, and it should be vigorously defended.

And what of the McElraths? I caught up with Lisa several weeks after her WEP orientation, wandering back into her homeless hotel. Rhafel had been arrested three nights previously for "hustling," Lisa said; she didn't explain further. Lisa's job assignment at Roosevelt Park had been short-lived. On the job, she stepped into a hole and hurt her leg. The city sent her by ambulance to Bellevue Hospital, even though she had walked back to the local Parks Department office after her injury. She has not been back to work since, despite a clean bill of health from her doctor. Her welfare case has now been closed, as she explained it, because Rhafel, who had applied for food stamps, had refused to work—an unlikely outcome, since their two welfare cases are independent of each other.

Lisa's muddled understanding of her muddled affairs is typical of people dependent on public assistance. They may be a lost generation. Though she told me that she enjoyed her WEP job and wants to return, the chances that she will stick to a WEP assignment and then find and keep a private sector job look slim. What will happen to the McElraths after the five-year time limit on welfare is anyone's guess, but both are able-bodied, and the notion that working taxpayers should support them indefinitely is no longer acceptable.

Half a continent away, Wisconsin, which welfare gurus laud as the foremost reform laboratory in the country, takes a diametrically opposite approach to workfare. No New York City–style public jobs program for it. Instead, Wisconsin puts welfare recipients to work in private and nonprofit sector jobs. Visitors stream into the state to see the system in action—to learn about Wisconsin's one-stop job centers, its diversion of applicants to non-welfare sources of support, and its so-called pay-for-performance model of workfare. Even the new federal law incorporates several of its reforms. Yet for all its successes, Wisconsin has had some disappointments, with serious implications for the adequacy of workfare as a tool of cultural renewal. And even the successes have only limited applicability to the inner-city populations that reformers worry about most, for they take place in rural areas where the scale of the welfare problem is minuscule compared with that of the South Bronx or Watts.

Wisconsin has been working at welfare reform longer than any other state. Between 1987, when Governor Tommy Thompson came into office vowing to stem the growing welfare crisis, and 1994, the state's caseload dropped 23 percent, more than double the nation's next largest decline. In some rural counties, the rolls dropped more than 70 percent over the seven years. However remarkable this may seem, it's important to remember that the state's robust economy, very different from New York's, made much of the reduction possible. Many Wisconsin counties have virtually no unemployment; companies are desperate for workers. But though the rolls surely would have dropped on their own, they wouldn't have dropped as far without the state's radical changes in policy.

The big idea at the heart of Wisconsin's reform is to get recipients off welfare fast—or, better yet, to dissuade applicants from coming on in the first place, a concept known as "diversion." Welfare department planners meet with an applicant before she even applies for assistance to analyze her budget, consider alternative sources of support—such as WIC, Medicaid, or soon, no-interest government loans—and to drive home the reality of the welfare work requirement. Equally important, applicants must spend 60 hours looking for work before seeing their first check.

In rural areas, this strategy has produced remarkable results. During a two-week period this October in Fond-du-Lac County, a dairy and light-manufacturing county in the middle of the state and the site of the state's most far-reaching welfare experiments to date, 16 people came into the county's welfare office to apply for support; only two ended up doing so, having been proselytized by the county's welfare workers to the new state religion of self-sufficiency. Much of Wisconsin's welfare bureaucracy is possessed by an almost holy zeal to move people into employment.

If diversion fails, Wisconsin immediately throws recipients into a flurry of activity designed to place them in jobs. If the pre-application job search has produced no offers, the client must enroll immediately in a daily program of job-readiness training, community service, or highly focused short-term job training. In Fond-du-Lac, for instance, the county provides two- to six-week courses in such skills as welding, printing, and nursing assistance. The smaller counties also provide customized service for the required work component: welfare workers phone local employers looking for an opening that matches a recipient's interests.

Wisconsin makes its job-readiness activities as job-like as possible with a "pay-for-performance" system. For every hour of unexcused absence from a job search program or a community service placement, a participant's check is docked $4.25. Result: in Fond-du-Lac, almost a third of the county's caseload opted to give up their welfare checks rather than participate in the intensely supervised job-readiness and workfare program. With predictable illogic, welfare advocates argue that this high rate of attrition shows that Wisconsin's reforms aren't working, as if the only acceptable reforms are those that keep people safely ensconced on the rolls.

Many welfare recipients, some of them migrants from large cities, are angry, too, about the reforms—just as angry as recipients in New York. I spoke with a middle-aged woman in the jobs center of Kenosha County, a reform showcase midway between Milwaukee and Chicago, who had been called in for quitting her telemarketing job after three days. "They make me sick—fuck them!" she spat out, after drawing heavily on a cigarette. "I do not understand why you would ask me to volunteer four hours a day and not pay me wages. It's slavery. I refuse!" The woman, a former postal worker who wouldn't say why she left her government job, is part of a large migration of inner-city Chicagoans who came to Wisconsin for its welfare benefits. Faced with the state's new workfare regime, many are now returning to Chicago. "They are trying to enforce work in Chicago," the woman explained, "but there's so many welfare recipients that it's hard to get them. It's still easier to find loopholes there."

In one of the most significant experiments for the new federal bill, two Wisconsin counties, Fond-du-Lac and Pierce, instituted a two-year time limit on welfare in January 1995. By October 1996, most Fond-du-Lac recipients were off the rolls, leaving only two people facing the mandatory cutoff in December. But after two years of getting the able-bodied off welfare, the county is left with a markedly changed clientele. More and more of those coming up to the mandatory cutoff in the months to come will be the truly dysfunctional. Some have mild mental illness or a low IQ; others, according to Roger Kowtz, a state project manager, "simply don't have a clue." When the county finds jobs for such individuals, they quickly get fired for absenteeism, tardiness, or recalcitrant behavior. While the 20 percent exemption from the federal five-year time limit, and the somewhat stricter exemption policy in Wisconsin's new round of statewide reforms, will soften considerably the limits' impact, the question of how to respond to the most dysfunctional segment of the population is one of the unanswered dilemmas of welfare reform.

Reporters who've trumpeted Wisconsin's welfare success have based their stories on places like Fond-du-Lac or Kenosha. These successes are real—but they are of limited relevance to the nation's urban areas. The numbers in Fond-du-Lac are microscopic: sure, the caseload fell by 64 percent between January 1994 and today, but in actual numbers it fell from a tiny 780 to an almost invisible 280. Moreover, the county's welfare population has a different character from inner-city populations. Fond-du-Lac has few people with no employment history and even fewer third-generation welfare recipients.

For a more realistic picture of the challenges of urban welfare reform, drive just 100 miles south of Fond-du-Lac to Milwaukee, the only industrial city in Wisconsin, where reform has had a much rockier course, one little reported in the national press. With a welfare population of 23,600—60 percent of the state's rolls—and an illegitimacy rate of 80 percent (the highest in the nation), Milwaukee has many of the same problems as Chicago, its neighbor on Lake Michigan, and New York.

Judging from the surface, you'd think Milwaukee's new programs are no different from those of Wisconsin's pioneering counties. Its four jobs centers are as clean and rationally organized as a corporate headquarters—blinking with computers, decorated in soothing mauves and pinks, and hung with cheerful cloth banners identifying the various services available to recipients. The contrast with the command center of New York City's WEP program— the battered, graffiti-bedecked Office of Employment Services—is heartbreaking. The centers offer a level of customer service unimaginable in New York: when a test-taker during a vocational assessment exam complained that the coffee was cold, the supervisor immediately called on his walkietalkie for a new thermos.

But beneath the trappings, the reality is quite different from Wisconsin's showcase counties. There, entire county administrations embrace reform and compete with one another to produce the most spectacular results. Milwaukee, by sharp contrast, suffers from fractious welfare politics. The city and county have fought Governor Thompson's reforms tooth and nail, arguing that they will increase child poverty. Local political leaders wouldn't take responsibility for the reforms, so state authorities cobbled together a consortium of 15 community service agencies to operate the new programs. Some agencies won inclusion not because of their experience or competence—which they sorely lacked—but because they lobbied successfully for a piece of the training and subsidy pie. The result is sometimes chaos. Employers find people whom they have never heard of showing up on their doorsteps expecting to work, claiming to have been referred by one of the community service agencies. Employers' calls to the agencies for assistance go unanswered. By comparison, the centralized approach of New York's workfare program looks like a model of efficiency.

Milwaukee avoids the problems of a big government jobs program, like New York's WEP, by putting workfare clients to work with nonprofit charitable organizations, such as soup kitchens or homeless shelters, or with the jobs centers themselves. But this solution has its own problems, as bad as or worse than those of a government jobs program. In contrast to WEP supervisors, some of Milwaukee's nonprofits cut absentee workfare workers an enormous amount of slack, not surprising from organizations that don't usually favor tough welfare reform. And private nonprofit workfare doesn't escape the make-work problem: welfare recipients empty the trash baskets in the county's jobs centers four times a day and mechanically clean the same windows over and over again.

As agents of welfare reform, Milwaukee's nonprofits range from the satisfactory to such woefully inept examples as the job-readiness class run by YWCA employee Oralann Caldwell in one of the city's huge jobs centers. Caldwell, a tall woman with long black hair, permed bangs, and an abundance of turquoise jewelry, is trying to teach the class how to call employers about possible job openings. "Youse can put this down," she announces, writing on the blackboard: "I am a very hard and consistant [sic] worker. I have very good people skills and highly motivated [sic]." Half of the girls in the room dutifully copy the phrases; the rest slump deeper in their chairs. "Or put this down," she suggests, writing: "My nam [sic] is ____. I am a highly motivated and consistant [sic] worker with fast learning skills." She is particularly proud of this one: it combines, she says, "two pitches in one." When members of the class compose and read aloud their own pitches, Caldwell makes them worse. One bright-looking young girl suggests: "I am bilingual." Caldwell's emendation: "I have bilingual qualities."

Mitchell Fromstein, chairman of Milwaukee-based Manpower, Inc., the nation's largest staffing or "temp" agency, heard this story without surprise. "It makes my stomach hurt," he responded. Fromstein has been a close observer of Milwaukee's welfare efforts, and the experience has left him pessimistic. Manpower has had a contract with the state to bring 5,000 job listings a month into the county's job center network, where welfare recipients and job seekers off the street can learn about them—this is full-employment Wisconsin, remember, where jobs go begging. Manpower did some assessments of welfare recipients' job readiness for its own information. Based on what it found, the company decided not to get further involved in Wisconsin's welfare reform effort. "I didn't want to be carried out in a stretcher," explains Fromstein.

Fromstein is an unusually authoritative judge of the challenges of welfare reform. His clients are just those businesses all welfare reform schemes expect to be the final destination of former welfare recipients. In addition, welfare reformers tout staffing agencies like Manpower as the magic solution to job placement for welfare clients, since such firms know the job market better than anyone else and have sophisticated assessment and training methods for placing people into jobs.

But what Fromstein says is troubling. "There is a big gap between the condition of the welfare population and job readiness," he concludes. Only about 40 percent of welfare recipients really want to work, he believes. Moreover, Manpower found severe limitations in welfare recipients' ability to think clearly. "Their cognitive skills are absent," says Fromstein. "Their schooling is limited, and they don't understand that at 9 AM the company opens and you've got to be there."

Fromstein's observations, echoed by employers across Milwaukee, point to a paradox of welfare reform: in itself, it is incapable of accomplishing its goals. Before welfare reform can succeed for a significant portion of the caseload, a far more basic revolution is necessary in the moral structure of families and communities. The cognitive deficiencies and lack of responsibility that Fromstein notes originate in miserable home environments and chaotic childhoods, years before an individual enters the workforce. No government or employer can change those conditions.

But in Milwaukee, a remarkable enterprise is meeting that challenge head-on, showing how to change a culture—as well as how much remains to be done. The program is part of no welfare reform plan, yet it cuts more directly to the core welfare problem than all of Wisconsin's official programs combined.

Deborah Darden, a velvet-voiced former welfare mother, is conducting an all-out campaign to restore traditional values to Milwaukee's troubled black community. Now the director of the Right Alternatives Family Service Center, a bare-bones day-care and adult education center in a north Milwaukee housing project, Darden conceived of her mission in the early nineties, when a group of friends began discussing how to respond to crime. Recalling what their grandparents had done differently to create stable families and communities, they drew up a list of 13 moral principles that once guided responsible adults. At the top was concern for children—and, above all, an awareness of adults' behavior in front of them. The discussion gave birth to Darden's Count Me In campaign. Members pledge to abide by the 13 principles and put a Count Me In decal in their window that signifies to the neighborhood: *If my child is raising hell, you can come to my house and tell me about it.* "People told us they were afraid to talk," explains Darden, "and kids were acting up because they knew no one would say anything."

Like the moralists of old, Darden aims to hold a mirror up to her community to show it its flaws. She has made public-service television announcements that skewer common destructive child-rearing practices. In one, a young girl in a silver lamé parka, full Tommy Hilfiger gear, and a bouffant hairdo, purrs at the camera: "My hair is always perfect, my nails are always done—I am divine, all of the time!" The camera pans down to two dirty children standing forlornly next to her, and the voice-over asks: "But what about your children?" In another ad, a woman screams at a child: "Your teacher tells me you've been swearing in class. Where'd you learn to speak that way?" The child answers in a very small voice: "From you, mommy."

The morally charged satire cuts even deeper in the powerful skits Darden stages at her day-care center. Part preacher, part dramaturge, she portrays the behavior that is tearing the ghetto apart—everything from drugs to child neglect, from promiscuity to illegitimacy. Her target: the lies people tell themselves to justify their complicity in illegal and antisocial behavior. Her usual audience (and supporting cast) is a single-mother support group that meets weekly at her Family Service Center. The skits confront the women, 85 percent of whom are on welfare, with the unacknowledged consequences of their own behavior.

Darden has an uncanny ear for hypocrisy and selfishness. At a weekly support group last Halloween, she started by standing in the middle of the room and whining self-righteously: "I have my needs. I'm frustrated! I took these kids to McDonald's; now these motherfuckers better leave me alone! I put a roof over they heads; that's enough." There ensued a discussion of what parents owe children. The women, ranging in age from barely 20 to middle-aged, spoke of leaving their children for days at a time when they used to take drugs, or of smoking marijuana around them.

The evening's main event was a skit called "Yo Money"—your money—with women from the group as supporting players. It begins as Darden puts on lipstick in front of a mirror—imaginary, like all the props. She hears a knock on her door. Two people are on the stoop, shuffling nervously. She opens the door, and they start feverishly pitching a $40 book of food stamps, as Darden looks on impassively. "How much are you selling them for?" she asks coolly. "Forty dollars," the girls stammer. "I don't have $40," Darden replies. "Here's $20." She hands them a white piece of paper with "YO MONEY" written across it in large letters. One of the girls grabs the paper; the other berates her for being such a pushover. Darden shuts the door, and the two girls take YO MONEY to a drug dealer and buy crack. They smoke their pipe voraciously, fighting over it, to roars of laughter from the audience.

After getting high, one girl asks, "Who TV is this?" The other answers, "Your sister's." "So what, does it have her name on it?" the first counters. In no time, they're back at Darden's door with the TV. "You don't have to come in," she says imperiously. They ask $100 for the set; she bargains them down to a much smaller sum, again paying with YO MONEY. The two crack-heads go back to the dealer and ask for some credit. He chastises them: "You know I never take credit, but you can give me some head"—an allusion to oral sex. That transaction presumably accomplished, the action returns to Darden's house, where a friend comes by and asks where she got the new TV set. "I'm not telling," Darden responds loftily. The two women settle down in front of the TV with a huge marijuana joint. "What is this?" Darden exclaims about the picture on the television. "Look at that—dope fiends! This is what makes our people look bad. I'm just embarrassed to be black." Meanwhile, the joint goes back and forth, and Darden announces in her silkiest voice, "But there's nothing wrong with taking a little hit."

At the end of the skit, a passerby compliments the crack dealer on his nice new car.

Darden then walks back to the center of the room. "Guess what we're talking about here," she asks the group. "'Yo money.' Guess where that woman [who sold Darden the food stamps] took it? The dealer." Then Darden starts mimicking the self-righteous TV watcher, who thinks she is above the lowly crack user. "But all I do is smoke a little weed; what's wrong with that? If I smoke weed, I look cool, my eyes close real sexy-like, I say interesting things," she whispers sultrily. The audience howls in appreciation. "But where'd I buy my dope from?" Darden responds in reproach. "Some drug man who made those other girls suck his penis." The ultra-cool, velvet voice comes back again: "But I'm not like them; I've got a degree!"

Then Darden takes up a favored ghetto complaint: "But it's the *white* man who's trafficking these drugs in the community," she pleads self-righteously. Again she responds: "But who distributes money to this pusher's hands? You did! How is he able to survive without my money? Forget who brings it in. Who keeps it going?"

Finally Darden stops the colloquy and drives home the moral: "If I said to my friends, 'I don't think you should buy those food stamps,' if a hundred doors said no, would food stamps have value in the community? We have to take a long look at what we're doing and what's going on here. If we didn't provide a market for stolen goods, they wouldn't be stealing. We are much more part of the problem than we're willing to acknowledge. It's not the drug addict's money that's keeping this going; it's because I wanted something quick and easy."

Then the stories start pouring in. One older woman says: "Deborah, you know how much I want a computer. The other day, a girl offered me a new computer with a printer for $30. But I kept thinking about 'Yo Money.' She was like: 'Are you crazy, girl? This has *everything!*'" A younger woman tells of being called at work by a friend who said: "You get over here real quick: they're selling $65 books of food stamps for $30." The speaker didn't go until after work. "The house was real nasty," she recalls. "You couldn't breathe, the place stunk so; the kids were dirty, running around—the woman was selling food stamps all day. I looked at those kids and just couldn't do it."

After each of these tales, Darden takes a Polaroid picture of the narrator and starts a big round of applause. Then a former addict says, "A friend of mine just bought a nice car for $30, with title deeds and everything, and I'll be honest: I really need a car, and if someone offers me one, I'm going to take it." Darden responds: "I respect your honesty, but my personal belief is, there's suffering involved with that car. I don't want to sound like a Goody Two-Shoes, because there was a time when I would've bought it. But our children are dying in the streets."

Before welfare reform can do much for that percentage of recipients unready to work, Darden's crusade needs many more adherents. The most telling statistic out of Wisconsin is this: even as the state's welfare rolls dropped precipitously, illegitimacy continued to climb. A perverse consequence of workfare, which exempts the mothers of children under a year old? Possibly. The head of the Manhattan Parks Department WEP program speculates that girls may be having lots of children now to get out of the work program, which exempts mothers with infants and toddlers. Indeed, the scariest words I heard out of Lisa McElrath's mouth were: "If I had a child, they wouldn't make me work." If we are to avoid repeating the errors of previous efforts at social betterment, people like Lisa McElrath must hear the imperative not just to work but also to behave responsibly.

—Winter 1997

HEATHER MAC DONALD

The Real Welfare Problem Is Illegitimacy

STANDING UNCERTAINLY in the middle of a lavish high school day-care center on Manhattan's Upper West Side is the future downfall of welfare reform. Eighteen-year-old Tamiesha has just dropped off her two-year-old and now watches impassively as the baby throws his bowl of Cheerios over his head. While a host of beaming day-care workers rush to clean up the child, Tamiesha, tall and so thin that her slacks hang from her hips in folds, distractedly pours a gold necklace from one hand to another. As usual, she has arrived late and is at that moment missing her second-period class, but no one seems in a hurry to get her on her way. The day-care director has tried to persuade her to come on time, without much of an impact. "I tell 'em I can't give them a 100 percent guarantee," Tamiesha explains. Tamiesha may not strike an observer as an overwhelmingly fit parent, but she has no intention of getting help from a husband. "I don't want to get married," she says emphatically. "My aunts 'n' stuff tell me what's going on, and it's, like, a hassle."

Unless girls like Tamiesha stop having babies, the 1996 federal welfare reform law will surely disappoint. The law unleashed a flurry of activity to get welfare recipients off the rolls; unfortunately, no one is watching the front door, where the next two generations of dependents are forming right now. Illegitimacy is the greatest cause of long-term poverty in this country; unless it comes down, the poverty rate won't, either. While some welfare mothers will thrive under the new welfare-to-work regime and will succeed in creating a stable home for their children, the majority will drift in and out of low-paid work for the rest of their lives, futilely seeking the grail of a permanent, "living-wage" job.

But the most pressing goal for welfare reform is ensuring the welfare of the children. While having an illegitimate child often dooms the mother to a life of poverty, illegitimacy may doom her child to far worse. Prisons, foster-care homes, and homeless shelters teem with fatherless children. Tamiesha's baby is three times more likely to fail at school, three times more likely to commit suicide, and from 20 to 33 times more likely to suffer child abuse than are the children of low-income married parents. His prospects in later life are just as grim: 70 percent of long-term prisoners, 60 percent of rapists, and 75 percent of adolescents charged with murder grew up without fathers. The risks to children living outside a two-parent home go beyond social failure, as witness New York City's never-ending cortege of tiny coffins containing children beaten, suffocated, and scalded by their mothers' boyfriends.

No urban reform could have a greater effect, if successful, than attacking the culture of single parenthood. Taking on the problem in New York City, however, requires great audacity. Not only does New York State have the sixth-highest incidence of illegitimate births in the nation—38 percent in 1995, just below such backwaters as Mississippi and Louisiana—but the city's official ideology has for decades treated single "parenting" as simply one "life-style" choice among many. What's more, social policy faces natural limits when confronting a problem as vast, complex, and personal as out-of-wedlock pregnancies.

Even so, the arena for action is large. New York's last mayoral term demonstrated the moral force that a strong leader in public office can generate. By speaking clearly about the obligations of people receiving public assistance, Mayor Giuliani shifted the ethic of welfare and made work part of the equation in New York. He should now set a national precedent and do the same for illegitimacy—the other, and much more important, part of the welfare equation. He should announce unequivocally that the most pressing issue affecting child welfare is the breakdown of the family. The persistently lagging well-being of the city's black children, he should point out—from low birth weight to school failure—is inextricably linked to the prevalence among blacks of teen pregnancies and illegitimate births. More social services, the mayor should emphasize, can never compensate for the absence of a father.

Such a message will amount to a declaration of war. Any political leader who dares to voice a preference for marriage over single "parenting" will face fierce opposition from the city's elites. Most perversely, the mayor can expect resistance from the city's child welfare advocates, who are determinedly agnostic regarding family structure. When asked if her organization takes a position on the two-parent family, Gail Nayowith, director of the Citizens Committee for Children, responded that family configuration "does not matter to us"—an astounding admission. She quickly added, "I shouldn't say it doesn't matter to us. We *will* say, you need a family"—not much of a concession, since the question is: what kind of family? Like virtually every advocate and service provider in the city, Nayowith apparently believes that government services are more important than a resident father: "When we talk about the family, [our goal] is to help them access services." Here, in a nutshell, is the ideology that New York's leaders must refute. To repeat: the city can offer "services" from here to eternity; they will never provide the crucial nurturing and support of two married parents.

Any defender of marriage can expect charges of racism and "classism." Emily Marks, head of the United Neighborhood Houses, a coalition of local settlement houses, accused me of bias against the poor when I asked if her organization was concerned about family breakdown. Then, displaying a favored debating tactic of the single-parent lobby, she established a precondition for marriage: "It all goes back to the job situation," she maintained. "Jobs are just not available."

This is doubly specious. First, plenty of poor people find jobs and marry. Second, Marks's reasoning presumes that children are an inevitability and marriage a mere add-on—when conditions permit. But if, as Marks claims, no jobs exist that would allow men to support a family, why are women having babies with them anyway? The question answers itself: because they expect the state to pick up the tab. Marks belongs to the right-to-have-a-baby school, which holds that regardless of the economic and emotional stability of the parents, a woman has a right to a baby at the government's expense. The question turns only on her rights, not the baby's fate.

It is this entire constellation of apologetics and destructive thinking that the city—in its role as a national model, if Mayor Giuliani chooses to assume it—will have to combat. City administrators should call in their social service contractors and ask them to fight vigorously the prevailing belief that unwed teens can raise babies, given the proper support. The city should also demand that the providers promote marriage for adults who want or have children. Those providers who put up an argument should be dropped. The city should also make sure that providers bring the concept of adoption out of deep freeze. From the moment an expectant single mother walks into a city health clinic, and above all if she is a teen, the nurses should make clear that she is embarking on a remarkably difficult path. City health workers should be required to discuss adoption as the most loving alternative for the child. Many illegitimate children will end up in foster care anyway, from which adoption is much harder to achieve.

Isn't it quixotic and self-destructive for the mayor to try to change attitudes so deeply ingrained and hotly defended as all these? Isn't he doomed to failure? In taking on this challenge, Mayor Giuliani can look not only to his own success in changing assumptions about welfare and work but also to the national campaign against smoking, which created a stigma practically out of thin air and virtually overnight. Today, no politician with a taste for media acclaim ignores teen smoking; yet if just one-quarter of the energy dedicated to that issue could successfully come to bear on illegitimacy, the public health benefits, not to mention the social benefits, would be vastly larger.

Accordingly, the mayor should have the city launch a media campaign, arguing that bearing a child out of wedlock is irresponsible and, for men, cowardly. Children need resident, married fathers, the advertisements should say; furthermore, the government will bring all the weight of the law against men who evade their parental obligations. The mayor should also call on church leaders, school principals, and youth leaders to join him in advocating marriage as the proper environment for raising children. Changes like this will take more than one mayoral term to achieve, but if Mayor Giuliani can begin to shift local attitudes, he will have won the hardest part of the battle.

But in addition to conducting a battle of ideas, the city should comb through its policies and eliminate all explicit or hidden encouragements for illegitimacy. To be blunt, rather than easing the way for single mothers, the city should restore the burden of having a child out of wedlock. Only in the last three decades did society facilitate illegitimacy, with predictable results. First to go should be the LYFE centers, as the high schools call their daycare centers. If there's any doubt that the centers have put an official stamp of approval on teen childbearing, just ask high school students what they think about them. A Brandeis ninth-grader, sauntering to class, summed up the prevailing attitude nicely: "Sure it's normal; schools are supposed to provide shit like that." Many of the nurseries are placed front and center; at Brandeis, the large, cheerful room is virtually the first classroom students encounter on entering the building. They are extravagantly funded at $10,000 a girl and boast lavish staffing ratios and employee perks. The obvious message is that the city considers teen parenthood a normal, highly valued part of school.

Like many of the city's social services, the LYFE centers embrace precisely the wrong values. Mothers don't have to feed or visit their children during their lunch hour (or at any time during the day, for that matter), so they can hang out with their friends. Such freedom, LYFE center advocates say, helps teen mothers preserve some of the "giddiness" of adolescence— just what a teen mother should lose as soon as possible. The LYFE workers don't even dare ask the mothers to stay after school for parenting classes, for that would infringe on their autonomy. Instead, some centers regularly pull the mothers out of class for parenting and group therapy sessions. But, after all, the ostensible purpose of the program is to help young mothers graduate by facilitating child-care arrangements; missing classes violates that purpose.

The LYFE centers are a corrosive presence in the schools. They should be closed. In their place, the city should open a school for pregnant teens and teen mothers in each borough and require all unwed teen mothers to attend. Those schools should insist on the highest standards of behavior for the mothers and include a mandated curriculum in child care, over and above the full academic curriculum.

Does such an arrangement "stigmatize" teen mothers, as advocates will immediately charge? Perhaps; and if it does, so much the better. By having a child out of wedlock, a girl has embarked on a course destructive both to herself and to her child. Society once understood this, and understood as well that attaching an onus to bad behavior was the best way to prevent it. (Stigma prevented illegitimacy from rising for the first three decades after the adoption of Aid to Families with Dependent Children.) But more important than the stigma, removing unwed teen mothers from their regular schools destroys the harmful fiction that they are still entitled to a carefree adolescence. Having decided to become mothers, they must become adults as quickly as possible.

The mayor should lobby the State Legislature for authority to withhold additional benefits from mothers who have more children while on welfare. In New Jersey the birthrate among welfare mothers has fallen more than 20 percent following the introduction of such a policy. As an alternative to cash payments for teen mothers, the mayor should issue a challenge to both the State Legislature and to the city's many philanthropists: let's build a public assistance system that actually ensures the well-being of children. Following the suggestion of *City Journal* editor Myron Magnet, the city should help create a pilot program requiring teen mothers on public assistance to live in group homes supervised by responsible adults (not by social workers imbued with the conventional don't-hold-the-poor-responsible attitude). The purpose of these group homes would be to give the children of children an upbringing that will allow them to break the cycle of poverty. They would, in other words, make good on the long-deferred promise of AFDC: that it protects children.

The homes' supervising adults would teach the teens how to be parents and provide them with the moral formation that may have been missing in the teens' own upbringing. They would strictly monitor the mothers' school attendance, homework, and alcohol and drug use. To learn household management and responsibility, the teens would help cook and clean. Again, the overriding point of such instruction is to teach the mothers how to provide cognitive and moral, as well as maternal, nurture for their children. The mayor should call on private donors to fund the experiment; the teens' government benefits could help defray the costs. The program should be rigorously evaluated. If the pilot succeeds in improving the welfare of teens' children and can be replicated cost-efficiently, it could be the best hope for breaking the perpetuation of the underclass.

The city should reward marriage, not illegitimacy. Each year, for instance, New York sets aside many thousands of public housing units and federal housing vouchers for homeless families, the vast majority of them, almost by definition, families without fathers. The city should give preference to married families in the distribution of public housing, explicitly articulating its reasons for doing so: that a home in which both parents have publicly committed themselves to each other and to their future children is the safest environment for children. So, too, with day care: many of the categories of applicants that now take priority for it, such as parents who have abused their children, teen mothers, and homeless families, are near stand-ins for single parents. Here, too, as in all its discretionary benefits for families, the city should give priority to married parents—and at the very least should not give preference to single parents.

It takes two to make a baby, yet the city has been lax in placing any responsibility on fathers. Fewer than 25 percent of the city's recipients of Temporary Assistance to Needy Families (TANF, previously AFDC) have child-support orders, in large part because many welfare mothers refuse to cooperate in establishing paternity, despite the law's requirement. Fewer than 5,000 have suffered any sanction for noncooperation. The city should step up enforcement of the cooperation requirement and institute an aggressive program to establish paternity in its hospitals. Elsewhere, such programs have had good results.

Once the city has established paternity and obtained a child-support order, it should enforce that obligation with the same zeal with which it enforces the welfare work requirements, for doing so strengthens the value that fathers, not the state, bear responsibility for their children. New York State has foolishly exempted low-income males from support obligations, as if poverty were an excuse for evading parental duties. Persuading the Assembly to remove the many roadblocks it has placed in the way of child-support enforcement is a distant hope. But the city should at least begin to make the case for encouraging responsible fatherhood. It should argue that if a father has little or no income, he should have to participate in the workfare program; if he is already in it, his hours should increase. If the mother is on welfare, she should have the option of requiring the father to perform her required workfare duties. Such a right would increase the mother's incentive to identify the father, and would give her greater bargaining power over him. If the unwed father is still a student, he should be banned from playing on his school's sports teams or from student leadership positions, as was the practice into the 1960s. In the schools, sex education should mean only one thing: etching indelibly into the teen brain that if you have a child out of wedlock, you will face extraordinary burdens, including having to pay years of child support. Kids should hear that sex is for adults, mature enough to accept its responsibilities.

Should the city decide to reward marriage instead of out-of-wedlock childbearing, it would reverse a local rule of social policy: the less responsible the individual, the more likely New York is to spend public dollars on him. Thus, the city funds programs for gay prostitutes with a drug habit, promiscuous mothers who beat their children, heroin-addicted shoplifters, female murderers, and teen thugs, among others. Reversing this indiscriminate social spending should be the mayor's next challenge, after removing the incentives to illegitimacy.

The undisputed beneficiaries of this largesse are the nonprofit social service agencies to which the government delegates its good intentions. The deal to date for the agencies has been: here's a problem; here's some taxpayer money; see what you can do. If, in the next fiscal cycle, the problem does not appear solved, the city will hand over more money. Officials rarely check to see what the agency actually accomplished. "It's easy money," confesses a youth-service provider in Brooklyn. The city Department for Youth and Community Development pays his agency one 20-minute visit a year—in the morning, when no programs are actually running—and writes a check for the next year.

As a result of this freewheeling generosity, the city's social service infrastructure is without parallel anywhere. State spending on social services accounts for twice the share of personal income as in the rest of the country, according to the Citizens Budget Commission. In 1994, the last year for which figures are available, New York City paid out $2.4 billion of local taxpayers' money for over 2,600 social service contracts—about the same as the city spent on the police and far exceeding the national norm. Including state and federal money would probably triple the total tab. A disproportionate amount of that sum went to executive salaries, far higher than the national median (and often even higher than the salaries of the city commissioners who oversee the agencies), according to a recent study by City Councilman Tom Ognibene. The city's nonprofits operate like fortresses, Ognibene observes, denying the public legally required access to their financial data. Their financial statements, he says, are so shoddy and incomplete that they would trigger an IRS audit in an instant if they came from the private sector.

Whole neighborhoods depend on the government money the nonprofits attract. Stand on the corner of Fulton and Nostrand Avenues in Brooklyn's Bedford-Stuyvesant section, and you stand in the principality of the decrepit Bedford-Stuyvesant Restoration Corporation, one of the Ford Foundation's opening salvos in the War on Poverty. This community development corporation rents out grossly overpriced, ramshackle office space to a host of government agencies and government-funded private agencies. Within a stone's throw, you can visit the Protestant Board of Guardians, Covenant House, the Brooklyn Bureau of Community Services, the Bedford-Stuyvesant Mental Health Center, and numerous small child-welfare and foster-care agencies. Walk a few blocks down Fulton Avenue, and you enter the principality of the Vannguard Urban Improvement Association, landlord to an equally large portfolio of government agencies and eponymous creation of social service kingpin Assemblyman Al Vann, chair of the Assembly's Committee on Children and Families from 1981 to 1992. Justifying his preference for social services rather than business development, Vann recently told *City Limits*: "The money needs to flow into our community. . . . We have to use the political power to impact on this economic system"—the same tired, anti-business, government-is-the-solution rhetoric that helped bring down a once-thriving borough.

It is impossible to exaggerate just how ineffectual the majority of the social service agencies are. Truly eye-opening are the results of a 1995 request from the city to contractors in four areas—HIV prevention, school health clinics, home care for the elderly, and Head Start—to set performance targets for themselves and to measure their success in meeting them. Many agencies found the concept of a measurable outcome baffling; others set goals so low and performed so poorly that they ought to have been ashamed to rebid for city funding.

The anti-HIV outreach group, Sub-Sahara AIDS Rescue, for example, serves 3,000 mostly male Africans in Brooklyn, many of whom live eight to a household and hire a communal prostitute for the weekends. The group's goal: to refer 200 customers during the year for services and counseling with other agencies. In the first quarter it had a grand total of five customers. After hustling in the next quarter, it referred 87 to unspecified "HIV services." (Of course, a referral to services is hardly a true performance target, since the question remains: what did the services accomplish, assuming the "client" even showed up?) Another HIV group, the Valley, serves 150 young people in Manhattan who are in trouble with the law and "who exhibit poor self-esteem." Its goal was to persuade 12 to accept HIV testing. After six months, five "customers" had been tested, a measly 4 percent of the sample. Project Return runs a "crisis intervention program" in Central Harlem to "engage" 3,000 black and Latina women who are drug users, prostitutes, or homeless. Its goal was to place 35 women in drug treatment—barely over 1 percent of the client base. Note well: completion of treatment was not an agency goal. After six months, 11 women had been placed. The agency did not disclose the outcome of those placements.

Just as ineffectual were the Head Start programs. The Children's Aid Society conducts "group discussions, brainstorming, and role playing" for welfare mothers in the Frederick Douglass housing projects. It planned that five of 20 women would "report a positive change in their coping skills," whatever that means. Only two did. Another program hoped that three of 23 Dominican single mothers would respond to questions in English and three would go back to school. Results? Nada.

However ludicrous, these efforts represent the most focused attention to outcomes that the city's service agencies have attempted in recent memory. Ordinarily, the agencies' accomplishments are even fuzzier. Part of the reason is that staff competence is often just a few steps ahead of their clients'. The youth leader in a Bed-Stuy family services agency, for example, can't write English. Her description of a teen "rap" group ran as follows: "LET'S TALK group will discuss issues that are of concern to young people, and there communities. All topics discussed expands their knowledge on current events topics. As will as help develop identity, and interact with other teenagers their age and of other ethnic background."

However high on good intentions, her after-school youth program appeared to the casual visitor extremely low on organization or standards. One day last October, four teens lolled in front of computers playing video games while a tall 18-year-old looked on. The 18-year-old admitted that he was unable to boot up a computer, though both the youth center and his school offer computer instruction. (Throughout the city, "computer instruction" seems to result primarily in video game proficiency.) The other 15 or so kids had not shown up. The radio was blaring pop music. Nothing else happened.

Fecklessness, however, is not the greatest flaw of the social service industry; moral agnosticism is. Most social service providers treat poverty exclusively as an economic condition rather than a moral one. Triple the welfare grant, or create more high-paying jobs, and voilà, we will have solved poverty. This is a gross, though seductive, lie. More than money, the long-term poor need values and self-discipline. They'll rarely get these tools for self-betterment from their city-funded social worker, however. I asked Deborah Rubian, preventive services director at Talbot Perkins, a private foster-care agency, if she talks about values with her clients—parents suspected of abusing or neglecting their children. Rubian was speechless. "I don't know how to answer. If [a parent] comes into the Administration for Children's Services [the city's child welfare watchdog], the system has already made a value judgment. ACS is a punitive system." Like most foster-care advocates, Rubian sees the potentially or actually abusing parent as no less a victim than the abused child. "People have to look at class issues," she retorted. "It's hard to have a discussion of morals unless you include class and gender." Rubian believes in sharing her identity-based apologetics with her clients: "When you give people information about class and gender, they eat it up." No wonder: for it means they can blame the system, rather than their own behavior, for their troubles.

The one value that the social service advocates hold dear? Self-esteem. Sister Mary Nerny runs a counseling program for women who have killed their abusive partners or who have allegedly been forced to commit a crime by those abusers. The program focuses on "practical concerns," except for what Sister Mary calls the "first value, really—how they value themselves." Murderers and felons might seem to need to learn how to value others, as well, but not in New York.

Given the reluctance of many nonprofits to teach personal responsibility, it is no surprise that some are on the warpath against the city's workfare program. Making people work for welfare benefits is "more like slave labor," says Sister Mary, speaking for many service providers on the city's payroll but opposed to its official policy.

New York's situation, then, is this: for all the billions that it spends on social services, it has literally no idea what it gains thereby. Some agencies may perform efficiently, but the city has few means of distinguishing the good from the bad. (To be fair, the city's own agencies are not necessarily more effective than its private, nonprofit contractors. I asked an employee in a clientless New York City Housing Authority job-training program what she did all day, and got the unapologetic response: "Nothing.") Many of those social programs bear the imprint of the advocates who fought for them: they seek to wring maximum benefits from government while making no demands on their clients. And though the city enjoys a budget surplus now, these expensive programs loom large in its multi-billion-dollar structural deficit.

Both financial and policy considerations argue for rethinking the city's social service efforts. City Hall should reevaluate all its programs according to the core values of individual responsibility and public accountability: bad behavior should never be rewarded, and the public interest, not some advocate's agenda, should govern how taxpayer dollars are spent. Then, the city should ruthlessly enforce performance goals.

In emphasizing individual responsibility, the city should establish a single principle of reciprocity throughout its benefit programs. Residents of homeless shelters should perform workfare, for example, and in the area of welfare, the city should begin strictly enforcing the school attendance rules for teen mothers. In all areas, the city should eradicate subsidies for irresponsibility. For example, the Administration for Children's Services should not be providing housecleaners, at a cost of $25.9 million in 1997, to mothers who beat or neglect their children. Though federal money helps pay for such services, the city should turn it down. Likewise, the city should stop paying for parenting classes for child abusers. It is not the government's role to try to reform such bad character; the burden should be on the parent, both financially and legally, to prove future fitness.

In addition to their moral dubiousness, court-ordered, city-subsidized parenting classes are unlikely to work. At the graduation ceremonies last October for a parenting class at Family Dynamics, a preventive services agency in Bedford-Stuyvesant, one-quarter of the "graduates" didn't show; another third were extremely late. A large-boned, broad woman with few teeth and wild dreadlocks was on her second tour through the parenting curriculum; many mothers make many more. Her first run-in with child welfare was around 1988, when she had two kids; in 1990, on her third child, she was charged with scalding and beating her children. Two more kids followed, and all five are now in foster care for neglect. Taxpayers should be free of her; but in one of the welfare system's greatest scandals, a recent New York State law says that, as long as a plan for reuniting parent and child exists, parents can keep getting their welfare checks, even while the children whose welfare is at issue are in foster care, at a hefty additional cost to the taxpayers.

The most powerful curb the mayor should put on the social service industry, however, is performance contracting. Only if an agency meets clearly defined goals should it get paid; it can wallow in class and gender injustice if it likes, but at its own expense. Yet the principle of performance contracting is easier to state than to implement. Since the social services industry has operated with so little accountability for so long, no one really knows what a reasonable goal in many fields is. In its own performance experiments, the city has mostly allowed nonprofits to define their own laughably low goals, or has used performance contracting only to reward agencies, not to penalize them. (One notable exception is the city's recent performance initiative for welfare-to-work job placement.) Clearly, getting 4 percent of a client population to take a desired action is not a good bargain by anyone's calculation. The city itself should establish more ambitious targets in its contracts and then make those targets the basis for compensation. Agency heads could use the "reasonable taxpayer" test for setting performance goals. Would the reasonable taxpayer, for example, be pleased with the existing 20 percent job-placement goal for welfare job clubs? Most likely not. If, after setting higher targets, the city finds that few agencies are eligible for contract renewal, so be it.

It may be that human services or charity work, faced with the difficult task of changing human motivation, has always had, and will always have, such a low success rate. In that case, a good argument exists for getting government out of the area entirely. Public officials have an obligation to use public funds for things that can actually be accomplished. If government does not have the tools to improve individual character, it should stop trying.

Where possible, the city should introduce competition into social services. In day care, for instance, the city should give mothers vouchers and let them choose their own provider—including, if they desire, a church- or synagogue-run nursery.

A final principle should govern the city's programmatic choices: fund opportunity for all, not rehabilitation for some. Faced with a choice between funding a sports or music program for children and drug treatment for addicts, the city should opt for the sports or music program, once integral parts of a child's formation. The drug addict made himself needy, whereas all children need education. America's great philanthropists and urban visionaries created enduring institutions that individuals could use for their own betterment—great libraries, museums, public parks, and universities. Cities are themselves such an institution; they squander their capital in catering to special-interest victim groups instead of the common good.

One program whose reform would send the right fiscal and policy messages loud and clear is the kinship foster-care program of the city's massively troubled foster-care system. Kinship foster care exemplifies just about everything that can go wrong with advocate-driven social services. No longer simply a means of protecting children, it has been fatally reconfigured as an anti-poverty program. Regular foster care places an abused or neglected child with an unrelated foster family, paid a monthly fee for the child's upkeep. In kinship foster care, the child moves in with a relative, who receives foster payments just as if she were unrelated to the child. Those payments happen to be many times higher than AFDC or TANF payments—in 1994, $547 a month for a 16-year-old child, compared with, say, the extra $37 that a child could bring into a welfare family of five.

The stated purpose of the program is to ease the child's difficulties by placing him within his own extended family. But note that the program keeps foster-care payments within the family as well. Economically, a single-parent family with three children on welfare is far better off with the children in foster care with their grandmother than it is with the children at home.

And these perverse economic incentives have taken over the program. Advocates see kinship foster care as a way to pump more government dollars into poor families. The child's well-being, as usual, takes second place. According to city officials, Legal Aid lawyers promote kinship foster care not as a temporary way station but in effect as a desirable, permanent status. Poverty attorneys counsel relatives who are willing to take their nephews or grandchildren for free to enter the more complicated, but far more lucrative, kinship foster-care program instead. By monetizing family obligation, kinship foster care is destroying the black extended family just as surely as welfare destroyed the nuclear family, former Human Resources Commissioner William Grinker has remarked.

Once a child is in kinship care, financial considerations keep him there, even though foster care is supposed to be as short-term as possible. In a current, sadly typical, case, the grandmother and drug-abusing mother live in the same building. The grandmother has her daughter's two children, for which she is getting $1,200 a month, plus clothing, medical, and transportation allowances. The grandmother lets her daughter visit her children at will and in all likelihood shares the kinship payments with her. Meanwhile, the drug-abusing mother has the right to receive her welfare check, even though her children no longer live in her home, because social workers have come up with a plan for the children's eventual reunification with her. If the grandmother either adopts the children or discharges them back to the mother's care—the ostensible goals of the foster-care system—the extended household loses an extra $14,400 a year in cash plus in-kind benefits. Not surprisingly, the grandmother is dragging her feet about discharging the children, and the mother has no incentive to get off drugs to get her children back. Moreover, though the grandmother may be a fine foster parent, the fact that she has raised a drug-abusing and child-neglecting daughter is reason for the city to presume her a suspect candidate for foster care until she proves otherwise.

Disgruntled city officials tell of families who have made kinship care into a cottage industry: the mother keeps having children, who, bundled with foster payments, go right to the grandmother. Private child-care workers complain that many kinship foster parents participate only for the money and are irresponsible caretakers. Indeed, a city-sponsored study revealed that only 58 percent of children in kinship homes attend school "nearly always."

Kinship foster care now drives the entire foster system. Kinship placements accounted for 72 percent of the dramatic rise in the foster caseload in the state (overwhelmingly concentrated in New York City) between 1986 and 1991, according to the Citizens Budget Commission. Kinship foster care also explains the enormous disparity in foster-care spending between New York State and the rest of the country—five times higher as a share of personal income.

The mayor should direct officials to end their current frantic search for relatives to nominate as kinship foster parents. Elsewhere in the state, county social service commissioners manage to keep children placed with relatives out of foster care, despite state law and regulations that promote kinship foster care. If a relative comes forward, the city should subject her to the same scrutiny as it would an unrelated foster parent. It should think carefully before certifying her, or anyone else, as a foster parent if she's on welfare, since the fact that she can't support her own children suggests that she may not be ready for more. The city should disqualify anyone investigated for abuse or neglect in the past. It should only place a child in a foster care relationship with a relative if the relative agrees to begin guardianship proceedings within a year. Ideally, the city would seek to change the rule requiring kinship-rate payments for relatives, thus removing the perverse financial incentives. Setting kinship foster rates at AFDC rates would also save $53 million a year.

The only thing we know for sure about New York City's vast social service effort is that it is a crippling burden on the local economy. Any other consequence—such as improving the lot of the poor—remains speculative. Given the certain negative effects of the city's disproportionate welfare spending and the uncertain positive effects, the burden henceforward should be on the advocates of any given program to prove its benefits. In the meantime, New York should return—and quickly—to its core function: providing opportunity for all through strong schools, a vibrant economy, and an efficient infrastructure.

As important as any specific reform, however, is the moral power of the mayoralty. For decades, New York's mayors have squandered that power with the tired plea: Washington, send money! Mayor Giuliani, however, has amassed enough political capital to try something radically new: speaking the truth about urban problems. If he were to speak honestly about illegitimacy, if he were to detail the ever-widening consequences of family breakdown, and if the city saw even a partial brake on the number of children born out of wedlock, Mayor Giuliani would leave an unparalleled legacy to the city and the country.

—Winter 1998

KAY S. HYMOWITZ

The Teen Mommy Track

FOURTEEN-YEAR-OLD TAISHA BROWN is thinking of having a baby. She doesn't say so directly, and it doesn't seem about to happen tomorrow, but she smiles coyly at the question. Around her way—a housing project in the South Bronx—lots of girls have babies. Her 16-year-old cousin just gave birth a few months ago, and she enjoys helping with the infant. "I love babies," the braided, long-legged youngster says sweetly. "They're so cute. My mother already told me, 'If you get pregnant, you won't have an abortion. You'll have the baby, and your grandmother and I will help out.'" What about school or making sure the baby has a father? "I want to be a lawyer . . . or maybe a teacher. Why do I need to worry about a father? My mother raised me and my sister just fine without one."

Taisha Brown seems likely to become one of the nearly half-million teenagers who give birth each year in the United States, a number that gives the nation the dubious honor of the highest teen birth rate in the developed world. About two-thirds of those girls are unmarried; many are poor. Americans debating welfare reform and the state of the family have no shortage of opinions about the cause of the problem: welfare dependency, low self-esteem, economic decline, ignorance about birth control—the list could go on and on. All these theories fail to explain the actual experiences of teenagers, because they ignore the psychology of adolescence, the differences between underclass and mainstream cultural norms, and the pivotal role of family structure in shaping young people's values and expectations.

To get a clearer focus on the teen pregnancy problem, I spoke with some 30 new or expectant young mothers and sometimes with their boyfriends, nurses, teachers, and social workers. (To protect their privacy, I've identified the teenagers with fictitious names.) I asked about their lives, their expectations, and their babies. The girls' stories vary widely: from a 15-year-old, forced to live in seven different foster homes over the last five years, whose sunken eyes hint of Blakean misery, to a 17-year-old college student who describes herself as "old-fashioned" and has been cheerfully dating the same boy for five years.

It gradually became clear that, however separated they may be by degrees of poverty and family disorder, these girls all live in a similar world: a culture—or subculture, to be precise—with its own values, beliefs, sexual mores, and, to a certain extent, its own economy. It is, by and large, a culture created and ruled by children, a never-never land almost completely abandoned by fathers and, in some sad cases, by mothers as well. But if such a culture is made possible by adult negligence, it is also enabled by mixed messages coming from parents, teachers, social workers, and the media—from mainstream society itself.

Sociologists sometimes use the term "life script" to refer to the sense individuals have of the timing and progression of the major events in their lives. At an early age, we internalize our life script as it is modeled for us by our family and community. The typical middle-class American script is familiar to most readers: childhood, a protracted period of adolescence and young adulthood required for training in a complex society, beginning of work, and, only then, marriage and childbearing. The assumption is not merely that young adults should be financially self-supporting before they have children. It is also that they must achieve a degree of maturity by putting the storms of adolescence well behind them before taking on the demanding responsibility of molding their own children's identity.

But for the minority teens I spoke with, isolated as they are from mainstream mores, this script is unrecognizable. With little adult involvement in young people's daily activities and decisions, their adolescence takes on a different form. It is less a stormy but necessary continuation of childhood—a time of emotional, social, and intellectual development—than a quasi-adulthood. The mainstream rites of maturity—college, first apartment, first serious job—hold little emotional meaning for these youngsters. Many of the girls I spoke with say they aspire to a career, but these ambitions do not appear to arise out of any deep need to place themselves in the world. Few dream of living on their own. And all view marriage as irrelevant, vestigial.

To these girls and young women, the only thing that symbolizes maturity is a baby. A pregnant 14-year-old may refer to herself as a "woman" and her boyfriend as her "husband." Someone who waits until 30 or even 25 to have her first child seems a little weird, like the spinster aunt of yesteryear. "I don't want to wait to have a baby until I'm old," one 17-year-old Latino boy told me. "At 30, I run around with him, I have a heart attack."

The teen mommy track has the tacit support of elders like Taisha's mother, many of whom themselves gave birth as teenagers. Even if they felt otherwise, the fact is that single mothers in the inner city don't expect to have much control over their kids, especially their sons, after age 13—on any matter. And, with few exceptions, the fathers of the kids I spoke with were at best a ghostly presence in their lives.

Commonly, mothers expect their older children to care for, and to socialize, younger siblings and cousins, a process that, as Ronald L. Taylor of the University of Connecticut speculates, disconnects children from adult control. Fifteen-year-old Rosie, now carrying a child of her own, describes how she had always taken care of her younger brothers, though their mother did not work outside the home. The youngsters started calling their sister "Mom" when she was nine. In a heart-rending example of this phenomenon, Leon Dash, in his book *When Children Want Children*, tells of a baby-sitting six-year-old girl hysterically trying to figure out how to mix formula for her infant brother.

Most adolescents are heartbreaking conformists, but kids with little parental supervision are especially vulnerable to their friends' definitions of status and style. As Greg Donaldson, author of *The Ville*, notes, the streets and projects of the inner city are dominated by kids; one sees few middle-aged or elderly adults. It's no wonder such children look to their peers from an early age for guidance and emotional sustenance. *Harper's* magazine quoted a pregnant 14-year-old, who had been taught about birth control, abortion, and the trials of single motherhood, and who captures the spirit of this teen world I saw so often: "All my friends have babies. I was beginning to wonder what was wrong with me that I didn't have one too."

In this never-never land, having a baby is a role-playing adventure. In the labor room, nurses say, younger teens sometimes suck their thumbs or grasp their favorite stuffed animal between contractions. The young mother's boyfriend, if he is still around, plays "husband"; the new baby is a doll that mothers love to dress up and take out for walks in shiny new strollers. In one high school program to discourage pregnancy, I was told, each girl had to carry around a five-pound bag of rice for a week, always keeping it in sight or paying someone to watch it. By the end of the week, several girls had dressed up their bags in clothes from Baby Gap. "It's like a fashion show," says one expectant 18-year-old. "At least for the first two years. Then they're not so cute anymore. After that, the kids are dressed like bums."

While the girls play mother, some of the lost boys of never-never land seek sexual adventure to test their early manhood. They often brag about their conquests, which they achieve with promises—sneakers, clothes, a ride in a nice car—and with flattery. "You know I love you, baby," they'll tell a girl. "You're so pretty." Fathering children is also a sign of manhood. A group of four disgruntled young Hispanic girls, strolling their babies down a shopping street in Brooklyn, say they have sworn off men forever and that they know of boys who get tattooed with their children's names like bombardiers tallying hits on the sides of their airplanes. Legend among these girls has it that the occasional adventurer surreptitiously punctures a condom to outwit his reluctant conquest.

But bravado, playacting, and fashion-consciousness are not the whole story, particularly for the older adolescents I met. For many of them, a baby stirs up a love they imagine will bring meaning to their drifting lives; it becomes an object of romance that beckons them away from the cynical, often brutal world in which they live. Frank, a 17-year-old African-American father, waxes joyful over his six-month-old daughter, who came as a sign that he must put away childish things. "Babies don't walk, they don't talk, but they get inside you so fast. Before she was born, I was a Casanova. I didn't even know who I was with. I was hanging out all the time, doing wild things. The baby slowed me down, put the brakes on things, and made me think about my future." According to University of Pennsylvania sociologist Elijah Anderson, some mothers actually want their teenage sons to have children in the hopes that they will settle down.

The early sexual activity of these unsupervised youngsters—it's not uncommon to hear of experienced 11- and 12-year-olds—is old news by now. Rape and abuse help fuel this precocity; some estimates claim more than 60 percent of teen mothers have been victims, with stepfathers or mothers' boyfriends often implicated. But early sex is also part of the accepted mores of teens on the underclass mommy track. Christie, a 16-year-old Latino whose tidy ponytail, shorts, white socks, and sneakers might lead one to look for a tennis racket rather than the month-old daughter she held in her arms, explained that she had her first sexual encounter two years earlier because she "was sick of being the only 14-year-old virgin around. I didn't really like the guy that much; 1 was just trying to get my friends off my back. When he started telling people, 'Oh, I had her,' I was really mad. I told everyone, 'No, I was using him.'"

Teenagers, as many can miserably recall from high school, rely on derisive name-calling to enforce conformity to their social codes. Inez, a tough, outspoken 20-year-old from a Washington Heights Dominican family, describes how her unconventional behavior was criticized in much the same way a black high achiever is accused of "acting white": "My sister and I are the only ones in my building who don't have babies. When I was younger, kids used to call me names. I never brought a boyfriend around, so they called me a lesbian. They told me I was conceited, that I thought I was better than everyone else, called me 'Miss Virgin.' I tried to stay off the streets." Elijah Anderson found that African-American boys reinforce the value of sex without emotional commitment by ridiculing those who look too enchanted as "househusbands" or "pussy whipped."

Marriage, as far as these kids are concerned, is gone, dead, an unword. Some observers, following William Julius Wilson, have suggested that this is because impoverished men with limited job prospects don't make likely husbands. But to listen to the kids themselves is to hear another theme—a mistrust of the opposite sex so profound that the ancient war between the sexes seems to have turned into Armageddon. Rap singers describe girls as "hos" (whores) or "bitches," but even some of the more modest individuals I spoke with see them as tricky Calypsos scheming to entrap boys—a view sometimes reinforced by a boy's own husbandless mother. The 35-year-old mother of an 18-year-old explains that she wants him "to have his fun. I don't care who he's sleeping with. I just don't want him to be trapped." For their part, girls see boys as either feckless braggarts and momma's boys or bossy intruders. "You're cursin' at me!" mocks Stephanie, an African-American from the Bronx, when I asked her if she thought of marrying her boyfriend of two years, father of a child due this summer. "Why would I want to have some man askin' me, 'Where you goin'? What you doin'?'"

Seventeen-year-old Roberto speaks woodenly throughout our conversation as he stands dutifully next to his expectant girlfriend, who is waiting to be seen by a nurse at Methodist Hospital in Brooklyn. But when I ask if he wants to get married, it is as if I have applied an electric shock. His eyebrows shoot upward and his mouth drops. "Married? Not until I'm 35 or 30 at least. You get married, the trouble starts. Marriage is a big commitment." But isn't a child an even bigger commitment? Evidently not. "A baby is from the heart. Marriage is a piece of paper, it's official. I'll be responsible for my child, make sure I support him and visit him, but marriage?" He shakes his head.

Stephanie plans to train to be an optician while leaving her child in the care of her mother—who, like many of these grandmothers still in their thirties, quickly shifted from anger over her daughter's pregnancy to delight over the imminent arrival of what she now calls "my baby." Like most of her sisters, when asked if she worries that a baby will get in the way of her plans, Stephanie answers emphatically, "No! Not at all!"

Nurses say they hear girls dreaming of "having their own budget" courtesy of welfare. But of all the new or expectant mothers I spoke with, only one shrugged when I asked if she had any thoughts about what kind of work she might do. About their economic futures, most girls seemed more unrealistic than demoralized or lazy. With no parents watching over them and cracking the educational whip, and with little intellectual drive or ability to organize their adolescent urges, their career notions seem hopelessly dreamy. Several said they wanted to be a lawyer or an obstetrician the way a four-year-old, asked what he wants to be when he grows up, answers he wants to be an astronaut.

Teenage dreaminess unchecked by adult common sense defines never-never land as much as conformity and bravado do. Lorraine Barton, a pediatric nurse at Methodist Hospital, describes a progression noted by many others in the field: "A lot of kids, and I mean boys and girls, are thrilled with having a baby. They love to dress them up and show them off; they like the baby carriages and all that stuff. But they don't seem to understand the baby will grow up. Around the time the baby begins to move around and be a separate person trying to go his own way, they lose interest. These are kids themselves, but they haven't had a chance to act like that. You can be sure they don't want to be chasing a toddler. It's also around this time that you see a lot of relationships end. The boys come around to visit, bring some Pampers, and later take the child for ice cream. But that's it." Even Frank, the chastened father of a six-month-old, says of his child: "I at least want to have a relationship with her. I want to know what's going on in her life." How could he envision anything more? He barely knows his own father.

The failure to understand the power of cultural norms over youngsters, especially norms that coincide so neatly with biological urges, has created a policy world that parallels but never quite touches the never-never land of underclass teenagers. Dwellers in the policy world seem unable to make the leap of sympathetic imagination needed to understand the mind-set of the underclass adolescent. Instead, they assume that everyone is born internally programmed to follow the middle-class life script. If you don't follow the mainstream script, it's not because you don't have it there inside you, but because something has gotten in your way and derailed you—poverty, say, or low self-esteem, or lack of instruction in some technique such as birth control.

According to this view, to say that teen pregnancy perpetuates poverty has it backwards. Instead, writes Katha Pollit in *The Nation*, "It would be closer to the truth to say that poverty causes early and unplanned childbearing. . . . Girls with bright futures—college, jobs, travel—have abortions. It's the girls who have nothing to postpone who become mothers." But evidence contradicts the notion that early childbearing is an automatic response to poverty and dim futures. After all, birth rates of women aged 15 to 19 reached their lowest point this century during the hard times of the Depression. And in the past 40 years, while the U.S. economy has risen and fallen, out-of-wedlock teen births have only gone in one direction—up, and steeply. Meanwhile, in rural states like Maine, Montana, and Idaho, the out-of-wedlock birthrate among African-Americans is low, not because there is less poverty but because traditional, mainstream norms hold sway.

A related but also flawed theory is that a lack of self-esteem caused by poverty and neglect is at the root of early pregnancy. But the responses of the girls I spoke with were characterized more by a naïve adolescent optimism than by a sad humility, depression, or hopelessness. Indeed, a study commissioned by the American Association of University Women found that the group with the highest self-esteem is African-American boys, followed closely by African-American girls.

Self-esteem has a different foundation in a subculture that, unlike elite culture, values motherhood over career achievement. To listen to some policy-makers, one might think that wanting to become a lawyer or anchor-woman—and possessing the requisite orderliness, discipline, foresight, and bourgeois willingness to delay gratification—are natural instincts rather than traits developed over time through adults' prodding and example. With little sympathetic understanding of the underclass teen heart, David Ellwood, an assistant secretary of health and human services, has written: "The over-whelming proportion of teenagers do not want children, and those who do simply cannot realize what they are in for. It is not rational to get pregnant at 17, no matter what the alternatives appear to be."

Ellwood's notion of rationality presupposes that a teenager is following the middle-class life script. This failure to understand the underclass teen's worldview leads him to embrace another deep-seated but mistaken theory: that unwed teen childbearing is the result of inadequate sex education. "Teenage pregnancy is a matter of information, contraception, and sexual activity, all of which might plausibly be changed," he writes. Most sex educa-tion curriculums, including those that "stress abstinence," rely on the same belief in a fundamentally rational teenager. They set out to train students in "decision making skills," "planning skills," or something mysteriously called "life skills." Explain the facts, detail the process, the bulb will go on, and the kids will get their condoms ready or just say no.

These approaches are not so much wrong as irrelevant, for they ignore the qualities of mind that are a prerequisite for developing complex skills. Christie told a story whose general outline I heard more than once. "I was on birth control pills. But then I slept at my cousin's house and missed a day. I took two pills the next day. I guess that happened a few times. The nurse had told me I had to take them every day, but I couldn't." Birth control, Christie unwittingly reminds us, requires organization, foresight, and self-control, often at precisely those moments when passions are most insistent. These are qualities that even adolescents from privileged backgrounds, much less those untutored in the ways of bourgeois self-denial, are often still in the process of developing. Something far deeper than simple ignorance or lack of techni-cal skill is at work here.

Governor Mario Cuomo took the fallacy of the underclass teenager with a bourgeois soul to its logical extreme when he remarked recently: "If you took a 15-year-old with a child, but put her in a clean apartment, got her a diploma, gave her the hope of a job . . . that would change everything." But it takes more than a governor's decree to transform an underclass 15-year-old into a middle-class adult. Many programs for teen mothers find it necessary to teach them not only how to interview for a job, but also how to shop for food, how to budget money, how to plan a menu, even how to brush their teeth. Programs like these point to the devilishly tricky problem of resolving the tension between the mainstream and underclass life scripts.

Moreover, instead of discouraging unwed teen pregnancy, such programs often end up smoothing it into an alternative life-style. If Taisha Brown does become pregnant, she will be able to leave her dull, impersonal school for a homey, nurturing middle school for pregnant girls like herself. Later, she will very likely find a high school with a nursery where she can stop by between classes and visit with her baby, attend parenting classes, receive advice about public assistance, and share experiences with other teen mothers in counseling groups. Kathleen Sylvester of the Progressive Policy Institute, who has visited such a school in Baltimore, says it is far nicer than ordinary public schools. "It's cheerful, warm; you get hugs and lots of attention." These programs have been introduced with the best of intentions—to ensure that teen mothers will continue their education. But because of them, it will seem to Taisha that the world around her fully endorses early motherhood.

Conservatives, most notably Charles Murray, see the roots of this normalization in Aid to Families with Dependent Children and other welfare subsidies that provide an economic incentive for illegitimacy. But even if welfare ignited the initial explosion of out-of-wedlock births in the 1960s, its role in shaping social norms today seems less vital. The Census Bureau reports that the number of children living with a never-married parent soared by more than 70 percent between 1983 and 1993. The birthrate among single women in professional and managerial jobs *tripled* during the same period. Increasingly America seems a land in which, as Mort Sahl has joked, the only people who want to get married are a few Catholic priests, and the only people who want to have babies are lawyers nearing menopause—and impoverished children. In a world so out of whack, welfare seems only a bit player.

All of the prevailing analyses of teen childbearing, both liberal and conservative, neglect a troubling truth apparent throughout most of human history: nothing could be more natural than a 16-year-old having a baby. But in complex societies such as our own, which require not just more schooling but what the great German sociologist Norbert Elias calls a longer "civilizing process," the 16-year-old, though physically mature, is considered an adolescent, a late-stage child, unready for parenthood. This quasi-childhood constitutes a fragile limbo between physical maturation and social or technical competence, between puberty and childbearing, one that requires careful ordering of insistent, awakening sexual urges. This century's gallery of juvenile delinquents, gangs, hippies, and teen parents should remind us of the difficulty of this project. Even now, social workers report seeing 14- and 15-

year-old wives from immigrant Albanian and Yugoslavian families coming to pregnancy clinics. The truth is that adolescent childbearing was commonplace even in the staid 1950s, when a quarter of all American women had babies before the age of 20, though of course almost always within wedlock.

But two related social changes occurred in the late 1960s: early marriage came under suspicion, and the sexual revolution caught fire. This meant that the strategies societies generally use to control the hormonal riot of adolescence—prohibiting sex entirely and encouraging marriage within a few years of puberty—both became less workable. The "shotgun wedding" became a thing of the past. As a result, American adolescence became longer, looser, more hazardous.

Adolescents at the bottom of the socioeconomic ladder were most harshly affected by these changes. Middle-class kids have more adult eyes watching over them during this precarious period. They also have numerous opportunities for sublimation—a useful Freudian term unfortunately banished along with its coiner from current intellectual fashion—of their urges: sports teams, church or temple groups, vacations, and camp, not to mention decent schools. Their poorer counterparts don't get that attention. It's much less likely that someone watches to see whom they're hanging out with or whether they've done their homework. Their teachers and counselors often don't even know their names. And "solutions" like contraceptive giveaways, decision-making-skill classes, and even abstinence training only ratify their precocious independence.

Far better would be programs that recognized and channeled the emotional demands of adolescence—intensive sports teams or drama groups, for instance, which simultaneously engage kids' affections and offer constructive, supervised outlets for their energies. According to some teachers who work closely with pregnant teens, births go up nine months after summer and Christmas vacation—further evidence of adolescents' profound need for structure and direction.

Given that unwed teen childbearing has become the norm for a significant subset of American society, the salient question is not why so many girls are having babies, but what prevents some of their peers from following this path. I explored that question with a group of five young black and Latino women in their twenties, all of whom had grown up in neighborhoods where the teen mommy track was common. All were college students or graduates acting as peer AIDS counselors for teens in poor areas of the city. None had children. All but one grew up with both parents; the other was the product of a strict Catholic education in Aruba. If the meeting hadn't been arranged by the New York City Department of Health, I might have suspected a family values agenda at work.

All of these young women said their parents, in addition to loving them, watched and prodded them. "My father used to come out on the street and call me inside," Jocelyn recalls, laughing. "It was so embarrassing, I just learned to get in there before he came out." Intact families seem to provide the emotional weight needed to ballast the increasingly compelling peer group. Clearly, two parents are vastly better than one at keeping the genie of adolescent pregnancy inside the bottle.

These experiences jibe with both common sense and research. Asians, who have strong families and the lowest divorce rate of any ethnic group (3 percent), also have the lowest teen pregnancy rate (6 percent). In a longitudinal study that may be the only one of its kind, sociologist Frank Furstenberg of the University of Pennsylvania periodically followed the children of teen mothers from birth in the 1960s to as old as 21 in 1987. His findings couldn't be more dramatic: kids with close relationships with a residential father or long-term stepfather simply did not follow the teenage mommy track. One out of four of the 253 mostly black Baltimoreans in the study had a baby before age 19. But not one who had a good relationship with a live-in father had a baby. A close relationship with a father not living at home did not help; indeed, those children were more likely to have a child before 19 than those with little or no contact with their fathers.

Some social critics, most forcefully Senator Daniel Patrick Moynihan, have insisted on the profound importance of fathers in the lives of adolescent boys. But for girls a father is just as central. Inez, one of the peer AIDS counselors, says she always bristled on hearing boys boast of their female acquaintances, "I can do her anytime," or, "I had her." Any woman who had grown up in a home with an affectionate and devoted father would be similarly disapproving. Having had a first-hand education of the heart, a girl is far less likely to be swayed by the first boy who attempts to snow her with the compliments she may never have heard from a man: "Baby, you look so good," or, "You know I love you."

The ways of love, it seems, must be learned, not from decision-making or abstinence classes, not from watching soap operas or, heaven forbid, from listening to rap music, but through the lived experience of loving and being loved. Judith S. Musick, a developmental psychologist with the Ounce of Prevention Fund, explains that through her relationship with her father, a girl "acquires her attitudes about men and, most importantly, about herself in relation to them." In other words, a girl growing up with a close father internalizes a sense of love, which sends up warning signals when a boy on the prowl begins to strut near her.

Further, a girl hesitates before replacing the attachment she has to her own father with a new love. I recently watched a girl of about 12 walking down the street with her parents. As she skipped along next to them, busily chattering, she held her father's hand and occasionally rested her head against his arm. The introduction of a serious boyfriend into this family romance is unlikely to come soon. Marian Wright Edelman's aphorism has received wide currency: "The best contraceptive is a real future." It would be more accurate to say, "The best contraceptive is a real father and mother."

If it is true that fatherless girls are far more likely to begin sex early, to fall under the sway of swaggering, unreliable men, to become teen parents, and quite simply to accept single parenthood as a norm, then we are faced with a gloomy prophecy: the teen mommy track is likely to become more crowded. Nationwide, 57 percent of black children are living with a never-married mother. In many inner-city schools, like those in Central Harlem where the rate of out-of-wedlock births is 85 percent, kids with two parents are oddballs, a status youngsters don't take kindly to. When Taisha Brown has her baby, that child may eventually repeat Taisha's question: "Why do I need to worry about a father? My mother raised me just fine without one." Indeed, it seems inevitable, without a transformation of the culture that gave birth to the teen mommy track.

—Autumn 1994

RITA KRAMER

In Foster Care, Children Come Last

WHEN POLICE FOUND four-year-old Shayna Bryant's body in March 1994, it was covered with blunt-force injuries, both old and new; some of her wounds may have been cigarette burns. She died, according to the New York City medical examiner, of "child abuse syndrome." Her parents, Orlando and Sherain Bryant, were indicted on murder charges.

Shayna died even though the city's Child Welfare Administration (CWA) had long before judged her to be at risk and had put her in a foster home when she tested positive for cocaine at birth. When she was one year old, her father petitioned successfully for custody, and at the time of her death, Shayna was living with—and apparently being brutalized by—both parents. Police said that when the girl misbehaved, her parents would make her choose between a beating and a day without food.

Sadder still, Shayna's story isn't an isolated instance. America's foster care system, originally set up to rescue endangered children, all too often returns them, sometimes over and over again, to abusive or neglectful parents. In New York City alone in the 12 months of 1992, 21 children were killed by a parent or mother's boyfriend *after* CWA had intervened.

The failures of the foster care system don't arise from any lack of resources. Nationwide, federal, state, and local agencies spend more than $10 billion a year caring for an estimated 460,000 children. New York City will spend an estimated $345 million in fiscal 1994 on its foster care caseload of some 50,000 children.

The problem isn't one of money but of purpose. The basic ideas that drive the foster care system have changed radically. Today, the "rights" of biological parents almost always trump their children's safety, and the "rights" of other blood relatives come before the child's interests. That's why urgently needed reform has to start by confronting the pivotal changes that have taken place in the way child welfare experts, policymakers, and social workers view foster care's mission.

The foundations of the foster care system were laid by studies in the 1930s and 1940s demonstrating that babies in orphanages failed to thrive. These infants, however well cared for by an efficient staff, seemed to take no interest in life. They languished physically and emotionally; some even died. What was missing, researchers showed, was an ongoing personal relationship with some particular nurturing adult. Child development experts concluded that it was time to end the "warehousing" of orphaned or abandoned children in institutions and instead place them with nurturing foster families.

By the 1960s, child welfare experts were finding that foster care had drawbacks of its own. Many foster care arrangements did not last—the children may have been hard to handle, or the foster parents' plans changed. Thus children were left in limbo, bounced from one foster home to another. The 1960s solution was the principle of "permanency planning," its goal to assure a stable home for every child. If a child could not be returned to his biological parents because the risk of abuse was high, their parental rights would be terminated so that the child could be legally adopted.

Ideology, racial politics, and societal prejudices, however, worked to undermine the concept of permanency planning. Most adoptive parents are white, while foster children are disproportionately black. Beginning in the early 1970s, the National Association of Black Social Workers objected vehemently to interracial adoption, labeling it "cultural genocide." Social workers, meanwhile, saw impoverished minority parents as victims of society; the stricture against "blaming the victim" militated against taking their children away. Further reinforcing resistance to adoption was society's general bias in favor of biological families—appropriate under normal circumstances but tragically misplaced in the case of parents who fracture the skulls or bones of six-month-old children; who have sexual intercourse with five-year-old daughters; who beat, burn, and starve their children.

Thus, over the course of the 1970s, permanency planning came to mean that a child's "stable home" should if at all possible be his biological parents'—or parent's—home. The federal Adoption Assistance and Child Welfare Act of 1980 formalized this outlook: it required state agencies to make "reasonable efforts" to avoid out-of-home placements and to reunite children with their biological parents as soon as possible.

New York City's policy toward "positive tox" babies—those born with cocaine or other drugs in their bloodstream—is an extreme example of this misguided approach. Until 1990, drug-addicted mothers automatically lost custody of their children at birth, on the assumption that addiction made them unfit parents. But since then, the city has followed a state directive allowing removal of such children only if there is proof of continued drug use *and* if social workers determine that the mother actually abuses or neglects the child. This policy means waiting for the worst to happen before rescuing the child.

To keep biological families together, child welfare agencies offer a variety of services designed to help them overcome crises. Family Preservation, as the effort is known, operates on the assumption that mothers or fathers who neglect or even torture their children will be redeemed by a class in parenting, some help with the rent, or a new refrigerator. Only after such measures have failed is a child eligible for adoption. Remarkably, officials measure the success of these efforts not by whether the child is safe and healthy but by whether out-of-home placement is avoided.

"It seems very naive to expect to correct a lifetime of disappointment, neglect, and dysfunction through a brief burst of social work attention and investment of resources," says Dr. Mark Simms of the American Academy of Pediatrics. Richard J. Gelles, director of the University of Rhode Island's Family Violence Research Program, points out that 30 to 50 percent of children killed by parents or caretakers perish after child welfare agencies have intervened and either left the children in their homes or returned them after a brief removal.

One of many such victims was a baby girl I'll call Darlene, born to a 15-year-old mother identified in official records as Jane Doe. At seven months, Darlene was brought to an emergency room with a double fracture of her left arm. A caseworker accepted Jane's explanation—that the child had accidentally fallen—and persuaded Jane, clearly a drug addict, to enter a rehabilitation program.

At her first session in the program, Jane admitted that she had caused Darlene's injury by angrily pushing over the child's stroller. The social worker saw the admission not as cause for alarm over the baby's safety but as "an encouraging first step toward rehabilitation" of the mother. Less than two weeks later, before Jane's second counseling session, Darlene arrived at the hospital again, this time suffering from a head injury. Her body was covered with old and new bruises, and Jane admitted that she had toppled Darlene's crib in a fit of rage at her persistent crying. The baby was pronounced dead on arrival.

Jane had three more children within the next five years. She physically abused all three, losing and regaining custody of each. When the children were finally removed for good, it was not because all three bore the marks of beatings, as was the case, but because Jane had been missing her drug rehabilitation sessions.

By returning children to abusive or neglectful parents—often more than once and with a succession of foster homes in between—the system not only subjects them to further danger but also deprives them of the permanent bonds that are crucial to psychological development. Consider the case of Errol, who entered a foster home at age two, after his third trip to the emergency room. CWA removed the boy from his mother's care when doctors found fresh welts and the scars of earlier blows inflicted, the mother said, by her live-in boyfriend. After a year in foster care, Errol had overcome his nightmares and his extreme shyness and was making up for lost time in developing both motor and social skills. At that point, he was returned to his mother's care: she had completed the prescribed number of counseling sessions.

Even when "preventive" efforts fail and parents lose custody of their children, social workers, guided by the same race-conscious ideology, still try to keep biological families together through the policy of kinship foster care. Both the 1980 federal Adoption Assistance and Child Welfare Act and the 1979 New York State Child Welfare Reform Act require caseworkers to consider relatives first among placement options for children needing foster care.

The number of such placements exploded with the crack epidemic of the mid-1980s. Before then, the illegal drug most commonly abused had been heroin, and its users were primarily male. The spread of crack among women sent the number of abused and neglected children soaring. Between 1985 and 1992, the number of children in foster care nationally jumped from an estimated 300,000 to some 460,000, with crack-exposed babies accounting for most of the increase. New York City's CWA saw its caseload triple. And by 1990, more than 22,000 New York City children were living in relatives' foster homes—almost as many as the 27,000 in traditional foster families.

The average biological mother of children in foster care is not the teenager, unable to cope with the responsibilities of parenthood, whom one might expect to find. More often, though she probably had her first child while a teenager, she is in her late twenties or thirties. The babies kept coming, along with the problems; the father or fathers left. As pressures mounted, she turned to drugs, and her behavior toward her children deteriorated. She might leave them unsupervised, neglect to feed or clean them, even beat or burn them. Family Preservation didn't work for her, so CWA turned to her relatives as the next option.

In a typical scenario, a harried caseworker arrives to find an unkempt and perhaps injured child in a roach-infested apartment, with the drugged mother and her current boyfriend about to be led away by police. If it is late in the evening, a placement cannot be arranged until the next day, so the child might have to spend the night in a makeshift cot in an agency office. Looking for an alternative, the caseworker will ask the mother if she knows of anyone with whom the child can be left. The response is often the name and address of her own mother, the child's grandmother.

By 1985, with the placement of children with relatives becoming commonplace in New York, the state established regulations for formally approving relatives' homes as part of the foster care system. But a 1986 lawsuit, *Eugene F. v. Gross*, established that, in emergencies, children must be placed with relatives immediately, without the usual investigation to assess whether those relatives could provide a suitable home. In 1989, the New York State Legislature made this no-questions-asked "emergency" policy the norm where relatives are concerned. Moreover, it required that child welfare agencies actively search for relatives to care for children who need foster care rather than place them with strangers.

But kinship foster care is often not in the best interests of a child. How can it be, if it automatically, unquestioningly places him in the same family that produced his abusive or neglectful parent? "Unless [relatives] are carefully selected, trained, and supervised, kinship care arrangements may expose children to potential risks similar to those from which they have been removed," says Dr. Simms of the American Academy of Pediatrics.

Though brochures from foster care agencies often picture smiling, middle-aged grandmothers with their arms around happy children, the reality is quite different, according to those who work within the system. "Some of these grandmothers are worn out, uneducated, and haven't a clue as to what the emotional needs of these at-risk children are," says a New York child welfare official. "For every grandmother doing a good job, there's probably another who shouldn't have these kids in her home, who fails to give them the stimulation they need to develop their minds. But the official policy is to place them with any relatives, as long as they're walking around and capable of changing a diaper." That policy may be said to be the Alice-in-Wonderland version of family values.

People tend to treat their children the way their parents treated them. An estimated one-third of parents whose children are in foster care were foster children themselves, evidence of an intergenerational cycle of dysfunctional families. Breaking that cycle requires rescuing children before they have been irreparably harmed, rather than leaving them in an abusive family until the worst has happened.

Not only is kinship foster care often bad for children; it is also an enormous boondoggle. Under the *Eugene F.* settlement, government payments for kinship foster parents are the same as for traditional foster parents—much higher than the welfare checks parents receive under Aid to Families with Dependent Children. Families, therefore, have a strong incentive to keep kids in kinship foster care, even if the children don't need it.

To illustrate the high costs of kinship foster care, consider the hypothetical case of a poor, single mother of three children, ages 4, 10, and 13, living in New York City. Under welfare, she would receive a $688 monthly check for their support. But if her sister took custody of the children under kinship foster care, the monthly payment would be $1,421, more than twice as high. The aunt would also receive a clothing allowance of $1,388 per year and could be reimbursed for the cost of new furniture for her nieces and nephews. (In addition, whichever woman has custody of the children would be eligible for a housing subsidy of about $300 a month and could apply for such means-tested benefits as Medicaid, food stamps, and school breakfasts.) The monthly foster-parent payment ranges from $401 per month for each child under five to $547 a month for children over 12. Those caring for "exceptional" children, those with severe mental or physical handicaps (including AIDS), get $1,332 per month. Other benefits for foster families include baby-sitting or child care, pediatric services, moving expenses, and a monthly diaper allowance of $47 for children three and under.

A private agency contracting with CWA to place children in kinship foster care issued a report that well illustrates the system's perverse incentives. "I don't have to plan for my kids," it quotes a parent saying. "They are with my family, and they are getting paid."

Particularly in New York City, inefficient, incompetent bureaucracies make misguided foster care policies even worse. CWA's social workers, in particular, are undertrained, underpaid, and overworked. Caseworkers come and go, sometimes even before they have gotten to know all of the children in their case files. Some caseworkers are responsible for as many as 30 children; the number recommended by the Child Welfare League of America is 17 to 20.

The background of the typical CWA caseworker? Consider: the starting salary is $25,000; the only requirements for employment are a bachelor's degree—in one case, a B.S. in agriculture from a third-world university—and a simple multiple-choice test. The test is graded on a curve, and a city regulation, designed to prevent discrimination, requires that CWA fill any position by hiring one of the top three scorers among available applicants. Sometimes this means the agency must hire the least unsuitable of three unqualified applicants instead of continuing the search. And city regulations make it next to impossible to discipline, remove, transfer, or suspend a worker.

The days when social work was one of the few professions open to educated women are long gone. Today, social work has become an entry-level job for many immigrants, some of whom have not mastered English, some of whom come from cultures that accept corporal punishment as routine and reportedly can be insensitive to signs of child abuse. After just three weeks of classroom instruction and three months of field training, new caseworkers must deal on their own with some of the city's most difficult families.

Necessarily, caseworkers are often out of their depth. I spoke to a CWA official on the day a *New York Newsday* headline about the Shayna Bryant case read: HOW THE BUREAUCRACY FAILED HER. "Why didn't they see it?" the official said, wearily repeating my question. "We expect these undertrained and overburdened caseworkers to make decisions doctors, lawyers, or psychologists are trained to make," she answered. "They can't recognize certain kinds of injuries." Few caseworkers stay in the job for very long. "They know they can go over to Probation and make $5,000 a year more right away, and they won't have to go out into scary neighborhoods at night," the official says.

The cumbersome bureaucracy that administers the foster care system is further paralyzed by federal and state regulations that require, one CWA staff member puts it, "a paper trail that is ludicrous." The number of people dealing with these requirements is vast, and the bureaucrats outnumber the frontline caseworkers. Family Court Judge Judith Sheindlin's voice drips with scorn as she describes what she sees every day in her courtroom: "The city pays for a CWA caseworker, three tiers of supervisors, and a lawyer in every child welfare proceeding. Additionally, when a private agency is involved in the case, it sends a caseworker, a supervisor, and a case manager — plus private counsel. Surely a few of the nine people present in court on a single petition could be spared."

A system whose failures jeopardize the lives of hundreds of children and the futures of thousands more cries out for reform. Children who are shifted from biological parents to foster parents and back, who see caseworkers come and go, readily fall prey to gang membership, violence, and criminal careers. Although no official statistics are available, experts familiar with the prison system say that an overwhelming number of prisoners have been through the foster care mill as children. Lacking the attachments in early life that form the basis for character and conscience, too many grow up with an abundance of rage, little empathy for others, and little sense of the consequences of their actions.

New York State has been experimenting with one approach aimed at reducing the length of time children stay in foster care. Instead of paying private agencies for the duration of a child's stay in a foster home, however long it may be, the state caps the amount it will pay for each child. The theory is that agencies will have an incentive to reduce the time a child spends in foster care and will more quickly return him to his biological parents or arrange for adoption. But this program makes no fundamental difference to the most pressing problem — children who remain too long with abusive or neglectful parents — since the focus is still on keeping the biological family together.

What would meaningful reform entail? Above all, child protection must replace family reunification as the guiding principle of child welfare policy. When children are found hungry, dirty, beaten, or sexually abused, they should be removed quickly. Those who would allow the equivalent of three strikes before terminating biological parents' rights ignore the fact that every strike leaves permanent scars on a child's mind and body. One serious incident of abuse ought to be enough to warrant termination of parental rights.

Kinship foster care should be strictly limited to those relatives who can demonstrate the capacity to provide a good home and who have a strong interest in the child rather than in a source of supplemental income. Adoption is the solution of choice for young children, because it provides them with a stable home and enables them to bond permanently with their new parents. The ties that bind are woven out of the myriad little transactions between infant and caregiver—the daily routine of feeding and cleaning, comforting and cuddling, talking and observing. Thus, adoption should be easier and should begin early enough in life so that a child can form these permanent attachments. Adoption is also a boon to taxpayers. Even though adoptive parents receive the same subsidy as foster parents, adoption cuts the cost almost in half because it entails far less administrative overhead.

Lawmakers should eliminate any rules that make race or ethnicity a criterion for adoption. The notion that interracial adoption is "cultural genocide" has deprived countless black children of the opportunity to be part of a permanent, caring family. Moreover, scientific studies have failed to demonstrate any significant difference in social or psychological outcomes for black children raised by black or white parents.

Senators Howard Metzenbaum of Ohio and Carol Moseley-Braun of Illinois have introduced legislation that would bar federally funded agencies from delaying or denying adoption solely on the basis of race. "Keeping a black child in a foster home because some black social worker doesn't believe it's right to cross the race barrier is horrendous," Metzenbaum says. "It means that the child [may go] from one home to another, without . . . a chance of ever having real parents." The bill was incorporated in the Senate version of the Minority Health Act, which, at this writing, awaits reconciliation with the House version.

For many older children, who are harder to adopt, institutions like boarding schools or group homes—vastly different today from Dickens's horrors—are the best option. "Instead of orphanages, call them long-term residential and educational placements," suggests Judge Bill Maddux of the Cook County, Illinois, juvenile court. "They allow you to take advantage of having a number of kids in one place to provide them with a real education. A kid realizes he's not the only one: there are others in the same boat. You remove him from the harmful community that caused his problems in the first place and let him grow up in an environment that can push a kid, give him confidence, move him forward, give him some spirit." Judge Maddux is well qualified to comment, having grown up in Nebraska's Boys Town.

These reforms would go a long way to reduce the costs of the foster care system. "What is needed is not more money but optimum utilization of what we have," says Judge Sheindlin of New York's Family Court. "Instead of trying to deal with 50,000 cases and doing it badly, why not eliminate the kind of ersatz foster care that goes on forever [kinship foster care] and concentrate on real foster care, limiting it to one year in a stable home and putting the savings into hiring better-trained caseworkers and paying them more?"

The financial costs, of course, pale to insignificance when compared with the system's heart-wrenching human cost. Sister Josephine Murphy, a social worker who administers Saint Ann's Infant and Maternity Home in Hyattsville, Maryland, tells of a seven-year-old boy with his back torn up by a beating with an electric cord. It took months to heal what he called his "mommy sores." A court order sent the boy back to his mother.

"Why do we leave children with mothers who can't or won't protect them?" Sister Josephine asks. "These children are orphans of the living, victims of the child slavery maintained by our legal system and our welfare departments." They desperately need a system that will put their interests first, that will find them a real family rather than condemn them to be further brutalized by their biological parents or turned into a subsidy for their relatives.

—*Autumn 1994*

MYRON MAGNET

Putting Children First: A New Direction for Welfare Reform

PRESIDENT CLINTON'S WELFARE REFORMS won't work, because they are the solution to the wrong problem. A workfare program, such as the president favors, only makes sense if you assume that welfare is fundamentally an employment problem of young women. Just get these women into the workforce, goes the reasoning, and that in itself will serve to make them independent. Their new independence will kindle in them the other qualities needed to make them good mothers and, even beyond that, good citizens.

Put aside for now the question of whether the means the president favors will achieve the employment goals he seeks—whether workfare as the Clintonites imagine it will ever get many hard-core welfare mothers into real jobs or will instead turn out to be a dismal progression of training programs of the preparing-to-write-résumé, preparing-to-go-to-a-job-interview variety, ending at last in a costly public jobs program whose clients will work as cynically and profitlessly as Moscow street sweepers under communism. The real point is this: the welfare problem isn't about employment. It isn't even about young women. It is, instead, about children and their welfare, realities ignored in the current welfare reform discussion. Listening to it, you can momentarily forget what an enormous price children often end up paying for the living their hard-core welfare mothers extract out of them. With the connivance of the system, many welfare children—when neglected, beaten, unimmunized, deprived of the moral and cognitive nurture that families normally provide small children—end up their parents' exploited victims.

Instead of solving the problem, the administration's outlined reform is the last gasp of a failed approach. Unintentionally, try as it may to cut through welfare's Gordian knot, it leaves intact the basic assumptions in which the current problem is enmeshed. Because it continues to subordinate the interests of children to the supposed economic interests of their mothers, it won't stop welfare from being a way of life. The trickle-down theory of nurture at its heart—the assumption that once the mothers are drawn into employment the children's welfare is assured—won't solve welfare's central ill: that it helps perpetuate an almost hereditary underclass of individuals whose childhood in fatherless families, nurtured by women too young and unprepared to be good mothers, so often dooms them to unfulfilled, unsuccessful lives.

The right way to reform welfare is not to tinker at the edges of an exhausted paradigm that created the problem in the first place. Reformers need to rethink the issue anew, outside the confines of the old orthodoxy.

That orthodoxy came into being in the 1960s, as part of a reformulation of the nation's most basic beliefs and values that it is only a slight exaggeration to think of as a cultural revolution. The reformulation took place in the name of two related liberations. First was a political liberation: a crusading effort to complete American democracy, to free the excluded Have-Nots, the poor and black, from marginalization. Out of that honorable impulse came developments ranging from the great 1964 Civil Rights Act to multicultural education to the National Welfare Rights Organization.

The second liberation was a personal one: an effort on the part of the Haves—by which I mean not the rich but the mainstream, the established—to achieve an inner deliverance from a sense of anxious, deadening conformity as organization men in gray flannel suits into a freer, more authentic, more spontaneous, more life-affirming, happier selfhood. Out of that impulse to escape from—or at least loosen—the limits of bourgeois discipline and morality came the sexual revolution and the counterculture.

Though these changes in the culture began with an elite, they rapidly diffused themselves into the college-going, newspaper-reading, TV-watching, popular-music-listening, church-attending portions of the population at large, as the explosion in the U.S. divorce rate beginning in the 1960s attests, to take only one example of how the new norms revolutionized behavior. Now the new norms radiate out from the most trivial expressions of our culture—from almost any perfume or underwear ad or popular song, for instance—as well as from the more official expressions, such as almost any federal social policy or almost any editorial in the *New York Times*.

Unfortunately for the worst-off, too many of the messages that came to them from the new culture only served to bind them more firmly to their poverty and marginality. The new culture devalued all the things you have to do to get out of poverty, like hard work at *any* job, and glamorized things that keep the poor poor and the marginal marginal, like careless promiscuity and "recreational" drug use. In the realm of public policy, it transformed the institutions—welfare prominent among them—that help shape the lives of the poor, so that they ended up degrading rather than uplifting the people they were intended to benefit.

And because of the moral fervor with which the new ideas are invested—because these ideas give many of the Haves, especially among the elite, their sense of moral worth, uniqueness, and justification—it has become too painful to admit what abysmal harm they inflict on the Have-Nots. So, even as the underclass became rooted and grew and deepened in degradation, the answer the new culture has given has been further doses of what was causing the problem in the first place, like pumping more gas into a flooded engine.

Both liberations, the personal and the political, worked together to produce the explosion of welfare dependency that took place in the mid 1960s. Indeed, the power of culture—the power of the new beliefs and values that have hardened into today's orthodoxy—was so great that it overcame the economic and racial currents that were flowing strongly in precisely the opposite direction. After all, this explosion of dependency, which was disproportionate among blacks, was something that a booming economy and falling unemployment rate, along with the opening of society by the 1964 Civil Rights Act, should have forestalled. But just at that moment, culture changed.

For one thing, mainstream culture began to be intoxicated with its own sexual liberation—premarital, extramarital, you name it. If marriages broke up, as increasingly they did, that was okay, because individual, personal fulfillment was more important than family stability. As for the kids—we were telling ourselves that as long as we were happy, they'd be happy; they were resilient, adaptable; they'd do just fine in any kind of family structure.

We could hardly turn to the poor and say, okay, fellas, all this is fine for us, but not for you—*you* have to cleave to the straight and narrow. So we destigmatized for everybody much sexual behavior that formerly had been kept in check by strong social disapproval. In the case of the poor, in particular, we destigmatized getting pregnant out of wedlock, even for 15-year-olds, even for 13-year-olds. Indeed, the distinction between the respectable and the scandalous lost much of its power to govern behavior when so many stopped respecting respectability and stigmatizing its opposite.

When it came to making social policy, the same new ideas prevailed. We saw no problem with lumping mothers of legitimate and illegitimate children together and giving an income to the latter with no questions asked. We saw no problem with abetting the proliferation of single-parent families, which the then-prevailing ideology said were just as good as any other kind. Today, of course, we have mountains of data proving conclusively that intact two-parent families are far and away best for children in every respect—emotionally, educationally, and in terms of later success in work and marriage.

Similarly, new beliefs from the political part of the 1960s' cultural shift contributed at least as much to the making of the welfare explosion as to most other features of the underclass. Take the key belief that the poor are, by the mere fact of their poverty, victims. Economic change has swept away their means of livelihood, goes this idea. Poverty gets inside them, filling them with feelings of futility and making them unable to take advantage of the real opportunities proliferating for the rest of society. These feelings, according to our new beliefs, lead them to self-destructive behavior and can only be changed by changing the economic circumstances.

Of course, telling the poor they are powerless victims of vast forces over which they have no control relieves them of the sense of personal responsibility and freedom we all need to summon the energy and initiative to change our fate. Further, when you tell people they are victims, the implication is that they've been damaged, that they're defective, unable to compete in the same ballpark with the rest of us. This implicit message (often an implicitly racist message, in my view) can only intensify the anxiety of those at the bottom and can make a life on welfare—or on drugs or drink, or of dropping out or crime—look like all they're capable of achieving.

That message is certainly contained in another baleful new idea of the political part of the cultural revolution: the idea that the victimized poor need reparations. In America, given its history, cockeyed Marxoid ideas of economic victimization got mixed up in the 1960s with an appropriate horror at the historical victimization of blacks to produce the belief that the state had to compensate the poor—and especially poor blacks—for their plight. That compensation, as Michael Harrington (among others) pronounced more than three decades ago, was welfare. In Harrington's phrase, we give it not out of charity but justice. With that formulation, another stigma against accepting welfare fell. It became no more than the recipient's due. Any shame attaches not to the welfare client but to the mainstream society that victimizes her.

But look at one key confusion embedded in this rationale. The reasoning here is fundamentally economic, energized with a powerful charge of race: people who are unjustly, through no fault of their own, closed out of an economy that allows their neighbors to prosper deserve their neighbors' support. One can certainly disagree with the factual underpinnings of this notion by pointing to the almost 40 million net new jobs created in the last quarter-century, many of them unskilled or low-skill, and many of them taken by millions of immigrants who have realized the American dream out of some of the humblest of those jobs. Nevertheless, disagree or not, one expects that the welfare system produced by such a rationale will be more or less similar to the dole as it exists in other Western industrial countries.

It isn't. What makes the American welfare system unique is that the economic rationale for the dole was used to expand an existing New Deal program aimed at protecting not the unemployed, but children. Eligibility for the principal American welfare program, Aid to Families with Dependent Children, doesn't hinge on simple lack of employment. Instead, it depends above all on having a child, along with no job and (usually) no husband, since the original Depression-era program was aimed primarily at children whose coal-miner fathers had died. In fact, as the focus of the program shifted away from the children, the original name of Aid to Dependent Children changed to Aid to Families with Dependent Children in 1962.

The requirement that you have to have a baby and, normally, no husband to be eligible is what has made the U.S. welfare system so destructive. It makes the next generation an inseparable term of the welfare equation. This isn't to say that the dole in Europe has been benign for society or the economy. But even though other countries have had an entrenched welfare population for longer than the United States, they haven't had anything like our social pathology until recently. That's partly because only recently have some welfare benefits, such as priority for public housing, become linked to having a child. Even more, it's because welfare's economic package, by itself, is not enough to produce the social pathology of an underclass.

For that, it takes cultural changes like those that have taken place in America over the last generation. Only now that the stigma against illegitimacy has fallen in England, for example, or that English judges and probation officers have begun to look at criminals as victims needing leniency, has England begun to show the explosions in illegitimacy and brutal crime that Americans first saw 30 years ago.

Once the new American culture destigmatized illegitimacy and presented asking your neighbors to support your illegitimate children as a right instead of a scandal, it transformed welfare into a machine for perpetuating an underclass by abetting the least competent women—those who have developed the least initiative and formed the weakest values—in becoming the mothers of the next generation. Fathers, especially crucial to the socialization of boys, are crossed out of the family equation altogether, so the families welfare encourages are weaker still. If you set out to design the most defective families you could imagine, you'd be hard-pressed to surpass this system.

This is the crux of the welfare problem: welfare's intergenerational transmission of a culture of failure. Anyone who looks at underclass children, with so deplorable a legacy of poor health, emotional and intellectual stunting, and failure in school and in later life, would have to ask whose welfare is advanced by a welfare system that proliferates such dysfunctional families—families that pass along the underclass state of mind and way of life from generation to generation. If welfare were producing sturdy children who grew up to have useful and fulfilling lives, the fact that several million able-bodied women were being supported by their hardworking neighbors while they raised kids would be, however uncomfortable, infinitely less problematic. You could argue that a rich society could afford this price of giving children the upbringing they need to succeed. But when the very mechanism designed to further the welfare of children puts it so at risk that the children regularly grow up doomed to fail, that's not tolerable.

To succeed in changing this malign system, welfare reform has to start by redefining the issue, shifting the focus from mothers to children. Welfare is not an unemployment benefit for "victims of society," as we often unreflectingly assume. It isn't designed to help adults but to protect children. That's why it isn't paid to all possible "victims of society" but only to households with children.

The real issue is: Can welfare be said to protect children adequately, when so many of its beneficiaries are so poorly cared for and, in consequence, grow up to be such dysfunctional adults? Isn't there something mad about a system that helps create the very condition it is designed to assuage—that in the name of relieving childhood misery calls forth ever more of it by enabling unmarried, often teenage, women who have no idea how to support or nurture or train children to bear and bring them up nevertheless? No wonder such a large percentage of American kids are classified as being in poverty: these are the children. Wouldn't the best way for American society to solve the problems of the underclass be to stop encouraging it to reproduce itself generation after generation?

Anyone who makes such a suggestion must confront head-on this specter haunting the Haves: that significant welfare reform will fill the streets with starving, homeless children. The answer is for welfare reform to create a system dedicated to nothing other than the welfare of children.

The bedrock of such a system would be communal hostels for needy kids—and their mothers. For the children, such hostels would provide structured, caring environments that would give infants and toddlers from the beginning the cognitive, verbal, and moral teaching that forms citizens with consciences and the ability to learn. By the time today's underclass children are in Head Start, and certainly by the time they start school, it's very late to begin teaching cause and effect, big and little, good and naughty, caring and cruel, sharing and selfish, and the whole array of cognitive and moral categories that it is the work of early childhood to learn, that families normally teach, and that underclass children don't adequately acquire. Without mastery of these categories, it is hard to think and therefore to learn.

The new communal hostels should be limited to children born out of wedlock and their mothers. Widowed or divorced mothers would be eligible for a cash welfare payment, as at present. The point would be to make a distinction between women who have made a public, legal commitment to the ideal of a stable family and those who have borne children with no such declaration of responsibility. Because what happens at the periphery of society helps define the norms for those at the center, a society that wants to encourage the strong families that are best for children has to make such distinctions.

Won't the new system stigmatize these mothers? I'm afraid so, but that is part of the point. When the state fulfills its responsibility of taking care of indigent children, it has to do so without condoning (and certainly without celebrating) the behavior of the mothers who, by bringing them into the world with no prospect of being able to support them, have disadvantaged them from the start. The new system aims to care well for the children in its charge while discouraging women both morally and economically from bearing children at the cost of the rest of the community.

The communal hostels will have rules of conduct for the mothers who live there, partly because the hostels should offer something very different from the life of license that the current welfare system offers young women, as it sets them up in their own apartments and gives them more purchasing power than a minimum-wage job (up to $27,000 worth in New York City). But since the hostels focus on the children rather than on the mothers, the rules are designed, above all, to ensure the order and structure children need.

In the same vein, the hostels will require mothers to take daily workshops on child care and child development to learn some of the basic truths about child rearing that young underclass women, not surprisingly, often don't know: that babies cry because they are needy, not because they are "bad," or that children need to be talked to and responded to—not ignored and not hit—if they are to grow up able to function as members of society. If a mother asks her neighbors to support her and her child, surely her neighbors can require her to take at least this much responsibility in return.

Mothers who don't want to conform to this system are free to take their children and leave. If they can support them, fine. If they can't, if the children are neglected or endangered, then the state, as it does now, will take them away. Unlike today's practice, however, such children should be cared for in group foster homes far removed from the influence of the underclass neighborhoods where they were born. To avoid the bureaucratic callousness, meanness, and lack of accountability that might make such institutions harsh or cruel, they should be run not by government agencies but private charities, including the religious ones that have proved themselves so effective at humanely helping the unfortunate.

I want to stress once more that the goal of this entire system isn't only to discourage unmarried women unable to support babies from having them. No less important for healing the pathology of the underclass, the system aims to ensure that the smaller number of such babies who will still be born despite all of society's discouragement grow up with a fair chance of becoming happy and productive citizens. However sweeping the changes I am suggesting may seem, they have to be weighed clearsightedly against the dreadful reality of the present system, which consigns millions to misery and failure, condemning them to grow up with so many human excellences unawakened, lost to themselves and to society.

—*Summer 1994*

V

HOMELESSNESS

Why did legions of the homeless suddenly appear in cities during the 1980s? Who are they? Why are they homeless? What should we do for them? Heated debate has swirled around these questions for years, debate made all the hotter—if not very illuminating—by advocates who've used the homeless as a political battering ram. The homeless are a combination of people with serious mental illness, who need treatment, and people who abuse drugs and alcohol, whose problem is their behavior, not lack of housing.

E. FULLER TORREY

Let's Stop Being Nutty About the Mentally Ill

THE EMPTYING of our public psychiatric hospitals has been the second-largest social experiment in twentieth-century America, exceeded only by the New Deal. The experiment, undertaken upon remarkably little data and a multitude of flawed assumptions, has received virtually no formal evaluation or assessment to ascertain whether it has worked. Once the spring of deinstitutionalization was wound, it just kept going and going and going. And it continues today—disastrously.

It is important to realize the magnitude of this experiment. In 1955 state psychiatric hospitals housed 558,239 seriously mentally ill persons. If the same proportion of Americans were hospitalized today, when the U.S. population is much larger, these hospitals would contain some 900,000 seriously mentally ill individuals. In fact the actual number is less than 70,000, meaning that the net deinstitutionalization amounts to some 830,000 people—more than the population of Boston, Baltimore, or San Francisco.

Some of those who were released fared better than in the state hospitals of the 1940s and early 1950s: most of these institutions were little more than human warehouses. Researchers had yet to develop antipsychotic and antidepressant drugs, and the hospitals had virtually nothing to offer patients except custodial care. That has changed dramatically in the intervening four decades. We now have an armamentarium of effective psychiatric drugs, and many state psychiatric hospitals have improved markedly. A few, such as the exemplary New Hampshire State Hospital in Concord, provide better care than most private psychiatric hospitals.

Many who were deinstitutionalized, however, are worse off than if they had remained in the hospital. They can be found talking to themselves in public streets and parks, living in cardboard boxes or subway tunnels beneath the city in the middle of winter, or escaping the cold in public libraries. They often end up victimized or in jail, charged with misdemeanors. Hundreds of thousands of the deinstitutionalized mentally ill have died prematurely from accidents, suicide, or untreated illnesses. All too frequently, the consequences of this failed social experiment have been tragic and fatal.

New York State is a typical example of deinstitutionalization, with a net effective deinstitutionalization rate of some 90 percent of all patients. Twenty-nine states have deinstitutionalized a higher percentage, led by Rhode Island, with a rate of almost 99 percent. Dr. Seymour Kaplan, one of the pioneers of deinstitutionalization in New York State, later considered it the gravest error he had ever made.

From the earliest days of deinstitutionalization it was clear that many persons discharged from New York's psychiatric hospitals were living marginal lives at best. A 1974 study found that one-quarter of those living in New York City's welfare hotels had once resided in psychiatric hospitals. By 1979 shocking newspaper articles had grown common. One typical story, headlined "21 Ex-Mental Patients Taken from 4 Private Homes," described the former patients as living in Queens "amid broken plumbing, rotting food, and roaches." The article further reported: "Last May the police found the decaying corpse of a former patient lying undisturbed in one home inhabited by six other residents."

New York State also provides abundant examples of the failures of deinstitutionalization, as measured by the number of mentally ill individuals who are homeless or in jail, the number of violent acts by mentally ill persons who are not receiving treatment, and the overall quality of life in the community.

A 1985 front-page story on the homeless in the *New York Times* featured a photo of a man named Vito, "who wears a suit and lives in a coffinlike cardboard box." It also described Antoine, who lived beneath FDR Drive, where he was training "for the rigors of a mission to outer space," and a homeless man who lived near the World Trade Center "because he believed it would be a good place to take off for outer space." As recently as 1995 a New York study reported that 38 percent of discharged psychiatric patients "have no known address within six months of their release."

Perhaps the ultimate symbol of the relationship between psychiatric hospitalization and homelessness in New York is the Keener Men's Shelter on Ward's Island. For three-quarters of a century the building was part of Manhattan State Hospital, serving individuals with severe psychiatric disorders. In 1981, as the state emptied the hospital under the banner of deinstitutionalization, the building became a men's public shelter. When I last visited the shelter in 1990, it housed 800 homeless men. Approximately 40 percent of them were severely mentally ill; several had once been hospital patients in the same building. Despite humane management by the Volunteers of America, the Keener shelter is merely a shelter and is neither staffed nor funded to provide the intensive psychiatric care that many of its residents need, including medication maintenance, vocational rehabilitation, social reeducation, and the transition to supported housing of their own or supervised group homes.

Another disturbing legacy of deinstitutionalization is the large number of the mentally ill in New York's jails and prisons. In 1987, Dr. Henry Steadman and his colleagues published the results of interviews with 3,332 state prison inmates and reported that 8 percent of them had "very substantial psychiatric and functional disabilities that clearly would warrant some type of mental health service." The consequences of jailing such people are often fatal. A study of inmates who committed suicide in New York State jails between 1977 and 1982 found that half of them had been previously hospitalized for a mental disorder.

Most of the mentally ill who end up in jail have committed misdemeanors like disorderly conduct or trespassing. For many of those charged with more serious crimes, there is a direct, and usually obvious, connection between their condition and their crime. For example, in Rochester a mentally ill man robbed a bank using his pointed finger in his pocket as a "gun," then took the money to the zoo and threw it into the enclosure for seals, "urging the animals to return home," according to a New York Correctional Association report. The report concluded that such acts were "more [the] pathetic expressions of mental illness than deliberate, premeditated crimes."

A small number of untreated mentally ill individuals, however, do commit serious crimes, including murder. Almost invariably, they are not receiving medication for their illness at the time of the crime. The incidence of such violent acts has grown in tandem with the number of untreated mentally ill individuals.

In New York such crimes have become a continuing commentary on the perversity of deinstitutionalization. Mary Ventura, three weeks after being discharged from a psychiatric hospital, pushed a woman she did not know into the path of a subway train. Reuben Harris, with 12 previous psychiatric hospitalizations, pushed another woman to her death in the same manner. Juan Gonzalez, who had been psychiatrically evaluated four days earlier, killed two and injured nine others on the Staten Island Ferry. Kevin McKiever, well known to the city's psychiatric services, stabbed to death a woman who was walking her dogs in Central Park. Christopher Battiste, psychiatrically treated at city hospitals twice in the previous two months, bludgeoned to death an 80-year-old woman on the steps of a church. Jorge Delgado, previously hospitalized seven times for his paranoid schizophrenia, ran naked into St. Patrick's Cathedral and killed an elderly usher. Dennis Sweeney, Lois Lang, Van Hull, Michael Vernon, Steve Smith, Da Pei Wu, Tatiana Belopolsky . . . the tragic litany continues year after year. There are an estimated 1,000 such homicides in the United States per year—4 to 5 percent of all homicides. The common denominator is a severely delusional mentally ill person not receiving treatment.

Finally, of course, deinstitutionalization has caused the quality of life for everyone in the community to deteriorate. Violent acts like those I've mentioned contribute to this deterioration, as noted by a *New York Times* columnist in 1995 in response to the Reuben Harris case: "If you are a New Yorker the fear is there somewhere, maybe buried deep beneath the surface of consciousness, or maybe right out there in the open. . . . The fear is that from out of the chaos some maniac will emerge to pointlessly, stupidly, inexplicably hurl you, blast you, cast you into oblivion."

But it is not only episodes of violence that sap community life under deinstitutionalization. It is Joyce Brown, mentally ill and addicted to drugs, living on a steam grate at the corner of East 65th Street and Second Avenue, urinating on the sidewalk and defecating in the gutter as she hurls obscenities at passersby. It is Larry Hogue, the "wild man of West 96th Street," with manic-depressive illness and cocaine dependence, masturbating in front of children and threatening to eat the dog of one local resident. As a woman writing a letter in the *Wall Street Journal* in 1994 summarized it: "A simple visit to the local elementary school, post office or grocery store . . . can be a Dantean journey through the dark underside of our society."

It is important to realize that the original underpinning for deinstitutionalization was political correctness, not scientific knowledge. When deinstitutionalization shifted into high gear in the early 1960s, only one study had been done on the effects of moving severely mentally ill individuals from public psychiatric hospitals to community living. Published in England in 1960 by Dr. John Wing, the study found that 20 schizophrenic individuals, selected because they were functioning at a high level and were able to work, did relatively well when moved from a psychiatric hospital to supervised community living facilities. Virtually every American advocate for deinstitutionalization in the 1960s and 1970s cited this lone paper, despite the fact that the 20 patients studied were far from representative of the vast majority of patients who were sent packing.

The policy of deinstitutionalization was in fact based on ideology. In 1961 psychiatrist Thomas Szasz published *The Myth of Mental Illness*, alleging that there really was no such thing as schizophrenia or manic-depressive disorder. That same year sociologist Erving Goffman published *Asylums*, in which he asserted that most of the behavior psychiatric patients exhibited was a consequence of their being in the hospital, not of their illnesses. The following year Ken Kesey published *One Flew over the Cuckoo's Nest*, which became an underground best-seller and further promoted the idea that most patients in state psychiatric hospitals were characters like Randle McMurphy, who had been hospitalized by mistake and who would function perfectly normally once released.

By the mid-1960s, then, it had become politically correct to denigrate psychiatric hospitals and assert that the patients would do just fine if moved to community settings. The ethos was similar to the British film *King of Hearts*, in which the inmates of the asylum are released en masse, take over the town, and live happily ever after. Civil libertarians and traditional liberals promoted this idea; fiscal conservatives, who saw deinstitutionalization as a way to save state funds by shutting down some of the hospitals, went along too.

In retrospect, it is easy to see the deeply flawed assumptions undergirding deinstitutionalization. One such assumption was that nothing much was wrong with patients in the psychiatric hospitals. At that time, the Freudian psychoanalytic theory prominent in American psychiatry held that bad mothering and social stresses by themselves could lead to disorders such as schizophrenia. Research in the past decade has shown this assumption to be false: studies using such techniques as magnetic resonance imaging (MRI) and positron emission tomography (PET) scans have proved that schizophrenia and manic-depressive illness are physical disorders of the brain in exactly the same way as Parkinson's disease or multiple sclerosis. Patients with such illnesses need medications to control their symptoms; without the medications, their symptoms usually get worse.

The second flawed assumption was that mentally ill individuals discharged from the psychiatric hospitals would voluntarily seek psychiatric treatment if they needed it. Psychiatric professionals in the 1960s and 1970s pointed to the newly funded Community Mental Health Centers (CMHCs) as places where the mentally ill could go to get continuing treatment.

In reality, however, most CMHCs had no interest in treating the patients being released from public psychiatric hospitals. Their staff psychiatrists aspired to do counseling and psychotherapy for individuals with more ordinary problems, just like psychiatrists in the private sector. One federally funded CMHC in Wisconsin even made individuals with schizophrenia use a separate clinic door and waiting room so that they would not offend the "worried well" going there for psychotherapy appointments.

More seriously, however, approximately half the patients discharged from state psychiatric hospitals did not seek treatment once out of the hospital because they did not believe themselves to be ill. In psychiatric terms, they lacked insight into their condition. Recent studies have confirmed that approximately half of all individuals diagnosed with schizophrenia and manic-depressive disorder have significantly impaired insight into their condition. They believe that the Russian KGB really *is* following them, or that they really *did* write songs for the Beatles and are owed millions of dollars in royalties. The fact that they lack such self-awareness is not surprising, since as we now know, these illnesses often afflict the same parts of the brain that we use to think about ourselves and our needs.

In practical terms, this means that approximately half of those who suffer from schizophrenia and manic-depressive disorder will not seek treatment voluntarily no matter how attractive the treatment facilities might be. And since lawyers working for the American Civil Liberties Union and the Bazelon Center in Washington, D.C., have changed state laws to make it exceedingly difficult to treat the mentally ill involuntarily, roughly half of these individuals are untreated at any given time. They constitute most of the mentally ill who are homeless or in jail, and who commit acts of violence.

Finally, advocates of deinstitutionalization wrongly assumed that the states would continue to take responsibility for treating mentally ill individuals after discharging them from public psychiatric hospitals. This was a reasonable assumption, since states had had virtually complete responsibility for treating these individuals since the early nineteenth century. For example, in 1963, when deinstitutionalization was getting under way, state and local government contributed 98 percent of the total cost for support and services for persons with mental illnesses, and the federal government contributed just 2 percent.

All that changed in the 1960s, when Washington made mentally ill individuals who had been discharged from state psychiatric hospitals eligible for a variety of federal programs. Funds from Medicaid, Medicare, Supplemental Security Income (SSI), the Disability Insurance Trust fund (SSDI), food stamps, and housing programs all became available to those with serious mental illnesses. States quickly learned how to shift the costs and the responsibility for providing public psychiatric services to the federal government, so that by 1994 the state and local share of total costs had decreased from 98 to 38 percent, while the federal share had increased from 2 to 62 percent. As the discharged psychiatric patients increasingly fell between the cracks in the treatment system, the states increasingly disavowed responsibility for them.

Given the vast scale of deinstitutionalization, one might have thought that both the federal and state governments would have been interested in evaluating the process and assessing the outcome, especially since this social experiment had been launched with virtually no empirical base. Incredibly, this did not happen. As late as 1981, when deinstitutionalization had been under way for over 15 years, an academic review of research on the subject found only five studies concerned with outcomes, three of which it deemed methodologically flawed. During these same years, the National Institute of Mental Health evaluated the Community Mental Health Centers program and discovered that patients being released from state psychiatric hospitals were not, with only occasional exceptions, receiving aftercare from the CMHCs. In other words, during the mass exodus of patients from psychiatric hospitals, nobody bothered to ask what was happening to them. It is doubtful whether, in the history of American medicine and social services, a policy of this magnitude has ever been implemented with as little evaluation or follow-up.

Given the debacle of deinstitutionalization, what can be done to correct the situation? Two changes would be most helpful.

First, responsibility for mental illness services should be fixed at the state and local levels, and the states should then be held accountable. Human services is not a function that the federal government carries out well. Let states with populations of under 10 million take ultimate responsibility for providing public services for individuals with psychiatric disorders. In states with populations of over 10 million, including New York, counties should take ultimate responsibility, as has happened in California.

States and counties cannot assume responsibility, however, without the necessary fiscal resources. Accordingly, federal funds now being used for mental illness services, including federal Medicaid and Medicare funds, should be given to the states in block grants. In most states more money than is presently being spent is not needed; what is needed is flexibility to spend the funds in the most efficient manner to provide good services. Turning federal funds into block grants would make it possible for patient needs, rather than reimbursement regulations (as is unfortunately the case today), to be the main force shaping the mental illness treatment system.

How would mental illness services change? States would doubtless discover that closing down all state hospital beds is ultimately not cost-effective and that a small percentage of seriously mentally ill persons need long-term inpatient care. The states would also discover that it costs less to maintain the mentally ill on medication—by making it a condition of their remaining at liberty—than to have them readmitted to the hospital every few months.

With responsibility should come accountability. State mental illness services should undergo an annual or biennial evaluation, funded by the federal government but carried out by a private contractor (RAND, say, or the University of Michigan's Institute for Social Research). Federal agencies cannot carry out such evaluations effectively because they are too susceptible to congressional pressure, White House mandates, and political correctness. Measures would include quality-of-life ratings (both by the patients and by their families), program evaluations, and data on the number of patients who are employed, homeless, or in jail. The results of the state evaluation would partially determine the size of the next federal block grant, with states being penalized for doing poorly and rewarded for doing well.

A second key reform that would improve today's bad situation is more controversial: the mental health system must provide for the occasional involuntary treatment of seriously mentally ill individuals. Of the approximately half of all seriously mentally ill persons who have impaired insight into their own condition, a significant fraction will need such treatment once initial attempts to persuade them to accept help have failed.

Involuntary treatment requires a court order for commitment, either as an inpatient or outpatient, or for guardianship. Outpatient commitment, commonly used in 12 states, requires the person to continue taking medication if he wishes to stay out of the hospital and has proved especially effective in reducing rehospitalizations. Thanks no doubt to the power of its civil-liberties lobby, New York has been the only state with a statute specifically *prohibiting* the use of outpatient commitment, although legislators modified this law in 1995 to allow a pilot program for outpatient commitment at New York City's Bellevue Hospital.

The crux of any commitment law is the conditions it sets for involuntary commitment to be legal. In many states, posing a danger to oneself or others is the only grounds for commitment, and courts often interpret this provision very strictly. In order to treat seriously mentally ill individuals before they have proved dangerous, it is necessary to include "need for treatment" or "substantial deterioration" as criteria for involuntary treatment, and several states have moved in this direction. There should, of course, be provisions for court hearings and public defenders to ensure that involuntary treatment is not abused, as it was in the Soviet Union. But as columnist (and psychiatrist) Charles Krauthammer has noted, the use of dangerousness alone as the criterion for involuntary commitment "is not just unfeeling, it is uncivilized. The standard should not be dangerousness but helplessness. Society has an obligation to save people from degradation, not just death."

A major danger in thinking about the disaster of deinstitutionalization is the temptation to accept it. An entire generation of young adults has grown up seeing homeless mentally ill individuals living on the streets and in the parks. From their perspective, why shouldn't these people always live there? To them, the Joyce Browns and Larry Hogues of the world are simply part of the urban landscape, along with broken-down cars at the curbs and refuse under the bridges.

It is important for those of us who are older to speak out. We remember when homelessness was rare, confined to alcoholic hoboes. We must not accept the debacle of deinstitutionalization and the inevitability of its consequences. We made this problem, and we can correct it.

—*Summer 1997*

HEATHER MAC DONALD

Homeless Advocates in Outer Space

IN EIGHTEENTH-CENTURY LONDON, aristocratic elites visited the mad in Bedlam Hospital and called it entertainment. In twentieth-century New York, professional elites visit the mad in the streets and call it homeless outreach. The results in both cases are the same: the objects of attention are left to rot in their own filth, perhaps to lose a limb or two to gangrene, or to die. The intention, however, could not be more different: in modern times, such hands-off treatment shows "sensitivity" and "respect."

Only by entering the realm of political myth can one understand how such deliberate neglect could constitute professional treatment. Contemporary homeless policy is one of the odder expressions of utopian political fantasy since Rousseau famously denounced society as oppressive and corrupting. For their advocates, the homeless are potent symbols of heroic alienation, concrete embodiments of the advocates' own adolescent longing for rebellion and nonconformity. The plight of the homeless, in the advocates' view, is a searing indictment of American culture. Should the Left ever lose interest in dramatizing the Rousseauian myth—an unlikely event—the homeless will disappear, removed to safer abodes.

A recent homelessness conference in New York City perfectly demonstrated how fanatically the advocates hold on to their myths. Called to discuss the failure of a model outreach program, the conference unwittingly showed instead why the homeless are still on the streets.

The Times Square Business Improvement District (BID), a coalition of business owners dedicated to the revival of New York's famed crossroads, has long prided itself on its generous homeless programs, aimed at getting derelicts off the district's streets. From 1992 to 1994, the BID funded an outreach program designed to coax the local homeless into temporary and permanent housing. The payoff was meager: some 200 long-term homeless, according to program estimates, remained on the streets around Times Square, impervious to the efforts of the outreach workers.

So in 1994 the BID decided to up the ante. It procured over $2.5 million in state and federal money to create what it and its government funders touted as a highly innovative homeless program. Under the plan, a brigade of gentle, well-meaning professionals from six local social service agencies would roam the streets 16 hours a day, spending an unlimited amount of time with their "clients" in their natural habitat. The outreach workers would try ever so delicately to persuade the homeless to visit the BID's renovated "respite center," located in the basement of a Times Square church, where they could get overnight shelter, showers, healthy meals, clothing, and medical attention—with no strings attached. For example, if a client wanted to booze on the streets during the day, that was fine, at least for his initial visits. Or if he wanted just to hang out and watch television, that was fine, too. On-site social workers would ensure that he was in receipt of every welfare benefit to which he was entitled, with nothing demanded in return.

If a client ultimately entered and completed detox, the center would require him to refrain from using drugs or alcohol and to attend group therapy sessions run by on-site psychiatrists and social workers. Ultimately, the BID hoped, the center's longer-term clients would deign to accept government-subsidized housing, lined up by the center's staff.

What was supposedly innovative in this utterly conventional program? The same people in the outreach teams would also work in the respite center, allegedly providing continuity and building trust with the homeless. In the hermetic world of homeless practice, such minor tinkering passes for radical rethinking.

One year and $700,000 later, only two people had accepted housing. The rest had staunchly balked. This remarkable result was certainly not for lack of trying. Over the year, the outreach workers had made 1,511 "contacts" with 206 individuals (only a handful of whom, it turned out, actually called Times Square home; the advocates and outreach workers' original estimate of the local homeless population had proved, as usual, to be wildly excessive). Those 1,511 contacts were seemingly more meaningful to the outreach workers than to the homeless: only 37 of the 206 contacted individuals agreed even to visit the BID's respite center, while a mere 15 condescended to stay overnight. The homeless, it appeared, did not really want housing, housing, housing.

To its enormous credit, the BID decided to publish a report on the year's efforts. This document, "To Reach the Homeless," written by Columbia journalism professor Bruce Porter, is a jaw-dropping account of state-of-the-art homeless rehabilitation techniques. Unprecedented in its honesty, it provides a rare window into the mad futility of the homelessness outreach profession. In the battle of wits between the wily homeless and guileless outreach workers, it's no contest, for the outreach workers will not infringe on the "autonomy" of the homeless, while the homeless feel no corresponding scruple.

As recounted in "To Reach the Homeless," a typical day of outreach resembles a Dantean pilgrimage through the underworld. One day, for example, outreach workers stop by a coffin-size box across from the New York Times building. "We know it's a person," reports Porter, "because we can discern a hand moving underneath some rags." The workers knock on the box and say hello but get no response. Because the hand is still moving, though, the team concludes that whatever it is attached to must be okay, so they move on.

They next come across "Shoeshine Bill," "an old man with a shoeshine kit and markedly swollen ankles who is sitting in a puddle of his urine." Shoeshine Bill assures the workers that he is doing "fine," so they move on. An old black woman is raving unintelligibly about drugs in Harlem. She's "not very open to help," says an outreach worker. A young white couple lying on the street banter off a suggestion that they visit the respite center; they'll go, jokes the gaunt male, "only if they could get a private room for an hour with a bed." The woman has deteriorated markedly from alcoholism over the previous months. The outreach worker drops a few condoms on their blanket and moves on.

Some of the homeless demonstrate admirable energy and persistence in avoiding the outreach workers' ministrations. "Heavy," a large black man who reigns, according to the report, as the "undisputed king" of Times Square, is one such vagrant. Heavy is highly visible: "[H]e is invariably dressed in a dark green jump suit, two or three canvas Post Office mail carts nearby heaped six feet high with his stuff—filthy quilts, dirty towels and plastic bags packed with plastic bottles, broken broom handles presumably used for defense, a half-dozen milk crates filled with wastepaper and tied on with bits of nylon rope, gallon ketchup bottles, some of the sauce still sloshing around the bottom. Sprouting up out of the pile is an eight-foot-tall iron pipe that is tied with long orange streamers fluttering in the wind."

Fortunately for Heavy, the outreach workers are also highly visible. Whenever he spots their bright red jackets approaching, he wedges himself behind a fence or other barricade, "prepared to resist the service providers at all costs." One time, the team tried to capture him with a pincer movement, but he dashed into traffic and nearly got hit. "After that, we seriously had to ask ourselves what exactly we were accomplishing by this," recalls the director of the program. Sadly, the workers' doubts were fleeting.

Other street residents avoid the outreach workers out of embarrassment. As an outreach team chats with three vagrants sharing a jumbo bottle of beer in a hotel garage, a 63-year-old man named Charlie hides nearby in back of a refrigerator. The workers have taken him to detox four times, and now he's ashamed to face them. The team leader is philosophical: "[H]e's smelling pretty bad these days, so we'll probably be hearing from Charlie soon. He usually comes in to take a shower when he gets that way."

Such repeated efforts are the norm. A lost soul from Rochester named Toni relies on the seemingly inexhaustible trust of the workers to avoid going to alcohol detox. The workers have given her subway fare to the treatment center, as well as fare home, many times, but each time she either never gets on the subway or gets off a few stops down and returns to her haunts. Toni's reception upon her return is not always gracious. "Last night I got the shit beat out of me, right here," she tells the workers. "Dutch did it. He's crazy. He hit me for no reason, just popped me in the face, no reason." The workers try to draw a moral from the situation: "You realize if you got out of detox and went home, this might not have happened?" they ask her. Toni half-heartedly assents to this proposition, so the workers once again give her fare to a detox center on Staten Island and see her on to the train. As usual, their homily vanished into thin air: one stop down the line, she got off and went straight back to Times Square.

Nothing, however, compares to the difficulty of enticing the homeless into housing. Time after time, a client deemed "housing-ready" will balk at the threshold of his new abode and plunge back into the most squalid street life. Only a few vagrants even get that close; most keep themselves safely removed from the housing process. The respite center's staff, faced with their meager record of accomplishment, have defined success down, to adapt Senator Moynihan's resonant phrase. The fact that the homeless sometimes return to the outreach center to "reveal how screwed up they've become" shows that the "staff has affected them in some positive way," the report concludes wanly.

The charity our society showers upon people living on the street makes possible this hardy resistance to seeking help. In true New York fashion, even vagrants can get home-delivered food: a do-gooder group from Dobbs Ferry called Midnight Run makes regular deliveries of sandwiches and juice, along with toiletries and blankets, right to people's cardboard boxes. The homeless know the hours and locations of every local soup kitchen, and the more enterprising work out deals for other personal needs. One older alcoholic would throw away a new pair of underwear every couple of days, secure in the knowledge that Midnight Run would soon bring another pair. Other homeless use more unorthodox approaches to street survival. When it gets cold, recounts a scraggly vagrant, "I smash a window with a brick and go to jail. I get along fine in jail."

Yet though no one is going hungry on the streets, vagrants' bodies often are disintegrating from a host of untreated maladies. Alcoholics lose toes, feet, and legs to infections they haven't even noticed. Workers at the BID's respite center work heroically to secure treatment for their clients, but the clients often disappear right before a scheduled operation. No one, of course, has the right to make them stay.

The costs of this charade to the larger society are enormous, too. To take only one example, Amtrak loses $11 million a year at Penn Station, just south of Times Square, because the homeless drive potential passengers away, according to Richard Rubel, community relations officer at Amtrak. And the repeated trips the homeless make to hospital emergency rooms for thoroughly avoidable medical crises also ring up a hefty public tab, as do their resultant disability benefits.

"To Reach the Homeless" proves beyond a shadow of a doubt that the homeless are not on the street because they can't find housing: desperate to give away subsidized apartments, the BID found almost no takers. Clearly, most vagrants prefer the streets to the responsibilities of a housed existence. Some may simply refuse to play by society's rules, like many hoboes of old; for others, speculates the respite center's director, housing may represent a scary reencounter with whatever psychological demons drove them to the streets in the first place.

But although the homeless may prefer the streets, that is not why they are still there. They are there because the advocates need them to be there. Should society finally decide to end street vagrancy, it could go far in that direction by facilitating commitment to mental hospitals and enforcing existing laws against street living. Though the average householder would surely welcome such a change, the average householder has no say in these matters; a vocal minority purporting to represent the interests of the homeless governs homeless policy. And those advocates, who range from single-issue advocacy groups to the ACLU to left-wing churches, fiercely resist any measure that would restrict the "rights" of the homeless to live on the streets.

They do so not just out of material interests—though many of them make a comfortable living off of homelessness—but out of a spiritual need. Homelessness confirms for the advocates their dearest beliefs: that American capitalism is corrupt and cruel, that the American Dream is a delusion, that American society deals harshly with its rebels and nonconformists. Remove the homeless from the streets, and Exhibit A in the advocates' brief against America also disappears. Even the outreach workers on the front lines, who would say that their fondest wish is to house the homeless, nevertheless reflexively take for granted a definition of autonomy suffused with left-wing romanticism and at odds with the best interests of the homeless.

The advocates' ideology has rarely been as visible as at a conference on homelessness that the Times Square BID organized last April. Provoked by the sorry results of its outreach program, the BID brought together some of the country's leading self-styled homeless experts for a good-faith discussion of the question, "What Do We Do When Homeless People Say 'No'?" What it got instead was an amazing and instructive display of deliberate duplicity and invincible self-righteousness. The advocates simply chose to ignore the BID's outreach program; wholly impervious to the facts, they brought with them instead their stock stories about housing shortages, a heartless society, and noble, helpless suffering. Their performance demonstrated why homeless policy has been so counterproductive.

Jack Coleman, former president of Haverford College and of the left-leaning Edna McConnell Clark Foundation, immediately set the tone of maudlin virtue. Coleman won acclaim in 1983 for living as a "street person" in New York City for ten days, an experience he wrote up as a cover story for *New York* magazine. The adventure was certainly a sociological "first": Coleman was undoubtedly the first "homeless" person to take a professional photographer on his rounds through soup kitchens and shelters to capture his every moment of despair—Coleman sitting next to a steam grate with forehead resting on fist, eyes closed, and face grimacing from fatigue and cold; Coleman gazing off pensively at a cheap diner; Coleman wolfing down his food in a shelter, surrounded by derelicts; Coleman staring hopelessly at the job listings in a minimum-wage employment agency (undoubtedly none called for his unique talents as a progressive foundation executive).

Now he once again put himself on display. He recounted his first moment back home after his "homeless" experience: he drew a hot tub, lay down in it, and started to cry. And lo! the tears began again, for everyone in the audience to behold. How many times Coleman had told this story to similar effect was anyone's guess, but it would prove a harbinger: if his tears spread Rousseauian "sentiment" throughout the conference, the subsequent speakers would suffuse it with Rousseauian self-righteousness. Before he left the podium, Coleman shared one further confession with us: he couldn't *really* lay claim to the full homeless experience, because he had always had change in his pocket with which to call his editor at *New York*! We the privileged can never really bridge the unfathomable gulf between ourselves and the homeless!

After Coleman's four-handkerchief histrionics, the next piece of drivel hit all the more painfully. It is our society's "intolerance of weakness and of the inability to compete in a free market" that causes homelessness, announced Mary Ann Gleason, an ex-nun who now heads the Washington-based National Coalition for the Homeless. If we were a gentler, more communal society, the implication seemed to be, the homeless would embrace our free housing. Yet the problem, in Gleason's view, transcends economics. It is spiritual. The reason the homeless don't come in off the streets, Gleason averred, is that "they don't have meaning in their lives." Translation:

we don't have meaning in our lives, and until we get some, the homeless will maintain their lonely outpost on the streets, "the only community they can find." (The fact that this "community" sometimes beats up its own members, as the detox-avoiding Toni discovered, did not seem to detract from its soul-enriching value, in Gleason's eyes.) Gleason especially admired the Europeans for having labeled the homeless the "socially excluded"—though she never explained why, given this progressive diagnosis, the Europeans haven't solved the problem by "including" the homeless.

With the homeless thus transmuted into Romantic critics of soulless modern life, the remaining speakers had their theme. Dr. William Vicic, a "community medicine" specialist at St. Vincent's Hospital and author of a book entitled *Memory of a Homeless Man*, turned the title of the conference, "What Do We Do When Homeless People Say 'No'?" upon itself. "Is 'no' from the homeless an answer," he asked dramatically, "or an echo of us and the society we maintain?" In truth, he implied, it is we who say "no" to the homeless, not they to us. That we may have some rational grounds for saying "no" to substance abuse, criminal behavior, chronic irresponsibility, and inability to follow rules did not register with Vicic; through his Rousseauian spectacles, he seems to see only enslavement and oppression in society's rules.

Like Gleason, Vicic identified the roots of homelessness not in the dysfunctions of the homeless but in the closed-mindedness of the housed: "Separatism causes a lot of our problems," he said darkly. As a response to the events that precipitated the conference, Vicic's diagnosis seemed all the sillier. It's hard to imagine a less "separatist" program than the Times Square outreach and housing project: it sought to include the homeless on their own terms, without imposing conventional social rules on them. Yet even such unconditional inclusiveness could not overcome the determination of the homeless to stay homeless.

The most vacuous variation on the "Homeless Saying 'No'" theme came from the Reverend James A. Forbes Jr., pastor at the nation's premier left-wing house of worship, Manhattan's Riverside Church. "We should value the one gift the homeless bring," Forbes admonished the audience— "the ability to say 'no.'" Forbes provided no clue as to how one "values" such a gift; he just reiterated his motif. The "ability to say 'no' is a strength," he said, adding that the burden was on us to figure out what the homeless are saying "no" to. One couldn't help wondering, if saying "no" is a strength, why the homeless are so beset by illness and fear. One wondered, too, if Forbes also celebrates as a gift the big "no" that criminals say to the law.

With excruciating predictability, Forbes went on to accuse society of a lack of compassion. This note rang particularly false in the most generous welfare city in the country, especially in the wake of a $2.5 million effort to house a handful of homeless people. Though money is a dubious measure of compassion, to be sure, it is the measure Forbes clearly had in mind.

Another speaker, Tena Frank, director of homeless services at Lenox Hill Neighborhood House, seemed to float far above the earth on a cloud of moral relativism. Our mainstream value systems regarding work and discipline, she explained, are just the way "*we* get *our* needs met"—exactly as the homeless get their needs met by using drugs. Our failure to see the similarity "allows us to blame the homeless," she concluded.

The only advocate to avoid romanticizing the homeless chose instead a bald-faced lie. Maria Foscarinis, director of the National Law Center on Homelessness and Poverty, is one of the shrillest advocates around. She lobbied tirelessly for the 1987 Stewart B. McKinney Homeless Assistance Act, a federal cash spigot that falsely identifies homelessness as a housing problem, and she wages a regular campaign in court and in the press on behalf of homeless "rights." At the conference, Foscarinis demonstrated the rhetorical techniques that have made her so successful. Cities have no right to enforce laws outlawing camping or urinating in public, she asserted, because the homeless are "people who literally have no place left to go." This was, without doubt, the most outrageous claim of the day. The very impetus for the conference was the fact that the Times Square homeless *did* have someplace to go but spurned the offer. Foscarinis, however, simply ignored that fact. Equally beneath her notice were the millions of public dollars dedicated solely to the small colony befouling Times Square. "The resources are not there," she announced grimly, "to provide an alternative place to sleep or eat." Again, a lie.

Such duplicity should disqualify its practitioners forevermore from having the slightest voice in determining policy. It hardly needs saying that the homeless are not lonely beacons of courage, taking their stand against a hypocritical world, but demoralized or broken creatures, fearful of the demands of adult life. Enslaved by their inner demons or the substances they abuse, they are the least likely to benefit from the sphere of absolute license their advocates have carved out for them. Yet self-serving fictions like those rampant at the Times Square conference have guided homelessness policy from the start, because few are willing to challenge the moral bullying of the advocates. The consequences for the purported beneficiaries have been dire.

A sane homeless policy would acknowledge two basic realities. First, many people on the streets need treatment, not housing. For the sickest, legislators need to change rules against involuntary confinement, and states need to recommission mental hospitals emptied by deinstitutionalization. Second, for the rest of the homeless the best medicine is the expectation of responsible behavior—the expectation of work and of civil and lawful conduct in public spaces. Accordingly, opinion leaders, from politicians to ministers, should decry all types of no-strings-attached handouts, such as no-demand soup kitchens and indiscriminate alms-giving to beggars, which simply subsidize self-destructive behavior. They should oppose allowing the homeless to turn public spaces into hobo encampments. Effective charity asks for reciprocity from the recipient, building patterns of work and discipline; to exempt the homeless from the rules that everyone else lives by infantilizes them permanently.

The advocates, clouded by ideology, may see the homeless as martyrs to American injustice or as free spirits marching to a different drummer, but by now most of the rest of us see them as disordered or confused souls who, for more than a decade, thanks to advocate-designed policies, have been marching to disaster.

—Autumn 1997

VI
THE ECONOMY

*Cities were once the dynamos of the nation's economy. As
they flourished, they came to see their principal mission
as helping the poor, either by giving them municipal jobs
early in the twentieth century or, later, by giving them
generous welfare benefits and services. But as the taxes
needed to pay for these wages and welfare benefits grew
ever heavier, companies and workers began to flee the
cities, tax rolls shrank, and budgets grew ever harder to
balance. The new urban thinking stresses the need to cut
taxes and city payrolls in order to create a favorable
economic climate that will attract new business and the
new jobs that are the poor's surest route
out of poverty.*

WILLIAM J. STERN

The Unexpected Lessons of Times Square's Comeback

ALMOST EVERYBODY rightly celebrates Times Square's revival as one of New York City's greatest recent success stories. Just a short while ago it was sleazy, blighted, and crime-ridden; today it is all but crime free, it has driven out the prostitutes and pornographers who made it so seedy, it bustles with tourists by day and night, and world-spanning corporations such as AMC, Disney, and Viacom prosper within it. But if everyone knows about Times Square's remarkable comeback, few understand what made it happen.

I thought I knew what the ingredients for success were back in 1984, when I worked for Governor Mario Cuomo as head of the Urban Development Corporation (UDC). On my watch, the UDC put in place a gigantic project, first conceived in 1981, to revitalize Times Square, then at its absolute nadir. The $2.6 billion 42nd Street Redevelopment Plan would extend tax-abatement deals to developers and direct them to transform Times Square by building grand office towers, a huge merchandise market, and a fancy hotel; by restoring historic theaters; and by revamping the dingy 42nd Street subway station. Also sponsoring the plan were Mayor Ed Koch and—unofficially but prominently—the *New York Times*, whose headquarters gave the square its name in 1905.

But almost nothing we planned ever came to fruition. Instead, Times Square succeeded for reasons that had nothing to do with our building schemes and everything to do with government policy that, by fighting crime, cracking down on the sex industry, and cutting taxes—albeit only selectively—at last allowed the market to do its work and bring the area back to life. The lesson: there's a right way and a wrong way for government to pursue economic development. It's a lesson that needs spelling out, since it's crucial to future economic recovery in New York.

It's important to recall accurately what Times Square was like when we officially launched our plan in November 1984, since today you still find a few people perversely nostalgic for it. Samuel R. Delany's new book, *Times*

Square Red, Times Square Blue, is a case in point: it is a lament for defunct Times Square sex clubs like the Capri, the Eros, and the Venus. These risqué establishments, Delany argues, provided a harmless, playful way to subvert stuffy bourgeois morality.

But the Times Square Delany mourns was anything but playful. The area began going to seed during the late fifties after the sex industry—waved on by ill-advised federal and state court decisions that extended First Amendment protections to pornography—edged out and took over once-lustrous theaters that had been economically struggling since the Depression. The decline was rapid thereafter: the porn establishments attracted to Times Square an unsavory and increasingly criminal crowd. Already by 1960, the *New York Times* was calling the heart of Times Square—42nd Street between Seventh and Eighth—the "worst block in the city." By the eighties, things got worse still, with an amazing 2,300 crimes on the block in 1984 alone, 20 percent of them serious felonies such as murder or rape. Dispirited police, at the time more concerned with avoiding scandals than fighting crime—especially low-level crime like the prostitution that was swamping Times Square—would investigate the serious felonies but mostly stood by and watched as disorder grew.

The lawless climate had devastating economic consequences. In 1984, the entire 13-acre area that we sought to revitalize employed only 3,000 people in legitimate businesses and paid the city only $6 million in property taxes—less than what a medium-size office building typically produced in tax revenue.

No legitimate business—indeed, scarcely a normal person—would willingly visit so blighted and threatening an area. As head of the UDC during the mid-eighties, I would walk through Times Square at night, a state trooper by my side, and feel revulsion. We'd hurry past prostitute-filled single-room-occupancy hotels and massage parlors, greasy spoons and pornographic bookstores; past X-rated movie houses and peep shows and a pathetic assortment of junkies and pushers and johns and hookers and pimps—the whole panorama of big-city lowlife. Everywhere I'd look, I'd see—except for female prostitutes—only men. A UDC study later verified my impression empirically: 90 percent of those who walked Times Square's streets were adult males. Times Square was haunted with them, like a circle of lost souls in Dante.

All of us involved in the redevelopment project were New Yorkers, born and bred. We remembered a better Times Square. In the early fifties, Times Square had been a childhood delight for me. On Saturday, my father and I would bus down from Harlem to see a movie, often a Roy Rogers or Gene Autry cowboy picture. Then we'd get something to eat at Nedick's and afterward just stroll around, gazing up at the giant signs that adorned Times

Square's buildings, then as now. Mario Cuomo and Ed Koch had similar happy memories. The mayor was old enough even to have heard firsthand accounts of Times Square's heyday during the 1920s, when 13 theaters studded 42nd Street between Seventh and Eighth and lit up in neon the legendary "Great White Way," as theatergoers crowded into the latest creations of impresario George M. Cohan or of musicians such as George and Ira Gershwin. The regret we felt over the passing of this glamorous world of our youth gave the project a powerful emotional boost.

Our plan was Neronian in scale. Its biggest component was to be Times Square Center: four giant office towers, containing 4.1 million square feet of floor space in all, looming over Times Square's southern border. Offered a $240 million tax abatement, George Klein's Park Tower Realty would develop the site. Perennial modernist Philip Johnson, together with fellow architect John Burgee, would design the buildings. In Johnson's controversial design, four-story red-granite bases would support glass towers topped with iron-crested glass mansard roofs. Each tower would light up at night to dispel the shadow world below; at street level, a pedestrian thoroughfare would connect the four towers and establish a new hub for subway travel.

Johnson's gargantuan buildings weren't the only part of the redevelopment project conceived on a grand scale. We also called for a 2.4 million-square-foot computer and garment wholesale mart between 40th Street and 42nd Street on the east side of Eighth Avenue, and a 550-room luxury hotel with additional office and retail space on West 42nd Street at Eighth Avenue. Nine historic theaters, including the legendary New Victory and the New Amsterdam, would get a $9 million spruce-up and reopen as nonprofit cultural centers featuring legitimate entertainment. The final component was a major $100 million makeover of the 42nd Street subway station, which would be outfitted with a computerized information center, scores of shops, and six new entrances, among other improvements. As part of the overall deal, Park Tower Realty would pick up most of the tab for the nonprofit theaters and the subway. Everything had to go forward at the same time, we felt, since the sheer momentum of the development would push out the sleaze for good.

Unveiling the plan early in 1984, we felt enormous pride. After all, how many people have the opportunity to leave such a deep and positive mark on the history—and in the landscape—of a world city? But, though I can't speak for the others, I felt doubt, too. Perhaps the pharaohs could contemplate such a mega-project with equanimity, but could a group of New York City kids really pull it off? But I suppressed my doubt: I had informed Governor Cuomo that I would soon step down as head of the UDC—I had grown disgusted with New York's pervasive political corruption and would leave public service for good in 1985—and I wanted to feel as if I had accomplished something big and worthwhile in government before I left. This project would be it.

On November 8, 1984, the now-defunct New York City Board of Estimate approved the project, removing the last political hurdle to its implementation. We all exhaled in relief, since reaching that point hadn't been easy. From the moment state and city officials first announced the redevelopment scheme in February 1981, it faced opposition from activists, who worried that it would displace lower-income people from their homes, and from the cultural left, who defended Times Square's sex businesses as constitutionally protected speech—speech that had the added virtue of subverting bourgeois proprieties. And after Johnson and Burgee's blueprint for the towers went public, civic groups lobbied for a less obtrusive design that took more account of smaller surrounding buildings. But none of these forces mustered enough support to defeat the project.

An internal disagreement had also broken out over who would get the potentially lucrative nod to develop the mart. The dispute was really part of a larger battle over who would predominantly shape the new Times Square. The city and the New York Times favored a team of Trammel Crow (a Texas-based developer) and George Klein; the state, thinking that Klein already had enough on his hands, preferred Paul Milstein, a major New York developer. An artful political compromise between Mayor Koch and Governor Cuomo—two politicians who harbored deep mutual suspicion from past political campaigns against each other—eventually settled on a consortium that brought together Klein and Milstein, though neither the mayor nor the governor ever questioned the idea that government should be picking developers in the first place. By the autumn of 1984, everything was set to go.

Yet after the Board of Estimate vote, the plan withered. The four new towers never went up, the wholesale mart never opened, the hotel never appeared, the subway renovations never happened, and the nonprofit theaters never materialized. What happened?

The commercial real estate market, perhaps already beginning to peak in 1984, tanked with the stock-market crash of 1987, and Klein hesitated to start work on what were now unlettable office towers. Already in 1986, the Dewey, Ballantine law firm, which was to have been a major tenant in Times Square Center, had withdrawn. In 1989, Chemical Bank, another anchor tenant, dropped out. By 1992, Governor Cuomo was letting the developers off the hook: "It doesn't make sense to go forward immediately with the building of the office towers—there's no market for them," the governor observed. "To hold these people to the contract is to ask them to commit an act of economic self-mutilation," he added. Later, after more than a decade on the project, Klein would leave, having built or renovated nothing.

But while the original building project remained stalled, something surprising happened: Times Square started to revive. First, it was a trickle of activity. In 1990, Viacom, the huge entertainment firm that owns Nickelodeon and MTV, signed a lease at 1515 Broadway. In 1992, the publishing giant Bertelsmann AG bought 1540 Broadway from Citicorp. In 1993, the Morgan Stanley investment firm purchased 1585 Broadway from Salomon Equities.

Then the trickle became a flood. On the last day of the Dinkins administration in 1993, the Walt Disney Company signed a memo of understanding with the city to refurbish and reopen the New Amsterdam Theater, though it didn't finalize the deal—which included a $25 million low-interest government loan—until 1995. In 1995, AMC, the entertainment conglomerate, agreed to move to the neighborhood; Madame Tussaud's Wax Museum decided to open a Times Square branch to join its famous London counterpart; the Tishman Urban Development Corporation contracted to build a big hotel; and the Durst Organization announced that it would erect a 1.5 million-square-foot office building, taking over one-quarter of the site originally intended for Times Square Center. By the summer of that eventful year, the left-wing urbanist Marshall Berman was complaining that Times Square had "become the focus of some of the most ambitious commercial development New York has ever seen"—and it hasn't stopped since.

The ever-accelerating development has brought back the whole neighborhood. Disney refurbished the New Amsterdam Theater, and it reopened with a wildly successful run of *The Lion King*. The 100-year-old New Victory Theater, which showed porn films in the eighties, reopened—beautifully restored to its original glory—as a venue for children's theater. And new restaurants like Caroline's Comedy Nation and the upscale Russian Firebird bustled from the moment they opened. By 1997, Broadway was having its best year in nearly two decades, as 10.6 million theater lovers flocked to 38 different shows.

Times Square was bursting with investment and renewal not because of the building project, since it had built nothing, nor even because the nation had entered into its present economic boom—42nd Street kept rotting away through the economic upswings of the 1960s and 1980s—but because government was at last starting to behave the way government should behave if it wants to nourish prosperity. Government began to do three things—two of them with the plan's help, though the city could have done them more effectively on its own—that ignited Times Square's revitalization: it started to fight crime, it kicked out the sex industry, and it lowered taxes selectively for big businesses willing to locate in the area. And as Times Square became safer and less sleazy, its natural advantages became strikingly apparent: at the center of the city's subway system, home to the Port Authority Bus Terminal, near Penn Station and Grand Central Station, it boasts a transportation infrastructure unmatched in the United States, and it has always been one of New York's cultural landmarks.

Mayor Abe Beame took the first hesitant steps to tame Times Square's disorder in 1977, when he enacted nuisance abatement laws to shut down some of the neighborhood's ubiquitous massage parlors. But the first really effective measures came courtesy of a now-retired deputy inspector named Richard Mayronne, assigned to the Midtown South precinct that includes Times Square during the mid-eighties. As former NYPD deputy chief John Timoney (now Philadelphia's police commissioner) remembers him, Mayronne was "a big tough guy, a cop's cop, and easily the most imposing police commander I've ever met." He was also something more, Timoney stresses: an innovator in police tactics. Mayronne covered his office with neighborhood maps, and used pins to chart crime patterns in order to employ his forces efficiently—creating a crude, pre-electronic version of Compstat, the computerized crime-tracking system that has since revolutionized New York City policing under Mayor Rudolph Giuliani.

Even more important, Timoney recounts, Mayronne instructed his men to make arrests for low-level crimes such as prostitution and minor drug transactions that, when left unpunished, create a climate of lawlessness that encourages criminals to act on their darker impulses, leading to ever more serious crime. Such quality-of-life policing, as most observers now recognize, is a major reason for New York's sharply lower crime rates, and the absence of it had contributed to Times Square's decay. The new techniques paid off: as Mayronne's Midtown South successors continued to monitor crime patterns and keep the pressure on quality-of-life infractions, crime dropped. By the end of 1991, Times Square's crime rate was 12 percent lower than in 1984—nothing like the 68 percent citywide reduction that Giuliani would achieve, but a healthy start nonetheless.

With Giuliani's election as mayor in 1993, the war on crime dramatically intensified. Together with his police commissioner William Bratton, the mayor completely transformed New York City's approach to policing: Compstat soon allowed the NYPD to deploy personnel and resources efficiently, and quality-of-life policing became the norm throughout the city. Thanks to the new techniques—a quantum improvement over Mayronne's early innovations—Times Square's crime rate dropped to an infinitesimal level. Felonies committed on 42nd Street between Seventh and Eighth—the "worst block in the city"—fell from 2,300 in 1984 to a mere 60 in 1995, prompting a city official to enthuse that "crime has reached such a low level on that block that we don't keep statistics anymore." In the entire Midtown South precinct, felony complaints fell 50 percent, from 20,000 in 1992 to 10,000 in 1997. Giuliani and Bratton also sent a powerful message through their public rhetoric that the city would no longer tolerate crime and disorder, heightening New Yorkers' and tourists' expectations about safety and soothing the jangling nerves of the business community.

Encouraged by dwindling crime, tourists began crowding back into Times Square—always potentially one of New York's biggest draws—bringing much needed revenue into the city. Giuliani had grasped the connection between cutting crime and reviving Times Square's tourism even before his mayoralty began. The mayor recently told me about how, during the 1970s, he watched Martin Scorsese's film *Taxi Driver*, which depicted Times Square as a hellish nightmare, and wondered how adversely it might affect tourism. During his 1993 mayoral campaign, Giuliani got a firsthand insight into the answer. Driving down Broadway in his campaign car, he saw a tourist frantically chasing a thief who had snatched his wife's purse, bruising her hand in the process. Giuliani, jumping from the car, joined the chase, but only caught up with the tourist, not the purse snatcher. No cops were around, and none arrived until 30 minutes had passed, assuring the crook's clean getaway. Again, Giuliani thought: what would these tourists think about visiting Times Square in the future?

But that was six years ago. Today, reassured investors and tourists no longer have reason to shun the area.

The 42nd Street Redevelopment Plan had nothing to do with this revolution in crime fighting and the safer Times Square it created—the main reason investment again started to flow into the neighborhood, just as it's the main reason investment has started to flow into a markedly safer 125th Street, also the site of an ambitious, but largely irrelevant, government redevelopment plan. But through the state's Urban Development Corporation, the redevelopment plan did play a key role in the second thing government did that helped revive Times Square: kicking out the sex businesses.

From 1984 on, drawing on the UDC's special powers to condemn for economic blight, the redevelopment project began to shut down Times Square's sex clubs. By 1990, after a hugely expensive six-year condemnation process, the UDC had taken title to two-thirds of the 13-acre project area, sending the sex businesses scuttling to other corners of the city. The ultimate cost reached nearly $300 million, a sum initially advanced by the developers, whom the plan would later reimburse through tax abatements. It proved so expensive because condemnation requires court-determined compensation for the owners of condemned properties and hefty legal fees to fight the protracted lawsuits when the owners resisted being kicked out.

Instead of condemning, why didn't the city just zone out the sex businesses? After all, throughout the nineteenth century—and indeed, for most of the twentieth—cities freely applied tough zoning regulations to the sex industry, viewing it, apart from any moral objection, as poisonous to other economic activity. In New York during the 1930s, Mayor Fiorello La Guardia, whom no one would accuse of being an early member of the religious right, waged war on the city's burlesque houses—the sex clubs of that era—because he knew that they drew in crime and drove away legitimate commerce.

But that was well before the late 1950s, when activist judges, in effect defining away the concept of obscenity, extended First Amendment protection to strip clubs and pornography. To apply zoning restrictions to sex businesses was henceforth different from applying them to, say, a slaughterhouse or a chemical plant, since now to do so supposedly violated the First Amendment. It also would invariably incur the wrath of the cultural left, loudly decrying censorship and the imposition of puritan values. The redevelopment plan allowed the city and the state to escape these invented First Amendment restrictions and deflect the criticisms of the cultural left, accomplishing indirectly what zoning would have done directly and far less expensively. Support for the project's condemnation efforts also allowed the *New York Times* editorial page to have it both ways: it denounced on economic grounds the sex businesses defacing its own backyard that it regularly defended elsewhere as constitutionally protected forms of speech. The *Times* stance seemed to be: "Yes to sex businesses, but not in our neighborhood."

Yet condemnation might not have been necessary after all. As early as 1976, the Supreme Court started to allow municipalities to subject "adult" businesses to zoning regulations for reasons of "secondary effects" on neighborhoods, with economic blight leading the list—the Fiorello La Guardia argument, we could call it. Looking back, zoning might have proceeded on the same rationale as condemnation and still have passed constitutional muster, though this certainly wasn't the high-priced legal opinion we were getting at the time (or the inclination of the governor, the mayor, or the *Times*, all averse to challenging New York's left-wing judicial culture). Later, in the mid-1990s, Mayor Giuliani did employ the "secondary effects" argument to pass sweeping regulations restricting sex-oriented video stores, X-rated theaters, and topless bars to a few isolated non-residential neighborhoods, where they'd cause the least economic damage. "They hurt the economy of the city; they cost us jobs; they cost us money," Giuliani bluntly explained.

But for Times Square, this was just sweeping up: thanks to the plan, most of the sex industry had already moved on by 1990, when the first signs of the area's economic rebirth became evident. The city had finally liberated Times Square from sleaze, though at a great, and probably unnecessary, expense. With the sex industry gone, Times Square could at last begin to develop its economic potential.

The redevelopment plan provided a second major spark to revitalizing Times Square: it reduced taxes for businesses willing to locate in the neighborhood. It did this, however, not by giving the city an overall tax cut, but instead by awarding special tax abatements, low-interest loans, and other subsidies to well-connected firms. From the original $240 million tax abatement given to George Klein to the $40 million abatement given to Morgan Stanley in 1992 to the $25 million low-interest loan given to Disney in 1994 to the $20 million incentive package offered to Ernst & Young just this year— everybody in the new Times Square has some kind of deal from the plan. The results show the power of supply-side tax cuts: more than $2.5 billion in private sector investment has poured into Times Square since 1995.

Any sensible economist would say: Why not cut taxes citywide? Giuliani, a defender of tax abatements, has a tough answer. There's no political constituency in New York for it, he claims, and polls show that he's right (though a mayor passionate about tax cuts could use his bully pulpit to begin to create a constituency for them). So if citywide tax cuts remain politically unfeasible, the mayor argues, the only thing the city can do to boost investment is to cut taxes selectively. The trouble with this approach is that the considerable political clout a firm needs to land a choice tax deal from the city means that it is invariably the older, already established, company, not the brash newcomer, that gets a break.

This favoring of the old and the well-connected over the new and the as yet unknown—it's really a form of state-directed capitalism, where government substitutes its bureaucratic thinking for the market's invisible hand— means that New York squanders enormous economic possibilities. Imagine a 29-year-old college dropout named Bill Gates coming to us in 1984 and asking for a tax abatement to build a 42nd Street office for his new computer-software company. "What's an operating system, and what's a Gates?" I can hear Koch sneering. We would have laughed Gates out the door. But for the last quarter-century, it has been the bold outsiders like Gates, usually bringing some undreamed-of service or technology to the market, who have fueled real economic growth and created most of the country's 70 million new jobs.

As great as the new Times Square is, what might it look like today if New York City's taxes weren't so anti-competitive and instead encouraged up-and-coming firms to locate in Gotham? If then-fledgling enterprises like Microsoft, Cisco, or Oracle, drawn in by low taxes, dropping crime rates, and a newly non-sleazy atmosphere, had moved into Times Square during the eighties and nineties, these upstarts would have created even more jobs and produced even more tax revenue than did the well-connected businesses that now reside in the neighborhood, lured in by politically negotiated tax abatements and sweetheart deals.

Giuliani asserts that "it will be perhaps 20 years" before Gotham's tax structure is competitively on a par with more business-friendly cities. But perhaps the mayor is too pessimistic. Even some of his detractors admit that he helped transform New Yorkers' attitudes on crime and proved that the city wasn't ungovernable. Perhaps some future mayor might build a political constituency to enact major, across-the-board tax cuts. He could use this argument: the *New York Times*, the state, and the city favored tax cuts for Times Square. Those tax cuts worked. Why not, then, try them for the entire city?

So what did the 42nd Street Development Plan really achieve? The four towers will eventually go up, but they won't look anything like those we proposed in the early eighties, and different developers will build them. No mart is on the horizon. The theaters have been given a new birth, but their parent is the market, not the government plan. The 42nd Street subway is still grungy.

The plan, in retrospect, seems like a giant Rube Goldberg device. It let public officials lower taxes without challenging the orthodoxies of New York's welfare state, and it let them drive out sex businesses without conflicting with court decisions on obscenity or unduly angering the cultural left. But Times Square's revitalization cost much more than it needed to—much more than if New York had simply abandoned the redevelopment project and pursued effective policing, smart zoning, and aggressive tax-cutting from the start.

—Autumn 1999

STEVEN G. CRAIG AND D. ANDREW AUSTIN

New York's Million Missing Jobs

NOTORIOUSLY, New York City's budget gives its taxpayers just about the worst deal in urban America. Not only do they pay startlingly high levies to fund it, but they also receive skimpy benefits from it in terms of the services that make urban life comfortable and convenient. Less visibly, the swollen budget, tumor-like, saps the city's economic health, depressing job growth, driving businesses away, and preventing the city from enjoying the expansive prosperity that buoys up much of the rest of the nation. The more money New York taxpayers spend, the less of a future do they seem to buy.

In outline, this tale is familiar enough, no doubt, if little regarded. Our goal here is to document and quantify these facts in dramatically concrete detail. Perhaps if New Yorkers can see graphically just how grotesquely out of whack municipal spending has come to be, how little of value it buys, and how catastrophic is the harm it inflicts on the city, they will summon the political resolve to change it. Doing nothing isn't a viable option: as our data suggest, this state of affairs can't endure forever. New jobs, proliferating in the other major U.S. urban centers, are not springing up in New York, which bodes ill for the city's long-term ability to sustain its bloated public sector.

New York's public sector is vastly larger than the public sector anywhere else. It employs a higher share of the workforce than in any other big U.S. city. Fully one in eight employed New Yorkers works for the local government, and an additional 3.4 percent of the city's labor force is in the social services sector, primarily funded by the city, bringing the total up to over 15 percent. By contrast, city workers account for only 8.7 percent of the average eastern big city's workforce and only 9.6 percent even of patronage-ridden Washington's. To pay the wages and unusually generous benefits of this vast army, and to cover the checks that so many public servants hand out to vendors and clients of every description, the residents of New York pay stupendous taxes. In their most whimsical moments, Gothamites take a perverse pride in being the most heavily taxed urban population outside Washington,

D.C. How gargantuan is New York's public sector? To find out, we compared the budgets of 18 of the largest U.S. cities (those with populations exceeding 500,000, in counties with populations exceeding 1 million) with the New York City budget. We also broke our comparison down into three geographic areas: eastern and midwestern cities (E&MW), southern and southwestern cities (S&SW), and cities of the West. The E&MW cities are most comparable with New York, with similar demographics and economic histories, shaped by similar changes in technology and industrial structure. The newer and quite different West and S&SW cities offer an instructive comparison, too, for they present a powerful source of competition for jobs and residents.

Finding comparable numbers on these matters is not easy or straightforward, and we have scrupulously tried to compare like with like. For those who take an interest in such things, this paragraph explains what we did. Because New York combines functions of both city and county government, you can't just compare New York's spending on hospitals with Chicago's, say, or Los Angeles's, because Cook County and L.A. County pay for that item, not the cities themselves. Therefore, we combine the per-capita levels of city and county governments for our 18 comparison examples (since in those areas the county per-capita expenses apply largely to the city). We also use county numbers for employment (since that is how they are available) and population (so that we can calculate meaningful employment-to-population ratios). The seven E&MW comparison cities are Baltimore, Boston, Chicago, Cleveland, Detroit, Indianapolis, and Philadelphia. For the West, the cities are Phoenix, Seattle, San Diego, Los Angeles, San Jose, and San Francisco. The S&SW cities are Jacksonville, San Antonio, Dallas, and Houston. We also include, in a category all its own, Washington, D.C. Our regional averages are simple averages across cities, rather than population-weighted averages. The fiscal data we examine are from 1994, the demographic data from the population census conducted in 1990—the latest comparable numbers available.

First look at New Yorkers' comparative tax burden. Gothamites paid $2,467 per person in city taxes during 1994—which means that for every $8 in income, they shipped almost $1 off to City Hall. Only Washington, D.C., burdens its residents more, with crushing taxes of $4,405 per capita. San Franciscans shoulder the next-highest tax burden after New Yorkers, but the $1,286 they pay is barely one-half the New York level. The tax level in New York is 2.75 times the average level of the E&MW comparison group, 3.3 times the level in the West, and a mind-boggling 4.36 times the level of the rising cities in the S&SW.

Of course, local taxes constitute only about 40.6 percent of New York City's total revenue, while grants from the state and federal government account for another 35.2 percent of it, and charges and other sources make up the remainder. When you add it all together, New York's total budget amounts to $6,682 per capita—2.4 times the E&MW, 2.1 times the West, and 2.97 times the S&SW.

One signal that the level of taxation is too high in New York is the extent to which the city strip-mines virtually every known revenue source. Only six cities out of 18 have city income taxes, and three of these half-dozen do not have sales taxes. Thus, the only four cities using all major sources of tax revenue are Washington, D.C. (the highest tax burden), New York (the second highest), Philadelphia (fifth), and Cleveland (sixth)—not a very prepossessing comparison group for the financial capital of the world. Three of these cities have been on the brink of bankruptcy sometime during the past 25 years, including New York; the fourth, Washington, D.C., isn't currently fit to govern itself, according to Congress.

The trend over time is not all that encouraging, either. Excluding education, since 1986 the city's expenditure has grown at a 2.3 percent annual rate in real terms (even faster when education is included), on top of the 3.85 percent annual growth due to inflation. Thus, not only is the public sector large, it is taking an ever-larger share of the income of New York taxpayers.

In an Autumn 1991 *City Journal* article ("Where the Money Goes"), one of us, Steven Craig, first detailed the disproportionate size of New York's budget and pointed out a further disturbing anomaly in New York's spending compared with that of other big cities. As the article showed, much of the city's spending didn't go to the basic services that most city residents use. Instead, vast sums flowed out to a multitude of activities most other cities don't perform. Consequently, the ordinary New Yorker faced a considerable fiscal deficit, meaning that the services government returned to him were worth far less than the tax cost to him. The fiscal deficit facing the average New York taxpayer, we find, remains dismayingly large in 1994—and in 1996 as well, though, as we'll show below, matters improved a bit in the intervening two years.

By the basic service budget, we mean expenditures on the core services cities traditionally provide, including police, fire, corrections, transportation, parks, and education (we have excluded utilities because, though New York City provides water to its residents, it provides neither gas nor electricity, as some other cities do). To compare New York with other big cities, we have had to subtract education, since in most localities, unlike New York, it is provided neither by the city nor the county government but by separate school districts. New York's expenditures on these basic services are $729 per person ($1,784 including education). This is 17 percent higher than the E&MW

average of $622 and comparably higher than the other regional averages in our sample.

But spending on basic services is nowhere near the stratospheric heights of the overall budget—17 percent higher is a far cry from the 110 percent to 197 percent by which the total New York budget exceeds the total average budgets of the comparison cities. Since basic spending is so much smaller a share of the budget in New York than elsewhere, the average resident is getting a much smaller return for his tax payment than he would in other large cities.

New York's basic service budget is only 14.8 percent of the total budget (after subtracting utilities and education for comparability), compared with 30.5 percent for the average city in the E&MW. Thus, New Yorkers are receiving only one-half the return on their tax dollars than the residents of a typical city in the region do. Even Washington, D.C., which has a public sector in much worse fiscal shape, is able to eke out 20.1 percent of its budget for basic services—though, of course, Washington's deplorable services remind us that expenditures do not necessarily equal quality. Still, New York would have to be twice as efficient as the average big city to equal the basic service level provided elsewhere—which is very far from the case.

If New York spends so little of its city budget on basic services, where is the bulk of the money going? Answer: to low-income assistance, to debt service, and to a host of activities that are not the usual province of city governments.

New York spends more than ten times as much per capita as the average E&MW city—and 58.5 times as much as the S&SW average—on low-income assistance, which comprises social services, hospitals and health, and housing. The difference between New York and cities in the West is less dramatic—because, like New York, California cities have significant local responsibility for welfare—but it is still more than 100 percent larger. New York's hospital spending is an astronomical $488 per capita, 312 percent more than cities in the E&MW, 214 percent more than the West, and 404 percent more than the S&SW. Similarly, public housing expenditures in New York amount to $349 per capita—over 350 percent of the level of spending in any other region in the country.

True, high levels of state and federal aid partially fund many of these low-income assistance programs. The total cost of these programs is $1,959 per capita, but state and federal aid lighten the net burden to New York's taxpayers to "only" $918 per person. Other cities benefit from these aid programs, too, of course. Subtracting out state and federal aid, the city faces an enormous net burden relative to other cities: the local taxpayer must pay 358 percent more for low-income assistance than taxpayers in other E&MW

cities, almost double what those in the West pay, and six times the level of those in the S&SW. And since the city is not getting back from Albany any more than Gothamites are paying in state taxes, in a very real sense state aid dollars are coming entirely out of city taxpayers' pockets, too.

New York spends a similarly disproportionate $494 per capita on "expenditures not elsewhere classified," a grab bag of goods and services completely outside the expenditure pattern for typical local governments—everything from crime-victim compensation to services to senior citizens who are not poor. The typical city in the E&MW spends only $180 per capita on this category, or just over one-third the amount spent in New York. Other cities spend even less: $112 in the West and a thrifty $73 in the S&SW.

Our comparative fiscal data come from fiscal year 1994, the last under Mayor David Dinkins's budgetary control. How have things changed with Mayor Giuliani in City Hall? Though we don't have the data to compare New York with other cities during the Giuliani administration, we can compare New York's 1996 tax and expenditure patterns with those of 1994. The following discussion, however, pertains only to the city's "on budget" expenditures, amounting to about three-quarters of the total. New York accounts for many big-ticket agencies, including housing and hospitals, elsewhere.

Overall, the picture is slightly improved. In nominal dollars, total taxes in New York were about constant in 1996 compared with 1994, indicating a drop in real terms (that is, after accounting for inflation) of some 5.2 percent—a modest amount but still a change in the right direction at least. Again in real terms, total revenue to the city fell slightly less, by 3 percent, because increases in state and federal aid offset the tax reductions.

But if total taxes haven't dropped much, the profile of what those dollars buy the taxpayer has improved. Spending on basic services has increased, mainly because police spending went up by 26.5 percent. With the murder rate down by over 60 percent and New Yorkers feeling that their city has a new lease on life as a result, at least some of these dollars appear to have provided a return to taxpayers. Fire department expenditures rose 8.3 percent, perhaps accounting in part for the fall in fire-related deaths to their lowest point in 37 years in 1996.

Social services expenditures fell by 1.6 percent in 1996 from 1994, or 6.7 percent in real terms. But by the end of the 1996 fiscal year on June 30, New York's highly successful welfare reforms had only recently really gotten under way: between March 1995 and June 1997 the city cut 280,000 recipients from its welfare rolls, representing meaningful future savings.

Worryingly, debt service expenditures grew 4.9 percent from 1994. Our comparison data show New York taking on debt as if it were building its infrastructure anew—which it clearly is not. Incredibly, New York has per-capita debt service expenditures 14 percent higher than the young and rapidly expanding cities of the S&SW, which you'd expect to have high debt and debt service levels, even though Gotham's population has not yet returned to its 1980 (or even its 1940) level. Compared with older cities, New York spent 2.3 times what the typical E&MW city paid for debt service per capita in 1994. Given the maturity of New York's economy and of its infrastructure, the $4,723 per capita of net general debt that weighs down New York taxpayers is tough to justify.

In a similar vein, pension contributions by the city ballooned 6.5 percent in 1996 from a 1994 base that was already over twice the level of the average E&MW city. Fattened pensions are one method the city has long used to shower more money on city employees without resorting to an immediate tax hike to pay for them. Some of these bills from the past are coming due.

New York, it is often said, is unique: so it's natural to ask whether, in comparison with the other major U.S. cities, its demographic and economic characteristics are special in ways that might justify its huge public sector and out-of-kilter budget. We again look at our 18 comparison cities, although for this comparison the data come from the 1990 population census (which contains income data from 1989). Relative income and demographic changes are fairly slow, however, so we believe the relative comparison is valid despite movements in the levels. Even though several comparisons show New York as unusual, the short answer is no, New York isn't different enough from other cities to require its unique spending level.

New York is a rich city, with per-capita income of $16,291, fully 33 percent greater than the E&MW average. Nonetheless, the average income level is not quite as high as in the typical city in the West. Further, if we took out the West's last-ranked Phoenix, New York's per-capita income would be only 93 percent of income in the West. Yet at the very upper end of the income distribution, New York sparkles; no city has a higher combination of share and level of wealth. For example, 1.88 percent of Gotham's families have income greater than $150,000, considerably above the E&MW rate of only 0.67 percent and even above the 1.72 percent rate in the millionaire-studded West. The rich in New York are richer as well, since the average income of the 1.88 percent of families with incomes above $150,000 is $300,048. This is greater than all the western cities and lags only Baltimore (with $315,000) and Cleveland (with $312,000), which have far fewer such families (0.77 percent and 0.15 percent, respectively).

To be sure, because the city is well endowed on the upper end, it can arguably afford a larger public sector than elsewhere. Slightly larger. If taxes were proportional to income, New York's taxes could be as much as 33 percent higher than the typical E&MW city. If the taxes were sufficiently progressive, the disparity could even be a little greater. Taxes 175 percent above average, however, are off the charts.

At the other extreme, while New York's poverty rate of 19.3 percent looks like a big number, it is lower than the 21.7 percent poverty rate in the other E&MW cities. Females head 8.5 percent of New York households, a whisker above the E&MW average of 8.4 percent. The poverty problem, in other words, is a national problem, not one localized in New York and thus requiring runaway welfare spending.

Demographically, the city's peculiarities are only at the margins—overwhelmingly, New York's demographics resemble, rather than differ from, those of other cities. The population of the five boroughs is 52.3 percent white, quite close to the 54.0 percent E&MW average. True, nonwhite New Yorkers are more various than elsewhere: blacks constitute only 28.8 percent of the city's total population, compared with 40.2 percent in the other E&MW cities, and New York's Hispanic population (both black and white) constitutes 23.7 percent, way above the E&MW cities and comparable with many California cities (though below Texas's numbers). And even more unusual, 28.4 percent of New Yorkers are foreign-born. Only Los Angeles and San Francisco have a higher share, and only two E&MW cities (Boston and Chicago) have even more than 10 percent. Similarly, New York has a disproportionate share of adults who do not speak English (10.6 percent) or are noncitizens (14.4 percent).

So, too, with New York's age distribution: despite its quirks, in the most important respect it is remarkably similar to other places. To be sure, it has fewer kids than most places: only 25.7 percent of its population is under 20 years old, compared with 28.4 percent for the average E&MW city. In addition, over 20 percent of those kids attend private school, compared with 18.6 percent for the average E&MW city (and much lower for the West and S&SW). But this relatively small young population is partially offset by a relatively large elderly population (65 and over), 13.0 percent of New Yorkers, compared with the 12.2 percent E&MW average. The net result—and this is the key point—is that New York ends up with a slightly larger than average working-age population.

This population, moreover, is relatively well educated. True, the 12.9 percent of the population with terminal college degrees is far below the West (and even the S&SW), but it is significantly above the E&MW. Moreover, the 10.0 percent with a graduate or professional degree is higher than all the regional averages. On the flip side, however, the 31.7 percent of the adult population that has not graduated from high school is also high, except compared with the E&MW, where it is average. Thus, as with the income-distribution figures, New York is slightly larger at both the upper and lower tail, although not by nearly enough to explain its bloated public sector.

What is the consequence for New York of its out-of-kilter taxation and public spending? To us, the most telling—and disturbing—comparative number is something called the employment-to-population ratio, which measures the relationship between the number of jobs in a given city (which may be held by commuters as well as by locals) and the number of residents (who may work elsewhere than in the city). The employment-to-population ratio is an excellent indicator of economic health, especially for a city that has distorted its housing market through extensive rent regulation and consequently has kept its population artificially low. A city that is thriving as the economic center of its region has a high concentration of employers, a high number of commuters flocking in to their jobs, and consequently a high employment-to-population ratio. Back in the 1960s, or the fifties or the forties, New York had an employment-to-population ratio higher than that of any U.S. city except Boston and San Francisco—some 20 percent higher than the average E&MW city in 1962. But this specialness had evaporated by 1979, when New York had an employment-to-population ratio slightly below the E&MW average, and by 1994, the city's ratio was 20 percent below the E&MW average and below the average of the other two regions as well. While 6.9 percent of New York's private sector jobs disappeared between 1962 and 1979, and employment kept on slipping until 1994, the E&MW metropolitan areas saw a 14.5 percent job growth until 1979 and a slight further rise since then.

What accounts for the difference? Vast technological and industrial changes—the decline of manufacturing, the revolutions in communications and distribution—swept over all old U.S. cities more or less equally. So why did New York suffer so great a relative decline in this key measure of economic strength, despite the magnitude of its regional economy, its ample access to suppliers and markets, its relatively well-educated labor force? Why didn't new industries grow up to take the place of the old in New York, as happened elsewhere in the E&MW?

Our data strongly suggest that the city's strikingly disproportionate level of taxation and its deep fiscal deficit are to blame. The numbers don't prove it conclusively, of course. But it is easy to see how such a cause might well produce such an effect. If business taxes (and the costs of complying with business regulation) exceed the economic benefit of being located in the city, businesses will decamp in search of higher profits elsewhere. In addition, high city taxes mean that employees will demand higher wages—even suburb-dwelling employees subject to the city's commuter tax. And that will drive firms to lower-wage areas.

The cost to the city of this ongoing economic erosion is enormous. If New York's employment-to-population ratio had remained equal to the current E&MW average—that is, if it had the average number of jobs given its residential population—its employment base would be 745,000 jobs larger. If it had remained the employment center it was in 1962, its employment base would be over 1 million jobs larger. At that employment level, if city taxes were 25.7 percent lower than today, the total tax revenue to the city would be the same as now.

This is a familiar conundrum: a rise in tax rates can in the long term produce a shrinkage of revenues. And as the employment tax base erodes, it starts a downward spiral from which it is very hard to escape. The residential tax base is likely in time to follow jobs out of the city. And just a few strategic taxpayers leaving can make a huge difference, since 5.5 percent of the taxpayers pay 47.6 percent of New York's personal income tax. As people and jobs leave the city, property values and tax receipts fall, as do income and sales tax receipts. And if the total tax burden remains the same, the per-capita burden grows even more insupportable.

Taxes and regulation, perennially cited as causes of urban decline, are problems that local government can affect relatively quickly, if not easily. Why not start by getting rid of either the city's sales tax or its income tax? The Giuliani administration could expand its move to exempt clothing from sales taxation to all the other sectors, or it could extend its move to repeal one of the income surtaxes to the entire tax. Sure, tax revenue would drop. But there's plenty of room in the bloated city budget to make corresponding spending cuts. General sales taxes, for example, raise $341 per capita. If the city cut $341 per capita (in 1994) from the unfocused "other" spending, the remainder would still be about average for E&MW cities (and above average compared with the remaining areas). Ending city income taxes would cut a heftier $828 per person out of the budget; but if New York reduced direct general expenses by $828 per person, it would still be spending over twice per capita what the average comparison city in the E&MW spends. Dropping one of the city taxes would start to make New York's fiscal situation a little less distinctive—just what it needs to give residents and employers something to smile about. And if it spent more of the remaining $5,854 per capita on the core service budget and less on pensions, low-income assistance, and its grab bag of nonessential government functions, New York might even start winning back some of those 1 million missing jobs.

—*Autumn 1997*

HOWARD HUSOCK

Let's Break Up the Big Cities

IT SOUNDS LIKE HERESY to say so, but maybe the consolidation of the five boroughs into the City of New York, whose 100th anniversary we celebrate this month, wasn't such a good idea. The question is not just of theoretical interest. Today prominent urbanists are urging a new wave of consolidation, exhorting cities to merge with their suburbs to form region-wide metropolitan governments. But equally energetic advocates have mounted fierce political campaigns to make exactly the opposite view prevail—to form smaller, decentralized city governments for neighborhoods that secede from a larger whole. There are good reasons to believe that the secessionists are right. Indeed, even New York, notwithstanding all the anniversary hoopla, would work much better split into pieces.

The idea of metropolitan government—a benevolent, expert central administration for urban areas—has tempted efficiency-minded urban theorists for generations. Here, they've argued, is a way of bringing order to the chaos of central cities surrounded by a crazy quilt of independent suburbs. Though in the 1920s the movement saw metropolitanism as a recipe for improved city services and non-corrupt leadership, by the 1960s advocates added two more goals: redistribution of wealth, with affluent suburbs supporting public services in poorer inner cities; and environmental protection, with enlightened planners dictating the shape of future development, preventing "urban sprawl" and keeping "ticky-tacky" suburbs from devouring farmland.

Today's foremost champion of metropolitan government, David Rusk, onetime mayor of Albuquerque and self-described former civil rights and anti-poverty worker, travels the lecture circuit spreading the gospel of his 1993 book, *Cities Without Suburbs*. A unified metropolitan government, Rusk proclaims, can "profoundly transform the long-term outlook for failing central cities and help re-energize American society." Cities that annex their suburbs, Rusk claims, adding his own twist to earlier arguments, not only will improve the lot of their poorest residents but also will be more prosperous overall than those that don't. As to how exactly the new metropolitanism will produce new wealth, he is disconcertingly vague.

Though big-city mayors and elite opinion makers like Rusk's views and consider them mainstream, on the political front lines these ideas don't carry much weight. Across the country local activists have been rejecting the push to create bigger jurisdictions. They want to retain—or create—smaller governments, by seceding from existing city governments, by incorporating new, smaller jurisdictions carved out of larger ones, or by resisting annexation by larger governments. New Yorkers are familiar with this move toward the local: five years ago the Staten Island secession movement blazed up fiercely, though the State Legislature eventually snuffed it out. But similar efforts are catching fire in many other locales.

Most notably, in Los Angeles, the ValleyVote movement, with Governor Pete Wilson's support, proposes to detach the entire San Fernando Valley (population: 1.2 million) from the rest of the city. Proponents say such a secession could come to a referendum vote in the year 2000. The next step could well be to split up the residential expanse of the Valley into 23 newly incorporated municipalities. In Florida four successful referenda since 1992 have given birth to four new municipalities within Dade County, the administrative district for 1.5 million residents of the suburbs surrounding central Miami. Six other new municipalities are in the works. Around Tucson, suburbs that have long resisted annexation by the central city leaped at the chance state legislation offered them last year to incorporate as independent towns. Two have already done so; six others have proposed or already scheduled votes. Suburban activists outside Houston and Atlanta have strenuously resisted the efforts of those cities to bite off pieces of their suburbs. Nor is localism limited to the U.S. In Canada, Citizens for Local Democracy (whose leaders include revered urban theorist Jane Jacobs) successfully organized resistance to the Ontario government's "megacity" plan to submerge, under the banner of cost reduction, six independent municipalities into a Rusk-like greater Toronto.

The conflict between localism and metropolitan government is a clash not over form but philosophy of government. To liberals like Rusk, localism reflects yet another example of what journalist Robert Kuttner has called the "revolt of the Haves"; it is a greedy retreat from the commonweal, sacrificing the city for the short-term improvement of the suburbs. But Rusk believes the revolt of the Haves is futile: it threatens the suburbs themselves, as inner-city chaos overtakes the surrounding communities. In this vein, Myron Orfield, a state legislator from Minneapolis and author of an influential text on metropolitan government, laments that "powerful resentments, based on class and race," have prevented cities from merging with suburbs to create efficiency and social justice. If the suburbs shared their often considerable riches, older, poorer neighborhoods wouldn't decline into dilapidated urban ghettos.

Orfield's view, the elite wisdom about secession and incorporation movements, is simply wrong. Localism is popular not because it promises a sweetheart deal for a few privileged suburbanites at the expense of the greater good, or because the unsophisticated fail to understand a demonstrably superior metropolitan approach. Instead, it rests on common sense—which economics and political science amply confirm. Voters' common sense tells them that the closer they are to government, the more it will respond to their demands. They will see their hard-earned tax dollars spent on the kind of projects they prefer and will have a greater assurance that interest groups—such as public employee unions—will not usurp local government for the benefit of their own members, who may not even live in the city in which they work.

In fact, there are good reasons to go one step further. To improve older neighborhoods in older cities requires not a single, bigger government but increased numbers of smaller ones. Rather than expanding cities, we should break them up into an array of independent, neighborhood-based governments that would set their own property-tax rates, elect their own officials, and give city residents the same control and sense of community that their suburban counterparts take for granted. City dwellers could direct public spending to the things they consider most important. They could ask the local public works director why their street went unplowed or unpaved, or push the local chief of police to deal with the rowdy playground gang before things get out of hand. Inevitably, such a system would favor economic growth over redistribution. Freed from centralized bureaucracies, these neighborhoods, including many of the older, poorer ones, would prosper. As for paying to maintain, or build, expensive regional infrastructure systems: for that purpose, these independent local governments could cooperate in a loose confederation, or "special purpose district."

I will admit to some personal bias in all this. As a resident and onetime minor elected official in Brookline—a Boston suburb of 56,000—I'm convinced that the town's decision 125 years ago not to merge with the central city is a key reason for our good schools, clean streets, and low crime rate, despite our closeness to the central city. My town is a living advertisement for the local control that leaders of today's secession, incorporation, and annexation campaigns seek.

These campaigns don't add up to a movement in the sense that metropolitanism is a movement, supported by foundations and promoted at conferences. The leaders of the new localism are responding to purely local conditions. Yet though they are generally unaware of their counterparts elsewhere, local activists make strikingly similar observations and complaints. Consider two of the most active and important sites of the new localism, both in areas of rapid population growth—southern California and south Florida.

In Los Angeles the head of the ValleyVote movement is a commercial real estate broker named Jeff Brain, whose office, in a converted toy store at the rear of a strip mall, overflows with clippings from the L.A. *Daily News*, the Valley newspaper, which has pushed hard for a secession vote. In his professional life, Brain rents out storefronts in this and other small strip malls along the length of Ventura Boulevard, one of the San Fernando Valley's main streets. Brain also helps organize a network of 30 local home owner and business organizations, with such typical LA names as the Tract 115105 Neighborhood Association. Though some affluent enclaves dot the Valley, on the whole this is Queens, not Westchester; New Jersey, not Connecticut. This is the valley of the shop-till-you-drop Valley Girl, where residents in small ranch houses and whitewashed apartments gaze up at the Santa Monica mountains, beyond which lies Beverly Hills. The Valley—white, middle-class, and heavily Jewish—is increasingly Latino and Asian. Some 27 percent of Valley residents are Spanish-speaking; 11 percent live below the poverty line. New restaurants sport signs in Farsi or Cyrillic characters; at Torah-land, a growing Orthodox Jewish community looks for bargains on yarmulkes and tallises.

Jeff Brain's complaints are very specific. Most nights, only two police cars patrol his own community of Sherman Oaks, which, like other residential areas in the Valley, has its own name but not its own government. Sidewalk cleaning in the commercial areas along Ventura Boulevard is dismal, even though merchants pay extra fees to the city for a private contractor to do the work. Brain also resents the private school tuition he pays for his four children to keep them out of the giant LA Unified School District, with its unmanageable 800,000 students. Moreover, the city pays little for Valley road repair (only $4 million out of a $28 million budget), even though the Valley contains a third of the city's total area. Look at the number of residents per City Council member, Brain complains: some 250,000 people per Council district. With fewer than 100,000 residents, nearby independent cities like Burbank and San Fernando have their own mayors and city councils, along with lower business taxes and an easier permit process. Brain looks enviously at older commercial main streets in these neighboring communities, where small beautification steps have paid big dividends by helping to attract and retain shoppers and businesses, while Van Nuys Boulevard, another of the Valley's main drags, grows shabbier by the day.

For Brain, being too distant from local government to get anything accomplished is more than a metaphor. "In order to get something for our area," he observes, "we have to go downtown. That's an hour's drive to start. Then we have to convince council members from all over the city. They say, 'Why should you get something if my neighborhood doesn't?' Then you reach an impasse."

Such frustration drove Brain to mount a successful campaign this past fall to persuade Governor Wilson to sign legislation allowing city neighborhoods to detach, without first getting the permission of their existing city councils. Next he'll try to get the more than 100,000 petition signatures necessary to get a regional advisory board to examine the issue, as required by law. Brain expects the petition drive—and then the secession vote—to succeed. And he believes that large parts of Los Angeles will follow suit, seeking to detach and incorporate on their own. "We've had interest from throughout the city and throughout the state," he says.

In Miami, localism has advanced even further. From his dark, wood-paneled office as chairman of one of the city's leading law firms, Eugene Stearns has already been through the fire of referenda campaigns like those Jeff Brain anticipates. A native Miamian who has watched the city change around him, Stearns is no political neophyte. He helped run the campaigns of former Florida Democratic governor Ruben Askew and served as his chief of staff. He thought he had left political life behind to build up his law firm—until 1991, when he heard that developers planned two new 800-room hotels close to his home in Key Biscayne, an enclave of 8,500 residents within so-called unincorporated Dade County. Key Biscayne had no local government: the county government, housed in a downtown Miami office tower, supplied the police force, firefighters, and garbage collectors.

"I figured I was a fairly connected guy, and I wanted to do something to get this hotel decision re-examined," he says—"not necessarily to block it entirely but to scale it down some. And I was told, 'This is a done deal: forget it.'" His unexpected sense of powerlessness led him to reflect on the overall quality of services in Key Biscayne.

Well-known and affluent, with luxurious waterfront condos and pastel Mediterranean-style homes, Key Biscayne nevertheless had embarrassingly pitted streets and shabby recreation areas far worse than in nearby independent municipalities—even blue-collar ones like Miami Shores, where many cops and schoolteachers lived. As in Los Angeles's San Fernando Valley, political representation was disproportionately weak, with just 13 out of 100 county commissioners representing the 1.5 million county residents who lived outside the core city of Miami (population: 365,000). Stearns grew convinced that centralized government made it too difficult for citizens to influence decisions about their neighborhoods. Moreover, he was certain that bigger government, with its layers of management, wasted on unproductive bureaucracies' funds that would otherwise flow into the capital improvements—new baseball fields, new public docks—that he and his neighbors wanted. "It all comes down to bigger isn't better," he says.

Stearns decided not to waste time fighting specific policies but to attack the underlying problem. He proposed to lead an independence movement to incorporate Key Biscayne as a village, with its own council and full-time manager. In November 1992 the incorporation referendum sailed through with a resounding 70 percent of the vote. Since then, Key Biscayne's assessed property valuation has skyrocketed by some $800 million, because local control has made the municipality a still more desirable place to live—and Eugene Stearns, from his nerve center in downtown Miami, has become the leader of an incorporation movement throughout south Florida. He has provided his law firm's services *pro bono* to leaders of four similar referenda, with others in the offing. Three of them succeeded, making Stearns the godfather to the new municipalities of Pine Crest, Aventura, and Sunny Isles, as well as his own Key Biscayne.

The referendum that failed is Stearns's most interesting battle. He served as advisor to Shirley Gibson, a black retired policewoman who sought to carve out an independent municipality called Destiny from the subdivisions surrounding the car dealerships and racetracks on Route 441, north of Miami. The area, 80 percent black, is a magnet for upwardly mobile African-American families from inner-city Miami neighborhoods like Liberty City and Overtown. But Gibson, an entrepreneur who had started a business that quirkily combined two of her own interests—a beauty-supply-shop-*cum*-private-detective-agency—believed that, for all the energetic striving of its residents, the area was suffering neglect.

"We had the worst bus service, the worst parks, the worst police protection," she recalls. "The kids couldn't drink out of the water fountains in the parks, and the bathrooms didn't work." Yet county planners told Gibson that she should be grateful for what she had—that the proposed new city was a "recipient community": it received services valued at $21 million but paid only $17 million in taxes. Gibson rejected this. She knew from experience that the high overhead costs of centralized county government gobbled up tax money before it could reach her neighborhood parks. "I'd been a policewoman; I knew that you had six layers of supervision in a big department and only two in a smaller one," she explains. Stung, too, by the condescending label "recipient community," with its insinuation of public assistance, Gibson, with Stearns's help, led the 1995 incorporation campaign.

And she would have won, had not the Miami Dolphins' Joe Robbie football stadium stood on the outskirts of the proposed new municipality. Owner Wayne Huizenga, concerned about how a new local government might tax his stadium, led an opposition that outspent the pro-Destiny forces by almost eight to one ($300,000-plus to $40,000) and emphasized the possible job losses middle-class black families, many of whom worked for government, might face. Destiny failed to gain incorporation by 700 votes of the 5,500 cast. Gibson does not rule out another referendum, although a change in the law now requires the permission of the sitting Dade County commissioners. Despite the loss, Gibson notes, services in her neighborhood have improved, a change she attributes to the mere threat of secession.

The reason to believe that these incorporation and secession leaders are right begins with history—even though the metropolitanists assert that history is on their side. But in fact the consolidation of formerly independent municipalities in New York, Philadelphia, Pittsburgh, and Boston, which metropolitan advocate Rusk cites to buttress his case, didn't arise from a Rusk-like belief that bigger was better. Rather, newly developing areas saw consolidation as the best means to plug into the services core cities offered. By the 1920s, as soon as suburbs discovered other means short of consolidation to hook up to regional infrastructure—typically special-purpose districts—they stopped joining central cities.

Even when given the option of voting for mergers and annexations, Americans historically have supported the creation of more local governments, not fewer. "The American system is one of complete decentralization, the primary and vital ideal of which is that local affairs should be managed by local authorities," wrote legal observer Thomas Cooley perceptively in 1868. Municipalities have differentiated themselves from one another for good reason. The formation of independent cities and towns fueled the explosive economic takeoff of the late 1800s; it defused tensions between immigrant and native-born; and it allowed the upwardly mobile to build communities that reflected their hard-won new social status. Industrialists, including the founders of Cudahy (incorporated so they could build a meatpacking plant just south of Milwaukee), have always sought safe haven from the hands of government regulators. A boon for owners, such municipalities also provided a living wage for employees and buttressed the property values of residential areas in nearby municipalities. Distinct ethnic and cultural groups established their own niches, as in the once "dry" towns of Pasadena and Compton, California, or Oak Bluffs, Massachusetts, where Methodists for many years used local control to keep out alcohol. The lesson is crystal clear: independent jurisdictions are a crucial means through which a nation as diverse as the U.S. can develop a modus vivendi among peoples of sharply different values and wildly various backgrounds.

Even as advocates (including the Department of Housing and Urban Development) beat the drums for metropolitan government, the number of local governments in the U.S. kept rising. From 1952 to 1992, the number of municipalities grew from 16,807 to 19,279. While a few core cities—Indianapolis, Jacksonville, and Nashville—have merged with their surrounding counties to form metro governments in recent years, citizens have overwhelmingly scorned the metro vision over the past half-century. Champaign and Urbana in Illinois twice rejected consolidation, even though they're often thought of as a single college town. Voters in the Knoxville and

Richmond areas refused city-county consolidation, as did voters in David Rusk's own Albuquerque (before Rusk's tenure as mayor). Even where citizens actually have embraced metro governments, suburbanization has inexorably continued, with metro governments generally stalled at their original lines.

There's no shortage of theory to explain why this long-standing American preference for localism makes sense. The key fact: we don't all want the same things from our local jurisdictions. Those with small children may care most about education, unmarried joggers may want to spend public money on parks, and the tidy-minded may want the streets cleaned three times a week. Forty years ago, in a brief but classic essay, economist Charles Tiebout argued that local governments do more than coexist side by side. Instead, they compete with one another for residents by offering different packages of services. Of course, wealthier communities can provide more amenities than poorer ones; that's part of the free-market incentive structure. But at equivalent income levels, governments can differentiate themselves, in terms of the kinds of services they offer and also the cost-efficiency with which they provide them. If they fail to provide what people want at reasonable cost, residents can "vote with their feet," wrote Tiebout. When municipalities lose residents, property values fall, leaving remaining residents with a powerful incentive to figure out what's gone wrong.

I can attest, through personal experience, that Tiebout's argument is sound. Several years ago, I agreed to join a volunteer financial-planning advisory committee to examine my town's costs for specific services. The committee immediately gathered cost data from comparable municipalities. Where our costs differed, we asked hard questions. Why do our police officers take twice as much sick time as those in other towns? Is it a management problem, a defect in our union contract—or are our police simply older than those on other forces? How can we improve matters? We were acting as Tiebout would have us act: "Public service agencies," he has written, "may be forced to compete over the service levels offered in relation to the taxes charged."

Daniel Elazar, director of Temple University's Center for the Study of Federalism, observes that some of the nation's most smoothly functioning cities may owe part of their success to competition of this sort. Elazar notes that in the Bay Area, three flourishing midsize cities—San Francisco, Oakland, and San Jose—compete (and also cooperate) with one another and with Silicon Valley towns like Palo Alto and Sunnyvale. Prosperous and efficient Minneapolis and St. Paul, along with a gaggle of nearby cities with populations between 100,000 and 150,000, do the same.

In other words, because of this competitive, anti-monopolistic mechanism, smaller—not bigger, as the metropolitanists contend—is more efficient. New research from the Institute of Government at Florida International University, located right in the middle of Dade County's wave of incorporations, soundly debunks the big-is-efficient argument that is the linchpin of the metropolitanists' case. Public administration professor Milan Dluhy examined the costs per resident for a wide range of core municipal services in metropolitan Dade County and in 24 "fragmented municipalities" within and around the county. Dluhy found that economies of scale existed in only two areas: fire protection and library services. Localities can provide all the other services—police, recreation, public works, waste management—at equal or less cost.

Evidence from other economists strongly supports the case that smaller is cheaper and more efficient than bigger. David Sjoquist analyzed 48 metropolitan areas in the South and found that competing local governments kept costs down. As he puts it: "The level of expenditures will fall as the number of jurisdictions rises." Conversely, Richard Wagner and Warren Webber, looking at counties in 16 southern states, found that consolidation and centralization led to greater spending, not less.

Why exactly would costs increase after governments merge? Jane Jacobs tartly gave one explanation in a recent talk: "Anyone who has had to deal with a big-city bureaucracy knows that the idea that bigger is more efficient is laughable." Another explanation invokes Tiebout's point about differing "packages" of government services. A newly consolidated government, replacing a group of smaller jurisdictions that had offered a variety of service packages with differing costs, comes under pressure to provide the same package of services to everyone—and always the highest level and greatest variety of services, since no community is willing to accept a service cut.

Tiebout's smaller-is-better theory finds interesting confirmation in National Bureau of Economic Research economist Caroline Hoxby's investigation of one key government service: schools. By Tiebout's lights, many small school districts should be better and cheaper than one huge one, because they will compete with one another to minimize costs and, within the confines of state regulations, to offer somewhat different educational "packages." Hoxby looked at metropolitan areas in which lots of small municipalities run their own school districts. Exhibit A: the Boston area, with some 70 municipal school districts half an hour from downtown. Many have only a few thousand students, compared with Dade County, Florida's Amalgamated District, with 400,000-plus students, or the LA Unified School District's 800,000 students. Sure enough, Hoxby found (after controlling for a wide range of factors, from race to income, that could explain variation) that even a fairly small increase in the number of districts—from three to 13, say—had a big effect. Costs per child dropped 17 percent, while reading and math scores went up 2 percent—perhaps, in part, because parents attended school meetings and other school events at a rate two-thirds higher than in larger districts.

But if you look at school districts across the country, you see relatively few Tiebout-style systems like the Boston area's but rather vast, centralized amalgamated districts that look like the metropolitanists' dream come true. And their performance doesn't do much to buttress the theory that big jurisdictions are efficient and cost-effective. Between 1952 and 1992, even though consolidation bypassed America's municipalities, it did descend upon the nation's school districts, reducing their number by over 75 percent (from 67,355 to 14,422). At the same time, costs skyrocketed and quality plummeted—not coincidentally. Nor is it a coincidence that teachers' unions swelled in power: larger jurisdictions put average citizens at a disadvantage, since even the most zealous unpaid neighborhood activist is little match for the full-time paid staffs of public sector unions, who know local officials and understand how the system works well enough to make the interest of their members prevail.

In the same way, as government jurisdictions get larger, control gradually melts away from voters; realizing the difficulty of influencing officials, and increasingly impotent against the organized electoral power of public employees, individuals give up. As Jeff Brain likes to point out, voter participation is much lower in the San Fernando Valley areas that are part of Los Angeles than in those that are independent municipalities. Growing voter apathy gives organized public employees and other special interests a clear field to advance their own agendas, while the higher campaign spending that comes with big government allows unions and government contractors to sway officials by providing campaign funds and volunteers.

Political science sheds further light on why voters tune out. Successful governmental systems, political scientists believe, have a high degree of political homogeneity—where voters generally share similar preferences—in contrast to political heterogeneity, with tightly wound tensions among many disparate voting groups. Given a large number of small jurisdictions, voters can sort themselves out according to what kind of place they want to live in, and they can pick the kind of representation they want. Homogeneity is high, and even losing voters are not violently disappointed and disaffected, since they live within the same universe of desires as the winners. There is no large group of voters whose dearest hopes have been dashed and who feel impotent and excluded. Maybe that's why polls consistently show that local government is much more popular than the federal government—which has taken on more and more tasks for itself but is not very likely to reflect a homogeneous preference. The title of a 1959 essay by James Pennock sums up this idea with still-unsurpassed brevity: "Federal and Unitary Government: Disharmony and Frustration."

Not only is metropolitanist Rusk mistaken when he asserts that bigger jurisdictions are more efficient than smaller; he is equally in error when he claims that they promote growth better. He contends that "elastic" cities—those empowered to annex new-growth suburbs—will economically outperform "inelastic" cities, frozen into historical boundaries. "Metro areas containing elastic cities," he pronounces, "have had higher growth rates than metro areas with inelastic cities." But economists John Blair, Samuel Staley, and Zhongcai Zhang have left this assertion in tatters. Rusk appears to have made the classic mistake of confusing correlation with causality. If cities that annexed their suburbs after World War II prospered, that does not prove that the annexations sparked the prosperity, and certainly Rusk offers no explanation of why they would. These economists observe that the cities Rusk singles out as elasticity success stories outperformed "for reasons unrelated to elasticity": Rusk compared newer-growth, non-manufacturing cities with older, manufacturing-based cities during a period of manufacturing decline, and he compared state capitals to non-capitals during a time of governmental growth. Finally, they note, if you compare the entire metropolitan areas of inelastic cities with the metropolitan areas of their elastic rivals, there's not much difference. Rusk himself notes that elastic metro Houston built new housing for 2.4 million new residents between 1950 and 1990, while inelastic metro Detroit built housing for 1.9 million. Not very persuasive evidence of elasticity's superiority.

The reverse of Rusk's proposition is closer to the truth: metro government is more likely to discourage than to foster growth. And further, quite possibly the older, inner-city neighborhoods Rusk is most concerned about—for him they are the most telling indictment of inelasticity—are depressed partly because of their imprisonment within the growth-stifling big-city governments we already have.

Why? Consider what I'll call the golden goose effect. Communities are willing (indeed, eager) to accept new development, the golden goose, so long as they can be sure of getting the golden eggs—strengthening their tax base and adding or improving such neighborhood amenities as schools, parks, or police protection. Metro government changes this whole calculation. Suddenly there is no guarantee that city hall will use new tax revenues the neighborhood generates to improve the neighborhood. Without the assurance that it will be able to make use of new taxes, a community's incentives change dramatically. Suddenly new developments bring a guarantee of costs but not of benefits. Areas asked to accept the new industrial park may get no improved services or new school buildings; the additional tax revenue, if not simply swallowed up in the day-to-day administration of the consolidated government, may well be spent in other parts of the city—probably those with the most political clout, which will probably not be the poorer areas.

In fact, poorer parts of cities, much as they would presumably be eager to attract new development, have reasons to be wary of it: they may get the smoke and noise, while more affluent and politically powerful neighborhoods get superior services. I recall, as a young newspaper reporter, covering the story of a home owner in Boston's Roxbury black ghetto who fought bitterly, and successfully, to close down a large neighborhood baking plant. Why should she put up with noise and trash, she reasoned—and still have to live in an area where streets were poorly swept and police response time poor? The same reasoning helps explain neighborhood opposition to new superstores in New York. Who wants the traffic without a guarantee of improved services?

Helping these poor neighborhoods is Rusk's real agenda for metro government, which at heart he believes will help them not so much by facilitating economic growth as by facilitating redistribution. Rusk discloses his true priorities in his book's conclusion: "It is not important that local residents have their garbage picked up by a metrowide garbage service or their parks managed by a metrowide parks and recreation department," he writes. "It is important that all local governments pursue common policies that will diminish racial and economic segregation. In baldest terms, sustained success requires moving poor people from bad city neighborhoods to good suburban neighborhoods and moving dollars from relatively wealthy suburban governments to poorer city governments."

Stripped of its pretenses about efficiency and economic growth, the metro movement turns out to be a campaign to support and enlarge the growing package of social services that our big cities provide—what might be called the municipal welfare state. Rusk asserts that those who have fled the crime and disorder of inner cities must be joined with those who have been "left behind." Even though these voters might prefer government that provides a menu of basic services—police and fire protection, public works, education—they should instead underwrite a social service edifice for the poor. Rusk never considers the possibility that these citizens recognize that the existing welfare state is an abject failure that has worsened urban life for everyone, taxing wage earners excessively and intensifying the dysfunction that Rusk deplores in underclass neighborhoods. He doesn't dream that expanding city borders to grab the wealth of those who have fled failed urban policies would simply extend the problem, not solve it. He imagines that middle-class habits will rub off on the poor if government drops them into middle-class neighborhoods, rather than understanding that it is the incentive of reaching a better neighborhood that encourages the habits of thrift and industry. Nor does he notice, or credit, the success of so many who by their own efforts have propelled themselves out of the inner city into the suburbs over the past two decades.

Instead of promising more of the redistributionist machinery that has failed so roundly over the last generation, breaking up the cities holds out a different, more valuable promise to poor neighborhoods: it offers them the incentive and the means to encourage economic growth. Knowing for sure, as suburbs now do, that they will benefit directly from new investment, poor municipalities would try to make their business climate accommodating—to developers, say, or street vendors or small, home-based businesses that might be zoned out elsewhere. Independent municipalities will have the option of limiting regulation and accepting employment-generating businesses, even waste-recycling centers or power plants, that middle-class areas may not want, but whose financial benefits a poor community might find well worth the costs. (State and federal health and safety standards would still apply, of course.) Neighborhoods would have the incentive to find the highest and best use of their land and buildings.

The fact that the Camdens and Newarks of the world have not prospered should not be taken as evidence that poor but independent cities can't succeed. For 30 years, such cities have focused on seeking state and federal aid for public works projects or the rebuilding of formerly middle-class housing, even after the middle class has fled, rather than on figuring out the economic advantages they might themselves offer. Poor but independent communities might, to be sure, become places where corrupt local officials take power; but they might, just as well, become places that can develop their own competent leadership, based on the exercise of real authority.

Whatever the complications very poor neighborhoods pose to creating a system of independent city neighborhoods, they should not obscure the tremendous benefits that such a system would bring the vast majority of neighborhoods. Not the least of these would be the new political cultures that will have a chance to take root, more communal and truly democratic than today's. Here's how it would work.

Neighborhoods that already have their own, informal identity, and often their own zip codes, would become formal municipalities. In New York, for instance, this would mean that the Upper West Side, Harlem, the Upper East Side, the Village, Canarsie, the Rockaways, Forest Hills—all the city's identifiable residential neighborhoods—would become independent municipalities, empowered to set their own property-tax rates, operate their own police and fire departments, make their own zoning and land-use decisions, pick up their own garbage, and clean and repair their own streets. This does not mean, however, that each municipality will in fact do all these things. Like suburbs, they will provide some services themselves and contract out others to either a private firm or another public entity, typically a county.

Just outside the Los Angeles city limits, for instance, a large number of so-called contract municipalities, members of the Los Angeles County Association of Contract Cities, contract for law enforcement services from the county sheriff's office. Cities like Bradbury and Rolling Hills have taken this as far as it can go: with but a handful of employees, they contract for all their services. Around Tucson, discussions are currently intense about what price Pima County should charge newly incorporated towns for, say, a week of a deputy sheriff's time. Over time, individual municipalities will doubtless figure out which services should remain local, which joint effort best provides, and what is the best way to pressure outside contractors to keep prices down. Key Biscayne attorney Eugene Stearns believes that ordinary police protection is best provided at the local level but that the cost of bomb squads or SWAT teams—operations that any single jurisdiction rarely uses—should be shared. Similarly, it may make sense for municipalities to operate their own school systems, as Caroline Hoxby's research suggests, but to form a buyer's pool for select educational goods or services. The costs and revenues of those services for which metropolitan economies of scale exist—as Milan Dluhy's research indicates—could be shared through special-purpose districts that would oversee airports, say, or libraries or arterial roads. Such districts have swiftly and steadily proliferated over the last two decades.

Key to any urban breakup would be figuring out which functions would be local and which would be regional. And what amount of the existing debt would each new municipality inherit? The residents of a jurisdiction containing the region's water treatment plant, clearly, would not become solely liable for the debt payments related to its construction. But what about school buildings or recreation facilities? "We expect," observes Richard Close, an attorney who has actively promoted San Fernando Valley secession, "that figuring out the terms of separation will keep a major accounting firm busy for several years."

Not every public facility or geographic area should come under the control of those who live in or near it. Voters in an entire metropolitan area should control what Eugene Stearns calls "regionally significant areas," either through regional votes or through appointed commissions chosen from the entire metropolitan area. In practice, this would mean that such entities as airport authorities, metropolitan-wide water supply and sewage districts, and port authorities would function as before.

It would also mean that a metropolitan area's central business district would be governed by a mayor and a city council whom voters from the entire metro area would elect. Who exactly would be eligible to vote? The Census Bureau already provides a framework for eligibility by delineating which municipalities—by virtue of their preponderance of economic ties—lie within a single "standard metropolitan statistical area." Those living within the New York SMSA, including those in parts of Nassau and Westchester counties—and perhaps parts of New Jersey and Connecticut as well—would have the right to vote for a metro mayor and council, who would set policy for midtown and lower Manhattan. Suburbanites would also get to vote for their own mayors, just as residents of the former City of New York would get to vote for their local neighborhood mayors, too.

Some new municipalities wouldn't have to raise all their tax revenues internally. Eugene Stearns—who envisions conjuring such new municipalities as Little Havana, Little Managua, and Coconut Grove out of Miami—proposes that well-to-do municipalities share a percentage of their local revenues with poorer communities. "I want to make clear," he says, "that this is not a rich man's attempt to avoid the cost of government." New municipal boundaries, he suggests, might divvy up poor communities among richer neighboring areas. Any municipal breakup campaign must recognize that some sort of regional revenue sharing will have to guarantee that all areas have decent schools and adequate police and fire protection. But assuring, say, a floor below which school spending must not fall is a far cry from aiming at overall tax equalization.

Stearns's proposal should serve as the start of a discussion, not the final word. What percentage of tax revenues should municipalities share? And who should pay it? All communities above a certain income level? All communities above the property tax median? How would cities like New York, which finance public assistance in part locally, finance it after breakup—and who would determine the levels of support, since cutting the size of the dysfunctional edifice of low-income assistance is a likely and desirable outcome of breaking up the cities? Only the winnowing of the political process will answer such questions.

The one thing we shouldn't do is to use the central business district's property-tax revenues to subsidize tax rates in residential neighborhoods. Such redistribution dampens business development. The better approach is to use Stearns's revenue sharing to accomplish desirable redistribution and to reduce, radically, central business-district taxes. Let the office buildings and residents of the economic heart of the city pay to support the actual services they require; beyond that, let the economic value they generate be reflected in the property values—and property taxes—of the residential areas. Keeping commercial taxes low will keep businesses in the cities—and preclude politicians from cutting deals with favored firms, offering lower taxes in exchange for staying put.

This is a radical proposal, true. The neighborhoods of our big cities have long been bound together; residents think of themselves as New Yorkers or Chicagoans. But they also think of themselves as residents of Flatbush or Canarsie—and in that capacity they lack the means of exerting political control over the places they call home, in contrast to people short distances away on Long Island or in Westchester County, who have, in effect, greater rights to influence where they live. Perhaps the strongest argument in favor of the unthinkable possibility of breaking up the cities is that the movement to do so has already, spontaneously, begun. David Rusk has written that we should not consider the "political geography of mature metropolitan areas" to be "immutable." Just so—but not in the way he believes.

—*Winter 1998*

VII
THE PHYSICAL
CITY

The city is arguably man's greatest work of art, expressing his ideals and aspirations even in such minute details as lampposts and phone booths. It is an ever-changing work of art as we adapt or tear down the old and build up the new, affirming both our dynamism and our connection to our past and traditions. How cities control that dynamic process is an important policy question, for (to paraphrase Churchill) we shape our cities, and then our cities shape us.

ROGER SCRUTON

Why Lampposts and Phone Booths Matter

THERE USED TO BE one object in every English village that stood out as a symbol of stable government and a refuge to the traveler: the telephone booth. This cast-iron structure in imperial red was designed in 1924 by Sir Giles Gilbert Scott, architect of Liverpool's Anglican Cathedral, itself the last great British venture in the Gothic style. Like many architects who worked in the Indian summer of the British Empire, Scott was eclectic, able to draw on classical, Gothic, and proto-modern motifs in order to provide a rich vocabulary of detail, responsive to the new demands of the industrial age. His telephone booth is a case in point: classical in outline and inspired by Sir John Soane's tomb for his wife in Saint Pancras Churchyard, it is nevertheless an unashamed product of the industrial age, with a suggestion of Bauhaus naughtiness in its fenestration. Raised on a slight plinth, and in the form of a classical column base, it is capped by a gentle pediment, beneath which a panel of opalescent glass, lit from behind, makes a kind of cornice, bearing the word "telephone" in sober classical letters. The door, divided into three parts by its mullions, has a brass handle set into the cast-iron frame, and above the cornice a little crown is embossed or perforated, symbol of national identity and promise of enduring government. So suitable did this form prove to the streets, countryside, and villages of England that it would often be seen on Christmas cards, upright in a sea of snow, beside the Gothic spire, the gabled cottage, and the five-barred gate. And it was a paradigm of what street architecture should be: permanent, dignified, and expressing an idea of public and legitimate order. With the privatization of the telephone network, Britain took a giant leap into the future. The first sign of this was the rapid disappearance of Scott's familiar landmark in favor of a barbarous concoction in alloy and shatterproof glass, of the kind familiar from the streets of New York. The new telephone booth is open to the elements and to the commotion of the city street. It offers neither shelter nor privacy to its occupant; it is void of style or architectural meaning and looks as impermanent and provisional as the activities that invade it. It represents not stability and lawful order but hectic movement and unceasing change. It is a visible reminder of the futility of listening for ancestral voices amid the din of a modern city. You do not enter the New York telephone booth but reach out to it as you pass. It is not the reassuring symbol of a permanent home, with which you can at any moment make soothing contact. It is a place from which you cry for help, into a void from which help can never come.

The contrast that I have just drawn illustrates a profound change in our perception of public space. The street is the public place *par excellence*, the place in which the city impresses its character on those who live in it and vindicates, if it can, the society that it exists to sustain. The design of a city street was never, in the great epochs of civilization, left to chance. The height, alignment, fenestration, and doorways of city houses were the subject of regulation, and the objects that were placed in the street for the benefit of passersby expressed and confirmed the sense of a common, legitimate, and public way of life.

This is one reason why the classical styles acquired such stability: they enshrined an idea of legitimacy. Gradually their forms and details came to have a permanent meaning and could therefore be relied upon to convey their messages without the benefit of words, and in a serene and genial idiom that mitigated the urgencies of city business. A classical doorway does not need the sign marked ENTRANCE; the classical steps need no supplement of words to direct the attention and the movement of those who walk on them. The use and meaning of a building were laid before the public in a series of visual cues that both expressed and endorsed the common understanding of the purposes of civic life.

That is why classical railway stations, like McKim, Mead, and White's Penn Station, destroyed during the sixties, had so few verbal markings: you knew at once, from the height and proportions of the arches, from the varied decorations and the dialogue of moldings, exactly where to buy your ticket, leave your luggage, or catch your train. Contrast this with the modern airport, in which a babel of words cries out on every side and in every style of lettering, precisely because the architecture, in its uniform stylelessness, is mute.

This babel of signs has erupted also in our streets. The facades of shops bear no mark of the goods contained in them; doorways are obscured, unembellished, scarcely noticeable without an explicit ENTRANCE sign. Bus stops are mere posts, on which BUS STOP must be written if we are to know their use. And the signs themselves have declined to the same level of impermanence as the functions they describe. The lettering is not weighty or dignified but imbued with motion; it seems to go whizzing past, throwing out a trail of sparks or dynamic shading, in some garish hue that clamors for attention. Even churches and chapels, whose Gothic porches make unambiguous display of their function, are now equipped with billboards, lest people should be unaware of their use. Contrast with this busy clamor the old enamel street signs of New York, which told us, though in a quietly authoritative whisper, that this street has been here forever.

At the same time, the design of street furniture has become subservient to function. The bus shelter in my village is a cottagelike cabin built of local stone and designed to blend into its surroundings. The modern bus shelter is an assembly of metal-framed screens, with no other meaning than its function—a function that it performs badly, precisely because it is the *only* function that it performs. Just as a house ceases to be a home when built as a "machine for living," so does a shelter cease to be a shelter when built as a "machine for standing in." Ever since Jane Jacobs mounted her devastating attack on the modernist theories of town planning in *The Death and Life of Great American Cities*, it has been clear that the "disaggregation of functions" in the modern city is a primary cause of social disaffection. Modernist planning, which places shops in one place, streets in another, parks in another, and offices in yet another, compels people to be constantly on the move and deprives them of the city as their collective home. It is the same with neighborhoods as with street furnishings: those designed purely according to an idea of their function are unable to fulfill it—unable to fulfill it, that is, in a human way.

Consider the English postbox—a wonderful structure that can be found, thanks to the Empire, in every corner of the globe, though not everywhere decked out in the imperial red that used to enliven it. Like the old-fashioned telephone booth, the English "pillar-box" has a permanent air. Its base and cornice, its solid cast-iron structure, and its open mouth emphasized by moldings are, from the point of view of the functionalist architect, entirely superfluous, a waste of labor and materials, which could not be justified by the box's use. In fact, however, they are precisely what is necessary to create confidence in the national post office: placing your letters in such a box, through such a decisive aperture, you feel that they are in safe hands and already on their way to their destination. This confidence has created a public expectation that the post office will live up to its promise, and that the royal insignia embossed on its boxes expresses a genuine spirit of public service and obedience.

And so it has always been. Our postal service has remained reliable, able to deliver a letter safely within a day. The contrast with the U.S. Postal Service is evident—and evident also to the eye, in the functional styleless-ness of the American postbox. During my first stay in America, I refused to place letters in that scrappy tin receptacle, unable to believe that anyone would take charge of delivering them. It looked like junk, seemed designed for junk, and promised to make junk of anything that was dropped in it. It provides a clear illustration of the way in which explicit functionality is the enemy of function. Maybe the American postbox has played its own small part in creating public distrust toward the federal service.

Such examples serve to show that solidity and self-confidence are every bit as important as style. This is illustrated by another American instance: the city fire hydrant. In the nature of the case, it is difficult to impose the discipline of the orders on such a structure, or to do very much by way of moldings and ornaments. Nevertheless, the fire hydrant has become one of the few reliable symbols of urbanity in American cities: the solid cast-iron structure, with its polished brass caps, standing rooted in its own inviolable space, expresses the vigilant guardianship of the city, durable, immovable, and prepared for every emergency. It is a visible pledge that the city intends to live longer than its local disasters.

When it comes to lighting, requirements of style are more directly involved, and easier to satisfy. The old gas lamp was a descendant of the architectural orders, with plinth, shaft, and capital, and an eruption of moldings at the places where they met. It was designed to stand in the street like a soldier, smartly dressed, unflinching, and reliable. The modern sodium lamp has a flimsy and slovenly appearance. It hangs above the street in a half-completed arch, its unembellished curve clashing equally with the upright housefronts and the horizontal pavement. In a high wind it will wave or rattle, and an air of precarious impermanence attaches to it: at any moment it might lose its balance and come crashing down. Its being has been absorbed into its function, and when it replaces the disciplined rows of gas lamps, the effect can be compared to replacing a row of uniformed policemen with a gang of efficient guerillas. In the heat of action, a policeman's uniform is far less functional than the jeans, guns, and ski mask of the urban guerilla. But it has a deeper function, which comes from transcending functionality. It reassures, elevates, and legitimizes: it reminds us that the power of the police is not arbitrary but authorized power, expressing the very same spirit of citizenship that prompts us also to submit to it.

Street lighting is a gauge of security, a sign that the city has eyes. Even so, people seem to be less interested in the quantity of light than in the urbanity of its source. The cold, hard stare of the modern street lamp is received more as a threat than a comfort. Its all-seeing shadowless glare seems to sweep the street of its social meanings, robbing us of intimacy and inviting the very danger against which it warns—for we instinctively sense that the distinctions between right and wrong, good and evil, crime and law, are wiped away by this soulless illumination. Modern street lighting is totalitarian, Orwellian; everything beneath it is pallid and impersonal. When people are allowed to choose their townscape, they frequently insist that gas lamps be retained, or replaced by electric lamps that copy traditional forms and soften the street with a familiar chiaroscuro.

One final instance: the public lavatory. In the street where I passed my childhood, there stood an iron chapel in forest green, the sections of which had been cast in the form of cathedral arches, decorated with leaf moldings and filled with sheets of perforated metal. Only the word GENTLEMEN, in black Gothic lettering on a framed window of opalescent glass, indicated the building's function. And not a soul objected to its presence, so much did this sanctuary add dignity to our undistinguished terraces. The Parisian *pissoir*, in the same soothing color, was a comparable triumph of street architecture. In place of these happy solutions to a permanent human problem, we now have transportable cabins of pale cement, with sliding metal doors that give the appearance of a space capsule. They have neither roots in the pavement nor orientation to the surrounding buildings but are merely dumped in the street like trash cans, vivid reminders of the garbage that we humans really are.

All is not lost, however. Firms now exist that specialize in street furniture and offer plausible simulacra of those fixtures, from gas lamp to cast-iron bench, that endowed our streets with their civic meaning. The old bishop's-crook street lamp and the World's Fair park bench are proliferating again in New York, and architects are beginning to take street furniture seriously. Quinlan Terry's development at Richmond Riverside, near London, pays as much attention to streets, steps, and walkways as to façades and is remarkable for its benches and litter bins, which have the same air of permanence as the buildings themselves. Nor is this revival of civic architecture confined to self-confessed classicists like Terry: witness the street lamps and railings whose beautiful rhythm lends festive dignity to the Battery Park esplanade in New York.

Nevertheless, we need to think hard about why the modern styles have so often failed to do justice to the street. Why is it that in this most simple matter, which had been so clearly understood by architects and city fathers from ancient Athens to the eve of the First World War, the wisdom of ages was so suddenly thrown away? Some will blame the corruption of popular taste; others will point accusingly to the market. But these are shallow explanations. In public matters there is no genuine market, since choices are made not by the citizens but on their behalf. And when the voice of the public is heard, it calls out for traditional designs and seems dissatisfied with their modern substitutes.

We are self-conscious beings, aware of our temporary nature and aware in our hearts that outside society, life is solitary, poor, nasty, brutish, and short. The city is the symbol of our defiance: the monument to human aspiration and the pledge that life will endure in something like its present mold. The city depends upon elaborate self-restraint and courtesy; it functions only because the millions who inhabit it make tacit bargains with their neighbors, renouncing force for agreement in countless tiny transactions as they jostle in the streets and markets, queue for buses, take their seats in theaters and cinemas, or pass one another in the park.

This amazing achievement comes about only because there is a general air of benign authority: a vigilant overseer who makes her presence known without officiously intruding. This overseer is the city herself, made apparent through streets and monuments and standing over the human commotion with an air of unruffled command. Through the city we relate to time, not as rural people do, through a consciousness of the seasons and their passing, but in another way—through a carefully constructed dialogue of permanence and change, in which enduring symbols of order play host to our most temporary transactions, and eternal remembrance stands above a sea of forgetting. That is the true meaning of monuments, churches, and the classical styles. And it is the meaning that should be captured by street architecture, if it is to be seen as *belonging* in the city, rather than dumped there.

When people refer to the trashy nature of modern street furniture, this is what they really have in mind. The garish signs, functional objects, disposable benches, phone booths, lavatories, and bus shelters do not belong to the permanent background of the city but only to the transitory foreground of human bargaining. As a result, our perceptions are confused. For the transitory foreground is occupied by people, not by the city. We perceive the ice cream stand or the fruit seller's stall as private property, part of the great sea of market dealings and movable from place to place. We cannot perceive street furniture in such a way, since we can attribute it to no one in particular. By its very nature it is removed from the world of private property and market dealings. If, however, it fails to speak of permanent things, fails to wear the badge of office that we witness in the classical styles, then we cannot perceive it as part of the background, either. It floats in a kind of no-man's-land between private foreground and public background, unowned and uncared for, without meaning or authority, adrift in the city like a piece of debris. No wonder modern mailboxes are so often smeared with graffiti and modern phone booths so often vandalized—changed from implicit to explicit rubbish as a kind of punishment for having failed to belong.

It seems to me that once we have understood the real nature of street furniture, as a symbol of permanent civil order in the stream of time, we will recognize that it matters very much how we design it. There are many reasons for the growth of crime and disorder in our city streets, and architecture is fairly low down the list of causes. Nevertheless, we should not ignore the fact that the standards of conduct and courtesy required by life in a modern conurbation are not easily produced. People can live peacefully at the accelerated pace of city life only on the assumption of elaborate good manners, rapidly established codes and conventions, and a general responsiveness to the collective good. The astonishing fact is not that people rob, rape, and murder in modern cities, but that they don't. However, only a constant and vigilant self-denial can make the arrangement work. And it has to work, since the city is the heart of modern society, the place where all decisions are made, and from which all government emanates.

The old street furniture engendered and endorsed a civic attitude among those who lived with it. People spontaneously imitated the dignified postures of the objects that stood around them and absorbed from the city herself a vision of public order and the common good. This can be seen from old films of Manhattan life—including the life of Harlem—in which the orderly forms of the city matched the uniforms worn by people, and in which the genial furniture of the street reflected the decencies of street behavior. Reflecting on our historical experience, I cannot help feeling that the growing disorder of the modern city stems at least in part from the fact that it has lost its air of permanence. The city has become as temporary and disposable to the eye as the discarded junk that drifts through its streets and alleyways.

—*Summer 1996*

DAVID GARRARD LOWE
Urban Lessons from Paris

BY EIGHT IN THE MORNING, the August sun is warming the Place Saint-Germain-des-Prés, brushing with gold the façade of the eleventh-century Romanesque church that gives the square its name, brightening the trees that surround the Picasso sculpture honoring the poet Apollinaire, turning up, as it were, the house lights for those fortunate enough to be having their *café au lait* on the terrace of the Deux Magots. Paris appears to sparkle; in fact, it *does* sparkle. The capital of France has about it the squeaky-clean aura of a just-scrubbed porch, a feeling one almost never experiences in New York. The reason is not difficult to discover.

There at the edge of the Boulevard Saint-Germain is one of the explanations. Dressed in pale green, a man is vigorously sweeping, pushing along the debris of the pavement and street with the help of a foot-wide stream of water flowing in the gutter. Parisians have begun calling the sweepers *vertes*—"greens." Similarly, a few years ago, the Parisian version of the meter maid was dubbed *aubergine*—eggplant—after the color of her smart new uniform. At first glance, the sweeper seems to be wielding a broom of twigs like those used by French peasants, but the brooms are in fact bundles of green plastic imitation twigs, now that the Paris Department of Sanitation has discovered that plastic brooms cost one-fifth as much as ones made of real twigs and last seven times as long.

The Paris Department of Sanitation has a reputation for being one of the most innovative in the world. This is, after all, the city of the mechanized municipal pooper-scooper, a Rube Goldberg marriage of motorcycle and vacuum cleaner. It is the city of the Gyrolave, a vehicle developed by the Department of Sanitation working with private manufacturers to deal with the animal-fat residue left by the open-air street markets, such as that in the rue de Buci, one of the shopping centers of the Left Bank. The Gyrolave mixes steaming water and soap and then directs it onto the markets' pavements. Afterward, it sweeps the street. The sanitation department has also, in cooperation with private manufacturers, come up with a truck that shoots a stream of water under parked cars to remove litter, allowing the streets to be cleaned when cars are in place. In contrast, those unwieldy behemoths, the New

York City mechanical street sweepers, can only be used on days when cars are not permitted to park on one side of the street or the other.

"The biggest difference between New York and Paris is the fact that Paris is clean," a New York editor now living in Paris observes. "The fact that Paris is clean gives Parisians a sense that things are not falling apart, that society is not doomed, that there is order in the universe and in municipal government."

The municipal authorities in Paris believe so strongly that public cleanliness is a statement of civic health that they spend 10 percent of the city budget, more than $2 billion annually, on sanitation. In contrast, recent cutbacks in New York's Department of Sanitation budget have produced the disgusting sight of overflowing trash baskets in midtown Manhattan. To stem the deluge, employees of the Grand Central Partnership, a private Business Improvement District, are now emptying the trash containers around Grand Central Terminal and bagging the refuse, neatly piling dozens of bags around the municipal litter baskets before the garbage trucks get around to hauling them away. The pervasive appearance of disarray, some think, has begun to damage New York's position as a world center of commerce and culture.

Paris's devotion to civic cleanliness teaches another lesson. Although Paris's Department of Sanitation has developed highly sophisticated equipment for some jobs, unskilled laborers still accomplish the essential task of sweeping the streets. Almost all of Paris's 4,500 sweepers are Arab or African immigrants. Here in New York, where unskilled workers abound, this is a lesson worth remembering.

Stretching for some 80 acres behind the French Senate—the palace that Salomon de Brosse designed in 1615 for Queen Marie de' Medici—the Jardin du Luxembourg exemplifies Paris's belief that municipal authority should be used to socialize and to civilize the populace by giving them a glimpse beyond the man-made, urban world to the natural order. "We are attempting to give the people of Paris something that people in most large cities lack," Paul Rissel, one of the Luxembourg's chief gardeners, explains: "contact with nature."

"Nature" in the Luxembourg plays by strictly French rules, of course. The garden's plants are carefully bedded arrangements of geraniums, dahlias, and petunias. At the center of the garden is a basin where children launch model sailboats, while around them adults sun themselves on those simple but superbly designed iron French garden chairs. The chairs, single, movable, some with arms, some without, in a way symbolize French individualism, but those who occupy them also play by the rules: though movable, the chairs remain in rows—ragged rows, but nevertheless, rows. People read or speak in low voices; usually on warm days, a band made up of members of the Paris fire or police department plays under a grove of trees on the side of the park nearest the Panthéon. The melodies are almost always by Gershwin or Porter or Kern. There are no loud radios, no running, no panhandling, no homeless asleep under the trees.

Two factors are at work here. The first is that Paris is one of the best-policed cities in the world, with some 21,000 police officers, or around one cop per 100 Parisians, compared with one per 270 New Yorkers. In the Luxembourg, one is very aware of the pairs of policemen routinely walking by. Second, the Luxembourg has more than one gardener for each of the park's 80 acres. The orderliness of the park, reinforced by the formal planting and the inescapable presence of the police, contrasts with New York's Central Park, which, with its radios and the electronic music of "The Summer Stage," turns what should be a calming, civilizing oasis into a jungle of noise. And though private agencies such as the Central Park Conservancy have valiantly attempted to step in where the city has failed, Central Park too often looks irreparably shabby. The labor-intensive rotation of flowers in Paris, which strikingly marks the seasons, gives way in New York to the bare maintenance of greenery.

In the self-denigrating lexicon of modern America, words like "progress" and "optimism" are forbidden. But a civilization that does not employ them, does not believe in them, is doomed either to the static condition of pharaonic Egypt or to the disintegration of nineteenth-century Venice. The French government embraces the idea that Paris—as well as the other cities of France—must give concrete evidence that conditions are improving, and that inhabiting a city makes ordinary human life better, not worse.

This is achieved in ways both large—such as the astounding expansion of the Grand Louvre —and small—as in the recent regilding of the 18 magnificent lamp standards gracing the Place de la Concorde. An outstanding example of an urban administration using its imagination to improve the lives of its citizens and to enhance a neighborhood is the recently refurbished Viaduc des Arts. Consisting of 60 high brick and stone arches, the viaduct carried a train line from the Place de la Bastille to the Bois de Vincennes from 1853 until it was abandoned in 1969. The vaults then quickly became a neighborhood nuisance, sheltering tramps and some noisome auto repair shops. The question was whether to demolish, at a high cost, the handsome, well-built structure or to find a practical use for it.

The solution was the Viaduc des Arts. The brick facades were cleaned, the soaring interior spaces were opened up, and the viaduct became a center for *métiers d'art*, that is, for the very craftsmen that cities need, but who all too often depart because of high rents and inhospitable locations. Now, in the vaults that once carried steam trains to the southeast corner of Paris, silver flatware is made in the Ateliers du Cuivre et de l'Argent, antique linens and laces are repaired at Marie Lavande, Atelier le Tallec has 12 painters who decorate and fire Limoges china for Tiffany & Company, while in still another vault rare musical instruments, including glorious French hunting horns, are sold and repaired. And, as always in Paris, there is a restaurant, Au Père Tranquille. The Viaduc des Arts, running along one side of the Avenue Daumesnil from numbers 9 to 129, has brought life, commerce, and style to a once-dull neighborhood.

But the real surprise of the recycled viaduct is the garden on top of it. Reached by both stairs and elevators, it is the creation of Philippe Mathieux and Jacques Vergely. The breadth and length of the viaduct surprises; the views, some four stories in the air, are sensational. Here is the fin-de-siècle Gare de Lyon, a new pastel-colored school, and an astounding postmodern police station topped with a couple of dozen gigantic copies of a single Michelangelo sculpture, *The Slave*. There are benches, fountains, tree-lined walks, places for children to play. It seems a modern version of the Hanging Gardens of Babylon.

This creative use of an obsolete urban structure is a lesson that Gotham could learn. After the Second World War, for example, when plans to demolish the Third Avenue Elevated were first announced, Buckminster Fuller and other imaginative urbanists suggested that, once the trains ceased to run, the structure itself should be kept. Paved over, they said, it would be a glorious pedestrian mall, separating people from the vehicular traffic in the street below. And since it was clearly foreseen that, once the El stopped running, Third Avenue would be rebuilt, the new structures would be required to have garage and delivery entrances at street level, while their lobby entrances would be at the level of the former Elevated. But the Elevated was demolished, and New York lost its chance for a unique urban amenity. Today, in a similar vein, neighborhood opposition, political infighting, and a general lack of vision have stymied a proposal to turn the spectacular vaults under the Manhattan side of the Queensboro Bridge into a market and shops not unlike those of the Viaduc des Arts.

The decision to find a creative use for the former railroad viaduct was a direct result of the terrible lesson that Paris learned from the destruction in 1971 of Victor Baltard's seminal glass and iron "umbrellas" of the 1850s that once housed Les Halles, Paris's central market. The loss of these majestic sheds, ordered by Napoleon III, and their replacement by the ghastly Forum des Halles, with its 200 shops and its cinemas, was an urban-planning disaster. The Forum des Halles, one guide has said, "manages to induce both claustrophobia and agoraphobia."

Since the debacle of Les Halles, Paris has striven to reuse its vast stock of fine buildings. A prime example is the transformation of Victor Laloux's ornate Gare d'Orsay into the Musée d'Orsay under President Valéry Giscard d'Estaing. The museum opened in 1986 as a space to display nineteenth-century art, and though the modernist brutalism of its interior by Gae Aulenti resembles an ambitious suburban mall, Paris has saved an important building, has preserved the Beaux Arts ensemble of the Quai d'Orsay on the Seine, and has gotten for itself an enormously popular new tourist attraction.

The imaginative recycling of structures, as well as Paris's desire to increase the number of green spaces within the city, has led to the hugely successful La Villette, site of Paris's vast cattle market and abattoir in the far northwest corner of the metropolis. Work began in the 1960s on a gigantic new slaughterhouse to serve the entire city, but construction stopped halfway through, when the authorities decided to ban such unpleasant industries from Paris. Thus, the city was left with some 36 acres lying on two sides of an old canal, a gargantuan, partially completed structure, and several handsome, empty nineteenth-century pavilions.

Late in the 1970s, the authorities decided to transform La Villette into a "Parc Urbain du 21e Siècle," a city park for the next century. The 20 concrete piers of the unfinished abattoir, each 80 feet tall and linked by 200-foot-long steel girders, were roofed and glazed, and the space converted into the new Museum of Science and Industry. The alluring hands-on displays, geared to appeal primarily to schoolchildren, include a delightful gaggle of robots, a transparent model of a particle accelerator designed to explain nuclear reactions, and a full-scale replica of an American space station. In front of the Museum is La Géode, a glistening 18-foot-high polished stainless-steel sphere that shows documentary films on a 10,000-square-foot curved screen within its dome.

Impressive ingenuity has also transformed the Grande Halle aux Boeufs, the former cattle market erected in 1867 by the architect Jules de Mérindol. The architects Bernard Reichen and Philippe Robert have kept its superb 24,000-square-yard iron and glass shed, reminiscent of Les Halles, and they have subtly tacked on bathrooms and other service areas needed for modern use. Now the Grande Halle is a much-sought-after venue for trade fairs, exhibitions, and popular music concerts. The park of La Villette, designed by Robert Tschumi, head of Columbia University's School of Architecture, is studded with pavilions of a deconstructivist design made of bright red enameled metal. Termed "Follies" by Tschumi, to recall the pagodas and Grecian temples that dotted the parks surrounding eighteenth-century French châteaus, the pavilions, practical as well as playful, serve as refreshment stands. An unqualified success, La Villette attracts thousands of children each year, as well as a growing number of Paris's 20 million tourists.

Over the decades, New York has squandered its capital of magnificent structures, mindlessly demolishing Charles McKim's staggering Pennsylvania Station, the resplendent old Metropolitan Opera, and Joseph Urban's wondrously chic Ziegfeld Theater on Sixth Avenue. There are signs, though, that even in New York the era of barbarity might be over: Trowbridge and Livingston's former B. Altman's department store, at the northeast corner of Fifth Avenue and 34th Street, has metamorphosed into a center for the New York Public Library's economics and business divisions, and plans to convert McKim, Mead & White's main post office building on Eighth Avenue into an Amtrak station are under consideration.

Paris, for the aware, is packed with lessons in sagacious urbanity. Walking up the gentle slope of the rue Soufflot from the Luxembourg Gardens toward the imposing dome of the Panthéon, the pedestrian receives a surprise as he approaches the rue Saint-Jacques. Automobiles, like ants leaving an anthill, stream out of the ground. They have been parked in one of the underground caverns the city has excavated beneath its boulevards, parks, and squares, including the tony Place Vendôme, the enticing Place Saint-Sulpice, and the Tuileries Gardens, which now, after years of being a construction site for Mitterand's Grand Louvre, are getting a much-needed restoration. In each of these projects, the Paris city fathers succeeded in preserving the grace and tranquillity of these splendid historic sites. These garages are no real solution to the problem of a population addicted to the automobile, but with parking choking streets ranging from the narrow rue des Saints-Pères on the Left Bank to the broad Avenue de l'Opéra on the Right, at least it is a constructive attempt to house cars off the street. New York might do well to imitate Paris and commission a survey of potential underground garage locations, beginning with the embarrassingly shabby park in front of City Hall.

Paris, like all world cities, is a place of breathtaking contrasts. It is a city both of charming corners where the very essence of civilized existence is concentrated into a glass of red wine and a yellow cat asleep upon a cash register and also of modern quarters whose banality makes one wonder if there are secret competitions among architects for the ugliest building.

Start with one of the most delicious experiences of city life anywhere: a stroll down the rue de Seine to the Louvre. The street opens with the flourish of an open-air market at the Boulevard Saint-Germain and then proceeds, like some wily conjurer, to present to the pedestrian an astonishing repertory of wonders: art galleries selling African sculpture and rare photographs, jewelers' windows filled with carnelians and carved jade, intimate cafés with brilliantly colored liqueurs glistening in tapering glasses, pharmacies dispensing cough drops laced with enough codeine to stop the heart, and charcuteries with mouthwatering displays of lark paté and cassis cakes. All are housed in the first floors of those tall, thin seventeenth-century French buildings that lean together like old maids at a dance.

At the river end of the street, one slips, like Alice, through an unobtrusive door into the elegantly curved courtyard of the Institut de France and enters a more expansive world. Behind looms Louis Le Vau's masterpiece, the high dome of the Institut, while ahead the rhythmical iron arches of the Pont des Arts carry one across the Seine to the side of Louvre called the Galerie du Bord de l'Eau. Passing through the Renaissance exuberance of the palace's Cour Carrée, one emerges onto the rue de Rivoli. There, a gigantic metallic plant bearing glass blossoms marks one of Hector Guimard's Art Nouveau entrances to the Metro.

Slip down into the spotless, art-filled Louvre métro station and hop on a glistening, comfortable subway car. The trip to La Défense, on the city's western rim, takes scarcely half an hour, but aesthetically it spans centuries. Left behind is the alluring human scale of the rue de Seine, the playfulness of the Pont des Arts, the classical balance of the Institut and the Louvre. La Défense is a visual cacophony of glass and metal office towers. Its centerpiece, La Grande Arche, completed in 1989 to commemorate the bicentennial of the French Revolution, is a 360-foot-high window of white marble designed by a Dane, Johan Otto von Spreckelsen. It resembles an awkward Danish modern side table from a discount store.

Despite its execrable design, La Défense teaches a valuable lesson in city planning. It exists because André Malraux, Charles de Gaulle's Minister of Cultural Affairs, decided to limit high-rise construction in the historic heart of Paris. Had he not made that prescient decision, the absurd structures of La Défense would have been scattered along the rue de Rivoli, the Boulevard Saint-Germain, even the rue de Seine, just as cousins in London have been permitted to obscure the view of Saint Paul's Cathedral from the Thames and, in New York, to destroy the splendid classical limestone ambience of Fifth Avenue, which once made it the retail and hotel glory of America. With wise planning, the energy so destructive to Fifth Avenue in the 1960s and 1970s could have created a new city west of Times Square.

Part of the planning lesson La Défense teaches is how to use a subway system to channel development. Until the beginning of the 1990s, the only way to reach La Défense was to take the métro to the l'Etoile stop at the Arc de Triomphe and then transfer to a suburban railway line, rather like a New York commuter changing from the subway at Grand Central or Penn Station. Now the métro's No. 1 line extends to La Défense itself. This new ease of access, combined with the need of companies such as the automaker Fiat and the giant oil conglomerate Aquitaine for vast floor space and twenty-first-century computer cabling, has led to a surge in rentals.

The Parisian authorities constantly and effectively use the métro to improve life in the metropolis. A new, fully automated train, for example, now connects Orly airport with the métro system, and a new line is under construction to serve Bercy, on Paris's eastern edge, a development begun to counter the city's relentless push to the west.

Though New York's subway system has made improvements to its constituent elements—especially by purchasing new, air-conditioned cars—the total system remains, to say the least, haphazard. After all, the subway began at the turn of the century as separate private companies, each serving a specific section of the city. It might have been expected that Mayor Fiorello La Guardia, after he took them over in 1940, would have corrected their astounding lack of integration. But no. There is still no east-west subway link in Manhattan above the southern boundary of Central Park. Anyone trapped in the arteriosclerosis-like flow of traffic from the East Side toward Lincoln Center as curtain time approaches will glimpse the enormity of this urban planning disaster.

Cities are more than the well-scrubbed cobblestones of the Place Saint-Germain, more than the perfect roses in the Luxembourg's parterres, more than the rubber-tired métro trains silently sweeping to La Défense. Cities are also the monument of—the celebration of—civilization. "It was divine nature which gave us the country," Marcus Terentius Varro wrote in the first century BC, "and man's skill that built cities." The ocean, a mountain, a grove of trees—all these make man aware of his limitations. How different is the sensation created by the Parthenon's Doric columns, Michelangelo's dome floating above Saint Peter's, or the mast of the Empire State Building flooded with light rising through the clouds. All these structures bespeak man the creator, man the innovator, man the reasoning being who has shaped and formed civilization.

Paris is a city overflowing with the monuments of civilization: Notre Dame, the Invalides, where Napoleon sleeps in his red porphyry sarcophagus, the Eiffel Tower. But Paris also celebrates the civilization of France, of Europe, of reasoning mankind in the most direct and logical of ways: in the names of streets and squares. To move up the Champs Elysées toward the Arc de Triomphe is to review a lesson in history, for the names reverberate with the power of cannons fired in an enclosed space: Place Clemenceau, Avenue Winston Churchill, Avenue Franklin D. Roosevelt, rue Lincoln, rue Washington, Avenue George V, Place Charles de Gaulle. Paris has thoroughfares named for writers—Proust, Voltaire, Victor Hugo—for painters—Van Gogh, Cézanne, Degas—for scientists like Pasteur and Alexander Fleming, for musicians like Poulenc and Berlioz, and even for quintessentially French performers Maurice Chevalier and the "Little Sparrow," Edith Piaf.

In striking contrast, New York suffers from civic amnesia when it comes to honoring such greatness. Perhaps it is not surprising that no street or square commemorates Henry James or Edith Wharton. But what can explain the fact that John Adams, who lived in the city when he served as vice president, rates not so much as an alley, and the street named for Thomas Jefferson is barely more than that? Such neglect says much about Gotham's civic consciousness.

The contrast between Paris and New York in this matter is perfectly exemplified at the Civic Center in Lower Manhattan, the city's administrative heart. Some of the center's buildings, such as Magnin and McComb's handsome City Hall and McKim, Mead & White's grand Municipal Building, are ranged along Chambers and Centre streets, but the focus of the government complex is an open space, designated a "square," which is surrounded by edifices housing various federal, state, and local courts. This square, little more than an unkempt traffic island, bears the name of a Tammany saloon-keeper friend of Al Smith's, one Foley. It is as though Adams or Jefferson or John Jay or Robert Livingston or even Chester Arthur or Dwight Eisenhower had never trod these streets and breathed this air.

Thinking of the first primitive settlement of the Gauls on the Ile de la Cité, Victor Hugo wrote: "To have once been Lutetia and to have become Paris—what could be a more magnificent symbol: to have been mud and to have become spirit." That spirit is revealed by things as complex as the Gyrolave squirting soap and steaming water beneath the stalls of the rue de Buci market or as simple as a name—Stendhal or Marie Curie—on a street sign.

—*Winter 1996*

HOWARD HUSOCK

We Don't Need Subsidized Housing

IT'S A SCENE that has been repeated time and again over the past four years, but it still seems almost too perfectly symbolic to be true. Secretary of Housing and Urban Development Henry Cisneros turns up to preside over the demolition of yet another "severely distressed" public housing project. But his speech directs attention away from what is actually happening. Just before the scarred blocks of apartments tumble down in a puff of smoke— such unequivocal failures that they aren't worth preserving—the secretary confidently paints a vision of improved design and management that will make a new generation of government-supported housing work out. Sure, we've flopped so far, the message goes—but give us one more chance and we'll finally get it right.

But maybe the whole idea is wrong. Maybe our housing programs haven't failed because of some minor management problem but because they are flawed at the core. The truth is, devoting government resources to subsidized housing for the poor—whether in the form of public housing or even housing vouchers—is not just unnecessary but also counterproductive. It not only derails what the private market can do on its own, but more significantly, it has profoundly destructive unintended consequences. For housing subsidies undermine the efforts of those poor families who work and sacrifice to advance their lot in life—and who have the right and the need to distinguish themselves, both physically and psychologically, from those who do not share their solid virtues.

Rather than confront these harsh truths, we have over the past century gone through at least five major varieties of subsidized housing, always looking for the philosophers' stone that will turn a bad idea into one that will work. We began with philanthropic housing built by "limited dividend" corporations, whose investors were to accept a below-market return in order to serve the poor. The disappointing results of such efforts—the projects served few people and tended to decline quickly—led housing advocates to call for public, not just private, spending for housing. Government first responded to their pleas with housing projects owned and operated by public authorities. These speedily declined. "Housers" then sought other solutions, such as using cheap, federally underwritten mortgages and rents paid by Washington to subsidize private landlords.

The expense of this last approach, which had its heyday in the sixties, and the resultant wave of decline and foreclosure led to the twin approaches of our current era. In the first of these, tenants use portable, government-provided vouchers to pay any private landlord who will accept them. In the second, federal tax credits encourage deep-pocketed corporate investors looking for tax shelters to finance new or renovated rental housing owned and managed by nonprofit community groups. Both approaches have had serious problems, but this hasn't deterred housing advocates from asserting that the way to fix the housing market is through even more such subsidies than the $12 billion that HUD already provides (out of its $25 billion annual budget) and the billions more in subsidies that state and local governments expend.

This mountain of government housing subsidies rests on three remarkably tenacious myths.

Myth No. 1: The market will not provide. The core belief of housing advocates is that the private market cannot and will not provide adequate housing within the means of the poor. The photos of immigrants squeezed into postage-stamp-size rooms in a recent New York Times series on housing for the poor strain to make this point. But housers have been making such assertions for more than 60 years, and reality keeps contradicting them. In 1935, for example, Catherine Bauer—perhaps America's most influential public housing crusader—claimed that the private housing market could not serve fully two-thirds of Americans and they would need public housing. The post–World War II era's explosion of home ownership quickly gave the lie to such claims, certainly with respect to those in the lower middle class and up.

As for the poor, a look at pre-Depression history shows that housing advocates get it wrong again. From the end of the Civil War up until the New Deal and the National Housing Act of 1937—which gave public housing its first push—the private housing market generated a cornucopia of housing forms to accommodate those of modest means as they gradually improved their condition. In those years Chicago saw the construction of 211,000 low-cost two-family homes—or 21 percent of its residences. In Brooklyn 120,000 two-family structures with ground-floor stores sprang up. In Boston some 40 percent of the population of 770,000 lived in the 65,376 units of the city's three-decker frame houses, vilified by housing reformers.

These areas of low-cost, unsubsidized housing were home to the striving poor. In Boston, as pioneer sociologists Robert Woods and Albert Kennedy describe it in their brilliant 1914 work, *The Zone of Emergence*, these neighborhoods teemed with clerks and skilled and semi-skilled workmen. "Over 65 percent of the residence property of the zone is owned by those who reside on it," wrote Woods and Kennedy, "and this is the best possible index that can be given of the end that holds the imagination and galvanizes the powers of a large proportion of the population. Doubtless the greater share of this property is encumbered with mortgage, but it is an index of striving and accomplishment."

Even in the poorest neighborhoods, housing, if modest, was rarely abject. A 1907 report by the U.S. Immigration Commission, for instance, found that in the eastern cities, crowding in such neighborhoods was by no means overwhelming, with 134 persons for every 100 rooms. "Eighty-four in every 100 of the homes studied are in good or fair condition," wrote the commission. True, many lived without hot water or their own bathrooms. But rents were cheap. A 1909 study by the President's Homes Commission of Washington, D.C., found that a majority of the 1,200 families surveyed paid but 17.5 percent of their income for housing costs. Many of the poor—just like the "emerging" class that Woods and Kennedy described—lived in small homes they owned or in small buildings in which the owner lived.

To be sure, as we know above all from Jacob Riis's powerful 1891 book, *How the Other Half Lives*, some families lived in hovels, even in unlit cellars. "It no longer excites even passing attention when the sanitary police count 101 adults and 91 children in a Crosby Street house," he wrote, "[o]r when a midnight inspection in Mulberry Street unearths 150 'lodgers' sleeping on filthy floors in two buildings." Many buildings did not have their own toilets, and large numbers of people relied on public baths to get clean.

But it is essential to remember that the conditions in which these poor families lived were not permanent—a fact unacknowledged by either Riis or present-day housing advocates. After all, the generation of children for whom Riis despaired went on to accomplish America's explosive economic growth after the turn of the century and into the twenties. By 1930 the New York settlement-house pioneer Lillian Wald would write in her memoirs of the Lower East Side that, where once Riis had deplored overcrowding, she now found herself surrounded by "empties": the poor had climbed the economic ladder and headed to Brooklyn and the Bronx. In other words, "substandard" housing was a stage through which many passed, but in which they did not inevitably remain. The arrival of Dominicans from Washington Heights in Hudson River Valley towns and Salvadorans from Queens on Long Island is proof that this process continues.

Perversely, housing reformers invariably make matters worse by banning the conditions that shock them. Insisting unrealistically on standards beyond the financial means of the poor, they help create housing shortages, which they then seek to remedy through public subsidies. Even Jacob Riis observed in 1907 that new tenement standards threatened "to make it impossible for anyone not able to pay $75 a month to live on Manhattan Island."

Though Riis's colleague Lawrence Veiller, head of the influential New York–based National Housing Association from 1900 to 1920, cautioned that "housing legislation must distinguish between what is desirable and what is essential," most housing programs since the New Deal have rejected this sensible advice. The high standards that have resulted—whether for the number of closets, the square feet of kitchen counter space, or handicapped access—have caused private owners and builders to bypass the low-income market. So stringent are the standards that, under current building codes and zoning laws, much of the distinctive lower-cost housing that shaped the architectural identity of America's cities—such as Brooklyn's attached brownstones with basement apartments—could not be built today.

True, even with relaxed building and housing codes, we still might not be able to build brand-new housing within the reach of those earning the minimum wage or those living on public assistance. Yet this is not an irresistible argument for government subsidies. Used housing, like used cars, gets passed along to those of more and more modest means. When new homes are built for the lower middle class, the rental housing in which they've been living (itself probably inherited from the middle class) historically has been passed along to those who are poorer.

In a subtle way, the very existence of subsidized housing is likely to contribute to the over-regulation that leads to constraints in housing supply—and to calls for further subsidies. When builders have plenty of work putting up high-cost subsidized apartments, they don't agitate for a less regulated market. Why should they seek an opportunity to build lower-margin low-cost housing? The rejoinder, then, to the myth that the market will not provide is that a greater supply of housing could be—and has been—created in a less regulated market.

Myth No. 2: By taking profit-driven landlords out of the equation, state-supported housing can offer the poor higher-quality housing for the same rent. Four generations of attempts to provide subsidized housing built to higher standards than the poor could afford on their own in the private market have proved that this idea just doesn't work. Each generation has seen the same depressing pattern: initial success followed by serious decline and ultimately by demands for additional public funds to cover ever-rising costs.

You can see the outlines of this pattern as early as 1854, when the New York Association for Improving the Condition of the Poor decided to build a "model tenement" at the corner of Elizabeth and Mott Streets. Constructed by a newly formed limited-dividend corporation, the building degenerated just 11 years later into what would be called "one of the worst slum pockets in the city." It was sold and soon after demolished.

Like its ill-fated predecessor, later public housing also aimed to do away with profit, financing construction through the sale of public bonds and then using the project's rental income to pay a public authority to provide maintenance. But the maintenance failures of public housing projects became legendary, to the point that a 1988 study estimated it would take at least $30 billion to remedy them. Instead of providing housing that rental income from tenants can maintain, the federal government has had to supply $4 billion in annual "operating assistance" to housing authorities for maintenance and administrative costs—and still the maintenance problems multiply.

The new public housing model that advocates favor retains the core—and fatal—dogma that the profit motive has no place in providing housing for the poor. In this model, nonprofit community groups run smaller, mixed-income apartment buildings, financed by monies raised through the Low-Income Housing Tax Credit, a program set up in 1986 to encourage corporations to support low-income housing. In New York City some 200 nonprofit groups manage 48,000 housing units. Though at this point such housing is widely viewed as successful, the New School for Social Research has found, in an examination of 34 developments in six cities, that "beyond an initial snapshot of well-being, loom major problems which, if unaddressed, will threaten the stock of affordable housing in this study." Predictably enough, more than 60 percent of the projects already had trouble maintaining their paint and plaster, elevators, hall lighting, and roofs.

Why does non-market housing founder? First, providing the poor with better housing than they can afford also saddles them with higher maintenance costs than they can afford. A newly announced state-financed "affordable housing" complex in Cambridge, Massachusetts, will cost $1.3 million—for eight units. That's $162,500 per apartment. Recent subsidized projects in the Bronx and central Harlem cost $150,000 and $113,000 per unit, respectively. These apartments may be built to higher standards, but their fancier kitchens, more numerous bathrooms, and larger space mean more maintenance. Not surprisingly, limited rents can't keep up with the need for service. The New York City Housing Partnership, which arranges private construction of housing for low-income buyers, has observed that nonprofit housing management groups in general "have no magic formula that allows them to manage property at less than cost. Ultimately they will need operating subsidies to remain viable."

Second, it is by no means true that cutting out the profit-making landlord reduces maintenance costs. On the contrary, public authorities and nonprofit management firms are bureaucracies with their own overhead expenses, and unlike private owners, they have no incentive to control costs. Nor have their employees any incentive to provide good service; and tenants, who are not full-fledged paying customers, have little leverage. Indeed, public housing authorities have demonstrated an ability rivaling any slumlord to disinvest in their properties.

Rather than being a source of ill-gotten gains, private ownership is a source of cost control. The expensive but ineffective maintenance regime of subsidized housing—with its formal bids and union contracts—replaces housing maintenance performed through a far less costly informal economy. Poor home owners and so-called "tenement landlords" (owners of small, multi-family buildings, many owner-occupied) contribute their own "sweat equity" or hire neighborhood tradesmen, not all of whom are licensed, let alone unionized. As one study of a low-income neighborhood in Montreal observed, "Owners can maintain their buildings and keep their rents low through the cooperation of their tenants on maintenance and through their own hard work." None of these factors comes into play in the bureaucratic environment of public or nonprofit ownership.

Far from being more cost-effective than private housing, subsidized housing is even more expensive than it first appears. Its cost includes the vast amount of property-tax revenue forgone when rental housing is held by public authorities or non-taxpaying nonprofit groups. By choosing to invest in housing, cities choose not to invest in other services, or not to leave money in the private economy to finance growth that would provide opportunity for poor and non-poor alike. Under the Rebuild New York program championed by the Koch and Dinkins administrations, the city "invested" an estimated $5 billion (much of it from its own operating budget) in housing renovation and gave up millions in property-tax revenues by deeding buildings to nonprofit organizations.

The rejoinder, then, to the myth of the public or nonprofit alternative is that gleaming new projects are bound to decay—and to have significant long-term public costs. But for housing advocates, this is really just a political problem: that of making clear to the body politic that perpetually escalating subsidies to guarantee a safe and sanitary environment for the poor are the cost of living in a moral body politic. Here we arrive at the nub of their mistaken ideology.

Myth No. 3: The moral qualities of the poor are a product of their housing "environment." The essence of the housing advocates' worldview, as the New York Association for Improving the Condition of the Poor put it in 1854, is that "physical evils produce moral evils." Improved physical surroundings will lead people to become upright, ambitious, and successful. Perhaps the quintessential myth of environmental determinism is that kids who might otherwise have no place to do their homework have their own room in government-assisted housing—and therefore succeed where they would have failed.

There is much that is appealing in this view, which has a powerful hold on the liberal psyche. But the track record of public housing—which by almost any physical measure is superior to the housing in which most of its residents have previously lived—has hardly borne out the notion that better housing uplifts the poor. The response of housing reformers to drug- and gunfire-riddled projects has been not to re-examine the premise but to tinker with the model. Having long dwelled on design, they now devote equal attention to the social "environment." Thus Secretary Cisneros has dreamed of new, low-rise, mixed-income subsidized housing that will correct the mistake of concentrating the poor in apartment towers now said to have encouraged crime. So, too, the nonprofit, "community-based" management of renovated apartment buildings is touted as a nurturing environment, in which the poorest are inspired by gainfully employed "role-model" neighbors to improve their habits and their lot.

Here is where housing advocates most radically misunderstand the nature of the unsubsidized housing market. They can't see its crucial role in weaving a healthy social fabric and inspiring individuals to advance. By pushing to provide the poor with better housing than they could otherwise afford, housers are blind to the fact that they are interfering with a delicate system that rewards effort and achievement by giving people the chance to live in better homes in better neighborhoods. In this unsubsidized system, you earn your way to a better neighborhood. In fact, you must help to create and to maintain better neighborhoods by your own effort.

Housing subsidies—whether in the form of subsidized apartments or even vouchers that you can take to a landlord of your choice—turn this system on its head and undermine it, for housing subsidies do not reward achievement; they reward need. Those who strive and save are offered the same subsidized unit as those on public assistance; the provident and the improvident become indistinguishable. Those who work must live alongside those who do not. To believe that this is just is to believe that the poor are fundamentally undifferentiated—that they are all the same in being victims of an oppressive system. Those done the greatest injustice by such naïveté are the hardworking poor, who find to their horror that their new neighbor in a housing project is a drug dealer, or that the house next door has been rented, through a housing voucher, to an AFDC mother who does not supervise her children.

Subsidies deny the self-sacrificing, working poor the chance to put physical and social distance between themselves and the non-working or antisocial poor. The *New York Times* cited the case of a hardworking woman who found herself in a bad neighborhood surrounded by gang violence as evidence of the need for increased housing subsidies, but it more likely demonstrates the opposite. By subsidizing troubled families, perhaps with criminal members, so that they can live in the same neighborhoods as those who hold modest but honest jobs, we expose the law-abiding to the disorder and violence of the undisciplined and the lawless, depriving them of the decent neighborhoods—decent in values if shabby in appearance—that their efforts should earn them. If we fail to allow the hardworking to distinguish themselves, by virtue of where they live, from those who do not share these traits, we devalue them. Even if we could somehow subsidize only the good citizens, the deserving poor, we would still do them a grave disservice, fostering the belief that they have moved to better homes in better neighborhoods by dint of largesse, not accomplishment—an entirely different psychology.

A neighborhood of good housing is not necessarily a good neighborhood. And a poor and shabby neighborhood is not necessarily a bad neighborhood. The terms on which residents have come to a place, as well as the extent to which they own property and have otherwise invested in the upkeep and safety of it, matter far more. It is worth recalling the distinctions sociologist Herbert Gans made among different types of poor neighborhoods. "In most American cities," he wrote, "there are two major types of low-rent neighborhoods: the areas of first and second settlement for urban migrants; and the areas that attract the criminal, the mentally ill, the socially rejected, and those who have given up the attempt to cope with life. The former kind of area[,] in which immigrants try to adapt to the urban milieu . . . [,] may be called an *urban village.* The second kind of area, populated largely by single men, pathological families, people in hiding from themselves or society, and individuals who provide the most disreputable of illegal-but-demanded services to the rest of the community, . . . might be called an *urban jungle.*"

Subsidized housing does not differentiate between these groups. In fact, it seeks to address the problems of the lawless by mixing them in among the law-abiding and upwardly mobile, who are regarded almost as mere instruments for the salvation of the disorderly. Because it is based on the myth that the lawless are victims rather than victimizers, such a policy makes victims of those who would build an urban village by enmeshing them in an unsafe, disorganized neighborhood.

True, the new subsidized projects run by community groups, with the advice of such sophisticated organizations as the Local Initiatives Support Corporation and the Enterprise Foundation, do seek to screen tenants so as to keep bad actors out of mixed-income developments. But it defies imagination to think that such a process will be as effective as the screening that the market does. Indeed, in its analysis of such housing in New York, the New School found that though 6 percent of tenants were in arrears on their rent, the eviction rate was still zero.

By remaining focused on the myth that physical conditions are the single most important quality of housing, housers have misunderstood the dynamics of neighborhoods—not merely as places where people live but as communities of shared ideals. As a result, they have blindly based new policies on old mistakes. Consider, for instance, recent housing initiatives that aim to promote racial integration by placing low-income minority families in apartments in the suburbs. These policies are a recipe for racial resentment, which has in fact developed. Asking working-class whites to accept the welfare poor—who would inspire discomfort whether white or black—as neighbors is the worst way to address the race issue. The right way is to enforce housing non-discrimination laws and thus allow the diffusion of upwardly mobile minority-group members into neighborhoods where, if they at first appear to be outsiders, it is only by virtue of race, not class.

A realistic housing policy would strive for a non-subsidized world in which many different sorts of housing form a housing ladder. The lower rungs will be modest indeed—as modest as the single-room-occupancy hotels that sprang up in San Diego when that city allowed dwellings with less-than-full bathrooms and limited parking. By relaxing its code requirements, the city catalyzed construction of some 2,700 new SRO units for the working poor—day laborers, cabdrivers, fast-food employees. The SROs have formed a housing ladder all their own: lower-rent buildings may have no TV or phone, while lobby guards in the better buildings enforce more stringent guest policies.

A sensible housing policy would purge housing and building codes of unnecessary barriers to construction. The New York City Housing Partnership, for instance, would like to build new versions of old-fashioned Brooklyn row houses, but handicapped-access laws forbid basement apartments, which allow for a less expensive overall design. Requirements for cast-iron or copper pipes instead of less expensive plastic ones, or for excessive numbers of electric outlets, increase the cost of housing needlessly. Hugely expensive environmental cleanup requirements discourage developers from building low-cost (or any other kind of) housing on the many "brownfield" sites of inner cities. Policy makers should push for safe ways to "minimally rehab" older buildings, so that they're not priced out of the reach of the unsubsidized poor. City Homes, a Baltimore developer, has tried this on a small scale, with the cooperation of local and state authorities that have held renovation requirements to a minimum. Because of its low costs, City Homes doesn't need the federal rent subsidies on which most low-income housing complexes depend. City Homes rents only to the employed and has created blocks—inhabited by nurses, city sanitation workers, and the like—that are oases of safety and civility in the midst of bad neighborhoods.

Even with building codes that focus on basic safety issues and try not to raise prices, there will be people who can't afford anything we think should be built. In some cases this may be the result of poverty despite effort. In others it may be the result of bad life choices and the wrong values. For those in temporary emergency situations, we should provide shelters, basic arrangements that ensure no one must live on the street. For those whose lack of housing is really a symptom of larger problems—the alcoholic, the drug addict, the teenage mother who cannot afford her own household—we can look to institutional ways, such as group homes, to deliver the combination of shelter, guidance, and treatment they need.

What about the subsidized housing we already have, including New York's 180,000 units of public housing? Ideally, it would be sold off. If that is impracticable—and it would be complicated given the public financing involved, as well as the politics of the situation—it may make sense to consider a limit on the time any person can live in a subsidized unit, especially now that welfare has a time limit. Or housing authorities might charge higher rents for apartments in "better" projects, so as to create a kind of housing ladder.

In this new order, we would understand that a large, variegated supply is the way to restrain housing costs. We would understand that modest housing is a stage that people pass through—and that, by trying to stamp it out, we threaten to short-circuit the process by which they improve themselves. It is superficially attractive to give the hardworking breadwinner a leg up, a housing subsidy, to help pay the bills and raise his or her children. But in practice, because subsidies are provided on the basis of need, not effort or accomplishment, such a policy threatens not to solve our social problems but to make them permanent.

—*Winter 1997*

KENNETH SILBER

When Cleanliness
Isn't a Virtue

FEDERAL AND STATE environmental rules have made it hard, sometimes impossible, to reuse old industrial sites. The result: economic and environmental decay in America's cities. Here's what to do.

For city dwellers, environmental issues often seem distant, involving such things as endangered species, wetlands, and old-growth forests. But cities have an "environment," too—indeed, environmental problems like garbage disposal or car and bus pollution are at their thorniest in areas of high population density. Though you might not think so, cities have an enormous stake in the raucous political debate over the costs and benefits of environmental regulation.

No urban environmental problem is pricklier, or more crucial for cities' economic vitality and competitiveness, than the "brownfields" issue: what to do about properties abandoned or underutilized because of real or imagined contamination. A web of federal and state law and regulation has driven development away from such properties—especially onetime industrial sites located in or near impoverished inner-city neighborhoods—and toward suburban and rural "greenfields."

Two powerful recent trends have engendered this state of affairs: a governmental tendency to impose environmental regulation without regard to economic consequences; and a litigation mania that assigns legal liability in defiance of commonsense notions of personal or corporate responsibility. Parties that had little or nothing to do with a site's contamination become liable for its cleanup—especially if they have deep pockets—while genuine polluters escape accountability. Some cleanup requirements are unnecessarily stringent; others, ambiguous and ever shifting. The division of authority among agencies and levels of government is frequently unclear. And sites that contain little or no contamination become caught up in labyrinthine procedures designed for severely polluted toxic-waste dumps.

As property developers around the country find themselves stymied by confusion, uncertainty, protracted delays, and burdensome costs when they seek to reuse brownfields, urban industrial sites stand idle and housing development hangs fire. And the environmental consequences are as bad as the economic ones: sites that require prompt cleanup stay contaminated. Moreover, development is diverted into pristine greenfield areas, bringing further environmental harm, and the infrastructure that already exists in the cities must be constructed anew, often at great expense.

Nationwide, the brownfields problem is most acute in northeastern and midwestern cities; New York, rich in properties with a long history of industrial use, ranks prominently among them. In these cities, environmental concerns swell the long list of factors—including crime, high taxes, and the quality of the local schools—that deter investment. Says John Norquist, Milwaukee's Democratic mayor: "You end up having companies locating their plants far away from the workforce, creating all kinds of transportation problems and creating unemployment in central cities. There's enough bias against cities as it is without having environmental laws hanging over them like a cloud. And, of course, the worst part about it is that the intended goal—cleanup of the environment—doesn't happen very often either."

Much of the trouble grows out of the federal Comprehensive Environmental Response, Compensation, and Liability Act, commonly known as the Superfund law, enacted in 1980 in response to the discovery of toxic chemicals beneath the residential neighborhood of Love Canal in Niagara Falls, New York. In subsequent years, numerous states, including New York, passed their own Superfund laws, which closely mirror the federal law.

The federal Superfund law derives its name from its establishment of a trust fund, financed by industrial taxes, for the cleanup of polluted sites. However, this fund is of secondary importance to the law's liability arrangements, which are aimed at requiring polluters, rather than the government and taxpayers, to pay for cleanups. Key elements of the law are "strict, retroactive" liability and "joint and several" liability. Retroactive liability holds parties responsible for land contamination that took place prior to the 1980 statute, even if their practices were perfectly legal at the time. The joint and several provision means that any party responsible for even a small portion of a site's contamination can be held liable for the entire cost of the cleanup. In practice, such provisions turn out to mean that property owners can be held liable for the cleanup even if they had nothing to do with the contamination.

This liability scheme, written into many state laws as well, generates lengthy, expensive litigation—a bonanza for lawyers but a disaster for both economic development and environmental protection. According to a RAND Corporation study, more than one-third of the $11.3 billion spent by the private sector on federal Superfund sites between 1980 and 1991 went for litigation rather than cleanup.

Like the interminable Jarndyce and Jarndyce lawsuit in Charles Dickens's *Bleak House*, some Superfund cases drag on for years. In North Hempstead, Long Island, for example, a property has been entangled in litigation since 1982—stalling a much-needed remediation of the site's severe contamination. A federal court initially held the property's current owner, Shore Realty Corp., liable for the cleanup of cancer-causing chemicals and other waste resulting from a previous tenant's unlicensed disposal business. A subsequent court decision shifted liability to a group of 90 companies that had originated the waste.

But the story didn't end there. State environmental authorities then initiated a new round of studies to determine the hazards involved. Wrangling over the site continues, and cleanup is far from complete. While millions of gallons of chemicals have been removed from above-ground storage tanks, the surrounding land and water remain contaminated. "We were willing to do a reasonable study and pay for the waste removal, and instead World War III broke out," says David H. Peirez, a Long Island attorney who represents Shore Realty. "Thirteen years later, litigation is still pending. Millions and millions of dollars have been spent—and the property is still sitting there, useless and barren."

Under the Superfund laws, virtually anyone even remotely connected with a contaminated property may be dragged into court and fleeced. Crucially, this includes financial institutions. In several cases, notably a 1991 federal lawsuit called *United States v. Fleet Factors Corp.*, courts have held that lenders foreclosing on a property may be held liable for cleanup costs. Even when banks avoid such an extreme liability nightmare, the discovery of environmental problems on a site can severely impair the value of a property held as collateral against a loan. Similarly, municipal governments that take over properties for tax delinquency or other reasons may subsequently discover contamination and become responsible for an expensive cleanup.

The overlapping jurisdictions of federal and state environmental authorities intensify liability worries. Developers receiving approval from one level of government may still face action from another level, and admitting wrongdoing in a settlement with one agency could increase one's liability with another agency. "A main problem, especially for some larger industrial sites, is the fact that nobody knows exactly who's calling the shots," says Mark D. Anderson, counsel for the Greenfields Group, an industry-backed lobbying organization based in Virginia. "Is it the U.S. Environmental Protection Agency, or is it the state agency? At times, it may be both."

Developers thus face a patchwork of cleanup standards: federal, state, and, particularly in large cities, local. Typically such standards are not clearly specified in legislation but left to the discretion of regulatory authorities. Often regulators take little account of the proposed use for a site, holding locations to be used for a warehouse or parking lot to the same standards as those planned for residential development. They often base risk assessments on grossly unrealistic scenarios. In 1994 the EPA concluded that one contaminated site on Long Island, belonging to Liberty Industrial Finishing, posed a health threat since trespassers might enter the location. The EPA's assumption: that a trespasser would eat or have dermal contact with soil on the site two hours a day, twice a week, for nine years.

The result of all this is that developers and financiers frequently shun properties that carry even the slightest hint of contamination. "People fear the uncertainty of what the environmental standards are going to be and what the environmental process is going to entail," says Diane L. Donley, assistant general counsel at Clean Sites, a Virginia-based environmental group. "Therefore, they simply avoid brownfield sites and go to a suburban site."

Determining the full dimensions of the brownfields problem is a difficult task. Information is scattered among a variety of organizations, public and private, and official statistics tend to cover only those already entangled in the regulatory machinery, ignoring properties that go undeveloped because of the mere possibility of entanglement. A well-intentioned if not altogether helpful estimate by the federal General Accounting Office places the number of brownfields in the nation at somewhere between 150,000 and 450,000. But efforts to quantify the problem within a particular geographic area have found disturbing news. The Regional Plan Association, for example, a nonprofit group that studies land-use issues, has inventoried brownfields in Union County, New Jersey, which includes the city of Elizabeth. The tally: 56 derelict sites in Elizabeth, totaling 824 acres—more than 11 percent of the city's entire land area.

Once landing on a federal or state list of actual or suspected contaminated sites, a property often remains unmarketable even after cleanup. The EPA's Superfund Tracking System list, for example, until recently contained nearly 40,000 sites, including many properties designated "No Further Remedial Action Planned." Yet these still carried the often fatal stigma of having attracted attention from the federal hazardous-waste bureaucracy. (Lately, in recognition of this problem, the EPA has begun removing such sites from the list.)

In New York City, federal and state Superfund laws have combined with the bureaucratic inertia of environmental agencies to form a powerful barrier to the cleanup and reuse of properties, especially along the Manhattan and Brooklyn waterfronts. Former industrial areas that could be converted into parkland, stores, or residences languish in disuse. While some sites on the waterfront and elsewhere are indeed thoroughly polluted and would require extensive cleanup before reuse, all too often properties descend into pariah status on slender evidence of contamination.

Among the parcels of land trapped in the regulatory toils are the 26 sites in the city currently on the New York State Department of Environmental Conservation's registry of "inactive hazardous waste disposal sites." They range from the 297-acre Fountain Avenue Landfill in Brooklyn to the half-acre Levco Metals property in Queens, onetime site of metal-finishing processes believed to have contaminated the nearby groundwater. Some properties sit on this registry for years before the degree of environmental hazard even becomes known. Take, for example, the 25-acre waterfront lot near the Gowanus Canal in Brooklyn, officially known as "the rear of the Bush Terminal Building." In the early 1980s, law-enforcement authorities compiled evidence of illegal dumping of solvents at the site. In 1985 a state environmental study recommended additional research, and a second study in 1990 confirmed the presence of contaminants but found "no significant threat" to the environment. The lot then attained its current status of a "class 3" hazardous waste location, meaning that further action may be deferred indefinitely. Meanwhile it languishes on the registry, its prospects for development virtually nil.

The same department has vastly complicated development of the West Side of Manhattan by a report labeling the entire West Side Highway between Battery Place and 59th Street a "hazardous substance waste disposal site," an assessment based in part on the presence of dead vegetation and discolored soil near the roadway and on the location of industries nearby. In addition, preliminary tests showed elevated levels of lead and other metals. But whether any actual threat to the environment or to public health exists, the report acknowledged, is unknown. Yet now any purchase of property adjacent to the highway—potentially valuable real estate with easy access to the Hudson River and the city's midtown and downtown business districts—entails enormous risk, including the possibility of becoming liable for exorbitant cleanup costs.

Not only properties with the singular misfortune of being officially identified as toxic-waste dumps but also hundreds of New York City sites listed in government databases as containing some lesser degree of contamination—even many sites that could become a problem once an environmental review occurs—hang in development limbo because of liability risks. "There's hardly a site for development in New York City that doesn't have some level of contamination that could under some scenario trigger liability," says Kathy Wylde, president of the New York City Housing Partnership. "If someone changed the oil in a car on the site, or threw away old tires or a battery, or if there was a building there that was demolished that had paint and asbestos or that had an oil tank left in the basement that percolated a little oil, or if there was a dry-cleaning establishment anywhere near the place, or if old paint cans were disposed there—all of that potentially triggers liability."

Some properties frozen by the regulatory climate do not require cleanup at all. The Housing Partnership, a nonprofit organization that works with the city and private developers to build low-income housing, set out in 1989 to build 50 two-family homes on a derelict, city-owned site in the South Bronx. The site passed three separate government environmental reviews. Yet a lender required the builder collaborating on the project to conduct an additional review, which revealed the presence of petroleum residues—probably from neighborhood residents using the vacant lot to park and repair their cars. "The environmental consultant the builder hired came out with a report that said the site wasn't 100 percent clean, but that he wasn't really sure if we had a problem or not," says Jody Kass, director of technical services at the Housing Partnership.

This ambiguous assessment deterred the bank from proceeding with the loan, and the project remained stalled during the next four years—generating some $100,000 in additional legal and consulting fees. "The builder hired several different environmental consultants, thinking maybe the consultant wasn't any good," says Kass. "He hired several different lawyers, thinking maybe he was getting bad legal advice." Finally, another bank provided the loan, after accepting a consultant's report that the site was safe for residential development. The housing was built and is now occupied. The only "cleanup" that occurred was the addition of six inches of new topsoil—something the builder had intended to do from the very beginning.

New York State and City have lagged behind much of the country in grappling with the brownfields issue. Numerous states have launched reform efforts aimed at expediting cleanup procedures and clarifying liability. Increasingly, urban states that have not undertaken significant reforms will face a competitiveness problem, as investment dollars migrate toward sites that can be cleaned up and redeveloped at reasonable cost and risk.

Key to reform is eliminating the most onerous liability provisions of the various Superfund laws. Some states have already taken action. Michigan recently passed legislation replacing joint and several liability with a provision holding parties liable only for contamination it is proved that they caused. While such an approach may in some instances result in cleanup costs being paid by the government when no liable party can be found, it also spares purchasers the threat of endless litigation that would make them avoid contaminated properties altogether.

More than 20 states have sensibly adopted voluntary cleanup programs, aimed at encouraging parties not responsible for the contamination of a site to purchase and develop the property. Such programs, which vary widely from state to state, typically allow prospective purchasers—or prospective sellers—to agree to clean up a site to a clearly specified standard in exchange for some form of assurance, to lenders as well as developers, that they will not become caught in open-ended liability arrangements. While most voluntary cleanup programs are still at early stages of development, some have already enjoyed notable success.

Minnesota, among the first states to undertake such an initiative, provides a model worth following. It gives developers and lenders who meet clearly defined cleanup standards an array of liability protections, from "no-action" letters that assure they won't be the subject of a state lawsuit to "off-site-source" letters, affirming that they aren't legally responsible for contamination known to have originated from a neighboring property. More than 450 properties have entered the program so far. At the same time, Minnesota has kept in place state Superfund provisions that enable it to take action against actual polluters. Says Ken Haberman, the voluntary program's supervisor: "We haven't released anybody who's really responsible for the contamination. What we've done is provided all sorts of cushions and parachutes for non-responsible parties to be protected from Superfund liability."

Such measures can determine whether a property gets developed. In Pennsylvania the enactment of voluntary cleanup legislation in mid-1995 opened the way for the sale of a northeastern Philadelphia food-processing plant that had been shut down for six years. Quality Foods, a frozen-meat company, purchased the property after state environmental authorities gave the company a "covenant-not-to-sue" for contamination existing prior to the purchase. Meanwhile the Pennsylvania Department of Environmental Resources required the previous owner to remove old storage tanks and tons of petroleum-contaminated soil. Says Quality Foods chairman and CEO Robert Gioia: "We saw the site and we realized it was perfect for our needs. Then we recognized that there were environmental problems, and we lost interest. Without the covenant the deal would not have gone through. If governments want to rebuild or rehabilitate inner-city industrial sites, they're going to have to do something like this, because no owner will ever touch these sites without some assurances that he's not going to be liable."

Making cleanup standards clearer and more realistic is another essential reform. Increasingly states are adopting standards based on future land use. Michigan, for example, recently established 11 categories of sites, representing varying degrees of residential, commercial, industrial, and recreational use. Each category requires a different cleanup standard, based on reasonable assumptions about how many people will be exposed to toxins and for how long.

Resolving the brownfields issue will also require federal action, for a significant weakness of state voluntary-cleanup programs is that they cannot shield participants from federal liability. What's needed is a delegation of authority from Washington to the states, reasonable enough when you consider that contaminated properties, unlike various other environmental problems, are inherently a local matter. Lately state environmental agencies and the federal EPA have begun trying to sort out lines of authority. Minnesota's Pollution Control Agency negotiated an agreement with the EPA's regional office that the MPCA would be the "lead agency" in handling sites that enter Minnesota's voluntary program. Still, a more sweeping change—for example, barring the EPA from any site already in litigation under a state Superfund law—is needed to reduce the uncertainty bred by overlapping jurisdiction.

Another promising avenue for reform—just beginning to be explored—is partial privatization of the regulatory process, making it cheaper and more efficient. Several states, including Ohio and Massachusetts, have established as part of their voluntary cleanup programs a system of licensing private environmental consultants to review sites and determine whether cleanup requirements have been met, tasks normally performed by government officials. Sites that pass such reviews will receive official state approvals, including liability protections. However, the private reviews will be subject to random audits by government inspectors; in Ohio, for example, some 25 percent of sites will be audited.

Such reforms build upon the private sector's ability to regulate itself. Throughout the country, banks routinely require environmental testing of properties as a precondition for lending—becoming, in effect, surrogate regulators. Insurance companies are taking on a similar role: some now offer environmental-liability insurance to developers and lenders and hence have an interest in ascertaining that cleanup occurs.

Government's traditional approach to contaminated properties, exemplified by Superfund, assumed that markets provide little incentive for cleanup; hence the emphasis on strict enforcement and punitive liability measures. In reality, however, the existence of large areas of urban land with severely diminished market value presents not only a problem but an opportunity for profit, once the uncertainties created by current laws and regulations are overcome. Says Robert Berger, a SUNY/Buffalo law professor: "There's a lot of money to be made in brownfields."

—Autumn 1995

VIII
IMMIGRANTS

In the nineteenth and early twentieth centuries, cities were the gateway to American opportunity for millions of immigrants, whose energy and creativity enriched their new urban homes immeasurably. A new wave of immigration has filled the cities, bringing dying neighborhoods back to life, revivifying languishing economies, and showing that the American Dream is still alive and well. The new urban immigrants remind us what moral qualities it takes to make that dream a reality—and what cities are for.

JONATHAN FOREMAN

Bombay on the Hudson

YOU DON'T HAVE TO BE a demographer to know that more and more New Yorkers these days come from the Indian subcontinent. Just hail a taxi in midtown: chances are, you'll find a man named Sarabjit, Uday, or Ali behind the wheel. The legions of South Asian taxi drivers are the most visible sign of an immigration that has been going on for more than three decades now. Today newcomers from India, Pakistan, and Bangladesh are a vital component of New York's mosaic: their vibrant communities enliven every corner of the city.

Begin in Manhattan, where Bangladeshis have settled into the old tenements of the Lower East Side and lined 6th Street in the East Village with their "Indian" restaurants. Then take the Number 7 subway across the East River to Long Island City, Queens, another Bangladeshi neighborhood, where new stores, auto workshops, and taxi garages are quickly supplanting abandoned factories and warehouses. If you continue on the Number 7—popularly known as the "Orient Express"—you'll find that Jackson Heights now contains a teeming and prosperous Little India whose turbaned Sikhs and sari-clad women make the main strip feel like Delhi's Chandni Chowk or one of Bombay's upscale shopping districts. Finally, hop on the B train to Coney Island Avenue in Brooklyn's East Flatbush. There Pakistanis have revitalized block after block, festooning their new storefronts with Urdu script.

South Asians have sunk roots in New York neighborhoods from Gramercy Park, Astoria, and Flushing to Brighton Beach, Richmond Hills, and Jamaica. All told, the city's population now includes some 500,000 souls—half of them Indian, the other half almost equal parts Pakistani and Bangladeshi—who come from the lands that formed the British Dominion of India until 1947.

But New York's South Asians are not just another large and exotic addition to the city's ethnic mix. They have prospered mightily in Gotham, as they have elsewhere in the United States. Their varied ranks include not only hardworking taxi drivers and shopkeepers but also thousands of accomplished engineers and entrepreneurs, physicians and academics. And their children excel in school, quickly entering the American mainstream.

What explains their success? South Asians have a double cultural advantage. They arrive not only with all the traditional immigrant virtues but also with an invaluable cultural and educational legacy from the days of British rule. That doesn't make assimilation an easy, trouble-free process for them, of course. As with other immigrant groups, it takes a painful toll. But the astonishing rise of these newly made Americans shows how resilient the American Dream remains and how much the nation benefits from an influx of such energetic new residents.

In 1965 Congress passed the Immigration Reform Act, an effort in part to deal with labor shortages in certain technical fields. The new law opened the door to the subcontinent's doctors, engineers, and pharmacists, accelerating a "brain drain" that began in 1947 and still afflicts the region. By the early 1970s, Indians, Pakistanis, and Bangladeshis—most of them highly trained—had established a modest foothold in the U.S. of some 45,000 residents. A decade later the South Asian community was around 500,000 strong.

By then the professionals who had come to the U.S. with little more than their talents had prospered and become citizens, enabling them to take advantage of the family-reunification provisions of the 1965 act. Thus began the second wave of immigration from the subcontinent, a gathering surge of brothers and sisters, cousins and in-laws. The result: a combined South Asian population in the U.S. that today exceeds 2.5 million. Indians alone now constitute a bigger American minority than Koreans or Vietnamese, and in New York they outnumber Koreans by 20 percent.

If the typical first-wave immigrant was a much-sought-after pediatrician or chemical engineer, the second-wave immigrant is likely to be less educated and less proficient in English. But make no mistake: the second wave hardly represents the subcontinent's poor, huddled masses. Almost all South Asian immigrants to the United States come from the region's English-speaking middle classes, from families able to send at least one child to college (many of the cabbies really do have degrees). As Farooq Bhatti, founder of New York's Pak Brothers Taxi Driver Union, explains, the rural poor of India and Pakistan are far too destitute to obtain a tourist visa and a plane ticket—or even a bus ticket from their villages to Bombay. Like the upper classes of these countries—who enjoy lives of extraordinary luxury and privilege—the very poor don't emigrate.

The social gulf between the two generations of immigrants can be profound, deepened by the rapidity of the first wave's success in "Amreeka." Ram Iyer, an Indian-born social worker who deals with South Asian families in New York, talks about a "disowning factor." As he explains: "People are embarrassed by their relative who works in a gas station." But such embarrassment is far from universal. For instance, Rahaul Merchant—who came to the U.S. in 1979, got a degree in computer science and an MBA, and is now head of technology at Sanwa Financial Products on Wall Street—is proud of his brother, who owns a convenience store in Queens. Merchant was pleased to have his siblings (two sisters came over as well) stay with him until they found their feet. The family still invariably comes together every Thanksgiving and Christmas, and, says Merchant, "we always talk on Divali," the Hindu festival of lights.

South Asians of both waves have wasted no time in climbing the American ladder of success. The 1990 census reported a median family income for Indians living in the U.S. of $50,000, compared with $35,000 for native-born Americans. Sixty percent of them had at least a bachelor's degree, and over a third had a graduate degree. Still more impressive, perhaps, this year the children of Indian immigrants won four of the ten prestigious Westinghouse prizes for high school scientists and placed second and third in the National Spelling Bee.

The cultural afterglow of the British Raj accounts for some of this rapid ascent. It is rare to find a South Asian immigrant who cannot speak at least some English—an enormous advantage. No less ingratiating in an America where language and manners seem to grow coarser by the day, most adult South Asians comport themselves with a certain old-world politesse, a courtesy redolent of Victorian tea parties. The consuming passion across the entire South Asian community for the game of cricket is emblematic: a slow, almost ritualistic sport of arcane rules, it typifies the immigrants' devotion to order and fair play, civility and good form. Finally, of course, South Asian newcomers tend to adjust quickly to the American political and legal scene: most have had experience with democracy and the rule of law, however imperfectly the post-independence regimes of the subcontinent have realized such ideals.

It is also hard to dispute the claim, common among South Asians, that America has received the cream of the subcontinent's migrants. Many of them have indeed demonstrated unusual initiative and perseverance to come here, and they have done so in order to build lives unimaginable back home. Thirty-five-year-old Joginder Singh, a Sikh taxi driver from the Punjab, has been in the U.S. seven years and plans to stay. He started out making sandwiches at a Blimpie's, drove a limo for a while, and now, like many Americans, dreams of moving to California. "There are more opportunities here," he says. "It really pays you if you want to work." The now-prosperous technologist Rahaul Merchant agrees: "I started from scratch. For the first few years I had nothing in my pocket. I could hardly afford French fries. But I made a go for myself. It's the meritocracy that attracts people like me."

The first decades of Indian independence were especially cruel to such

strivers. The Congress Party subjected the new country to one socialist experiment after another, including nationalization. Protectionist policies and an
obsessive fear of multinational corporations kept out capital, products, and
ideas from abroad. And the so-called licensing Raj made setting up any kind
of business a bureaucratic nightmare, made worse by endemic corruption
and nepotism. By the mid-sixties, India couldn't even keep pace with other
developing nations like Turkey and Mexico. In the last several years the
country's political elite has begun to open up the economy, but India still
has far to go if it is to hold on to its entrepreneurs. As the Indian-American
novelist Bharati Mukherjee says of one of her characters who emigrates to
the U.S., "Success had meant to him escape from the constant plotting and
bitterness that wore out India's middle class."

The Hindu caste system has done even more than socialism and bureaucracy to stifle Indian enterprise and social mobility—and to drive out
the ambitious. A complicated form of hereditary ranking linked to occupation, caste effectively sets Hindu society in stone. As a guest at a Brahmin
house in Rajasthan, I once watched in amazement as food spilled on the
floor one hot afternoon remained there for hours: the servant whose role it
was to clean up was out. Under this rigid system, any effort to improve your
status is pointless—once a member of the floor-mopping class, always a
member of the floor-mopping class. Such distinctions exact an enormous
psychological toll on those of higher rank as well. The British author V. S.
Naipaul, an Indian born in Trinidad, has noted that Indian scientists who
win Nobel Prizes for work done abroad go home and produce little of value
ever again; achievement ceases to have any bearing on their social standing.

The concept of caste is particularly hard for Americans to understand,
the U.S. being in so many ways the antithesis of a caste culture. Indeed, caste
identities tend to dissolve quickly once Indian immigrants arrive, in part because it becomes impractical to follow the system's elaborate codes of purity.
Traveling abroad was itself once considered a defiling experience. After
decades of official disapproval, caste is finally losing its grip in India—but
not fast enough for thousands of middle-class emigrants.

Physicians were among the first to flee the subcontinent and the earliest
Indian immigrants to flourish in the U.S. Today the 32,000 Indian doctors
practicing here are a formidable presence in the profession, especially
among anesthesiologists, 10 percent of whom are Indian. With years of experience in the U.S. and plenty of money, they are an unrivaled organized influence in their community, acting through the powerful American
Association of Physicians from India.

Dr. Mukhund Modi, an ethnic Gujarati from Bombay, has practiced
pediatrics in the tough Brooklyn neighborhood of East New York for 25
years. Working in the borough was not his first choice, but he did his resi-

dency at King's County Hospital there and decided to "hang around" while his wife, a pathologist, completed a fellowship at Columbia. "I went for the first five years thinking I would go back to India and live happily ever after," he says. "I think that was true of most of my Indian colleagues too. But this country has given us a lot. Things changed—we had kids. It wasn't a sudden decision. The opportunities we had here and the quality of life were very important to us." His wife now works at University Hospital on Staten Island, where the Modis have lived for the past 19 years.

Modi has gradually come to identify with his new country. Though he remains the head of a New York organization that raises funds for the BJP—India's Hindu nationalist party—he is also involved in local Republican politics, having long been good friends with his next-door neighbor, Staten Island borough president Guy Molinari. After many years Modi has finally decided to become an American citizen. "I didn't apply before because of the dream of going back to India," he says. "Now I feel that I'll go back to visit but not to stay forever, so why should I lose the chance to vote in the U.S.?" Like many Indian professionals, he and his wife have settled comfortably into suburban life. They sent their daughters to local public schools—after a stint in Catholic primary schools—and then on to Amherst and Wesleyan. "Indians are typical middle-class people," observes Modi. "We want a house, a good school, and a safe neighborhood. I'd call that the American Dream."

Dr. Unni Moopan, a urologist and general surgeon who teaches at the Brookdale University Hospital in Brooklyn, remembers well the advertisements for doctors in the Indian press that drew him from the southwestern state of Kerala to America in 1976. Already a surgeon in India, he came for additional training and to do research. Five years later he had become a U.S. citizen. "The best part about New York is its mixture," he says. "You don't feel as though you are in a thoroughly foreign place suddenly. In New York everybody can feel at home. You are not the odd one, standing out in the crowd." Moopan and his wife lived in Brooklyn and Queens before moving to Hewlett, Long Island, attracted by the public schools. The father of two children, he knew just what he was looking for when it came to their education: "The class size is small, and the rate of going to Ivy League schools is very high."

Engineers formed a second large contingent in the professional exodus from the subcontinent. Today more than 20,000 Indian engineers work in the U.S., many of them graduates of the elite Indian Institutes of Technology. Unable to find work at home, these superbly trained technologists have made key contributions at such American high-tech giants as Sun Microsystems, Intel, and Bell Labs. The U.S. job market continues to place a premium on computer experts from South Asia, who now outstrip physicians among the professionals who choose to emigrate.

Kersh Birdie came to the U.S. in 1971, an early refugee from India's high-tech sector. Formerly a partner at First Boston and head of technological development at Morgan Stanley, he took an MBA at night and now runs his own software and consulting company, Northstar Technologies, which employs 25 people in Manhattan. "Back in India they have tremendous computer-science education," says Birdie. "They can compete with anybody. But in the Third World, opportunities were very limited in the technology business. Coming here was great—the market was wide open. I made up my mind to stay as soon as I got here, and I became an American as soon as I could." Many others followed suit, Birdie notes, reeling off a list of senior Indian technologists at Wall Street firms like Fidelity, First Boston, and Bankers Trust.

South Asian immigrants who lack professional qualifications have gone into an array of traditional immigrant occupations. Crucially for the day-to-day life of New York City, they have nearly taken over the taxi industry: some 30,000 of the city's 45,000 yellow-taxi drivers are now of South Asian descent. When a Pakistani "taxiwallah" was murdered in 1993, as many as 10,000 drivers protested outside City Hall. As for service, this takeover has made it almost universally possible once again for drivers to communicate with passengers in English.

Gaining entry into the taxi business is easy, but it's a grueling way to make a living. After getting a New York hack license—a process that takes about six months—a new immigrant will lease a medallion taxi, keeping what he can, after expenses, from fares and tips. In a slow seven-day week, a cabbie can make as little as $300, which partly explains why so many of them compete recklessly for fares. "You must remember that we have the medallion owner on our back," says a Bangladeshi driver named Imran. "I pay $112 per day for the cab, $3 for the union, $20 for gas, and $10 for food—plus taxes, TLC tickets, parking violations, and summonses. I'm driving 90 hours a week, and I cannot make $2,000 a month."

It's a physically and mentally exhausting job. Because the city has so few public restrooms, every cabdriver must carry a mental list of restaurants whose facilities he can use—without getting a parking ticket or a Taxi and Limousine Commission citation, which means at least a day of lost income. The rudeness of city officials, especially the police, baffles and pains the South Asian drivers. A Pakistani driver called Ahmed told me he was "stunned" the first time a cop told him to "move your fucking car." The cabbies often find their passengers abrupt and unfriendly too, especially by South Asian standards. And because impatient passengers and their own financial interest push them to drive as fast as they can, they live in fear of tickets.

Taxi driving tends to be a bachelor's profession, a fallback job for younger men in need of work. A Bangladeshi named Rahim came to New York to study aeronautics but had to drop out of school and start driving a cab. "I needed more money," he tells me over a 2 AM dinner at the Kasturi restaurant on Lexington Avenue, a favorite hangout of Bangladeshi drivers. "My family back home is dependent on me." Ponytailed, bespectacled, and sweatshirt-clad, he looks like a graduate student. Rahim lives with four Bangladeshi friends in a four-bedroom apartment in Astoria, where he pays $300 a month for his spartan quarters. He and a partner recently borrowed money to buy a medallion—no mean expense at the going rate of $200,000. It will take them ten to 15 years to pay off the debt, but once they do, their incomes will shoot up. If Rahim can make enough money in the next couple of years, he would like to return to school part-time and find a wife to bring over from Bangladesh.

Most South Asian taxi drivers dream of being in business for themselves someday, whether with a medallion of their own or some other enterprise. Karnal Singh drove a cab for five years and then opened the Punjabi Palace restaurant on Houston Street, where he employs a brother, a nephew, and two cousins, as well as a Bangladeshi chef. Still only 25, he recently opened a second restaurant at Tenth Avenue and 27th Street. Though a Sikh, he retains only one visible sign of his faith: the steel bangle, or *kara*, on his wrist. His Pakistani friend and frequent customer Riaz Ahmad, who wears the traditional *shalwar kameez* pajama suit and a backward Yankees baseball cap, has a master's degree in Islamic studies; he has been driving a taxi for five years. A restaurant is not in his future; he imagines instead going into "something like a car service—because I know this business." Many drivers pool their resources to make the down payment and pay off the loans needed to start a business. "Four drivers making $30,000 a year will get together and buy a $100,000 workshop," explains Farooq Bhatti, "and then they are on their way. In Pakistan we have become very good at repairing cars, because parts are so expensive." In the westernmost avenues of Chelsea and the Garment District, Pakistanis and Indians now run dozens of small auto-shops-cum-taxi-garages.

South Asians have also turned New York's newsstand business into a virtual ethnic monopoly. According to the Department of Consumer Affairs, they now operate an astonishing 300 of the city's 330 street newsstands.

Eight years ago I found myself in Penn Station after midnight, waiting for a delayed Amtrak train. The main hall was a dirty, unwelcoming place, full of the homeless and prowled by other unsavory types. I noticed a new shop on the concourse, with a sign announcing: HUDSON NEWS. It was an oasis of cleanliness and light, with a handsome selection of magazines. Best of all, it contained several young Pakistani men in uniform, keeping a watchful eye on what was clearly a place of refuge for the respectable. Since then, Hudson News has gone on to revolutionize the terminal newsstand business, with a hundred stores in train stations and airports nationwide. Almost all of its employees are South Asian. The managers of the Penn Station, Grand Central, and Port Authority stores are "Joe" Khan, "Bob" Khan, and "Mo" Khan, respectively. Unrelated to one another, all are Pakistani immigrants and vice presidents of the company.

Joe DiDomizio, son of the chain's founder and vice president of marketing and operations, is quick to give credit for the company's expansion to its employees from the subcontinent. "They have a tremendous work ethic, they work very long hours, they are very dedicated, and they treat the business as if it were theirs," he says. "We hire them at every level."

The assistant manager of the Grand Central store is Waris Khan. A Pathan from Pakistan, where his people are famous for their martial qualities, he is a former high school math teacher. Today the mustachioed Khan stands a short distance from the store in his smart tie and navy blazer, keeping a fierce watch over the whole operation. He commutes each morning from Westchester Square in the Bronx, arriving in time to open the store at 5 AM, and he doesn't usually leave until early evening. "We are from the Northwest Frontier, and we are very strong," says Khan. "We don't mind doing anything. I am 63 and still working." Would-be robbers have tried to hold him up several times, but he so intimidated them that they left empty-handed. "You have to show that you are ready to fight," he insists, mindful perhaps of the famous Pathan motto, "If someone gives you a pinch, respond with a blow."

Sponsored by his four brothers—two of them lab technicians, one an accountant, and the fourth a supervisor at an Atlantic City casino—Khan came to New York in 1988, largely to get his two boys away from the guns and drugs endemic to his corner of Pakistan. The breaking point for him came when his 11-year-old returned from school one day talking about the Kalashnikov rifle that he and his friends had been playing with. Both of Khan's sons now attend City College, and one of them recently applied to medical school.

South Asians man the ranks of many other businesses in New York. Many work behind the counter at neighborhood delis and grocery stores, and at chain stores like Duane Reade and National Wholesale Liquidators. The more entrepreneurial of them have bought into Blimpies, International House of Pancakes, and other restaurant franchises; Baskin-Robbins reports that some 250 of its operators nationwide are now South Asian. In the low-income neighborhoods of the outer boroughs, Pakistanis have made a specialty of under-a-dollar retailing, with successful stores like 99¢ Dream, 99¢ World, and 99¢ City. And should you venture into such porn emporia as remain in Times Square, you will find that a Sri Lankan runs almost every one of them.

Young South Asian men of the second wave have made a niche for themselves in several of the city's more dangerous occupations. After taxi driving, the most common lines of work for Pakistani immigrants are construction and trucking. Sikhs have established an empire in the gas station business: the city's Department of Consumer Affairs estimates that immigrants from India's Punjab region—the great majority of them Sikhs—now own nearly half of New York's gas stations.

Sikhs seem well qualified for such work, where the possibility of robbery is a constant. Observant male Sikhs take the surname Singh upon admission to a quasi-military order called the Khalsa, and they are famously macho: "We are kind of like the Klingons in *Star Trek*," one young man told me. A fifteenth-century offshoot of Hinduism, the Sikh religion demands that observant males wear unshorn hair under a turban and, most important, carry a dagger. The Sikhs developed their proud military tradition through years of armed struggle—against India's Moghul rulers, against the British, and then against the Empire's enemies in India and abroad. Since independence, Sikh separatism at home has accelerated their emigration: many left amid the anti-Sikh sentiment that followed their bloody attempt to establish an independent state in 1984 and the assassination of Indira Gandhi shortly thereafter by one of her Sikh bodyguards. But even Sikhs have their limits. One told me that he started working at a gas station after two armed robberies in his cab, only to be robbed twice more "by black guys with guns." He wants to move back to India.

South Asian community leaders are quick to liken themselves to the Jewish immigrants of yesteryear, and there are indeed some pronounced parallels. Like Jews, members of the Indian "diaspora"—especially Gujaratis and Sindhis—have played the role of middleman in international commerce, trading and settling throughout the world. Their economic success has often stirred resentment, giving rise to harassment and confiscations in the Caribbean, in Burma and Malaysia, and most notoriously, in Uganda and Kenya, which expelled South Asians by the tens of thousands in the 1970s. Having been driven now from several homes, many South Asian immigrants to the U.S. are multiple exiles. Here they rarely encounter serious discrimination or racial hostility (though this hasn't prevented some South Asian campus activists from declaring that their communities share the victimhood of other "people of color").

Like their Jewish predecessors, people from all three countries of the subcontinent have a special reverence for teachers, whom they often address as "masterji" (the suffix "ji" indicating great respect). Keshavan Narayan, a Tamil Brahmin who works as a journalist in New York, touches the feet of his former schoolteachers when he encounters them back home. Farwana, a 14-year-old Bangladeshi girl whose family moved to Long Island City a year ago and who attends the Newcomers' School there, misses the respectful ways of her old classroom: students would stand up when the teacher entered and quiet down immediately when the teacher spoke. But she doesn't miss the beatings that Bengali teachers sometimes give their students.

Such attitudes translate into sterling academic performance. As anyone who has spent time lately on the NYU or Columbia campus knows, South Asians make it into the top schools in disproportionately large numbers. Like youngsters from China, Korea, and Vietnam, they are more likely than other Americans to excel in the hard sciences and mathematics (though as native English speakers, they are more comfortable with liberal arts subjects than many other Asian children). Solid early schooling accounts for some of their success in these fields—primary and secondary education on the subcontinent is often superb—but so does parental pressure. Like generations of Jewish parents, South Asians strongly prefer their children to take courses that promise secure professional careers. Engineering, medicine, and business administration are clear favorites. The idea that a college student should study, say, theater arts because he or she finds it personally fulfilling is an utterly alien, American idea that causes considerable generational strife.

South Asians pursue many traditional Jewish trades. The Jains—members of an Indian religious sect famous for its ascetic vegetarianism, nonviolence, and business acumen—have become a powerful force in the diamond industry, as cutters, polishers, and importers. Their connections extend from Antwerp and Tel Aviv to the cutting workshops of India and Manhattan's 47th Street, where they do business with Hasidic Jews. "Our philosophies are pretty close," says Arun Kothari, a Jain in the gem business, of his Jewish associates. "We have been working with them for 25 years. We trust them implicitly, and they trust us implicitly. We know their families, and they know our families." Punjabis in New York, like Jews before them, sell textiles and apparel in dozens of shops west of the Port Authority.

Natives of Gujarat, in northwestern India, have distinguished themselves as the premier shopkeepers and small-scale entrepreneurs of the South Asian diaspora. Wherever one finds immigrants from the subcontinent, a Patel—the most common Gujarati surname—is likely to run the neighborhood store. On the corner of 7th Street and First Avenue, one Mr. Patel has recently expanded the hardware store that he bought from a Russian Jewish family eight years ago. Both his sons and one of his daughters-in-law work in the store and have helped him open a second one in Gramercy Park. They presently employ workers from Mexico, Ecuador, Bangladesh, and Ukraine, and one can only listen with wonder as Mr. Patel's son Muk yells down to the storeroom in a mixture of English, Gujarati, and Spanish. Though he sports a long gray beard, Mr. Patel still puts in a 12-hour day between his two stores.

Most South Asian immigrants come to this country with at least a vague idea of returning home once they have made their fortunes. Yet few go back, especially if their children have gone to American schools. They do visit, however—and that can be a traumatic experience. In Bombay I met an Indian-American businessman who had just come "home" from a successful career as a management consultant in Manhattan. After only three days he had decided to go back to New York: he could no longer handle what now struck him as unacceptable chaos, filth, and deprivation. Sunita Mukhi, a scholar at New York's Asia Society, tells the story of an Indian businessman who went back for the funeral of his father. The sympathy of his relatives, many of whom he had never met, overwhelmed him. Mukhi asked him why he didn't move back. "Are you crazy?" he replied. "I cannot breathe there. Too many people, too much corruption. Even the priests were asking for money to facilitate my father's passage to the next life."

Other Indian-Americans forget what made them migrate and romanticize the old country. Like tourists, they see only the colorful trappings and cultural confidence of the life they left behind. The result, very often, is a kind of pan-Indian identity that even the Indian state, for all its efforts since independence, has failed to generate. For the children of such immigrants in particular, what matters ethnically is that they are from the subcontinent— not that they are Keralites or Kashmiris. In an effort to recover their roots, many will take classes in Hindi—India's official language—even though their parents speak, say, Tamil or Bengali. This softening of ethnic differences has carried over to the region's most combustible conflicts. "We get on fine with each other all over the world," a Pakistani taxi driver told me of his community's relations with Indians. "It's only on the border back home that we have a problem." South Asians from all three countries often refer to themselves as the *desi* community or just as *desis*. The term means "countryman," like the Yiddish *landsman*.

Like previous immigrant groups who have made a quick success of assimilation, South Asians struggle to hold on to their heritage. Pride drives much of this effort, but so too does a certain unease with their new home and its alluring but often destructive mass culture. As the British writer Theodore Dalrymple has observed, "Immigration across half the world is very stressful and disorienting, and old customs therefore become to some immigrants what soft toys are to children in the dark—a source of great comfort."

South Asians rely heavily on religion to transmit traditional values to their children. Families worship together at their local temples and mosques (hundreds of which are scattered throughout the New York area), and parents often send their children for cultural instruction—weekend religious school for young Muslims and classical Indian dance for Hindu girls.

For Hindus, such training has met with mixed success. Anand Mohand—a professor of philosophy at Queens College who is a Purohit, or hereditary Brahmin priest—argues that a meaningful Hindu education requires a Hindu social setting: "In India we are raised by tradition. You don't ask questions, and if you do, you are told 'because it is so.' Indians are Hindus more by osmosis than anything else. This means that immigrant parents are not equipped to answer the questions raised by their children. They spend millions of dollars building temples, but the youngsters are unwilling to sit through the ceremonies." Journalist Keshavan Narayan, who has observed the community for two decades, believes that many of these young Indian-Americans eventually give tradition a second chance. "After college, when they are looking for relationships and establishing careers, they undergo a change in thinking," he says. "They look at their roots and realize that their background gives them enormous strength in a society where family structure is falling apart."

Growing up in New Jersey, Anu Anand, 25, went to some kind of Indian cultural event every weekend while attending Catholic school during the week. Her parents, worried by stories of South Asian students unable to deal with the newfound freedom of school away from home, insisted that she pick a local college. A recent graduate of Fairleigh Dickinson University now bound for law school, Anu is fascinated by her roots. "I would like to have a traditional wedding ceremony if I marry another Hindu," she says. And though she is not devout like her Brahmin parents, who pray every day, she studies Indian classical dance with her mother, Lakshmi, and insists, "I'm not an atheist, and I pray on my birthday." Whatever the differences between herself and her parents, Anu generally approves of the traditional upbringing that Indian parents provide: "Overall, our parents did very well. We don't have too many drug addicts, teen pregnancies, or alcoholics."

Najma Sultana, a psychiatrist and a prominent member of the Indian Muslim community in the U.S., applies a practical test to her faith. Yes, South Asian families "lead a boring life," she tells me as we sit in her living room in Jamaica, Queens, decorated with framed verses from the Koran, family pictures, and posters from the recent International Women's Congress in Beijing, which she attended. But such a life "comes in handy: we hold on to our money, and we hold on to our families." Islam helps them navigate American culture. "For us, religion is a positive force for dealing with all the temptations. We go to the mosque, we pray, we share—and half the battle is won."

Nothing is so fraught with the tensions between the old life and the new as relations between the sexes. When an Indian couple come to New York and take an apartment, it is often the first time they have enjoyed any privacy; on the subcontinent, even the wealthy live with their extended families, a constant source of company and help. Life in the city thus brings on feelings of intense loneliness, straining many marriages. For men who come here alone and work until they can bring over their families, the solitude can be unbearable, as one after another told me. This is the flip side of the family-values coin—not having your family with you is extremely painful.

Yet for South Asian women, these new arrangements can also be profoundly liberating. "In India, whether you are married or not, there are too many people guarding you," explains the novelist Susham Bedi. "And there are constant social and familial obligations, constant pressure from your parents, from your peers." Most immigrant wives go out and work, a practice still relatively rare on the subcontinent—and a sore point with husbands whose ideas of family life took shape in very different circumstances. "We feel strong here," continues Bedi. "Men, on the other hand, feel unnourished. In India, even if his wife weren't around, his mother and a sister would take care of him." To appreciate just how revolutionary this change in family structure is, consider that in a Hindu marriage the wife promises to worship her husband "as a god." "It's tough for an Indian man," says Sunita Mukhi. "He comes to this country, and it doesn't fly anymore that he is a god, and the law doesn't say that he is a god."

The humiliations inherent in immigrant existence also bedevil South Asian men in their family lives. Not knowing how to do things—paying taxes, registering the kids for school—makes them feel unmanned in the eyes of their wives and children. Nor is it easy for someone with a college degree to find himself driving a cab year after year. Many weave lying stories of corporate advancement to pass along to family back home. Social worker Ram Iyer says that it is hardest for immigrant men in their forties or older, many of whom "have to come to terms with the fact that they are always going to be working at a newsstand or in a garage." They transfer their ambitions to their children.

Unfortunately, such frustrations often contribute to domestic violence—a serious but largely unacknowledged problem in the South Asian community. According to Prema Vora, the program director of Sakhi, a Manhattan-based South Asian women's group dedicated to combating such abuse, it is not uncommon to encounter battered South Asian wives whose husbands have deliberately refused to sponsor them, thus depriving them of legal-immigrant status. The women "are terrified to go to the police because they're afraid they'll be deported." Domestic servants—many of them illiterate and brought over illegally—are vulnerable in the same way and often suffer under atrocious conditions.

Almost all South Asian parents would like their children to marry within the community. When pressed, they will admit that they would prefer them to marry within the same caste and ethnic group. This is true even of people like Susham Bedi, who comes from a generation of Indian intellectuals that pointedly rejected other forms of caste and religious prejudice. Among her friends, she says, "the hardest thing to accept is a black or a Muslim. A Christian or a Jew is okay." According to Professor Mohand, marriages between young *desis* and Jews are especially common.

Most South Asian immigrants, even many of the second generation, continue to believe that you love the person you marry—you don't marry the person you love. A modified version of arranged marriages thus remains the norm in their communities. Parents do not simply impose husbands on their daughters, of course. Rather, they introduce her to a man after they've checked his background and met his parents. The young people then decide whether to pursue the relationship.

The South Asian press in New York—Indians alone sustain seven English-language papers and a dozen more in Malayalam, Bengali, Gujarati, and Urdu—bristles with matrimonial ads. "Sikh parents request correspondence from handsome Sikh professionals (no Jats), for their daughter, 27, 5'9", educated and family-oriented." "Brother invites alliance from respected Sindhi families for sister, 28, 5'2", attractive, highly educated, working in US. Prefer early marriage." "Parents seek tall MD/MS/MBA match for beautiful, tall, slim, fair, Agarwal citizen girl, born/raised in India, 25/5'5", BS, MBA (US) Senior Executive." Sometimes parents describe their daughter as "homely"—meaning not that she is plain but that she would be content as a traditional homemaker. And having a "fair" or "wheaten" complexion is a definite advantage for a woman, especially among those northern Indians who consider their light skin and greater height a sign of racial superiority over southern Indians.

South Asians are quick to defend these old-fashioned alliances. "You have a 50 percent divorce rate in this country," gloats a cabbie named Ali. "Our system is working much better." It must be said, however, that the sexes divide in their support for traditional marriages. The South Asian press often notes the continuing preference of young Indo-American men for wives from the old country, women who have not been "spoiled" by Western ways. Prizing their newfound liberty, Indo-American women have begun to marry out of the community at a much higher rate.

Sexual liberation is a foreign and deeply disturbing notion for South Asian parents. Most do not allow their children to date, and many will not even allow their daughters to have male friends. Coming to terms with American sexual license is especially hard for those who are observant Muslims. As Farooq Bhatti puts it, sitting in his tiny, windowless office behind the Port Authority, "We don't want to raise our daughters in all the vulgarity and nudity, the boyfriend/girlfriend concepts. It is hard to remain pure in this culture." He remembers a friend who was so disturbed by the kissing that his seven-year-old boy and three-year-old girl had seen on television that he packed up and returned to Pakistan.

Most South Asian immigrants adjust more easily to life in the U.S., fending off the more pernicious elements in our culture while embracing the opportunities that attracted them in the first place. They have become model Americans in many ways. Well-educated and industrious, they contribute prodigiously to the wider economy and society while at the same time maintaining the vitality of their own communities.

Each year in mid-August, the Indian and Pakistani communities celebrate the independence of their home countries with parades down Madison Avenue to Union Square. Crowds picnic in the park. There are stalls all around, selling samosas and kebabs. Small children with American accents cling to their parents' knees and wave little flags. Teenage boys in baggy jeans affect boredom, hoping to impress the girls. Many of the women wear brightly colored traditional dress, while older men look crisply Anglo-Indian in Nehru jackets or coat and tie. Modest by New York standards, the event has an authentic feeling that has long been missing from most of the city's other ethnic parades.

No doubt the day will come when New York's South Asians, like sundry Polish-, Greek-, and Irish-Americans, will parade down Fifth Avenue as thousands of their fellow citizens cheer them on. With the mayor on hand to praise their contributions to the community, the marchers will feel a certain self-consciousness as they display their distinctive costumes and food, dances and songs. They will have crossed the invisible cultural line that divides the immigrant from the hyphenated American. Such assimilation has always taken place with astonishing speed. It has its tragic side, to be sure, as traditions fall away. But it has an intensely American glory—well worth parading every year.

—*Summer 1997*

HEATHER MAC DONALD
Why Koreans Succeed

KYUNG T. SOHN was one of the first Korean greengrocers in New York City. A 1968 forestry graduate of the University of Maryland, he was unable to find a job in his profession. So in 1975, using $5,000 his brother had saved, he bought out a retiring Italian grocer in the northern Bronx. "I didn't know what romaine was," recalls the affable, pear-shaped Sohn. He asked the former owner to stay on as a wage worker for two months and teach him the business. Sohn bought a truck and learned the daily grind, rising at 2 AM to go to the Hunt's Point wholesale produce market in the Bronx, going to bed at 11 PM. His wife worked by his side.

Two years later he gave the store to his brother and bought one in Kew Gardens, Queens. A year after that, a friend asked him to take over a store in Jamaica, Queens, for $8,000. In 1981 and 1982, Sohn sold the two stores for nearly $200,000. By then he was operating the city's first Korean "cram school" for boosting test scores.

Such unflagging enterprise, multiplied many times over, has powerfully boosted the economy of New York City. The Korean deli turned the traditional produce store—previously the province of Italian- and Greek-Americans—into an art form and put New York's shabby supermarkets to shame. Korean-Americans opened stores in inner-city neighborhoods that other retailers had long shunned. And when Wall Street boomed in the eighties, Koreans and other immigrant entrepreneurs worked around the clock providing services to the financial industry.

Korean-Americans have proved that the American Dream is still alive. "If ever I want to know where the American work ethic went, I know where to find it," says Stephen Solarsh, a business and real estate consultant who has advised dozens of Korean-American business owners. "The Koreans just keep moving in a wonderfully disciplined way. Anyone who sees them can think back to the time when our forefathers came to this country."

The Koreans' success in New York and across the country provides a partial blueprint for how we can rebuild our cities. But of late, New York's Koreans have experienced some economic and cultural jolts that make clear just how big the task of building the urban future will be.

Sitting on the balcony above their sparkling new deli on Third Avenue and 43rd Street while their two-year-old daughter scrambles up and down the stairs, Doug and Haesu Choi reflect on their life in New York. As for many Korean-Americans, that life has alternated between unstinting cooperation and cutthroat competition with other Koreans.

Haesu Choi, a statuesque woman with short straight hair framing an angular jaw, moved to New York with her family in 1975. Haesu's brother built a supermarket empire in Brooklyn that at its peak comprised five stores. Doug Choi, lanky and soft-spoken in a black leather jacket and black aviator glasses, spent 12 years in the U.S. Army as a field nurse.

A few years after their 1983 wedding, the Chois started a produce business in Bay Ridge, Brooklyn. Unable to get a bank loan and fed up with the red tape for a GI loan, Doug invested his $20,000 army savings in two *gaes*, Korean communal savings pools. At each monthly meeting of a *gae*, members contribute whatever they can afford, usually $400 to $500. One person draws the pot, based on a list made up at the start of the *gae* and on how much the recipient has contributed. There is no interest on the loan, but whoever collects that night buys dinner for the 20 to 30 members.

Stephen Solarsh says he has never seen Koreans use bank loans or other conventional financing. The *gae* has become less common today, however, since many immigrants now bring money with them from the sale of a house in Korea or from personal savings. The Chois raised much of the $75,000 they put into the produce store from the gae. Haesu's family contributed the rest. Haesu's brother helped Doug learn the business. Working an 18- to 20-hour day, they just covered the rent on their store and apartment.

Having started their grocery business with help from other Koreans, the Chois soon encountered the second face of Korean business experience: ruthless Korean competition. A recent immigrant opened a produce store almost next door, igniting a brutal four-month price war. "We don't mind working hard," says Doug Choi, "but every day, we were selling 36 boxes of very good cantaloupe at a negative price margin." News spread quickly. "Everyone in Hunt's Point knew," he explains. "They said: 'Hey, there's a price war in Bay Ridge. We don't need to go to Hunt's Point; we'll just buy there!'" The Chois tried unsuccessfully to reach an agreement with their competitor. "Finally I burned out," says Doug. They sold in 1988.

The Chois next opened a stationery store on Second Avenue and 94th Street in Manhattan, but the business suffered from a dismal economy and the lack of a stable client base. In 1993 a friend asked them to take over his Lexington Avenue deli in trouble with the Health Department. They jumped at the opportunity and gave their stationery business—with no strings attached, they say—to Byong Lim, a friend from Maryland.

Once the Chois stabilized the deli, however, the previous owner wanted it back, leaving the Chois unemployed for six months. Donations from friends and family poured in—$500 here, $2,000 there. Eventually the Chois borrowed $65,000 from three *gaes*, enabling them to open their deli on Third Avenue in September 1994. They also owe $50,000 on 15 credit cards for equipment. With weekly revenues of $15,000, "we are just standing still. Every penny, we put back in," says Doug. "But we have to succeed because of all the people who put their trust in us and tried to help," explains Haesu.

The Chois' business experience in New York is typical. Korean-American small business is fluid and dynamic: businesses often pass between friends and family; owners who take a loss at one location try again in another. This give-and-take reinforces the mutual obligations that knit the Korean community together.

According to the National Bureau of Economic Research, 28 percent of Korean-American men and 20 percent of Korean-American women own their own business—the highest rate of entrepreneurship in the country. Census data put the rate of self-employment among Koreans in New York City at 14 percent. According to the Korean-American Small Business Service Center, Koreans own 85 percent of produce retailers, 70 percent of independent grocery retailers, 80 percent of nail salons, and 60 percent of dry cleaners in New York City. The Korean food business in the New York area has sales of $300 million annually, according to the Federation of Korean Food Businesses of Greater New York.

The flowering of Korean enterprise in the United States defies most theories of immigrant entrepreneurship. Unlike what Harvard sociologist Nathan Glazer calls the "great migrating nations" of Jews, Chinese, and Italians, the Koreans have no tradition of wandering the world as commercial middlemen. Indeed, in the eighteenth and nineteenth centuries, while commerce and banking flourished in China and Japan, these Asian neighbors viewed Koreans as neither industrious nor intelligent.

Korea's official support for Confucianism, which disdains commerce, did not end until 1972, when military dictator Chung-Hee Park declared it contrary to the goal of economic development. Yet Confucianism gave Koreans one trait that would both propel them to the New World and ensure their success here: a passion for education. "Our main concern?" asks Doug Choi. "Education—Number-One quality. Most people, that's all they think about. Even if you mop floors or work as an auto mechanic, if you have an education, you will be better."

In Korea this commitment to learning results in close to a 100 percent literacy rate and a nearly comparable high school graduation rate. Yet the government allows only 30 percent of high school graduates to enter a university. Competition is ferocious. The primary reason why Koreans emigrate to America is to ensure a place for their children in college, preferably Harvard or Yale—household words in Korea.

Many Korean immigrants have sacrificed white-collar or professional careers, difficult to pursue here because of language and licensing barriers. Often a grocery cashier or dry cleaner is a former engineer or nurse. Retailing requires little English: "There's no need to communicate," says Doug Choi. "If you have good products, the customers know."

Few Korean immigrants had any previous retailing experience. A 1983 survey of 40 New York greengrocers by Philip Young of Pace University found that only 20 percent had run a business in Korea, none in the produce area. Ninety-five percent had college degrees—a level of education that sets Korean immigrants sharply apart from traditional immigrant entrepreneurs. Koreans' advanced degrees make up in part for their lack of business experience. "Why have a master's in engineering to succeed in produce?" asks Young. "Because small businesses require a lot of thinking to plan and organize."

Abandoning white-collar professions imposes psychological costs: in Korea, as here, status differences between professionals and shopkeepers are sharp. Some Korean-Americans are bitter that after so much hard work in the United States, their social status isn't higher. Others hold tight to their former professional identity. Bokyung Kwon, a pharmacist in Korea, opened One Merchandise, a variety store on Broadway at 98th Street, when she got to the city. "I always felt I was a pharmacist," she says of her ten years selling handbags and mufflers.

The Koreans have followed the time-worn formula for immigrant success—grueling hours, a willingness to work for low wages or profits in hopes of success later, and the extensive use of family labor, essential in a highly competitive market. "If you use someone else's labor," explains Kyung T. Sohn, "your profit goes out as wages." Of the 40 greengrocers Philip Young surveyed, all but three employed family members.

Families work together for non-economic reasons too. For the past two years, Yo Chung, 24, has managed a produce store in Flatbush, Brooklyn. Though he graduated from Queens College in computer science, he didn't even look for a computer job: he wanted to work with his 61-year-old father, a former engineer, who sits outside, watching the store. "My father could not work alone," Yo explains. "People do not want to hire older people, and he does not speak English."

Devotion to family is part of the "social capital" that Koreans have brought to America. Parents sacrifice for their children and expect them to reciprocate. "My sons are doing well," says Doug Choi with pride. "I may not be doing so well, but they go to a good school. That's all that matters." Jane Kim, a 28-year-old tax consultant at Price Waterhouse, came to Cleveland with her parents when she was six. "I like the idea of taking care of family and one's elders," she says. "I would never put my parents in a nursing home."

Armed with strong family ties and an indefatigable work ethic, Koreans fanned out across New York. Looking for low rents, they penetrated inner-city markets that other retailers had abandoned or neglected. "A Korean will own a business anyplace in town," says Frank Vardy, a demographer with the City Planning Department. Adds consultant Stephen Solarsh: "The Koreans know how to buy property. I've seen them go to a site and eyeball it and know exactly what they want to do." Solarsh's clients have erected thriving supermarkets in East New York buildings that had become roach-infested drug-shooting galleries. In East Harlem, Korean enterprise revitalized entire blocks with a one-two punch of a produce store followed by a fish store. This cluster then attracted other businesses.

Korean retailers closely tailor their businesses to local demands. Grocery stores in Flatbush and Crown Heights, with their open boxes of salt cod, their banana flour, yucca, and herbal aphrodisiacs, bear little resemblance to those on Manhattan's East Side or in Queens. The Koreans pioneered the 24-hour deli for fast-track Manhattan consumption—no such business form exists in Korea. They introduced the deli salad bar when grocery sales flattened. After the first Korean entered flower wholesaling, Korean delis blossomed with flowers. The ubiquitous nail salon is another Korean creation; by taking nail care out of the full-service beauty salon, Koreans made such pampering available to middle-class women.

Koreans' eye for opportunity led to the resurgence of Manhattan's West 32nd Street. Twenty years ago the long block between Broadway and Fifth Avenue was decaying fast. Tony Pecorella, owner of Santorellos, a 60-year-old leather repair store, says his women customers had stopped coming, fearful of crime. But spotting potential, Koreans started opening businesses to serve the export-import firms clustered nearby. Wholesalers lined up along Broadway between 27th and 32nd Streets, a stretch now known as the Korean Trading Avenue, and retailers on 32nd Street.

Now the block is ablaze with Korean signs advertising restaurants, bookstores, recording studios, cosmetic stores, and printing establishments. Two lavish Korean banks sit within a short walk of each other. The ornate Stanford Hotel keeps its lobby clock on Seoul time. "The Koreans really cleaned up the street," says Pecorella. The area is safe, its restaurants busy around the clock.

West 32nd Street is the smaller of New York City's two Korean business centers. The other is Union Street in downtown Flushing, Queens, the heart of the Korean-American residential community. Like 32nd Street, Flushing's downtown had hit hard times in the seventies. Today it is densely packed with Korean as well as Chinese businesses. Signs in Korean advertise insurance agencies, driving schools, hair salons, bakeries, bridal salons, and law offices.

Many Korean-Americans who came to New York City in the early wave of Korean immigration—from the late sixties to the early eighties—have achieved that most tangible accoutrement of the American Dream: a house in the suburbs. "All Koreans have the dream of moving out," says John Lee, a Flushing Realtor. "If they're making money in the city, they prefer living in the suburbs, where it is quiet, clean, safe, the schools are good, and [there are] no racial problems." The high earners—attorneys and doctors—go to Long Island; merchants with stores in Manhattan look for lower taxes in New Jersey. The Korean population of Bergen County, New Jersey, increased fivefold from 1980 to 1990; Palisades Park now has a Korean business district. The Chois spent two years scouring the metropolitan region for the best schools before settling in affluent Mountain Lake, New Jersey.

Koreans have triumphed as well by the measure of success most important to them—educational achievement. Korean students dominate the city's best schools. Stuyvesant High School is over 50 percent Asian, the Bronx High School of Science 40 percent, and the Juilliard School of Music 33 percent. Koreans are the largest Asian group at all three. Members of the second generation and "1.5 generation"—Korean-Americans born in Korea but raised in the United States—are graduating from Ivy League and other top colleges and returning to the city as attorneys, doctors, computer analysts, and artists.

Behind the younger generation's achievements lies the keen—a few critics argue, overweening—interest that parents take in their children's schooling. Haesu Choi spends two or three hours each night tutoring her two sons, ages ten and eight. "They complain that their friends get to watch TV, but I tell them because we're Asian, they have to do better," she says. During the summer the family spends a month going over math and English. But the Chois don't regard their family simply as an academic factory. "My kids are having fun," says Doug Choi with great pleasure. "In the summer they ride their bikes all over. I like to let them grow like Americans."

Most Korean parents have no time to tutor or even supervise their children because of grueling work schedules. Whereas few wives work in Korea, here most do. But the Koreans brought with them another institution for promoting academic success, the *hagwon*, or prep school. (The popular term—"cram school"—is viewed as derogatory by the schools' principals.) Several dozen such schools have sprung up in the city.

Kyung T. Sohn founded the first—C.C.B. Prep School in Woodside, Queens—in 1980. The school is in a small brick building on Woodside Avenue, plastered with placards in Korean and Chinese, as well as large pictures of Sohn. Inside, every available wall is covered with snapshots of students in class and accepting awards—and more pictures of Sohn advertising his English-language program on the Korean cable station. The classrooms, mostly in the basement, are unheated in the winter.

C.C.B.'s main purpose is to ensure that younger students get into the city's competitive high schools and, once there, ace their college admissions exams. In 1994, 95 percent of C.C.B.'s junior high students were admitted to Stuyvesant, Bronx Science, or Brooklyn Tech. Tuition is $595 for eight weeks of Saturday instruction, $695 for eight weeks of Tuesday and Thursday instruction. Half the Saturday students come from the suburbs, dropped off at the school, upon occasion, in Rolls-Royces and BMWs. Most weekday students are Queens residents whose parents are shopkeepers. Parents keep their children in the school for years. Fifty percent of the pupils are Korean; 40 percent are Chinese; and 10 percent Caucasian.

The school teaches math, English vocabulary and grammar, and some literature and writing. Students review the same material over and over. "By the time these kids walk into a placement exam," says one teacher, "they have no anxiety, because they've been doing it for five years." But some of the teachers—most of whom are from city schools—complain of too little emphasis on creative thinking. "This is not real teaching; it's just rote," says one. "It's too cramped and too cold to learn." Though the teachers all express admiration for the Korean parents' involvement, some feel such involvement can backfire. "The graduates of this school are neurotic," one teacher told me. "The culture is not rosy."

The students I met at C.C.B., though, seemed neither unhappy nor anxious. Unlike hagwons in Korea, the class atmosphere is informal—students banter incessantly with the teacher and one another. When the bell rings, students dash upstairs, returning to their classes with hot dogs, candy bars, and soup.

Soo Young Kang, a striking 14-year-old with a flapper haircut, has been at C.C.B. for eight months. At first Soo resisted an interview mightily, claiming poor English. In fact, she speaks fluently, though she has been in America only three years and speaks only Korean at home. Soo's father is an "international trader," she says, but also helps in her uncle's grocery store near the Kangs' home on Manhattan's East Side.

Soo has absorbed her culture's passion for education: "I wanted to come to America because of college; I heard they had high standards." Which college does she want to attend? An explosion of energy follows. "Harvard," she laughs, a little embarrassed. Her first goal, however, is to get into a competitive high school. "In a regular high school," she explains, "it's harder to get good SATs for Harvard and Yale."

Soo keeps a demanding schedule. After the three-hour session at

C.C.B., she studies another two hours when she goes home. On Friday she has a piano lesson; on Saturdays, a flute lesson. Sunday she practices the piano: "It's the only whole day I have for it," she explains regretfully.

Soo says her parents never pressure her to study. But her habits belie this perception, if one assumes that studiousness is not a natural trait in children. High parental expectations are apparently so integral a part of Korean culture that children don't regard them as noteworthy.

Despite her rigorous schedule, Soo says she studied harder in Korea. "The competition and expectations are higher there," she explains. Her American classmates called her a "math nerd" when she arrived in the seventh grade, because her scores were so high. "Some kids say: 'Why do you work so hard?' If I try to explain, they don't listen. So I say to them: 'I do my stuff, you do your stuff.'" The hardest part of American school, she says, is the group projects: "They're fun, but you waste a lot of time in groups. In Korea there's more emphasis on the individual."

Schools such as C.C.B. have quietly taken on a second function: keeping young people off the streets. That highlights a paradox of Korean immigration: though parents came to the United States for their children's sake, heavy work schedules don't leave them enough time to supervise their kids. Community leaders speak with alarm of the appearance of teen delinquency. Though an infinitesimal problem compared with other teens in the city, it terrifies parents and teachers nonetheless.

For parents who can't afford private prep schools, or students who can't pass the entrance exams, churches have stepped into the breach. The 12-year-old Chodae Church in Corona, Queens, has 85 students in day care and after-school programs. Located in a single-story box under the Grand Central Parkway, the church charges $180 a month tuition. The school helps students do their homework and meet citywide standards in reading and math. "We are also reluctantly functioning as baby-sitting," laments the Reverend John Paik, a diminutive, ebullient 72-year-old.

Several of the students I spoke with at Chodae share the enthusiasm for learning that Soo Young Kang exhibited at C.C.B. When Paik asked a class of third-graders for a volunteer to be interviewed, the room erupted. The students pounded their feet, waved their hands in the air, and cried, "Me! Me!" After a whispered consultation with the teacher, Paik chose eight-year-old Christina. Asked if she liked the church school, Christina clasps her hands together in delight. "I enjoy it very much," she says. "I get bored at [public] school. Here we learn math and English and have workbooks for when we finish our homework. Teachers at public schools just say 'Quiet!' or 'Sit down!' They're not very demanding. The teachers at after-school really care about us."

Christina might offer some hope to Korean elders worried about the lack of supervision. Her parents don't get home to Whitestone until nearly 9 PM from their grocery store in Yonkers, and her father leaves the house between 2 and 4 AM. But their message gets across: "They're always saying, 'Christina, you better learn something instead of watching TV.' " Her mother worries about her grades, though the worst she's gotten is a B. What if she got a D or F? A shiver of horror runs through her. "They would spank me," she whispers. Tellingly, she adds: "My parents are not very strict." Like Soo Young Kang, Christina does not perceive her parents' pressure to succeed as a burden but as a sign of concern.

Korean-Americans' worry about what happens to children when parents work such long hours is part of a larger debate about the preservation of Korean culture. The eternal immigrant tension between assimilation and cultural preservation is particularly wrenching for Koreans, whose values seem so alien to contemporary American culture. Although by American standards Korean children are paragons of self-discipline and courtesy, many Koreans find the attitudes of the young alarming.

They're most worried about the erosion of parental authority, difficult to preserve in a nation mesmerized by youthful rebellion. Many parents have gone back to Korea because they could no longer control their children. In Korea corporal punishment is an accepted part of child rearing. But students in America learn in school that if a parent hits them once, they are victims of child abuse and must report it. Numerous Korean parents have been dragged before family court judges, to their utter humiliation.

Joseph Min, 35 and a member of the 1.5 generation, grew up in the crossfire between Korean and American culture. Now the director of the Korean Y, part of the Flushing YMCA, he came to the Bronx with his family when he was nine. At first the habits he learned in Korea stayed with him. There, he went to school at 7:30 AM; after school he went straight to a tutor for additional work; then he did his school homework. He did not watch TV. "I was so disciplined," he says. "And for the first two or three years in the Bronx, I was too." But his parents worked all the time, and they couldn't afford an after-school program. In school he "observed people loosening up and not getting as much homework." Eventually he started watching a lot of TV.

He also learned a completely different attitude toward authority. "The thing that shocked me was the [lack of] respect of the students," he says. "In Korea the teacher is God; students don't talk back. Here, in junior high, when the teacher is writing on the blackboard, the kids just laugh and are allowed to hit each other. It took me ten years to get over my respect and joke about teachers." Says Judy Yoon, who works in her cousin's dry-cleaning store in Manhattan: "My kids tell me about their friends at school, who don't respect their teachers and use very bad language. They hate it, just hate it. I have to keep telling them that is not the good way."

The Korean church plays a key role in cultural transmission. Many non-Christians converted in America, when they saw how central the church was in the community. Whereas in Korea only about a quarter of the population is Christian, nearly three-quarters of Korean-Americans attend church. The New York area has nearly 500 Korean churches; some have 2,000 congregants.

The Korean Methodist Church and Institute on West 115th Street is the oldest Korean church in New York. Founded in 1921, it occupies a small townhouse on the hill down to Riverside Drive. It holds its Korean-language service in an auditorium across the street. The chapel, where the smaller English-language service is held, is a long, plain white room; quilted banners and a wooden cross hang over its simple altar.

The church is divided by generations. Attending large Korean-language services are mainly first-generation immigrants who joined the church while studying at Columbia and other local colleges. Now successful professionals, they drive in on Sundays from the suburbs. Since some are the only Koreans in their suburban communities, the church provides an essential link to other Koreans. The 1.5 and second generation make up the smaller English-language congregation. Most are in their twenties, living in the city. The young congregants, casually but neatly dressed in corduroys, khakis, and bulky sweaters, seem wonderfully self-confident; their English is fluent. All speak of a desire to hold on to their culture.

Hyung Park, 27, started coming to the church, he says, "because after college I needed an outlet to meet Koreans. Then I became more religious." A graduate of Pratt School of Architecture whose center-parted hair gives him a rakish Edwardian air, Hyung came to New York when he was six. He lives with his parents in Brooklyn and helps in their hardware store. Hyung wants to marry a Korean woman. "I would teach my children Korean. A lot of Koreans tend to lose their heritage, but I don't want to."

Hyung's desire to marry a Korean woman is not accidental. According to Chun Soo Pyun, chairman of Korean Community Services of Metropolitan New York, daily conversation between parent and child consists of: "(1) study, study, study; (2) eat well, eat well, eat well; (3) best school, best school, best school; and (4) marry Korean, marry Korean, marry Korean." "My parents would have disowned me if I had married a non-Korean," says 28-year-old Jane Kim, whose husband, David, is a violinist. "I dated an American boy seriously for two or three years. My parents liked him, but they were really getting worried."

The Korean language itself is a source of both division and unity within the Korean-American community. Korean parents show a range of responses to the eternal immigrant dilemma of how much to preserve the native language. Ann Song, a 27-year-old freelance graphic designer, speaks no Korean. She grew up in Short Hills, New Jersey, attending bar mitzvahs rather than Korean-language school. When she and her parents go to dinner, her parents' friends greet her in Korean and stare disapprovingly when she is unable to respond.

The Chois spoke Korean with their boys until they were five years old. But when the boys' teacher wanted to put them into an English as a Second Language program, Haesu begged her to wait. "After that we spoke only English," she says. Doug Choi adds: "Speaking Korean is important, but the primary thing is, they have to do well in school." By contrast, Judy Yoon, the dry cleaner, kept her children in Korea with their grandmother until they were ten so they could master Korean.

In some families, parents speak Korean while their children respond in English. For such children, Saturday Korean-language school is an important means of maintaining or improving their rudimentary skills. Since Korean is inflected according to the status of the addressee, losing the language means losing a way of marking the culture's gradations of social respect. Some English-speaking children find themselves estranged from Korean-speaking parents.

Outside church, the other certain place to meet Koreans is on the golf course. "Even in the middle of the winter, you'll see a lot of Koreans playing," says Peter Choi, owner of Golf Town on West 32nd Street. Choi, a former managing editor at *Korea Times*, competes with six other big Korean-owned golf stores in the area. In Korea a shortage of courses makes golf very expensive. Here golf cuts across social classes. Early-rising greengrocers are on the course by 5 AM; Korean doctors hold their annual conferences at golf resorts; the few who don't play find themselves shut out of discussions. Women are learning fast, and fathers teach their children.

For all their energy, Koreans aren't exempt from the economic cycle. While early arrivals have prospered, recent immigrants face a more uncertain future. Battered by New York's punishing taxes and regulations, more and more Korean businesses are succumbing to a stagnant economy. Between 1991 and 1994, Korean leaders estimate, at least 1,600 Korean-owned stores in the city went bankrupt. "Koreans don't announce their bankruptcy, because they feel shame and want to disappear," says Bong Jin Sa, executive director of the Korean Produce Association. "But we see the doors closed." Sales at Korean grocers have declined 30 percent in the past three years. Because three out of four Koreans depend on small business, the slow-down touches nearly every family.

The story of Byong Lim, who took over Doug Choi's troubled stationery business on the Upper East Side, is typical. "I feel really trapped," he says. Lim and his American wife would like to close the store on Sundays, but they can't afford to forgo the $250 to $300 the day brings in. He pays $4,500 in rent and $500 in taxes each month; the city's 8.25 percent sales tax drives many would-be customers to illegal street vendors. Lim looks enviously upon the late seventies and early eighties, when Korean-American business was booming.

In good times and bad, all Korean retailers worry about crime. "I've never been to a place like this," Lim says. "You can't let your hand down for an instant." He and his wife have been threatened several times, and children are always trying to steal merchandise. Anecdotal evidence suggests that Koreans stores are disproportionately victimized because of their location in poor neighborhoods.

According to Bong Jin Sa of the Korean Produce Association, Koreans feel ashamed if they are attacked and will report only the most serious incidents. Store owners fear revenge if they call the police. If they report a crime, they rarely get satisfaction, Sa says, so they have stopped bothering. The Produce Association has launched a campaign to persuade shop owners to report all crimes and not to resist or chase criminals, who may be armed.

But however dangerous, shop owners feel they must fight back against criminals. Doug Choi experiences constant shoplifting. "People ask, 'Why go after someone for 60 cents?' But if I let him go, he comes again. By the time I'm leaving him alone, my store is empty." Choi has paid a price for his vigilance. In late 1994 someone filled up a tray from the salad bar and walked out of the store. Choi followed him outside and asked him what he was doing. The shoplifter knocked him unconscious. Choi's face was swollen for two weeks, and he still has a scar.

Though Koreans don't report most crimes, news of them spreads like wildfire. In a six-month period in 1993, three store owners were killed by robbers. Koreans are still angry over the city's lack of response to the destruction of Chong Sook Kim's variety store in Washington Heights during rioting in 1992. And they remember as well the torching of Tong Kwang Kim's store and the bludgeoning of his wife in Bedford-Stuyvesant in 1991. The press covers such events thinly, if at all.

While crime is worst in the outer boroughs, the city's punishing business tax and regulatory structure hits everywhere. Small businesses in New York pay 14 different taxes. Merchants especially loathe the city's 6 percent commercial rent tax, unique in the nation. A typical grocery requires four to eight licenses—each of which requires a visit to a different agency.

Korean business associations have long sought an easing of the tax and regulatory burden on store owners. Korean leaders charge that the city views its business regulations as a revenue source, noting that a recent Giuliani administration budget earmarked $150 million in additional fines without any mention of increased offenses. Owners particularly object to the laws subjecting them to fines for dirty sidewalks.

Dispirited by all these problems, between 4 and 5 percent of the Korean population is returning each year to Korea, where word of Korean-Americans' long hours and decreasing returns has begun to spread. Those who return are in for a surprise: Koreans who stayed are doing better than those who left, thanks to Korea's booming economy. As a result, immigration has slowed to a trickle: the City Planning Department estimates that only 1,500 Koreans have been entering the city annually in the nineties.

One final problem that is leading would-be or actual immigrants to rethink the U.S. is racial tension. Koreans who do business in the inner city have been the target of racial extortion — thinly veiled threats to "give back to the community" or face boycotts and even violence. "Koreans are the most successful business group in the black community, which is why they target us," says Kee Young Lee, a vice president of the *Korean News*.

Though business concerns have galvanized Korean-Americans over the years, racial hostility has most sparked their political coming-of-age. "Flatbush was the first time we realized we needed political power," says Chun Soo Pyun of the Korean Community Services of Metropolitan New York, referring to the nine-month racial boycott in 1990 that drove two Korean produce stores in Brooklyn out of business. Black activists, led by the Reverend Al Sharpton, charged that employees of the Red Apple market had beaten up a Haitian woman without provocation; the manager denied the charge. The Dinkins administration refused to enforce a court order banning protests within 50 feet of Red Apple and a neighboring store that had been drawn into the dispute. When Pyun organized a City Hall rally to demand that Mayor Dinkins enforce the order, between 7,000 and 10,000 protesters showed up; voter registration was brisk.

But nothing has had as profound an impact on Koreans' ideas about America as the 1992 Los Angeles riots. Six hundred Korean-American businesses in South Central Los Angeles and 200 in Koreatown were damaged or destroyed; Koreans sustained 45 percent of all riot damage. In New York an armed gang vandalized a Korean dry cleaner in the South Bronx in sympathy with the Los Angeles rioters, and vandals shattered the windows of a Korean grocer in Bedford-Stuyvesant as they taunted him with a racist rap song.

Though deeply shaken, the Korean business community has turned the other cheek. In February 1993, Al Sharpton gave the invocation at the annual awards dinner of the Korean-American Grocers Association of New York. Last year the Korean Association of Greater New York sent three students selected by the *Amsterdam News* to Kyung Hee University in Seoul.

For four years Korean grocers have distributed "love turkeys" at Thanksgiving through 3,000 churches in minority neighborhoods; they also sponsor spots on black radio stations honoring black heroes.

No other group of small-business owners is subject to such pressure to redistribute its resources, and no other has responded with such a variety of initiatives. Yet these efforts provide no more certain a guarantee against racial animosity than did similar efforts in Los Angeles before the riots. When Mayor Giuliani ousted more than 1,000 illegal street vendors on 125th Street in Harlem in October 1994, a local Nation of Islam mosque organized a short-lived "Buy Black" boycott of non-black merchants on the street. Won Duck Kim, owner of Guy and Gal clothing store, was one of the targets of that boycott. A short man with basset-hound eyes and a quick smile, Kim is hardly insensitive to black concerns: he proudly displays pictures of himself with former Mayor Dinkins, Congressman Charles Rangel, and other black leaders. Awards from black organizations line the top of one 40-foot wall. "Malcolm Lives" and Martin Luther King posters cover his cashier stand. He supports the Harlem Boys Choir. In 1990 he helped organize a nine-day trip to Korea by 37 black preachers. He advertises in the *Amsterdam News*, though his ads there, he says, bring him no business. Asked his opinion of the demand to "give back to the community," he merely says that "new immigrants can't jump over buildings." Tony, one of his two black employees, is more outspoken: "My boss is supporting the community by being here. He has done more than his share—he gives 300 percent. Even in Buy Black stores, the owners don't support the community."

Many Koreans feel that their political power lags far behind their economic status. Korean culture does not emphasize democratic participation; Koreans have little expectation that government institutions can help them. Many Koreans are afraid to fill out the census or register to vote. If they do register, their grueling hours make it hard to get to the polls. Little wonder the two major centers of Korean-American population, the cities of New York and Los Angeles, have no Koreans in public office.

But that is starting to change. The Flatbush boycott and Los Angeles riots showed that hard work and discipline alone do not guarantee permanent success. After the riots, Diamond Bar, California, sent the first Korean-American, Republican Jay Kim, to Congress. Across the country 11 Korean-Americans, nearly all Republicans, hold government office.

On the local level, commercial worries have spurred some New York Koreans to get involved in politics. The Korean-American Small Business Service Center, joined by 22 other organizations, presented Mayor Dinkins and candidate Giuliani with a Korean Bill of Rights in September 1993. It demanded, among other things, an end to the commercial rent tax, stricter regulation of vendors, and protection from ethnic boycotts and violence.

The Korean-American Small Business Center has been one of the most forceful voices for all small business in the city; its president, Sung Soo Kim, organized the Small Business Congress of New York.

Though Korean leaders donated over $1 million to the Giuliani campaign, many have been disappointed that so far Mayor Giuliani has taken no action on his promise to roll back the commercial rent tax, a $600 million revenue source for the city. Also galling to Koreans is city hall's promotion of mega-stores. Says Sung Soo Kim of the Small Business Center: "The big supermarkets abandoned the city in the 1970s, leaving a vacuum that immigrant business filled. Now they want to come back, but only with a host of unfair subsidies" such as tax abatements and energy rebates.

Despite these setbacks, some Korean-American leaders are optimistic about their community's political future. "Five years ago our political involvement was invisible," says Chun Soo Pyun. "Now it's totally different." Round-faced and balding, with a quick sense of humor, Pyun points proudly to the fact that he helped raise nearly $100,000 for Giuliani and $30,000 each for George Bush, Dan Quayle, and George Pataki.

Pyun is buoyed by the results of the 1994 elections. When he ran unsuccessfully for the City Council in 1990, Koreans hadn't heard of the GOP, because it is so minor a party in Queens. "People laughed at me. 'You in wrong line,' they said." But in the two most recent elections, he estimates that Koreans voted 70 percent for Giuliani and Pataki.

Pyun is as optimistic about Korean-Americans' business prospects as he is about their political future. Asked to show a visitor the Korean community in Flushing, his first stop is Korea Town Plaza, a giant, controversial wholesale and retail outlet for Asian food and hardware. Owned by Rhee Brothers, a Korean-American corporation based in Maryland, the 100,000-square-foot, $10 million complex deeply divided the Korean community long before it opened in December 1994.

Korean leaders accuse the store of violating both the city's zoning laws and its certificate of occupancy as a wholesaler by operating a huge retail operation. In January 1995, the city Buildings Department issued Rhee Brothers two criminal summonses for zoning violations. Certainly, all the shoppers I questioned were buying for home use, and the gleaming white shelves were lined with individual portions of yogurt, pickled cabbage, and noodles. Korean grocers have formed a federation to lobby the city against the store. As Sung Soo Kim puts it, the Rhee Brothers are "carnivores trying to take away our business."

But Pyun brushes off such squabbles. Bounding through the aisles, he is clearly relishing the Darwinian struggle unfolding in Queens. "Within the entire world, the free enterprise system is springing up," he says. After Korea Town Plaza, he took me to Flushing's two chains of midsize Korean supermarkets. These stores had themselves put many thriving small owners out of business; now, to the grim satisfaction of the smaller owners, they, too, fear competition from the mega-store. But again Pyun is sanguine: "Mega-stores may destroy some businesses temporarily, but then the situation will stabilize." Besides, "Rhee is small business compared with Home Depot."

Pyun's belief in the compatibility of big and small retailers is a minority view within the Korean community. But though he understates the pain and dislocation that giants such as Rhee Brothers will cause, the evolution of Korean entrepreneurship seems, as he says, inevitable. Many Koreans are going into the wholesale business; they also set up computer systems for big stores and service their equipment.

Despite America's racial conflicts and Korea's increased economic strength, Pyun believes the United States will continue to attract Koreans. South Koreans still fear conflict with the North, and Korea's economy is volatile. "America remains the land of opportunity," Pyun says. "It's harder to make money here, but it's steady."

Doug and Haesu Choi are more cautiously optimistic. Asked why they don't move their business out of New York closer to their home, Haesu exclaims: "I love this city. In the whole world, you can't find another like it." But she rues its decline: "It's changed so much since 1975. It's really a shame. People used to pay more attention to each other and their surroundings." Can the Koreans contribute to the city's revival? "The Koreans are still a small percentage compared to other immigrants," Haesu says. "But we hope that as the second generation grows up, they will do something to make it better."

Stephen Solarsh agrees: "Hopefully we will get our quality of life back, and the Koreans are all part of it."

—*Spring 1995*

IX
QUALITY OF LIFE

When people live cheek by jowl with one another, packed closely together in cities, it matters all the more how they treat one another, since they can't escape the presence of others. They must make hundreds of tiny mutual adjustments every day to keep the great urban mechanism humming harmoniously. For cities to flourish, the public space citizens share must be orderly, safe, and clean. All must understand civility: the art of living in a city.

HEATHER MAC DONALD
BIDs Really Work

IN 1983, the management of Mobil Oil Corporation produced a videotape that would change the face of midtown Manhattan. Mobil's leaders, having resolved to abandon the company's headquarters on East 42nd Street in favor of an office park in Fairfax, Virginia, decided to show the city why the company was leaving. Exhibit A: the videotape.

Filmed in and around Grand Central Terminal, directly across from Mobil's headquarters, the short, un-narrated tape reveals a city that has lost control of its public spaces. Cigarette butts decompose in pools of urine outside the terminal; newspaper cyclones swirl wildly down the street; illegal vendors hawk cheap toys from overturned cardboard boxes; crumpled men lie hopelessly on the sidewalk; legions of commuters try unsuccessfully to open terminal doors mysteriously tied shut with twine. The tape then flashes to the pastoral suburban headquarters of Exxon and Bell Labs. Finally, a question appears: "What do we tell our employees?"

The tape got the city's attention. In response, aides to Mayor Koch convened a meeting of midtown business leaders in 1984 to discuss how to clean up the Grand Central area. Improvement was imperative. The terminal and its surroundings provided the first glimpse of New York to thousands of visitors and commuters daily—and what they saw was the largest homeless encampment in the city, hustlers flocking upon tourists and demanding payment for flagging down a taxi, graffiti splattered across stores, filthy sidewalks, and broken streetlights.

In an implicit admission of governmental defeat, the city implored midtown business leaders to craft a remedy. They responded by organizing a business improvement district, or BID—a special taxing district that would raise additional revenue for cleaning, patrolling, and improving the district's streets and providing services to the homeless. Today the squalor around Grand Central is just a bad memory. The BID—officially called the Grand Central Partnership—put an army of cleaners to work scouring the sidewalks and removing graffiti within 24 hours of its appearance. The BID's security patrol has produced a 60 percent drop in crime. Taxi dispatchers today operate orderly queues outside the station; and new lampposts, planters, and trash receptacles, paid for by the BID, are sprouting up across the district.

BIDs have emerged as one of the most important developments in urban governance over the past two decades. They have created a mechanism for harnessing private-sector creativity to solve public problems, and their success has sharply highlighted the failures of city government. Today some 1,000 BIDs operate in the U.S.—in big cities like Houston and Philadelphia as well as in small ones, in rich neighborhoods as well as in poor. Increasing in number monthly, BIDs are trailblazers in solving such urban quality-of-life problems as aggressive panhandling, graffiti, and vandalism.

Little wonder that they've also generated controversy. Critics charge that the additional tax burden they impose on business will prove fatal to business's long-term viability; that BIDs represent a dangerous concentration of private power in public spaces; and that they will further balkanize cities into wealthy and poor districts.

Yet the great advantage of BIDs lies in their private characteristics. Unlike government, BIDs possess finite goals, which they can accomplish free of civil service rules and bureaucratic procedures. More important, they negotiate labor contracts from a clean slate: unbound by decades-old municipal labor deals, they can reward—and fire—employees according to their productivity, not their civil service status.

Nowhere are these questions debated more violently than in New York City, which boasts the continent's largest concentration of BIDs—34 in operation, with up to 39 more in the wings. Their success and power have threatened a host of existing interests, from community boards and the City Council to the social service industry. The ongoing fight over BIDs, centered on the Grand Central Partnership—the city's most ambitious BID— has brought out every atavistic anti-business instinct in the city and thrown an X-ray on those forces that impede an improved quality of life. New York's BID movement was a response to deteriorating municipal services. In the 1960s and 1970s, the city started devoting an increasing share of its budget to employee salaries and pensions and to social services. The growth of municipal unions meant that it cost more and more to provide less and less service. At the same time, court rulings regarding loitering and police procedure seriously damaged the city's ability to keep order.

New York's first BID grew out of Con Edison's efforts to clean up the then-troubled 14th Street area in Manhattan in the late 1970s. In a valiant effort to beat back the grime and crime engulfing the area, Con Edison and other major property owners around Union Square started sweeping the streets and sidewalks. The local merchants' association tried to persuade neighboring businesses to contribute to the initiative, costing $10,000 a month, but donations were sporadic and paltry. Finally, a dispirited Con Edison gave up the effort—provoking an uproar from the same merchants who originally wouldn't pitch in.

Con Edison and other property owners then decided to take advantage of laws that the state and city had passed in 1980 and 1982, authorizing merchants to form self-taxing districts for the provision of services. Under the new laws, local merchants would have to agree to form the BID, but once it was formed, their contributions would be mandatory, collected by the city under its normal taxing powers, like any other levy. Bringing to public spaces the techniques of "common space management" that made malls and office parks so successful, BIDs would maintain security and cleanliness in the area and oversee group marketing and facade improvements. Today, thanks to the 14th Street BID, the area around Union Square is cleaner and safer than it has been in decades.

After the 14th Street BID, the next few BIDs were in even less affluent areas of the city—Washington Heights in Manhattan; North Flatbush Avenue and Grand Street in Brooklyn. All were facing similar problems—government money for business improvement was scarce, city services were declining, and voluntary merchants' associations were strapped for cash. Then, as now, many BIDs began with the homely goal of raising enough money for Christmas lights.

The small BIDs, such as White Plains Road in the Bronx and Grand Street in East Williamsburg, perform an essential, if modest, role in keeping neighborhoods together. The North Flatbush BID, for example, with the second smallest budget in the city, stretches its $83,700 over a variety of services. Director Richard Russo has organized local teens to paint stores' graffiti-covered roll-down security gates in decorative designs. He has printed up attractive shopping guides and shopping bags for the district. And the North Flatbush BID's solitary sanitation worker is having a real effect: traffic and light poles on the avenue are free of the illegal fliers that one block away, on Seventh Avenue, flap from the poles like papier-mâché.

Had BIDs remained only small-scale enterprises, they might never have become a flashpoint of controversy. But at the same time that property owners in North Flatbush and Grand Street were organizing BIDs, a far larger BID was taking shape in midtown Manhattan with the explicit aim of restoring social order in a public space. Bryant Park, a large Beaux Arts greensward behind the New York Public Library on 42nd Street, had become a glaring symbol of the city's inability to control its public spaces. The park was a haven for drug dealers and petty criminals; shootouts and assaults were common. Law-abiding workers in the area feared and shunned the park, and surrounding property values had taken a nosedive.

In 1980, Andrew Heiskell, vice chairman of the New York Public Library and chairman of Time, Inc., proposed, as part of the library's own renovation program, that a nonprofit corporation of adjacent property owners should restore and manage the park—an idea that eventually evolved into a BID. L. Robert Lieb, co-owner of 81 West 40th Street and one of Heiskell's original backers, explains the difficulties the plan faced: "To go into a down area and put additional taxes in was a gamble. Even some of the smartest developers were hesitant to sign on; we had to sell them on the idea that to make money, you have to spend money." The hard reality, however, says Lieb, was that "if we didn't clean up the park ourselves, it wasn't going to happen."

City Hall welcomed Heiskell's idea, but elsewhere it brought out the city's most virulent anti-gentrification sentiment. Though the park would remain city property, open to all, civic groups such as the Parks Council, as well as academics and the press, accused the project's sponsors of seeking a private enclave for the rich. A proposal to build a restaurant in the park, whose revenues would contribute some $2 million toward park renovation, drew dire warnings of the imminent privatization of all public spaces. Critics conjured up Dickensian scenes of the ragged masses pressing their noses up against the restaurant's large windows, while fat bankers consumed huge quantities of goose liver and Bordeaux inside. Why this scenario should represent more of a taking of the public domain than leaving the park the exclusive province of criminals was never explained.

Nevertheless, the Bryant Park BID won approval, and it finished the restoration in 1995. Overnight, the park became the most successful public square in the city, showered with awards. Round-the-clock security and an exacting standard of maintenance keep the space safe and immaculate— even down to its public toilets. The crowds thronging the park throughout the day and evening have belied the charge that it would become the exclusive province of the rich. "I have yet to see turnstiles," muses Lieb. "No one has ever said: 'You can't go into the park.' They *have* said: 'You can't urinate on the bushes and attack people.'" Property values around the park have risen; many buildings have waiting lists for tenants. Former critics of the Bryant Park BID are now unabashed supporters.

This fight was a dress rehearsal for a larger, more bitter battle. As the Bryant Park BID got under way, city and business leaders were discussing the Grand Central problem, whose solution would pit the eventual Grand Central BID against one of the most powerful, and retrograde, forces in the city—the social service industry.

At the urging of the Koch administration, Peter Malkin, a lawyer and eventual chairman of the Grand Central BID, began organizing local property owners in 1985. Malkin hired Dan Biederman, the Bryant Park BID's young director and president, to serve the same roles in the Grand Central

BID. The plan Malkin and Biederman devised was the most ambitious yet: a sweeping renovation of the streetscape, including specially designed street-lights and signage throughout the district, new trees in pits that allow deep watering during droughts, ornamental planters, trash receptacles, redesigned food carts and newspaper kiosks, restoration of the Pershing Square Viaduct that leads traffic from the elevated roadway around Grand Central Terminal back to Park Avenue, floodlighting the terminal, and replacement of all side-walk wheelchair ramps.

In late 1988 the Grand Central Partnership—a 50-block district extend-ing roughly from 39th Street to 48th Street and from Second Avenue to Fifth Avenue—began operations. Only one of the 181 property owners had filed an objection in accordance with the law. With some 51 million square feet of commercial real estate, the district constituted 14 percent of Manhattan's total office space, valued at approximately $7.8 billion in 1994.

The partnership, today with a $10 million annual budget, has trans-formed the district with a fanatical sense of mission. Biederman is a perfec-tionist and has assumed an unmistakably proprietary attitude toward the district. Pointing to an elegant new lamp pole crowned by a clutter of park-ing signs, he sighs: "The city has been putting things on our poles that we don't like." Characteristically, the partnership has offered to provide alterna-tive poles.

In a city where official indifference to the broadest assaults on human dignity had until recently been the norm, such devotion to detail should be welcome. But for many New Yorkers, such an attitude signals a sinister in-tention to usurp the public domain. The partnership's imperialistic designs on midtown Manhattan seemed confirmed when Malkin and Biederman announced plans in 1990 to establish another BID on 34th Street. No mat-ter that City Hall backed the plan, recognizing that it was incapable of clean-ing up the area around Madison Square Garden in time for the Democratic National Convention in 1992.

Then the Grand Central Partnership and the 34th Street BID an-nounced their intention to issue some $55 million in bonds to finance their capital improvements program, with interest and principal to be paid with the BID assessments. Since the bonds are not backed by the full faith and credit of the city, the city would not be liable in the case of a default. Yet all resulting capital improvements would become city property—a gift to the city. Even so, State Senator Manfred Ohrenstein introduced anti-BID legis-lation, with a specific anti-Biederman clause. "You've got one man running a private government for public purposes in the center of Manhattan," Ohren-stein told Crain's New York Business in 1992. "It's just too much power with no control, no accountability, no review." The legislation ultimately went nowhere, for even the Democratic Assembly realized the value of BIDs to the city. In 1992 and 1993 the partnership and the 34th Street BID issued $32 million and $24 million in bonds, respectively, receiving a credit rating of A1 —far higher than the city's.

The Grand Central Partnership's greatest infraction lay in its attempt to offer an alternative to existing services for the homeless. From its inception, the partnership had acknowledged a duty to help the homeless who congregated in and around Grand Central. Then-Manhattan borough president David Dinkins had made his support for the BID conditional on its involvement in homeless services. Robert Hayes, founder of the Coalition for the Homeless, the city's most powerful homeless advocacy and litigation machine, had urged the partnership's involvement in social services.

In 1985 —the same year that the partnership was starting to organize— the Coalition for the Homeless had begun a feeding line outside Grand Central on Vanderbilt Avenue. Unruly and dangerous, the line brought hundreds of men each night to the area; fights —one of them fatal—often broke out. Businesses and restaurants complained that the men were defecating in their doorways. Several other charitable organizations in the neighborhood also offered food, with the result that men were racing around the district to collect three dinners in one evening. The food line invited the public to dislike the homeless; advocates predictably complained of "backlash."

To improve the district, the partnership needed to get the food line off the streets. "I realized that if you attack Robert Hayes, he only grows bigger," explains Jeff Grunberg, director of the partnership's social service programs. "Instead, we decided to compete by providing the homeless what they want indoors." In 1989 the partnership opened a 24-hour, multi-service drop-in center on East 44th Street. It is the only drop-in center in the city that turns no one away except those who show up drunk or threaten violence, and one of the few programs willing to cater predominantly to young black men, many of whom have psychiatric disorders, criminal records, and addictions. Yet it is also among the city's safest.

Three months after the partnership opened its Social Service Center, Hayes, to his credit, moved the coalition's feeding line to the center. But the agreement between the coalition and the partnership was extremely fragile. Hayes soon left the directorship, replaced by Mary Brosnahan, a far more confrontational advocate with a deep disdain for "muckety-muck business people," as she calls them. Periodically, the coalition's food line would reappear on Vanderbilt Avenue—in protest over the partnership's policy of metal detection for weapons, or the partnership's allowing the "coalition's homeless" into the building early (the coalition preferred that they wait on the street), or over the air-conditioning, crowding, or alleged lack of safety in the center. When the line returned to Vanderbilt, the partnership would try to lure the "coalition's homeless" back inside by passing out menus for the center's meals on the food line—a bourgeois tactic viewed with Olympian disgust by coalition officials. The partnership had encroached upon the advocates' universe by opening a competing shop: its center offered not only hot meals and a place to stay overnight but also job training and a program to prepare people for, and place them in, housing. The partnership's record in hiring the formerly homeless is unparalleled among service providers. Given these incursions into the advocates' territory, the chances of peaceful coexistence between the coalition and the partnership—in the same building, no less!—were slim.

Writing in *New York Newsday* upon the occasion of the food line's reappearance in 1994, columnist Murray Kempton spoke for the city's entire left wing in his contempt for the partnership's efforts. The partnership, he said, ran a human "waste disposal program" whose main goal was "to find a place to hide" the homeless. The center's purpose, he claimed, was "obscuring the homeless with cosmetology"—never mind that its "cosmetology" included giving the homeless drug treatment, mental health counseling, housing, and jobs, as well as food and shelter.

It began to seem that for the advocates and their allies in the press, the only place the homeless belonged was on the streets. Several months before the Democratic National Convention, the partnership had begun an innovative program to persuade people living in homeless encampments to seek help. The partnership's outreach workers would give the encampments' occupants a coupon for $5 and a hot breakfast, redeemable at a social service "network fair," where the homeless would meet an array of service providers and learn about their programs. If a person actually hooked up with a provider, the partnership offered to reimburse the provider at the city rate and pay the homeless person's first month's rent if the organization found him housing. The coalition would have none of it. A "passive sweep!" cried Mary Brosnahan. The advocates charged that the network fair program—like the Social Service Center—was intended simply to get the homeless out of sight for the convention. The Coalition for the Homeless, by contrast, planned to *create* a homeless encampment on the periphery of the convention, a sort of Potemkin Village in reverse.

What was at stake in the battle between the Grand Central Partnership and the city's traditional service providers was not just ideology, but money—lots of it. The partnership supplemented its own assessments with government grants—in 1995 the Social Service Center received $1.7 million from the city's Department of Homeless Services and $300,000 from the Federal Emergency Management Agency for nutrition. When Peter Malkin and Dan Biederman announced their intention to form a BID on 34th Street, the advocates and their allies on local community boards decided that this was the moment to get their hands on that money. Peter Smith, then president of the Partnership for the Homeless, began an all-out campaign in the press and the community boards to tar the Grand Central Partnership. Smith warned that if the 34th Street BID was approved, New Yorkers "will lose a huge chunk of Manhattan." The Social Service Center was one of the "worst in the city," he falsely charged. Smith demanded that the 34th Street BID sponsors give *him* the money they had set aside for social services. He found an ally in the local community boards, often populated by representatives of social service agencies. During board meetings about the 34th Street BID, people screamed at Jeff Grunberg, director of social services for the Grand Central Partnership, that he was "causing homelessness."

After the advocates' political attacks came the legal ones. In February 1995 the Urban Justice Center sued the Grand Central Partnership for violating minimum wage laws in its homeless job-training program. "I've never seen exploitation as bad as at the partnership," deadpanned Doug Lasdon, executive director of the Urban Justice Center, to a sympathetic City Council. The advocates charged that the partnership was trying to get rich off its homeless, paying highly capable workers slave wages to perform needed tasks. A ludicrous charge: the partnership's trainees are initially incapable of holding down a job—no more than a third show up for their kitchen and maintenance jobs on any given day. The program gives the trainees needed discipline and confidence: a tall, thin man working in the center's kitchen drew himself up and told me emphatically, "This is not a homeless shelter; this is a self-help center." The partnership has a highly credible record in moving people into full-time jobs: 400 former clients are working to date, 200 of those doing menial or administrative jobs for the partnership itself.

In December 1995 the Urban Justice Center sued again, charging the partnership with violating the Constitution by not giving residents in the district equal representation on the BID's board of directors. BIDs revive America's "tradition of non-democracy," Lasdon told me. "For hundreds of years, we haven't had democracy but landowners voting." Of course, the partnership's bylaws merely follow the state and city BID legislation in requiring that over half the board consist of property owners, and the U.S. Supreme Court has upheld property qualifications for voting in special assessment districts.

But these suits, for all their cost and negative publicity, cannot compare in destructive force with the brilliant public relations coup launched on April 14, 1995—the day the *New York Times* published its by now infamous "goon squad" article on page one. Noting that the partnership trains its own homeless clients to do homeless outreach, in the belief that the formerly homeless can best persuade those still on the street to seek services, the *Times* charged that the partnership encourages these trainees to beat up the homeless and drive them off private and public property. Four former partnership outreach workers—brought to the *Times* by the Coalition for the Homeless and the Urban Justice Center—claimed to have kicked and bludgeoned the homeless who resisted services as part of their expected duties. The partnership vehemently denied the charges, pointing out that two of the self-confessed "goons" had been fired for stealing partnership vans, and all had axes to grind. Three of the accusers are parties to the Urban Justice Center's minimum wage suit.

The *Times* article resembles nothing so much as the Salem witch trials, with no charge too fantastical to print. A former secretary of the partnership who had been fired for being in the office after hours says that the director of homeless outreach dispatched his workers in the morning with the cry: "OK, goon squad! Go get 'em!" The partnership, charges the *Times*, referred to its outreach workers not only as "goon squads," but also as "wrecking crews" and "vigilantes."

With the publication of the *Times* article, a glad cry went out across the city. The allegations immediately entered city lore as the gospel truth. The City Council Committee on General Welfare, chaired by Councilman Stephen DiBrienza, the social service industry's mouthpiece, held a circus-like hearing on the partnership's "goon squads," and the Finance Committee declared a moratorium on new BID approvals and ordered a review of BIDs, targeted undisguisedly at the Grand Central Partnership. The federal Department of Housing and Urban Development, working closely with the City Council Welfare Committee, yanked a half-million-dollar grant to the partnership. "There's no doubt that these things happened," announced Andrew Cuomo, assistant secretary of HUD and a former New York homeless advocate.

The question is: what "things" happened? In one of the incidents alleged by the Coalition for the Homeless—a fight between an outreach worker and a homeless person in front of the Philip Morris building on 42nd Street and Park Avenue—the partnership outreach worker filed a police report and a criminal complaint for assault. The alleged "victim" filed a cross-complaint; neither party pursued the matter further. The partnership made no effort to cover up the incident. In another—an alleged assault on a man under a box in the snow—although the partnership had no record of the event, it now believes its outreach worker feared the man was dead and sought to rouse him. Out of 70,000 contacts between partnership outreach workers and the homeless, these are the only charges for which any evidence has been found. They do not support the fundamental indictment against the partnership: that it sanctioned a policy of aggression toward the homeless. Homeless advocates have been videotaping alleged abuse of the homeless on the streets for years; they recorded none of the beatings allegedly routine among the partnership's outreach workers. Likewise, hundreds of hours of videotape by banks inside their ATM vestibules, the most frequent site of partnership outreach services, yield no record of the goon squad activity. The partnership has asked the Manhattan district attorney to investigate the charges; that report has yet to issue. No one has denied that the partnership encouraged abuse more adamantly than the partnership's own homeless outreach workers.

The episode has further damaged the partnership's reputation and isolated it within the BID community. Some of the big competing BID managers have taken to delivering gratuitous and sanctimonious potshots at the partnership. Ultimately, however, the partnership will ride out the storm — it is too effective to be destroyed.

The greatest damage from the smear campaign is not to the partnership but to the city itself, which will lose a highly promising alternative approach to homeless services. The partnership's outreach effort had succeeded in striking a unique balance between the needs of the homeless and the interests of property owners and public order. But now such balance is forbidden, thanks to a report by Robert Hayes, whom the partnership, in a striking show of good faith, had asked to evaluate its outreach and social service programs in the wake of the goon squad charges. Though Hayes's report unequivocally supports the Social Service Center and dismisses the goon squad allegations as "demagoguery," it reasserts the prevailing, destructive social service orthodoxy that homeless outreach must concern itself solely with the interests of the homeless, without reference to the public interest.

As the Hayes report details, when an outreach worker found a homeless person on private property, such as a bank ATM vestibule, he would try to persuade the homeless person to accompany him to the partnership's Social Service Center. So far, so good. But if the homeless person refused to move, the outreach worker would counter: "You're on private property; I am therefore obligated to notify the bank security officer, who will evict you. So you might as well come with me now where you may get shelter and food."

That argument, said Hayes, violates the most fundamental tenet of homeless outreach: the outreach worker may not "mix outreach and security." Telling the homeless person he is trespassing would jeopardize the precious bond of trust that the outreach worker hopes to establish with him. In fact, states Hayes, quoting several social service "professionals," the fondest wish of the outreach worker is that the homeless person will still be trespassing in the same spot the next day, so that he can re-administer his services (thus, one might note, filling up his quota of requisite homeless "contacts" for the month).

The absurdity of this argument is overwhelming. Nothing could be less conducive to reintegrating the homeless into society than exempting them from the rules that others have to live by. To treat the homeless as sensitive plants that may be damaged by learning that they are breaking the law is profoundly "infantilizing," to borrow a word from Hayes. Equally nonsensical is the implicit assumption that the homeless person is better off either left in a bank vestibule or evicted by a security officer, rather than being persuaded by the invocation of the law into shelter. Before the partnership persuaded bankers to try its more compassionate approach, banks used dogs to evict the homeless.

Hayes's report subtly reaffirms a basic tenet of the left: business will always oppress the powerless, even when it claims to be working for the common good. He cites with concern the statutory purposes of BIDs: to "restore and promote business activity" and to enhance the "enjoyment and protection of the public"—purposes that, he says, may put the BIDs in conflict with the mission of helping the homeless. Thus, he concludes, BIDs should not deliver social services on their own; any such efforts must be directed by "experts" and "professionals." Unsurprisingly, those "experts" acclaimed the report as the definitive statement on homeless outreach.

In response, the partnership meekly capitulated: its outreach workers have stopped telling homeless people that they are on private property. As a consequence, Chase Bank canceled its contract with the partnership for outreach services, now relying solely on its security officers—hardly a victory for the homeless. The partnership has also reconstituted the board of directors of its Social Service Corporation with a large majority of "seasoned social service experts," including a director who once headed the radical Mobilization for Youth—the original failed War on Poverty program—and it is considering Hayes's recommendation to find a "sophisticated outreach agency" to replace its own former homeless clients.

Game, set, and match to the advocates: the Hayes report preserves a huge pot of money for social services and reestablishes the social service industry's hegemony over it, as HUD awarded the grant money it had stripped from the Grand Central Partnership to the Partnership for the Homeless. And a move is afoot in the City Council to prohibit BIDs from direct involvement in social services, thus locking up the advocates' monopoly over government money. This proposal, still in its early stages, would be a heartbreaking loss to the city. The partnership, which started delivering services because it couldn't persuade existing organizations to take on the challenge of its universal drop-in center, has provided some of the most creative solutions to homelessness in recent years. Requiring all BIDs to contract out with existing service providers, as Councilman DiBrienza would like to do, would limit new ideas in a field desperately in need of them.

By now, about the only people willing to support the partnership publicly are BID managers in other cities—many of whom also see dealing with the homeless as central to their mission. Nationally, the reaction to the uproar in New York is one of utter incomprehension. "West of the Mississippi, we think: 'You guys are nuts!'" exclaims Margaret Mullen, executive director of the Phoenix BID and chairman of the International Downtown Association. "Tell them in New York to grow up and call our social service people— and leave Dan Biederman alone!" If such a smear campaign were ever waged against the Phoenix BID, Mullen says, "the business community would be so offended that it would stop giving money to social services."

Indeed, what the Hayes report finds so objectionable in the partnership's operations—allegedly combining "outreach" and "security" is far more innocuous than what BIDs in other cities do, without protest. The BID in Portland, Oregon, a bastion of liberalism, sends out its security guards to give morning "wake-up calls" to the homeless—in other words, to roust them from the doorways of businesses. Phoenix's downtown guides—like roving ambassadors—evict the homeless from private property and call the police if a homeless person is panhandling or urinating in public. Baltimore's downtown guides ask panhandlers standing in front of businesses to move along. If a panhandler refuses, the guides station themselves on either side of him and discourage pedestrians from giving money. In 1993 the ACLU sued the Baltimore BID over its practice of asking panhandlers to move along; the BID board refused to settle out of court. "Our board felt it was a battle worth fighting—the community had to find out what its rights are," explains Frank Russo, the Baltimore BID's head of security. The BID won.

All these cities, like New York, have extensive systems of help for the homeless, but they also recognize what many in New York are still oblivious to: "If you emphasize individual rights," Baltimore's Russo argues, "the city goes bankrupt. You have to do what needs to be done to see that the city survives."

While the Grand Central Partnership's social service program should have been a non-issue, BIDs do pose genuinely serious questions for cities. Critics within the business community charge that BIDs impose a second tax on businesses for services they are already paying the city to provide. In the long run, these critics say, the double taxation, rather than the enhancement of services, will determine whether firms stay or leave.

But the BID assessments are tiny compared with the city's own tax burden. Real estate taxes in midtown Manhattan run between $6 to $14 a square foot compared with the Grand Central Partnership's assessment of 14 cents a square foot. BID assessments range from a few hundred dollars a year for small buildings to $500,000 for the Empire State Building. A sensible proposal floated in 1994 by Deputy Mayor John Dyson to allow at least part of BID assessments to be tax-deductible would further defang the double-taxation argument.

The evidence at least partly confutes the economic argument against BIDs. Buildings are starting to advertise membership in the most successful BIDs: the law firms of Simpson, Thacher & Bartlett and Davis, Polk & Wardwell say the existence of the Grand Central Partnership figured in their decisions to relocate to midtown. Property owners in some areas, such as the perimeter of Bryant Park, point to the existence of the BID to explain the zero vacancy rates of many buildings. Even small-property owners view the additional expense as a worthwhile investment: "I have no problem paying more if it upgrades the area," says Howard Somers, owner of Grand Book Center, a 40-year-old business in the Grand Street BID. "The more the area is worth, the more my property is worth."

And BID revenues don't only duplicate what city taxes are supposed to provide. Even the best-run city is unlikely to provide, as many of the larger BIDs do, continual sidewalk cleaning and graffiti removal for over 12 hours a day, peripatetic visitor guides, special events, and help with store upgrading. Many BIDs aim at a standard set not by the ideal city but by Disney World or a premier shopping mall. And if midtown merchants want, say, floodlighting at Grand Central Terminal, they'd be politically naive to expect taxpayers in Jamaica, Queens, to pay for it.

It's true that many BID activities are things the city should be doing. But what is the alternative? If all BIDs were to cease operations tomorrow, it is fanciful to think that New York would revamp its work rules, civil service policies, and spending priorities fast or fully enough to prevent further business decline. Forcing businesses to die a slow death in order to highlight the city's failings is unlikely to make the city refocus its priorities.

Yet BIDs make the situation *worse*, respond critics, by taking pressure off New York to reform its ways. By providing basic services themselves, critics argue, BIDs "enable" the city to continue pouring money into salaries, pensions, and a massive welfare apparatus while ignoring the essentials of municipal government. Furthermore, opponents say, BIDs "co-opt" out of the political process the most powerful citizens. The large real estate interests, the argument goes, which otherwise would be screaming at City Hall about the filth in the streets, fall suddenly silent once in a BID, because their neighborhood is clean. Meanwhile the rest of the city continues its long decline.

The first argument—that BIDs enable dysfunctional spending priorities—has some bite. BIDs conceivably allow the city to shift resources even further from basic services in the knowledge that others will pick up the slack. Some people have argued, analogously, that the Central Park Conservancy, a private philanthropic organization that contributes millions to the maintenance of Central Park, has allowed the city to slash further its entire parks budget, though proving the claim is virtually impossible. But again, the response has to be pragmatic: *not* picking up the slack is unlikely to produce a positive result. And conceivably, BIDs could force reform of city priorities by creating a higher standard for neighborhood cleanliness and safety. New Yorkers have grown accustomed to a barbaric level of litter and filth; the best BIDs show what a city should look like. With any luck, residents will start demanding that the entire city look as clean.

As for the argument that BIDs co-opt people out of the political process, the opposite has proved true. BIDs involve business as never before in the day-to-day operations of cities. The BID becomes a watchdog for service delivery because it is so close to the ground. When New York cut trash pickups in midtown, the Times Square BID fought—with some success—to get them back. Rather than fostering just a parochial commitment to turf, the New York BIDs are working together on citywide solutions to citywide problems, such as illegal street vending.

Another argument against BIDs is that they are elitist, allowing wealthy areas of the city to help themselves *at the expense* of less wealthy areas. BIDs do not simply add to the total pot of city services, charge critics such as Robert Solomon, a law professor at Yale who is bringing the suit against the Grand Central Partnership over its board representation; they are a zero-sum transaction: the BID's gain is someone else's loss. Solomon's reasoning: when a city proposes to raise taxes, members of a BID—who are already paying an additional tax—will fight against the increase all the more strenuously. "If the city currently has a revenue pie of 100 pennies," complains Solomon, "and the BIDs self-tax, raising the pie to 110 pennies, they get to keep all those additional pennies and will pressure the city against the tax increase."

So much the better! one hastens to reply. The more pressure against tax increases, the better for the city. And surely Solomon is naive to think that without BIDs, property owners would be any more amenable to tax increases. More important, Solomon's zero-sum analysis of BIDs is utterly wrong. BIDs are a net gain to urban well-being, because they operate in the public realm, adding benefits available to all city residents, not just BID members. We are all free riders on BID expenditures. Solomon also ignores BIDs' potential effect on a city's tax base. If they increase the value of commercial property, they will contribute additional revenue to city coffers and allow continued funding of those (often counterproductive) welfare programs that Solomon cherishes.

Anti-elitists also argue that BIDs exacerbate existing disparities in the city, because some BIDs have big budgets, others small ones, and some areas can't afford BIDs at all. Accordingly, Doug Lasdon, executive director of the Urban Justice Center and professional scourge of the Grand Central Partnership, recommends raising taxes citywide 1 percent, so that every neighborhood can be given a $10 million budget like the Grand Central Partnership. This proposal illustrates that at bottom, BIDs offend left-wing sensibilities because they violate the redistributionist principle of ordinary taxation. BID taxes are virtually the only taxes in the city that are spent locally: those who pay more, get more. The absence of redistribution is a strong argument in BIDs' favor. Certain areas of the city are economically more important than others, and increased spending on them is in the entire city's self-interest. The big Manhattan BIDs target resources where they can stimulate the most economic activity to the benefit of the whole city.

Leaders of the smaller BIDs are the first to recognize this. Stan Bonilla, manager of the East Brooklyn Industrial Park BID, says he "absolutely does not agree with Lasdon's redistribution argument. The Grand Central Partnership is at the doorstep of the world. If they can afford to spend $500 million, go ahead—it's not affecting East Brooklyn." Leonard Battle of the Grand Street BID agrees: "It's unfair to redistribute; that's taxation without representation. My needs are different from those of the Grand Central Partnership or Metrotech [the largest BID in Brooklyn and sixth largest in the city]."

The City Council's Finance Committee added one last set of criticisms, in a November 1995 report on BID operations. Based on a telephone survey of some 6 percent of property owners and BID managers, the report purported to find widespread ignorance and less than overwhelming support of BID operations. In addition, the report charged some BIDs with such improprieties as paying excessive salaries to BID managers (a swipe at Biederman), employing illegal aliens, conflicts of interest, excessive spending on administration, and lax management. The report recommends that a vote be taken on the continuation of a BID every five years, and threatens regulation if BIDs don't improve their accountability to their members and the public at large.

But property owners say the report is based on a sloppily conducted survey, and one looks in vain in it for evidence of systemic problems that might require government intervention. The improprieties alleged in some of the outlying BIDs remain hotly disputed; the complaints about the midtown BIDs center on a rehash of the "goon squad" lie. And the council's report holds BIDs to a standard of accountability and efficiency that city government can only dream of achieving. Unless more persuasive evidence of member dissatisfaction surfaces, the current procedures for operating a BID—which already provide for extensive public and governmental oversight, including political appointees on their boards—should remain in place. Above all, it would be a gross mistake to let the City Council get its hands on the BIDs, so it can do for BIDs what it and other branches of city government have done for New York.

BIDs have channeled an enormous amount of private-sector energy toward the solution of public problems. They have disproved the notion that the public interest and private interests necessarily conflict. And in a city that has often been swayed by anti-business sentiment, BIDs have given business a needed voice in the provision of city services. BIDs may also offer some lessons for the future. They suggest the advantages of giving smaller areas of the city more control over the raising and spending of revenues. And they point further in the direction of privatizing city services.

Perhaps one day BIDs will not be necessary. But for now, as Dan Biederman says, they "provide the West Berlin to the city's East Berlin."

— *Spring 1996*

JULIA VITULLO-MARTIN

Quiet, Please

NOISE POLLUTION is the great ignored urban problem, dismissed as a minor annoyance, unworthy of policy-makers' serious attention. But to physiologists, it is a much weightier matter. They describe loud noise as a trauma, a warning that provokes the body's reflexes to prepare for an emergency. In most people, sound levels over 70 decibels constrict blood flow to the extremities while increasing it to the brain. The adrenal and pituitary glands rush hormones into the bloodstream. The liver releases glucose for energy. The fear persists after the noise stops, fading only gradually as the body waits for a recurrence.

Not only is loud noise a trauma; it can do permanent physical damage as well. Hearing loss, often caused by noise, is the country's most common chronic physical disability, affecting one in eight Americans, according to the Council on the Environment.

A certain amount of noise is inseparable from the urban ambience — hot, young, energetic. But if people are to live peaceably in a close-packed urban setting, they must be able to count on limits to the noise their neighbors make. Accordingly, from the Babylonians forward, cities have routinely sought to outlaw unnecessary, excessive, offensive, or unreasonable noise. English common law deems freedom from noise essential to the full enjoyment of a dwelling: acts that diminish that enjoyment may expose the noisy to legal action. In modern times, precise new technology to measure noise has paved the way for more precise ordinances, such as New York City's 1972 law.

But technology to create louder noise than ever before has developed even faster than measurement technology, and today noise is seriously marring New York City's quality of life. "I hear more complaints about noise than I hear about murders and drugs," says Deputy Inspector James F. McShane, commanding officer of the 47th Precinct in the Bronx. Bob Leitman of the polling firm Louis Harris and Associates calls noise a "real top-of-the-consciousness" issue. In a quality-of-life survey Leitman conducted for the Commonwealth Fund, 62 percent of New Yorkers said noise bothers them; half of those said it does "to a great extent." Physicist and preeminent acoustical engineer Cyril M. Harris, who lives in a superbly quiet apartment high above the East River Drive, says he has concluded that every New Yorker has at least one exasperating noise problem.

Much of the city's noise is unnecessary. For example, ambulance sirens often project their sound so inefficiently that it awakens residents 20 stories above, even while a driver three cars ahead may be unsure of where the sound is coming from. Noise intended to express oneself has hit unprecedented levels in amplified sound trucks for political candidates or music coming from rock clubs and discos. Some of that self-expressive noise has an explicitly aggressive edge: teenagers with boom boxes, for example, or motorcycles with "straight pipes," an illegal resonant exhaust device.

The city's environment includes almost limitless sources and kinds of noise. But when the city government tries to quiet noise, it quickly runs up against the difficulties of measuring it accurately and claims of First Amendment rights. Add to that the irrational split in jurisdiction between two separate city agencies: the Department of Environmental Protection (DEP) regulates what engineers call "community noise," like outdoor concerts, honking, construction, motorcycles, discos, and car alarms; the police, reluctantly, regulate private noise inside apartment buildings and single-family dwellings. But the bulk of DEP's 5,500 annual complaints are in the area of private noise, where the department has no jurisdiction, notes Commissioner Marilyn Gelber.

You have to measure noise before you can regulate it, and, even with the new technology, that isn't easy. Sound is measured in decibels, named for Alexander Graham Bell. Because the scale is logarithmic, not arithmetic, a 10-decibel increase means that a sound has roughly doubled in loudness. Quiet breathing registers 10 decibels; quiet conversation, around 60; shouting across a room, 75. Midtown traffic ranges from 80 to 95 decibels, while an express subway train rumbling through a local station can reach 105. Registering 120 decibels are: a jet at takeoff; a rock band playing "normally" with amplifiers and loudspeakers; and a thunder-clap, the loudest natural sound on earth. The specifications for sirens on New York City fire engines call for 118 decibels at 50 feet.

A sound of 40 decibels will awaken sensitive people; 70 will wake up almost anyone. Noise of 120 decibels causes discomfort and sometimes injury; 140 is acutely painful. The National Institute for Occupational Safety and Health says that two years of regular exposure to 90 decibels will produce hearing loss.

Measuring urban sound is especially difficult because inspectors have to measure the prevailing background noise before they can measure the additional noise generated by, say, a rock concert or street fair. Once the inspector has established the ambient level, he must take measurements at intervals and calculate the difference from the ambient level at each, an operation requiring much preparation.

Another complication: because some noise is the result of expressive activity, the city must design its regulations so as to control noise without running afoul of the First Amendment. Regulation of outdoor rock concerts is a frequent source of legal challenges, for at least since the 1960s popular music has often presented loudness itself as a political protest.

The U.S. Supreme Court has consistently held that governments may impose "reasonable time, place, and manner" restrictions to regulate nuisances attendant upon expression. A court will uphold such a regulation if it is tailored to meet a significant governmental interest, such as noise abatement, and if it does not discriminate based on the content of expression. The rule that applies for a rock concert, for example, must also apply to an equally loud opera performed at the same time of day.

New York's most famous recent noise case, *Ward v. Rock Against Racism*, demonstrates how furiously these issues can clash in practice. In the mid-1980s, the Parks Department was issuing some 175 permits a year for public performances in Central Park's Naumburg Bandshell. To avoid excessively disturbing the neighbors in the buildings that surround the park, the Parks Department needed a way of limiting the noise the concerts generated. Measuring the sound level and intervening during a performance had proved impractical, so the department came up with a different way to keep a hand on the volume control. In 1986 it hired its own professional sound engineer, or "mixer," who would regulate the level of sound of every performance. If citizens complained, the mixer could make instant adjustments.

Rock Against Racism, an advocacy group that held annual all-day concerts in the park, balked at the requirement, because it regarded the mixer as a skilled band member, just as important as a musician. With William Kunstler as its high-profile attorney, the organization won a preliminary injunction against the required use of the city's mixer. Three years later, the case reached the Supreme Court.

In a six-to-three decision delivered by Justice Anthony Kennedy, the Court held the regulation reasonable and constitutional. But the disagreement within the Court reflects a fundamental conflict in viewpoints over the relationship between individual rights and the common good where noise is concerned. In a furious dissent, Justice Thurgood Marshall quoted musician and lexicographer Nicolas Slonimsky: "New music always sounds loud to old ears. Beethoven seemed to make more noise than Mozart; Liszt was noisier than Beethoven; Schoenberg and Stravinsky noisier than their predecessors."

But today's musicians not only sound loud to old ears; they *are* loud. The electronic technology they use to project their music is far more powerful than anything imagined by previous generations. Indeed, when asked what he would consider too loud, Rock Against Racism's mixer had replied: "I think a volume that would cause people's ears to bleed would be too loud." While music is unquestionably a form of expression protected by the Constitution, free expression does not entail a right to be as loud as one wants in any public place.

Rock bands aren't the only users—and abusers—of powerful amplification technology. For a few thousand dollars, a driver can equip his car with a stereo system capable of projecting music at outdoor-concert sound levels. These "boom-box cars" represent a step up in aggression from the portable stereos popular among urban youths. Ironically, once it became clear that Sony's huge, powerful portable radios had become noisy blights, Akio Morita, Sony's CEO, had the Walkman developed as an alternative. But the Walkman didn't displace the boom box, selling like hotcakes instead to middle-class joggers. Morita had missed the cultural implications of the boom box, often used to attract attention or stake out territory.

By the early 1990s, complaints about boom-box cars were pouring into precincts all over the city, especially in Washington Heights and Greenwich Village. The city's response was ineffective, owing to the convoluted system of jurisdiction. DEP inspectors had the meters to measure the noise, but only the meterless police could issue summonses.

In 1992, Jeremy Travis, then deputy police commissioner in charge of legal affairs, devised a strategy dubbed Operation Soundtrap to give officers meters and train them to use them, so they could enforce a long-standing state law allowing police to confiscate cars if their stereo sound measured more than 80 decibels at 50 feet. The campaign began in Washington Heights and Greenwich Village on Friday nights in mid-summer 1993. Police ship the seized cars to the distant Whitestone Pound, and owners cannot reclaim them until after paying a $100 fine Monday morning.

Police in Washington Heights seized 40 cars in 1993 and have seized 103 so far in 1994, according to Captain Terry Monahan. In Greenwich Village, officers confiscated up to ten vehicles every Friday night early in the program, but the effort was so successful that by the end of the summer of 1993 police were facing Fridays with no offending vehicles to confiscate. By the beginning of the following summer, the window-rattling, ear-shattering cars were back, and the police started in again. Village police confiscated 33 cars in 1994 and by the end of summer had eliminated the blight. "On Saturday night we were out to 4 AM, and the only boom car we found measured 76 decibels," Lieutenant Robert McKenna said in early September.

Soundtrap is an important step forward, but an early technical decision has constrained its effectiveness. Although the law's 80-decibel limit is itself beyond most people's tolerance, the Police Department has chosen to enforce a higher level—83 decibels—in order, it says, to make its cases iron-clad. But because of the logarithmic scale, the three-decibel difference represents an exponential increase in loudness.

The sum total of noise that boom-box cars make pales to insignificance compared with the braying of countless automobile alarms, which can be as loud as 100 decibels. They are intended to deter theft, but most insurance actuaries and criminologists deem them ineffective: many alarms go off so easily and repeatedly that people no longer associate them with danger. Some make purely gratuitous noises, beeping hello when the driver enters the car. And some, like the Invisibeam Plus, claim public space as the domain of the car, barking orders at pedestrians who merely walk by. "It works in two languages," says a Brooklyn merchant who sells the Invisibeam—"English and rap." The rap version begins: "Yo! I know you want to look inside, but I suggest you step away from the ride." If a passerby fails to comply, the voice continues: "You violated the perimeter beam; you now have five seconds to leave the scene." If this warning fails, a noisy alarm starts wailing.

Though alarms that go off without the car being touched are illegal in New York, state law actively encourages drivers to own conventional alarms. A law passed in the late 1970s requires insurance companies to give discounts to owners of cars equipped with them. Alarms have become standard equipment on most cars sold in the city.

Adding $200 to $2,000 to the cost of a car, they can save 10 percent annually in insurance premiums.

New York City's current noise code requires that alarms cease after three minutes, and periodically City Councilman Sheldon Leffler of Queens reasonably proposes banning alarms outright. The city could ban their use within city limits, subject to fines. At the very least, the State Legislature should end the mandatory insurance discount. Quiet anti-theft devices are available—steering-wheel locks like the Club, for example. Lojack, a silent tracking system that sends radio signals out from the car, allowing police to locate it on a computer screen, may well be the wave of the future in auto security.

Honking, another automotive nuisance, is meant to annoy. "Don't honk, Bobby," Senator Robert F. Wagner once told his son, the mayor, when they were caught behind a slow-moving car. "The man is a voter." Honking is illegal in New York City, except in an emergency. But New York drivers routinely use their horns to notify the driver ahead of a changing light, to express outrage at bad driving, to ward off pedestrians in the crosswalk, to assert their manhood, or to blow off steam.

Nearly everyone who challenges a honking citation at the city's Environmental Control Board gets off, usually on the grounds that an officer couldn't know for sure who was honking. Other cities, however, particularly in California, effectively punish honking under the same provisions that cover amplified sound and barking dogs.

City officials attribute the worsening honking by taxi drivers over the past few years to the many new drivers from countries where honking is commonplace. But even if drivers arrive thinking honking is fine, the Taxi and Limousine Commission should instruct them otherwise in its mandatory training courses and should enforce the noise code against them. Right now it does neither.

Noise generated by many kinds of business is usually controlled by a combination of regulation and negotiation. Restaurant air conditioners venting outside, for example, cannot exceed 45 decibels. In the mid-1980s, after the city had persuaded the *Daily News* to keep its printing plant in Brooklyn, angry residents complained that the huge trucks that deliver newsprint were too noisy. When an environmental study confirmed their complaints, the *News* provided double windows to some 60 local households and spent hundreds of thousands of dollars to soundproof its facility. Not every business, however, would be so accommodating or have as strong a reason to be concerned about its public image.

Noise is at the very heart of businesses like rock clubs, discos, and aerobics studios, all of which regularly register 110 decibels and above. Proprietors tend to look on complaining neighbors as neurotic nuisances, but DEP inspectors take complaints seriously. For a period in the 1980s, inspectors visited the Jeff Martin Studio on Manhattan's West Side every week. The studio's solution was an expensive renovation that included tightly sealed double-glazed windows. Most complaints ceased.

Deputy Commissioner Travis's noise-abatement teams are targeting clubs and discos, but here the law explicitly constrains the police, who must measure noise inside an apartment, not on the street. The practical complications are enormous: police must find someone, preferably ahead of time, who will let the team come in, perhaps repeatedly, in the dead of night when noise is worst.

The Police Department faces the same problem in regulating loud businesses as it did with boom box cars before Operation Soundtrap: various state and city agencies have jurisdiction over different parts of the process. The Police Department should develop an assertive program for regulating loud clubs and discos, starting with a simple change in the city's administrative code eliminating the requirement that noise from a commercial club can only be measured from inside an apartment.

An astounding amount of noise comes directly from public agencies, which are, unfortunately, exempt from the noise code. Shrieking brakes on city garbage trucks, an order of magnitude louder than those of almost any other vehicle, frequently awaken citizens as sanitation workers make their morning rounds. Despite empty streets and green lights the whole way, five fire engines barreled up Amsterdam Avenue at 8:15 on a recent Sunday morning, blaring a symphony of noise in which horns and sirens blended with an accompaniment of little yelps. On another Sunday, a fire engine roared down Columbus Avenue, lights flashing and horn honking, en route to Poulet Away for an emergency take-out chicken.

Sirens are perhaps the most notorious governmental noisemaker. Their purpose, of course, is to signal an emergency and induce vehicles to yield. But drivers often have trouble locating the siren's wail, a problem caused by the modulating frequency. Cyril Harris says a far better device is the loud-speaker, which can be directed at a particular vehicle: "You, in the red car, move to the right!"

Sirens sometimes panic people into doing the wrong thing. And because their overuse teaches people that a siren often doesn't mean an emergency, New Yorkers have learned to disregard them. This, in turn, becomes a justification for even more aggressive use of sirens. Solution: use sirens and horns only in true emergencies, and configure them to be as inoffensive as possible to get the job done. At present, the Police and Fire Departments don't consider their siren noise a problem and refuse even to measure it.

Ambulance sirens are an even more vexing problem. Emergency Medical Service spokesman Charles DeGaetano says that "indiscriminate use of the siren is strongly frowned upon," but acknowledges that some of the agency's ambulance drivers put their sirens "on continuous mode so they don't have to fiddle with the siren while they're driving." In addition, the ambulances of voluntary hospitals and organizations like Hatzoloh, essentially unregulated, can mount any siren or horn they like, no matter how loud, and use it whenever they want.

So loud is the subterranean din of the subways that a transit policeman recently couldn't hear the calls for help of two fellow officers being attacked 140 feet away. Decades of poor maintenance have created the mind-numbing noise. While not subject to city control, the Metropolitan Transportation Authority is subject to New York State's 1982 Rapid Transit Noise Code, which it violates on many counts despite the $1.47 billion it has spent to bring itself into compliance. The state's overly lenient code requires that most cars maintain noise levels below 85 decibels. Instead, cars average in the high 80s. The MTA was supposed to be in compliance by this year, but is still far from that goal. Arlene Bronzaft, a psychologist who did the original research on the damaging effects of noise that led to the 1982 code, says the MTA refuses to measure subway noise. Moreover, she says, one can verify that the subways are too loud by taking a rough measurement with an amateur's meter. "I did—on the A train—and measured 100 decibels, way over code."

Neighbors' behavior is the most common source of noise complaints, according to Harris. The best solution is usually private negotiation. Diplomacy, however, may not be enough. Many indoor sounds are both persistent and elusive. The loud television you blame on your upstairs neighbor may be several stories away; its sound has traveled a circuitous path to reach your apartment.

A key to indoor quiet is good construction. Harris says that New York's standards are acceptable, but California's are better, requiring, for example, more sophisticated insulating materials. And many New York City apartments were built between World War II and the 1960s, when standards sagged.

Renters have some protection under the statutory right called the "warranty of habitability," which requires the landlord to provide a dwelling "fit for human living," and under a common-law right to "quiet enjoyment" of an apartment. These provisions obligate the landlord to police the behavior of other tenants. But in practice, if private negotiation fails, tenants must generally take their landlord to court in order to enforce their rights—a costly, time-consuming process that doesn't guarantee success. One solution for the noise-bedeviled is to move to a co-op with strict rules: some, for example, ban the playing of televisions and radios late at night and have boards willing to take on noisy shareholders.

The police are traditionally reluctant to intervene in disputes about private noise. In many precincts, operators will simply tell callers it is not a police matter. But when James McShane arrived at the Bronx's 47th Precinct in January 1994, he decided to do something about the precinct's most frequent citizen complaint: deafeningly loud backyard stereo systems installed to entertain parties of 400 to 500 people, who often pay $5 each to attend. McShane and the NYPD counsel's office developed a legal strategy to control noise by seizing private property.

Police frequently seize property as evidence, but the offending sound equipment was huge. "You'd need a truck to carry it away," McShane says. The counsel concluded that police could also seize property to abate a nuisance, taking just the speaker wires, turntable, or whatever would render the equipment inoperable.

McShane created a noise-abatement unit that worked in three stages. First, police identified "recidivist locations," where parties had produced complaints in the past. Second, they posted signs saying noisy parties were against the law. Third, they did "preemptive work," warning the householders who had offended before. Only after these efforts failed would they resort to seizing property.

On an average Saturday when the weather is nice, the unit handles 50 noise complaints. McShane says the program has been a striking success: "I heard constant complaints about what we weren't doing in January, but I got only one irate call this summer. There was a party, it was bad, and we didn't do anything. We'd had an off-duty cop shot, a homicide, and we didn't have the manpower to handle the party."

McShane's experience demonstrates that police assertiveness can have a powerful deterrent effect on noisemakers. The unit's officers have not had to seize any sound equipment because lesser measures have been so effective.

If the public demands a quieter city, their elected officials will eventually respond. Anger about noisy garbage collection prompted the Lindsay administration to mandate garbage bags instead of cans for apartment buildings. Bensonhurst residents calling themselves the Big Screechers pressured the Transit Authority into modifying the brakes on subway trains in the mid-1980s.

Harris suggests Mayor Rudolph Giuliani begin by calling the city's own employees to account. He should ask bus drivers not to honk; he should demand that all city vehicles adhere to the muffler ordinance; he should instruct drivers of emergency vehicles to minimize the use of their sirens; he should order the Sanitation Department to fix the brakes on its trucks.

At the same time, the mayor should put the onus on nongovernmental sources of noise that depend on government services. Street fairs, for example, are a tremendous source of noise during their high seasons in spring and fall, in part because they have become too frequent and in part because traffic is not alerted properly to street closings or directed properly at jammed intersections.

And what about the noise that private citizens generate, from car alarms to honking to blaring music in the apartment upstairs? A forceful public-awareness campaign could make noise a front-burner issue and embolden the 62 percent of New Yorkers who are troubled by noise to speak their minds. Such efforts, combined with strictly enforced ordinances, have reduced noise significantly in Memphis, Chicago, and throughout California. The NYPD has made noise abatement part of its recently announced strategy for combating quality-of-life crimes. Active police involvement is crucial: as Inspector McShane found, the vast majority of people will comply with reasonable requests from officers.

Excess noise is a form of pollution, not an inevitable part of urban life. Environmentalists have succeeded in cleaning the city's air and water; they have one more frontier to conquer. Mayor Giuliani was elected to improve the quality of life in New York—and that means making the city not only wealthier and safer, but quieter as well.

—Autumn 1994

JONATHAN FOREMAN

Toward a More Civil City

INNOVATIVE SUGGESTIONS about fixing New York's then-ragged quality of life that Nathan Glazer, George Kelling, Peter Salins, and other urban thinkers outlined in a special issue of *City Journal* six years ago influenced one of the great successes of Mayor Giuliani's first term. *City Journal*'s authors argued that seemingly trivial irritations—from aggressive panhandling and lackadaisical garbage collection to public drinking, excessive noise, and de facto decriminalized drug selling—gave citizens the impression that things were falling apart and hinted, almost subliminally, that they were vulnerable to greater harms. "If the city doesn't care about one aspect of its citizens' lives," former *City Journal* editor Roger Starr wrote, "it probably doesn't care about others." The inevitable result was soaring crime. The devil-may-care atmosphere emboldened wrongdoers, and a pervasive demoralization made ordinary New Yorkers anxious, pessimistic, alienated from civic life, slow to go out into the city for pleasure, and quick to leave town for good.

In response, Mayor Giuliani directed the police to enforce aggressively the laws against low-level crimes—so-called quality-of-life offenses or what used to be called "victimless" crimes. It turned out that there really was a victim: the social order. The most visible, dramatic consequence of the mayor's new policy was the drop in crime to levels unknown since the early 1960s. Just as important, law-abiding New Yorkers began to feel that their city belonged to them once again. No longer did they have to watch thieves flaunting their invulnerability by selling their booty in full view of impotent passersby on Columbus Avenue or St. Mark's Place; no longer did every subway ride make them cringe under the aggressive mockery of graffiti-scrawled trains, proclaiming that lawlessness ruled; no longer did every walk on the sidewalk involve facing a gauntlet of deranged or drugged beggars; no longer did motorists have to submit to extortion by squeegee at every intersection. Central Park, Tompkins Square Park, Bryant Park all became pleasant and safe. Trade picked up at the city's restaurants and theaters. Hotels burst with tourists, formerly repelled by Gotham's crime and grime but now drawn by its newly restored metropolitan glamour. New Yorkers no longer believed that their city was poised on the brink of anarchy; instead, it had a future.

What can a second Giuliani administration do to improve the city's quality of life further? It can make New York a more civil place. Civility sounds old-fashioned, calling to mind Victorian gentlemen tipping their hats, and the word is alarming to those who believe bourgeois values are a prison from which we have recently, and thankfully, escaped. Indeed, for three decades a culture war has raged against bourgeois civility, under attack from moral relativism and multiculturalism, from the idea that people should be "authentic" rather than conventional, from the growing primacy of rights over duties, and from the fractiousness of identity politics. But civility is the preeminent urban virtue: both "civility" and "citizen" derive from the same Latin word for "city." Civility means behaving in a non-aggressive, mutually forbearing way toward your fellow citizens. Since cities draw together large numbers of strangers in a small area, civility is the mutually respectful behavior required of all if urban life is not to become disordered and dangerous, as it did over the last three decades.

The mayor should focus on three main civility-enhancing strategies. First, two large classes of the public incivilities that infuriate New Yorkers — dangerously inconsiderate driving and excessive noise — are in fact illegal, and the mayor should push the police to enforce existing traffic and noise laws seriously. This is an extension of his first term's quality-of-life strategy of enforcing already-existing but largely disused laws. Just as taking minor crimes seriously sent the message that the authorities really were in control, so too will increased police attention to cars with ear-pounding sound systems. Stopping motorists from skidding around corners and cutting off pedestrians in crosswalks will send an equally salutary message. Right now, the fact that you can get away with me-first, in-your-face behavior that isn't just thuggish and inconsiderate but plainly illegal encourages people to let loose their thuggish but legal impulses, if only in retaliation. Enforcement would underline the principle that society has standards for your behavior toward fellow citizens.

Second, the mayor should demand civil behavior from all city employees, who should be models of right conduct for the public. If the representatives of public order show no respect, then why should anyone else? Third, schools should teach the rules of good behavior, as they did in the recent past. Contrary to the romantic ideology of the day, children are not born knowing all moral truths intuitively.

Now that New York has the lowest violent crime rate of any major American city, residents are less afraid of being mugged and more afraid that they or their children will get run down crossing the street. They feel under constant assault from motorists who run red lights, cut them off, or honk at them in crosswalks. They know that they have to walk defensively, because the near misses they experience every day sometimes turn into something really dangerous. Motor vehicles kill 250 pedestrians in New York annually and put a startling 13,500 more in the hospital. By comparison, Tokyo, with 12 million people, averages around 150 pedestrian deaths annually. London, with a population close to New York's 7.5 million, experiences the same. Even Paris, noted for its crazy drivers, and with 2 million more people in its metropolitan area, has fewer than half New York's pedestrian deaths. Gotham's streets are the most dangerous for pedestrians in America, and lethal for children: every year, motor vehicles injure 3,500 kids between the ages of five and 14 in the city.

Enforcing the traffic laws would make New York's streets a lot less anarchic—and a lot safer. Traffic engineers point out that a decrease in vehicle speed from 40 to 30 miles per hour—the speed limit on New York City streets, though few motorists know it and very few signs proclaim it—increases the chance a pedestrian will survive being hit from 40 to 70 percent, so just slowing speeders down will lead to fewer lost lives. A city with fewer speeders will be less scary not only to the elderly, to parents, and to out-of-towners but to all New Yorkers.

Oddly, the New York Police Department does not see traffic enforcement as a priority, despite the pedestrian casualties. Police issued a mere 650 summonses for failure to yield to pedestrians in crosswalks in 1996—fewer than two a day—despite the 70 percent of traffic fatalities that occur there. Police should punish crosswalk violations ruthlessly. Despite the regular speeding on city streets of the city's 2 million motorists—on Manhattan's upper Broadway, the Department of Transportation alarmingly discovered, vehicles regularly zoomed by at 50 miles per hour—90 percent of the city's 84,227 speeding tickets were for violations on the city's limited-access expressways, not its pedestrian-heavy main streets, though more pedestrians than motorists die in city accidents. The NYPD hands out only 44 speeding tickets a day on the five boroughs' local streets, and it should aggressively increase that number. As John Kaehny of Transportation Alternatives explains, "the police feel overwhelmed by the general lawlessness of the streets"—but their ticketing policy makes them complicit in the chaos.

New Yorkers must especially beware of the city's buses and taxis, which frequently operate with little concern for the law. Buses, in particular, terrify motorists and pedestrians. Bullying juggernauts of the road, they pull out from the curb without regard for oncoming traffic, plow through red lights—causing gridlock along with endangering lives—and straddle lanes with impunity. Such reckless driving may well stem from a sense of legal invulnerability: police almost never ticket bus drivers, who share unionized civil servant status with them—albeit under state, not city, jurisdiction. And municipal bus drivers who have injured or killed people in multiple accidents still ride the streets, for civil service rules make dismissing them next to impossible. But when bus drivers, as civil servants, flout the rules of the road, it sends exactly the wrong message—that the official representatives of society have contempt for the law. More reason, then, for the mayor to direct the police to enforce moving violations against them vigorously.

By contrast, the police shower taxi drivers with tickets, but not for bad driving—though taxis often careen through the streets as if traffic laws didn't exist, frightening pedestrians and passengers alike. Cabs killed 48 New Yorkers in 1994 and 1995, 70 percent of them pedestrians or bicyclists, and 5,000 taxi accidents occurred annually from 1988 through 1993. Yet most taxi citations are for ripped seats, parking illegally while the driver looks for a bathroom, or letting passengers get in at a bus stop. To take only one month as an example: of the 1,500 summonses police gave taxi drivers in April 1995, only 38 were for moving violations. If police would intensively penalize reckless taxi drivers now, they could ease up in the future, just as strict enforcement of the pooper-scooper law when it was introduced changed dog-owners' behavior permanently, even though enforcement has now greatly relaxed. If word got out that police no longer tolerated irresponsible taxi driving, taxi drivers would drive lawfully and civilly—and other motorists would get the message too. Instead, the NYPD's Traffic Control Division—which includes taxi enforcement—operates at half strength.

Bikes join the motorized forms of transportation in terrorizing pedestrians, even more so since a Chirping Chicken bicycle deliveryman recently killed an elderly man on the West Side. The NYPD has cracked down on bicycle road crime, issuing around 10,000 summonses to cyclists for running red lights, driving on sidewalks, and other infractions in 1997—an almost 50 percent increase over 1996. Of the 100,000 bicyclists on the city's streets on any given day, the messengers and deliverymen, rather than the amateur riders, scare pedestrians the most, as they whiz the wrong way down a one-way street or plow onto the sidewalk with somebody's Chinese dinner. Not surprisingly, they cause most of the city's bike accidents, according to Transportation Alternatives. Commercial bikes should prominently display the employer's name, and new laws should hold companies liable for the reckless driving of their cyclists, who work under heavy pressure to be speedy. Police should register all bikes ridden on city streets.

More than half the callers to the Police Department's recently established, though under-publicized, quality-of-life hot line (888-677-LIFE) complained about excessive noise. Some of the noise is designed to be uncivil: boom-box cars, for example, or motorcycles and "muscle cars" with engines altered to make them sound as loud and raucous as possible. Mayor Giuliani moved in the right direction when he signed into law a noise pollution bill last November. The new law trebles the penalties for excessive noise, with a maximum individual fine reaching $2,100 for a third offense.

Police can now slap a riotous nightclub with a $24,000 penalty. But police need to take excessive noise more seriously: early in 1997, only five of Queens's and Brooklyn's 39 precincts had meters to measure whether a noise was louder than the 80 decibels within 50 feet established by city ordinance as legal.

One major noise problem needs a new law to rein it in. The piercing wails of car alarms serve no purpose in most of the city. As much as graffiti or squeegee men, they send the message that no one is in charge: burglar alarms wail constantly, yet no one comes, as in some dystopian science-fiction movie. The chronic false alarms proclaim the intensely uncivil message several times a day (and night) that the peace and quiet of an entire neighborhood weighs as nothing compared to the anxieties of individuals about their property. Though in 1992 the City Council passed a law requiring car alarms to shut themselves off automatically after three minutes, it should go further and forbid entirely the use of car alarms within city limits and permit police to tow offending vehicles.

The city needs to look at its sirens, too, and ensure that they are the least bothersome possible and that they wail only during real emergencies. This holds true of the private ambulance services, whose noise-making remains unregulated. The mayor should also push to curtail street fairs sharply. They have turned into honky-tonk franchises. The mayor can also send a message that the city will no longer tolerate stores that blast music out front, except during Christmas and with a special permit.

If New York's 200,000 public employees were to behave more civilly, it would soften some of the harshness of city life and set an appropriate example to citizens. Of course, the incivility of public servants is often systemic and impersonal. I once tried to report a broken fire hydrant and called the Brooklyn telephone number suggested by my local police precinct, but no one ever picked up. The Fire Department gave me another number in the same area code. It too rang unanswered in some dusty Brooklyn office. My experience was not out of the ordinary. One survey found that the city Finance Department put callers on hold for 27 minutes on average, and a 1996 City Council survey found that, out of 173 complaint and question letters sent to 21 different city agencies, only 31 percent had received the courtesy of an answer within six weeks. Of 16 letters sent to 16 agencies offering to donate books and other items, none received a response.

Sadly, if Mayor Giuliani tried to emulate his predecessor, Mayor La Guardia, and fire uncivil civil servants, he'd have a tough time. La Guardia, the well-known anecdote runs, once dropped by incognito on a Lower East Side relief station, where insolent officials ignored him. Eventually, one of the city workers went up to the angry La Guardia, who shouted, "Take off your hat when you speak to a citizen!" striking the hat from the bureaucrat's head. La Guardia fired the civil servant on the spot. These days, regulations make it hard even to reprimand civil servants, much less fire them. Yet regulations do not tie the mayor's hands completely. Managers can fire city officials "for cause," though the process is arduous. The mayor could make it a potentially terminal offense for a civil servant to be rude to the public. Symbolically, such a gesture would show what city government expects when its employees deal with citizens. Nor are all city workers civil servants: some work part time or on contracts, so civil service regulations don't shield them from public dissatisfaction.

The city's managers can work at creating a culture of civility within their agencies. They should criticize boorish employees and lavish praise on those who treat the public as valued customers. Former Transportation Commissioner Ross Sandler recalls a senior transit executive who, whenever he rode the subway and heard a particularly friendly announcement, rewarded the driver with a star to wear on his uniform. The executive's gesture might seem corny today, but it expresses Management 101 common sense about human motivation. Wherever civil service rules permit, positive reinforcement could also take the more material form of promotions and pay increases.

Private businesses spent the last decade figuring out how to "meet and exceed customer expectations," as the management mantra has it, and businessmen have much to teach bureaucrats about how to be polite to taxpayers. The New York State Department of Motor Vehicles engaged Eastman Kodak to train DMV employees to see license applicants as customers rather than as irritating distractions. Kodak's program transformed DMV employee attitudes, with a happy result: the opening of the efficient, friendly, License X-press office on Manhattan's 34th Street. In 1993 the average waiting time in a DMV office was one hour. In 1996, after Kodak's creation of a new corporate culture in the department, the average wait shrank to only 11 minutes. Service companies offer other lessons from the private sphere that city agencies might borrow as well, including comment cards, 800 numbers, and monitored phone calls, to ensure satisfied customers.

The NYPD has already developed a civility program called "CPR"—"Courtesy, Professionalism, and Respect"—which, properly instituted, could be a model for city government. But CPR has yet to permeate the entire Police Department, and it currently expresses more of a hope than a reality. Police, because they are the literal embodiment of the civil order, need to exemplify civility more than any other city employees. As the community's monopolists of lawful force, they must hold themselves—and be held—to the highest standard. They must strike a delicate balance, making law-abiding citizens feel that the authority of society is on their side, while inspiring fear in criminals—all while the policeman is himself apprehensive.

Cops must be civil even as they inspire respect, and sometimes fear—like FBI agents, for example, who address adult members of the public as "sir" or "ma'am," even when they are about to arrest them, without in the least compromising their reputation: their very self-restraint is intimidating. The police force must not appear to be the meanest, best-armed gang in town, but something higher than that. Sure, this is New York, not never-never land, but when cops are rude or vulgar or dismissive to law-abiding citizens, whether rich or poor, it's as if society has surrendered to thuggishness.

Under Mayor Giuliani, the Taxi and Limousine Commission has also launched a commendable quality-of-life campaign to improve cab drivers' civility. The TLC banned burning incense in cabs and posted in all of them a "Passenger's Bill of Rights," which grants, among other things, a right to a quiet, radio-free ride. The city's yellow-cab drivers now attend a mandatory four-hour course in customer relations at La Guardia Community College. The campaign has been a success, according to TLC Assistant Commissioner Allan Fromberg. Serious complaints are down by 20 percent. "We are getting more praise and pleased phone calls," Fromberg reports. "The business is getting more professionalized."

Any city effort to foster civility should have a public school component. Resistance would be fierce: New Yorkers who believe that school uniforms are fascistic doubtless will object that teaching children to give up their seats to elderly people or pregnant women on the bus embodies unacceptable cultural bias. Already, though, public school teachers instruct their charges about the wrongs of racism, pollution, and cruelty to animals. Surely, civility is somewhere on the modern moral continuum, even if up-to-date teachers do not avow it. Some schools teach "conflict resolution" to prevent fights—a last-ditch course in civility. Any civility course would in fact convey a basic principle essential to coexistence in the city: do unto others as you would have them do unto you. Even teenagers in chaotic schools can understand that if everybody littered, held open subway doors or sprawled across two subway seats, talked in movie theaters, and blasted music, cities wouldn't work. Where schools have abandoned civics, as have all elementary schools in the New York system, the mayor should push them to reinstate it.

Teachers should teach civility as early as possible. With an increasing proportion of New York's schoolchildren arriving here from abroad, the need for such education grows more urgent, though many immigrant children come from societies that are far more civil than our own. Immigration's past success resulted in part from the schools' effectiveness in instructing newly arrived children in the norms of democratic urban life. New York will have fewer inflamed and resentful egos if all its citizens share a common ideal of civility.

Each of these initiatives is in the mayor's power to begin right away.

Since he knows from the experience of his first term what valuable consequences flow from an enhanced quality of urban life, he'd be well advised to
set them going now.

—*Winter 1998*

Contributors

BRIAN C. ANDERSON is senior editor of *City Journal* and the author of *Raymond Aron: The Recovery of the Political*. His writings have appeared in *First Things*, *The Wilson Quarterly*, and *The Public Interest*.

WILLIAM ANDREWS, a *City Journal* contributing editor, has worked at the New York City Transit Police and the New York Police Department. He now works at First Security Consulting, which advises police departments in the United States and abroad and is helping to introduce New York City–style policing to Brazil.

D. ANDREW AUSTIN is visiting assistant professor of economics at Bowdoin College.

WILLIAM J. BRATTON has managed five police agencies in Boston and New York, serving as police commissioner in both cities. He has written an autobiography of his crime-control successes, *Turnaround*, and is now president and chief operating officer of CARCO Group, Inc.

STEVEN G. CRAIG is professor of economics at the University of Houston and has published extensively on state and local public economies in the *Journal of Urban Economics*, the *Cato Journal*, the *Wall Street Journal*, and the *New York Times*, among other publications.

JONATHAN FOREMAN, a former lawyer and contributing editor of *City Journal*, is a movie critic for the *New York Post*. He has written for the *Wall Street Journal*, *National Review*, *New Yorker*, *Reader's Digest*, and *Salon.com*.

NATHAN GLAZER, professor of education and sociology at Harvard University, is co-editor of *The Public Interest*. His many books include *Beyond the Melting Pot* and *We Are All Multiculturalists Now*.

PATRICK J. HARNETT, a thirty-two-year veteran of the New York Police Department, is now the first deputy director of a federal program that helps coordinate anti-drug activities by federal, state, and local law-enforcement agencies.

HOWARD HUSOCK is director of case studies at Harvard's John F. Kennedy School of Government and a *City Journal* contributing editor. An Emmy Award–winning journalist, he is the author of *Repairing the Ladder: Towards a New Housing Policy Paradigm*. He has also written for the *Wall Street Journal* and *The Public Interest*.

KAY S. HYMOWITZ, a contributing editor of *City Journal*, is the author of *Ready or Not: Why Treating Children as Small Adults Endangers Their Future and Ours*. She has written for the *Wall Street Journal*, *The New Republic*, and the *New York Times*.

JOEL KOTKIN is a senior fellow with the Pepperdine University Institute for Public Policy and a research fellow at the Reason Public Policy Institute. The author of several books, he writes regularly in the *Los Angeles Times* and *Inc.* magazine.

RITA KRAMER, a former contributing editor of *City Journal*, is the author of numerous books, including *Ed School Follies* and *At a Tender Age: Violent Youths and Juvenile Justice.* She has written for the *Wall Street Journal*, *The Public Interest*, *Commentary*, and the *New York Times Magazine.*

DAVID GARRARD LOWE, whose books include *Beaux Arts New York*, *Lost Chicago*, *Chicago Interiors*, and *Stanford White's New York*, writes and lectures widely on architectural and cultural history. He is president of the Beaux Arts Alliance, an organization that celebrates the cultural links between the United States and France.

HEATHER MAC DONALD is a contributing editor of *City Journal* and John M. Olin Fellow at the Manhattan Institute. Her articles have appeared in the *Wall Street Journal*, *The New Republic*, *The New Criterion*, and the *New York Times.*

MYRON MAGNET is the editor of *City Journal* and author of *The Dream and the Nightmare: The Sixties' Legacy to the Underclass.*

RICHARD E. MORGAN is William Nelson Cromwell Professor of Constitutional Law and Government at Bowdoin College. He is at work on a book about the Supreme Court in the 1980's, *Constitutional Conservatism: The Counterrevolution That Couldn't.*

PAUL E. O'CONNELL is assistant professor in the department of criminal justice at Iona College.

PETER REINHARZ is chief of the Family Court division of the New York City Law Department, an adjunct professor at Fordham University's School of Law, and a *City Journal* contributing editor. He is the author of *Killer Kids, Bad Law: Tales of the Juvenile Justice System.*

MATT ROBINSON is currently a Phillips Foundation Journalism Fellow, at work on a book on media and the polls. His writings have appeared in *Investors Business Daily*, the *Los Angeles Times*, *National Review*, and the *Washington Times.*

ROGER SCRUTON is a writer and philosopher living in England. He is a contributing editor of *City Journal* and editor of the *Salisbury Review.* His many books include *An Intelligent Person's Guide to Modern Culture* and *The Classical Vernacular: Architectural Principles in an Age of Nihilism.*

FRED SIEGEL is professor of history at the Cooper Union for Arts and Sciences and the author of *The Future Once Happened Here: New York, D.C., and L.A. and the Fate of America's Big Cities.*

KENNETH SILBER writes about politics and economics. His articles have appeared in *Commentary*, *Insight*, the *New York Post*, *Reason*, and other publications.

SOL STERN, a contributing editor of *City Journal*, has written for *Commentary*, the *Wall Street Journal*, and the *New York Times*, and has served as a policy analyst for the governments of New York City and New York State.

WILLIAM J. STERN is a contributing editor of *City Journal.* He chaired New York governor Mario Cuomo's 1982 campaign and from 1983 to 1985 headed the state's Urban Development Corporation.

FRANK STRAUB is executive deputy inspector general in the Office of the New York State Inspector General.

E. FULLER TORREY, a psychiatrist, is president of the Treatment Advocacy Center in Arlington, Virginia, and author of numerous books, including *Surviving Schizophrenia* and *Nowhere to Go: The Tragic Odyssey of the Homeless Mentally Ill.*

JULIA VITULLO-MARTIN is director of the Citizens Jury Project at the Vera Institute of Justice, a nonprofit organization based in New York. She is the editor of *Breaking Away: The Future of Cities.*

Index

NOTE: Noncontinuous discussions are sometimes abbreviated using *f*, *ff*. *f* indicates "and on the next page"; *ff* indicates "and on each of the next two pages."